REASSERTION OF CONTROL OVER THE INVESTMENT TREATY REGIME

Driven by public opinion in host States, Contracting Parties to investment agreements are pursuing many avenues in order to curb a system that is being perceived – correctly or not – as having run out of control. *Reassertion of Control over the Investment Treaty Regime* is the first book of its kind to examine the many issues of procedure, substantive law and policy which arise from this trend. From procedural aspects such as early dismissal of claims, the establishment of appeals mechanisms or State-State arbitration to substantive issues such as joint interpretations, treaty termination or detailed definitions of standards of protection, this book identifies and discusses the main means by which States do or may reassert their control over the interpretation and application of investment treaties. Each chapter tackles one of these avenues and evaluates its potential to serve as an instrument in States' reassertion of control.

ANDREAS KULICK is a senior research fellow at Eberhard Karls University Tübingen. He has published extensively on various aspects of public international law, including a previous monograph, *Global Public Interest in International Investment Law* (Cambridge University Press, 2012). He has advised and represented States with regard to various matters of public international law before international courts and tribunals, as well as before domestic courts.

REASSERTION OF CONTROL OVER THE INVESTMENT TREATY REGIME

Edited by

ANDREAS KULICK

CAMBRIDGE
UNIVERSITY PRESS

CAMBRIDGE
UNIVERSITY PRESS

University Printing House, Cambridge CB2 8BS, United Kingdom

One Liberty Plaza, 20th Floor, New York, NY 10006, USA

477 Williamstown Road, Port Melbourne, VIC 3207, Australia

4843/24, 2nd Floor, Ansari Road, Daryaganj, Delhi - 110002, India

79 Anson Road, #06–04/06, Singapore 079906

Cambridge University Press is part of the University of Cambridge.

It furthers the University's mission by disseminating knowledge in the pursuit of education, learning, and research at the highest international levels of excellence.

www.cambridge.org
Information on this title: www.cambridge.org/9781107172654
10.1017/9781316779286

First published 2017

A catalogue record for this publication is available from the British Library.

Library of Congress Cataloging-in-Publication Data
Names: Kulick, Andreas, 1982– editor.
Title: Reassertion of control over the investment treaty regime / edited by Andreas Kulick.
Description: Cambridge [UK] ; New York : Cambridge University Press, 2016.
Identifiers: LCCN 2016042171 | ISBN 9781107172654 (hardback)
Subjects: LCSH: Investments, Foreign – Law and legislation. | International commercial arbitration. | BISAC: LAW / International.
Classification: LCC K3830 .R43 2017 | DDC 346/.092–dc23
LC record available at https://lccn.loc.gov/2016042171

ISBN 978-1-107-17265-4 Hardback

CONTENTS

CONTRIBUTORS

FREYA BAETENS (Cand/LicJur (Ghent); LLM (Columbia); PhD (Cantab)) is an associate professor of law and Director of the LUC Research Centre at Leiden University and visiting professor at the National University Singapore (NUS). As an associate lawyer with VVGB Advocaten/Avocats (Brussels Bar), she regularly acts as counsel or expert in international disputes.

PAUL BARKER is a barrister in independent practice at Doughty Street Chambers. He specialises in international arbitration and public international law. He has acted as counsel to both investors and States in investment treaty arbitrations. He read law at Emmanuel College, Cambridge, and Columbia Law School, New York, and was formerly a visiting fellow at the Lauterpacht Centre for International Law, Cambridge. He is a guest lecturer at Stanford Law School and City University of Hong Kong.

FERNANDO LUSA BORDIN (PhD, Cantab) is a John Thornely Fellow and Lecturer in Law and Director of Studies in Law at Sidney Sussex College, Cambridge. He is, in addition, an affiliated lecturer at the Faculty of Law of the University of Cambridge and an associate fellow of the Lauterpacht Centre for International Law.

ERIC DE BRABANDERE is a professor of international dispute settlement at the Grotius Centre for International Legal Studies at Leiden University. He is also attorney-at-law at the Ghent Bar, practicing in international law and arbitration, editor-in-chief of the *Leiden Journal of International Law*, visiting professor of international investment law at the University of Trento in Italy, and a member of the Board of Editors of the *Journal of World Investment & Trade*, the *Revue belge de droit international* (Belgian Review of International Law), and the Martinus Nijhoff Investment Law Book Series.

DIANE A. DESIERTO is Michael J. Marks Distinguished Professor in Business Law, tenured associate professor of law, and co-director of the ASEAN Law and Integration Center (ALIC) at the University of Hawaii William S. Richardson School of Law. She is a member of the Scientific Advisory Board of the *European Journal of International Law* and editor of *EJIL:Talk!*, member of the Academic Council of the Institute of Transnational Arbitration, head of the International Economic Development Law Interest Group of the Asian Society of International Law, co-chair of the Oxford Investment Claims Summer Academy, and legal expert for the ASEAN Coordinating Committee on Investment.

MELANIE ECKARDT is Rechtsanwältin and holds an LLM from King's College London and a doctorate from the University of Erlangen-Nürnberg. She is an associate in the arbitration practice of Gleiss Lutz, Frankfurt (Germany). Her practice focuses on international commercial and investment arbitration as well as cross-border litigation.

ANDREAS KULICK (Doctor iuris, Tübingen; LLM, NYU School of Law; First and Second State Exams, Berlin) is a senior research fellow at Eberhard Karls University Tübingen. He has published extensively on various aspects of public international law, including a previous monograph, *Global Public Interest in International Investment Law* (Cambridge University Press, 2012). He has advised and represented States with regard to various matters of public international law before international courts and tribunals, as well as before domestic courts.

NIKOS LAVRANOS is secretary general of EFILA, Brussels, and head of legal affairs at Global Investment Protection AG, Zug. Until 2014, he was chief negotiator and senior advisor for all investment issues at the Ministry of Foreign Affairs (formerly Ministry of Economic Affairs), the Netherlands. He studied at Goethe University Frankfurt, Germany, and obtained an LLM and a doctorate, both from Maastricht University, the Netherlands.

ELENI METHYMAKI is a research associate at the University of Glasgow, a graduate of the universities of Athens and Cambridge and a lawyer at the Athens Bar advising on matters of international law.

MARTINS PAPARINSKIS is Reader in Public International Law at the Faculty of Laws, University College London, and a visiting senior fellow at National University of Singapore. He is a generalist international lawyer with a particular interest in international dispute settlement and international investment law. He is the book review editor of the *Journal of World Investment &Trade*, a member of the Academic Review Board of the *Cambridge International Law Journal*, a member of the ILA's Study Group on the Use of Domestic Law Principles for the Development of International Law, a member of the ILA's Committee on Non-State Actors and a member of the Panel of Arbitrators of the International Centre for Settlement of Investment Disputes.

FRIEDRICH ROSENFELD practices arbitration with Hanefeld Rechtsanwälte in Hamburg, Germany. He acts as counsel, expert witness and arbitrator. He holds a PhD in international law and is Global Adjunct Professor at NYU Law in Paris, visiting professor at the International Hellenic University in Thessaloniki and Lecturer at Bucerius Law School in Hamburg. In 2014, he was appointed Global Hauser Fellow from Practice & Government at NYU School of Law. Since 2015, he is alternate member of the ILA Committee on Rule of Law and International Investment Law.

MAVLUDA SATTOROVA (LLM, PhD) is a senior lecturer in law and co-director of the Liverpool Economic Governance Unit at the University of Liverpool School of Law and Social Justice. Dr Sattorova's most recent research examines the impact of international investment law on domestic governance, with particular focus on empirical approaches to investigating the variety of factors shaping the evolution of investment treaty norms.

ANTONIOS TZANAKOPOULOS is associate professor of public international law at the University of Oxford and Fellow of St Anne's College, Oxford. He advises States, international organisations and other entities on matters of international law.

MICHAEL WAIBEL is a university senior lecturer in law at the University of Cambridge, Deputy Director of the Lauterpacht Centre for International Law and Fellow and Director of Studies at Jesus College. His main research interests are public international law, international economic law with a particular focus on finance and the settlement of international disputes. He teaches international law, WTO law and European Union law.

STEPHAN WILSKE is Rechtsanwalt, attorney-at-law (New York) and Partner with Gleiss Lutz, Stuttgart (Germany). He is Maître en Droit (Aix-Marseille III) and holds an LLM from the University of Chicago Law School (Casper Platt Award) and a doctorate from the University of Tübingen. He is admitted to the US Supreme Court, Fellow of the Chartered Institute of Arbitrators (CIArb), Member of the American Law Institute (ALI), senior committee member of the *Contemporary Asia Arbitration Journal* and Lecturer at the Universities of Hanover and Heidelberg and visiting professor at the National Taiwan University (spring 2010).

RUMIANA YOTOVA (PhD, Cantab) is Fellow, Lecturer and Director of Studies in Law at Lucy Cavendish College, University of Cambridge, and an affiliated lecturer at the Faculty of Law. She teaches international law, investment law and external relations of the European Union. Her research interests are in the areas of sources of international law, international dispute settlement, investment law and the interaction between different legal regimes within international law, including EU law.

PREFACE

This book, as many books, has taken a long journey from its first inception to eventual publication. First ideas regarding a project on States' reassertion of control over investment treaties and investment arbitration ripened in the spring of 2014, when I was still working as a full-time practitioner, and academic endeavours were, at the time, reserved for weekends or late nights. What appeared to be a growing trend then, in early 2014, seems to be an almost all-pervasive phenomenon in late 2016. Driven by public opinion turning from indifference towards investment protection and investor-State dispute settlement to scepticism or even fierce opposition, Contracting Parties to investment agreements are pursuing many avenues in order to curb a system that is being perceived – correctly or not – as having run out of control. What are these avenues? How do Contracting Parties pursue them? What is their potential for reasserting control over the investment treaty regime? What are the limits that public international law sets to their pursuit? This book offers answers to these and many other questions pertaining to Contracting Parties' reassertion of control. To my knowledge, it is the first one to do so systematically, from a distinctively doctrinal perspective and with a view towards covering the crucial doctrinal and theoretical issues of the phenomenon of reassertion. Its contributions focus on the various avenues to reassert control and evaluate their viability through the lens of public international law – in particular, albeit far from exclusively, the law of treaties. For this purpose, it takes an almost monographical approach – with a plurality of authors – in targeting the most pertinent issues of reassertion of control over the investment treaty regime with respect to theoretical, procedural, substantive and policy issues.

I am proud to say that for this task I have assembled a brilliant team of authors who come from a variety of different academic and professional backgrounds and who hold a variety of different views on international investment law and arbitration: academics and practitioners, investment law specialists and general public international lawyers, investment arbitration enthusiasts and investment arbitration sceptics, among others. The result is, so I hope the esteemed reader agrees, an edited volume that offers new insights into this now all-pervasive phenomenon of reassertion of control by tackling the pivotal doctrinal and theoretical questions emerging from the various approaches and avenues that Contracting Parties do or might consider.

This book has profited from various sources of support. First and foremost, I extend my utmost gratitude to the German Academic Research Association (Deutsche Forschungsgemeinschaft (DFG)), which provided funding for this project. Such funding permitted financing, *inter alia*, access to specialised databases that considerably enhanced and facilitated the research, as well as a considerable amount of the costs of the authors' workshop I had the honour of organising and presiding over at Hohentübingen Castle in June 2015. Further, I wish to thank the Juristische Gesellschaft Tübingen e.V., particularly its president, Professor Dr Hermann Reichold, and Gleiss Lutz, for additional funding of the workshop; Michel Boven and Björn Ebert for their organisational support; and, of course, all participants of the workshop for spirited and inspiring discussions that further shaped the project. My academic mentor, Professor Dr Martin Nettesheim, inspires me every day with his academic and intellectual brilliance, inquisitiveness and innovation to push my own boundaries. He permitted me to pursue this project among many other academic extravagancies. Ms Isolde Zeiler and Mr Xu Tengfei were of great assistance with the proofreading. Parts of the work on the manuscript, including work on copy-editing and proofreading, were completed during research visits at the Lauterpacht Centre for International Law and the NYU School of Law in the late summers of 2015 and 2016, respectively. I thank both institutions for their hospitality and their vibrant intellectual communities. Finally, I extend my gratitude to Cambridge University Press's anonymous readers, who provided very valuable and thought-provoking comments at the peer-review stage, and last but certainly not least, I thank Elizabeth Spicer of Cambridge University Press, who supported this project from the very beginning and helped to turn it from a few sketchy ideas into the book the esteemed reader holds in his or her hands.

Andreas Kulick
September 2016

PART I

Introduction, Theory and Domestic Law Approaches

1

Reassertion of Control: An Introduction

ANDREAS KULICK

A. The Current State of International Investment Law: Rough Waters or Catharsis?

(1) *The Legitimacy Crisis of International Investment Treaty Law and Arbitration and the Public Law Debate*

International investment treaty arbitration is undoubtedly one of the most vibrant mechanisms of international dispute settlement to date. As of September 2016, the total number of investment treaty disputes has reached 739,[1] with the very first award having been issued only about twenty-five years ago, in 1990.[2] While having a relatively slow start, from the late 1990s onwards the number of awards increased, and so did the amounts claimed,[3] providing a constant flow of investment treaty arbitration disputes and awards, with about forty to fifty being issued annually over the course of the past five years,[4] including seventy in 2015.[5] Further, investors started to realise that the international investment agreement (IIA) provisions did not merely sanction expropriation without compensation but allowed, through clauses such as fair and equitable treatment and indirect expropriation, targeting more subtle ways of deprivation of investors' rights by the host State. Consequently, and arguably a success

[1] See United Nations Conference on Trade and Development (UNCTAD), Investment Policy Hub website: http://investmentpolicyhub.unctad.org/isds (accessed 22 September 2016).

[2] *Asian Agricultural Products Ltd.* v. *Republic of Sri Lanka*, ICSID Case No. ARB/87/3, Final Award of 27 June 1990.

[3] See United Nations Conference on Trade and Development (UNCTAD), World Investment Report 2015, 114, fig. III.7, available at http://unctad.org/en/PublicationsLibrary/wir2015_en.pdf (accessed 22 September 2016).

[4] United Nations Conference on Trade and Development (UNCTAD), World Investment Report 2016, 104, fig. III.4, available at http://unctad.org/en/PublicationsLibrary/wir2016_en.pdf (accessed 22 September 2016).

[5] See UNCTAD Investment Policy Hub website: http://investmentpolicyhub.unctad.org/ISDS/FilterByYear (accessed 22 September 2016).

attributable to the increasing web of IIAs,[6] nationalisations or other direct expropriations became rather rare. Instead, governmental measures of a more general nature, including legislation or other regulatory activity, came under scrutiny in investor-State disputes.[7]

As these disputes shifted in focus, from targeting nationalisations absent (adequate) compensation to frequently addressing general regulatory measures of the host State, it became increasingly apparent that the host of them were fundamentally different from both commercial disputes between private actors and classical public international law disputes between sovereign States but rather displayed a considerable resemblance with domestic public law litigation.[8] These disputes permit the control of the exercise of public authority, followed by a sanction (usually monetary damages or compensation), the enforcement of which is quite effective.[9] Indeed, if the claims target, for example, a statute or even far-reaching governmental responses to a financial crisis,[10] what

[6] See A. Lowenfeld, 'Investment Agreements and International Law', *Columbia Journal of Transnational Law*, 42 (2003–4), 123, 129–30.

[7] See M. Valenti, 'The Protection of General Interests of Host States in the Application of the Fair and Equitable Treatment Standard', in G. Sacerdoti, P. Acconi, M. Valenti and A. De Luca (eds.), *General Interests of Host States in International Investment Law* (Cambridge University Press, 2014), 26, 38–54; S. Hindelang and M. Krajewski, 'Towards a More Comprehensive Approach in International Investment Law', in S. Hindelang and M. Krajewski (eds.), *Shifting Paradigms in International Investment Law: More Balanced, Less Isolated, Increasingly Diversified* (Oxford University Press, 2016), 1, 2–9.

[8] See G. Van Harten, *Investment Treaty Arbitration and Public Law* (Oxford University Press, 2007), 48–50; S. W. Schill, 'International Investment Law and Comparative Public Law: An Introduction', in S. W. Schill (ed.), *International Investment Law and Comparative Public Law* (Oxford University Press, 2010), 3, 10–17; A. Kulick, *Global Public Interest in International Investment Law* (Cambridge University Press, 2012), 94–7; *ibid.*, 'Book Review: International Investment Law and Comparative Public Law', *European Journal of International Law*, 22 (2011), 917–24; see also, generally, D. Schneiderman, *Constitutionalizing Economic Globalization: International Investment Law and Democracy's Promise* (Cambridge University Press, 2008); S. Montt, *State Liability in Investment Treaty Arbitration: Global Constitutional and Administrative Law in the BIT Generation* (Oxford, UK: Hart Publishing, 2009).

[9] Cf. Articles 53 and 54 of the ICISD Convention and Article V of the 1958 New York Convention.

[10] See e.g. *CMS Gas Transmission Company* v. *Argentine Republic*, ICSID Case No. ARB/01/8, Award of 12 May 2005 and Decision of the Ad Hoc Annulment Committee of 25 September 2007; *G&E Energy Corp., LG&E Capital Corp., and LG&E International, Inc.* v. *Argentine Republic*, ICSID Case No. ARB/02/1, Decision on Liability of 3 October 2006; *El Paso Energy International Company* v. *Argentine Republic*, ICSID Case No. ARB/03/15, 31 October 2011; *Poštová banka, a.s. and Istrokapital SE* v. *Hellenic Republic*, ICSID Case No. ARB/13/8, Award of 9 April 2015; see also the pending case *Cyprus Popular Bank Public Co., Ltd.* v. *Hellenic Republic*, ICSID Case No. ARB/14/16.

makes the dispute functionally different from administrative or even constitutional judicial review?

However, while function and effect are similar to domestic public law disputes, adjudication in investor-State disputes is beyond the host State's sphere of influence: it is first and foremost an international dispute settlement mechanism. In addition, the treaty instruments on which the claims are based in the vast majority of cases focus on investor rights. Only to a limited extent do IIAs take into account the various interests at stake if issues of public interest are brought before an investor-State tribunal. Elsewhere I have called this the 'public interest challenge'.[11] Combined with the model of private adjudication, the ad hoc nature of the arbitral panel and the often still limited level of publicness of the proceedings,[12] these factors fuel what has been discussed for more than a decade now as the 'legitimacy crisis' of international investment law.[13]

Since the early 2000s, calls from the literature and public opinion to take issues of public interest and the specificities of democratic decision-making into account in investor-State dispute settlement have significantly grown in number. Indeed, there is evidence that these calls are increasingly being heard in arbitral practice. To name but two examples, decisions such as *Electrabel* v. *Hungary* and *Paushok* v. *Mongolia* of 2012 and 2011, respectively, emphasised that the inherent political and hence

[11] A. Kulick, *Global Public Interest in International Investment Law*, 50–2.

[12] However, transparency has improved significantly in investment arbitration with the amended ICSID Arbitration Rules of 2006, the recent UNCITRAL Rules on Transparency of 2014 and most notably with the conclusion of the United Nations Convention on Transparency in Treaty-Based Investor-State Arbitration (so-called Mauritius Convention); see ICISD Arbitration Rules, as amended and in effect since 10 April 2006, available at https://icsid.worldbank.org/ICSID/ICSID/RulesMain.jsp (accessed 22 September 2016); UNCITRAL Rules on Transparency in Treaty-Based Investor-State Arbitration, in effect since 1 April 2014, available at www.uncitral.org/uncitral/uncitral_texts/arbitration/2014Transparency.html (accessed 22 September 2016); United Nations Convention on Transparency in Treaty-Based Investor-State Arbitration, adopted on 10 December 2014, opened for signature on 17 March 2015, available at www.uncitral.org/uncitral/uncitral_texts/arbitration/2014Transparency_Convention.html (accessed 22 September 2016). See also on recent developments regarding transparency in international investment law and arbitration D. Euler, M. Gehring and M. Scherer (eds.), *Transparency in International Investment Arbitration* (Cambridge University Press, 2015).

[13] See S. D. Franck, 'The Legitimacy Crisis in Investment Treaty Arbitration: Privatizing Public International Law Through Inconsistent Decisions', *Fordham Law Review*, 73 (2004–5), 1521; D. Schneiderman, 'Legitimacy and Reflexivity in International Investment Arbitration: A New Self-Restraint?', *Journal of International Dispute Settlement*, 2 (2011), 471; generally, G. Van Harten, *Investment Treaty Arbitration and Public Law* (Oxford University Press, 2007), 175–84.

more volatile nature of democratic decision-making in itself cannot serve as an indicator that the host States frustrated the investor's legitimate expectations.[14] Further, in the award of 9 April 2015 in *Poštová banka and Istrokapital* v. *Hellenic Republic*, pertaining to the Greek financial crisis, the tribunal adopted an interpretation of what constituted an investment under the respective bilateral investment treaties (BITs) that was much more restrictive[15] than interpretations of similar clauses by tribunals dealing with Argentina's sovereign default of 2001–2.[16] However, the case law, not least due to the ad hoc nature of proceedings, still lacks a consistent, generally accepted and practiced approach of how to include public interest considerations absent detailed treaty language to that effect.[17] Further, and particularly important for the purpose of this book, as the ensuing section will demonstrate, what drives a growing trend in international investment law is the *perception* among IIA Contracting Parties that investment law and arbitration are out of control rather than whether or not this is actually the case.

(2) A New Generation: Reassertion of Control

Hence, this book will depart from the premise that we are currently witnessing a paradigm shift,[18] a new generation of international investment law and arbitration. After three decades of proliferation of investor-friendly IIAs enfranchising the investors to bring themselves international claims against their host States and, accordingly, proliferation of investor-State

[14] *Electrabel S.A.* v. *Republic of Hungary*, ICSID Case No. ARB/07/19, Decision on Jurisdiction, Applicable Law and Liability of 30 November 2012, para. 8.23; *Sergei Paushok, CJSC Golden East Company and CJSC Vostokneftegaz Company* v. *Government of Mongolia*, UNCITRAL, Award on Jurisdiction and Liability of 28 April 2011, para. 299. See also, for further references, A. Kulick, 'Investment Arbitration, Investment Treaty Interpretation, and Democracy', *Cambridge Journal of International and Comparative Law* 4 (2015), 441.

[15] See *Poštová banka a.s. and Istrokapital SE* v. *Hellenic Republic*, ICSID Case No. ARB/13/8, Award of 9 April 2015, paras. 228 *et seq*. and 248 *et seq*.

[16] See e.g. *Abaclat and Others* v. *Argentine Republic*, ICSID Case No. ARB/07/5 (formerly *Giovanna a Beccara and Others* v. *Argentine Republic*), Decision on Jurisdiction and Admissibility of 4 August 2011, paras. 352, 354–7.

[17] Which, however, is not to mean that there is a shortage of conceptual and theoretical approaches offered in the literature. For maybe the most prominent one in the past years, see S. W. Schill (ed.), *International Investment Law and Comparative Public Law* (Oxford University Press, 2010).

[18] See also S. Hindelang and M. Krajewski (eds.), *Shifting Paradigms in International Investment Law: More Balanced, Less Isolated, Increasingly Diversified* (Oxford University Press, 2016).

disputes, the public opinion is changing from indifference or ignorance towards international investment law and arbitration to predominantly scepticism or even fierce opposition.[19]

This is spurred by the fact that over the course of the past ten to fifteen years the old capital-exporting countries of the West are realising that BITs are no one-way street but indeed thus: bilateral. Originally intended to warrant investors from wealthy, predominantly Western countries a certain standard of protection, IIAs, so the old proponents of investment protection realise, can be targeted as much at their policies as they have been targeted at the policies of their treaty partners from the so-called developing world. Regulatory States with complex regimes for protection and conciliation of a myriad of different interests existing in a modern civil society, so it is submitted by many, are particularly prone to fall prey to a system of international investment law and arbitration that is not designed to make the careful balancing choices required of judicial decision-making in complex societal structures.[20] To name but a few examples from recent years, Germany has been seized to pay damages for its decision to phase out nuclear energy,[21] Australia faced a claim by Philip Morris for its plain packaging legislation[22] and Spain is subject to numerous claims for withdrawal of subsidies to the solar energy sector.[23] The pressure on decision-makers to recalibrate treaty

[19] Note that even an economically liberal publication such as *The Economist* has started to doubt the added value of investor-state dispute settlement and is promoting an exclusively inter-State dispute settlement system modelled on the World Trade Organisation (WTO) Dispute Settlement Understanding; *see* 'A Better Way to Arbitrate', *The Economist*, 11 October 2014; and also 'The Arbitration Game' from the same issue.

[20] I only refer to the numerous submissions by non-governmental organisations (NGOs) to the consultations by the European Commission on investor protection in TTIP, which in the vast majority expressed general concerns with regard to investor-state dispute settlement and investment law in general, see online public consultation on investment protection and investor-to-state dispute settlement (ISDS) in the Transatlantic Trade and Investment Partnership Agreement (TTIP), EU Commission website: http://trade.ec.europa.eu/consultations/index.cfm?consul_id=179 (accessed 22 September 2016); on this complex, see also generally A. Kulick, *Global Public Interest in International Investment Law*, 77–167.

[21] *Vattenfall AB and Others* v. *Federal Republic of Germany*, ICSID Case No. ARB/12/12.

[22] *Philip Morris Asia Limited* v. *Commonwealth of Australia*, UNCITRAL, PCA Case No. 2012–12. However, the claim has been rejected by Award of 17 December 2015.

[23] E.g. *AES Solar and Others* v. *Kingdom of Spain*, UNCITRAL; *RREEF Infrastructure (G.P.) Limited and RREEF Pan-European Infrastructure Two Lux S.à.r.l.* v. *Kingdom of Spain*, ICSID Case No. ARB/13/30 (a Decision on Jurisdiction has been issued on 6 June 2016; *Antin Infrastructure Services Luxembourg S.à.r.l. and Antin Energia Termosolar B.V.* v. *Kingdom of Spain*, ICSID Case No. ARB/13/31; *NextEra Energy Global Holdings*

standards and dispute settlement is high – not only in democracies but, due to (social) media, in almost every society with widespread Internet access.

Moreover, the world economy is becoming more and more complex and intertwined. Not only is the classical dichotomy between capital-exporting (developed) States and capital-importing (developing) States severely blurred, but there is a growing tendency among developing or emerging economies to conclude BITs among each other.[24] These changes in economic realities and IIA parties bring about changes in IIA design and IIA policy, as well as in approaches to investor-State dispute settlement by the Contracting Parties to the respective agreements.

Examples for this paradigm shift are myriad. Contracting Parties are increasingly introducing inter-State arbitrations, such as the *Ecuador* v. *United States* arbitration[25]; they make use of, or are seriously considering making use of, joint interpretations of specific treaty provisions[26] and are increasingly including express provisions to that effect in the IIA text[27]; they terminate their IIAs and/or the Convention on the Settlement of Investment Disputes between States and Nationals of other States (so-called International Centre for Settlement of Investment Disputes (ICSID) Convention) or launch a general overhaul of their BIT regime[28]; they make

B.V. and NextEra Energy Spain Holdings B.V. v. *Kingdom of Spain*, ICSID Case No. ARB/14/11 (all pending).

24 See United Nations Conference on Trade and Development (UNCTAD), World Investment Report 2016, 101–04, http://unctad.org/en/PublicationsLibrary/wir2016_en.pdf (accessed 22 September 2016).

25 *Republic of Ecuador* v. *The United States of America*, PCA (award not public); further information is available on the PCA website: www.pca-cpa.org/showpage.asp?pag_id=1455 (accessed 22 September 2016).

26 Joint interpretations will be the subject of Chapter 7 but are also touched upon in Chapters 2 and 6. See also on this issue generally J. R. Weeramantry, *Treaty Interpretation in Investment Arbitration* (Oxford University Press, 2012), 2.39–2.51; and Article 31(3)(a) and (b) of the Vienna Convention on the Law of Treaties: 'There shall be taken into account, together with the context: (a) Any subsequent agreement between the parties regarding the interpretation of the treaty or the application of its provisions; (b) Any subsequent practice in the application of the treaty which establishes the agreement of the parties regarding its interpretation.'

27 See e.g. Articles 9.24.3 and 27.2.2(f) of the Trans-Pacific Partnership Agreement (TPP), signed on 4 February 2015, available at https://ustr.gov/trade-agreements/free-trade-agreements/trans-pacific-partnership/tpp-full-text (accessed 22 September 2016).

28 See on this issue Chapter 9. See also generally UNCTAD, World Investment Report 2015, 106, UNCTAD website: http://unctad.org/en/PublicationsLibrary/wir2015_en.pdf (accessed 16 March 2016); see also UNCTAD, IIA Issues Note No. 2 (December 2010), 'Denunciation of the ICSID Convention and BITs: Impact on Investor-State Claims'.

increasing use of frivolous claims mechanisms such as Rule 41(5) of the ICSID Arbitration Rules or consider introducing similar mechanisms into IIAs[29]; they include definitions of standards such as fair and equitable treatment or indirect expropriation into their (model) IIAs[30]; they consider introducing appeals mechanisms or facilitations to challenging an investment treaty arbitration award[31]; and on the EU level, the European Commission has started to implement a regime for extra-EU BITs that foresees a number of control mechanisms for the Contracting Parties over investment disputes and the interpretation of the agreement, pushes for termination of all EU Member States' (intra- and extra-EU) BITs altogether and considers introduction of a so-called investment court system (ICS) into all its future IIAs, which shall replace investor-State arbitration.[32] All these observations are evidence

[29] See on this issue Chapter 4. See generally ICSID Arbitration Rule 41(5), introduced in April 2006; see also R. Dolzer and C. Schreuer, *Principles of International Investment Law*, 2nd edn. (Oxford University Press, 2012), 282–3. See also the EU Commission, 'Concept Paper: Investment in TTIP and Beyond – The Path for Reform', available at http://trade.ec.europa.eu/doclib/docs/2015/may/tradoc_153408.pdf (accessed 22 September 2016).

[30] See on this issue Chapter 12. See also generally European Commission, DG Trade, 'Investment Provisions in the EU-Canada Free Trade Agreement (CETA)', dated 26 September 2014, available at http://trade.ec.europa.eu/doclib/docs/2013/november/tradoc_151918.pdf (accessed 22 September 2016).

[31] See on this issue Chapter 5. See also generally European Commission, DG Trade, 'Factsheet on Investor-State Dispute Settlement', dated 3 October 2013, 4–5, available at http://trade.ec.europa.eu/doclib/docs/2013/october/tradoc_151791.pdf (accessed 22 September 2016): '[T]he EU believes that on the basis of the agreements we have signed with our trading partners there should be a debate setting up an appeals mechanism for ISDS disputes. This would also lead to greater consistency in how the provisions of investment agreements are interpreted'; see already the discussion within the ICSID dating back until 2004: ICSID Secretariat, 'Possible Improvements of the Framework for ICSID Arbitration', Discussion Paper, 22 October 2004; see generally K. P. Sauvant (ed.), *Appeals Mechanism in International Investment Disputes* (Oxford University Press, 2008).

[32] See on this issue Chapter 13 and also Chapters 5 and 14. See also generally European Commission, DG Trade, 'Factsheet on Investor-State Dispute Settlement', dated 3 October 2013, available at http://trade.ec.europa.eu/doclib/docs/2013/october/tradoc_151791.pdf (accessed 22 September 2016); European Commission, 'Towards a Comprehensive European International Investment Policy', Communication COM(2010)343 final, dated 7 July 2010, available at http://trade.ec.europa.eu/doclib/docs/2010/july/tradoc_146307.pdf (accessed 22 September 2016); European Commission. Press Release 'EU Finalises proposal for Investment Protection and Court System for TTIP', dated 12 November 2015, available at http://europa.eu/rapid/press-release_IP-15-6059_en.htm (accessed 22 September 2016). According to Ingo Venzke, the ICS 'make[s] good sense from the perspective of a public law theory of international adjudication'; see I. Venzke, 'Investor-State Dispute Settlement in TTIP

indicating that this approaching or already present new generation of international investment law and arbitration is characterised by the Contracting Parties' reassertion of control over IIAs and international investment treaty dispute settlement.[33] Moreover, developments such as the Brexit vote and the Trump election signal that we have by no means reached the peak of push-backs against trade and investment liberalization.

It appears that for the first time in the past five decades of modern IIA practice the interests of Contracting Parties to agreements regulating foreign investment are to a large part aligned or at least approximated.[34] This includes Contracting Parties with a traditionally very liberal IIA policy that used to be the frontrunners of investment protection. Germany, for instance, the world's BIT champion, with over 130 such treaties concluded,[35] has recently dispelled considerable scepticism with regard to the current prevalent investment treaty regime and called for re-introduction of the local remedies rule in new IIAs to which it or the European Union may become a party.[36] In addition, its government is opposed to including a chapter providing for investment protection and investor-State dispute settlement mechanisms in the Transatlantic Trade and Investment Partnership (TTIP).[37] This does not sound fundamentally

from the Perspective of a Public Law Theory of International Adjudication', *Journal of World Investment & Trade*, 17 (2016), 374, 399.

[33] For a similar assessment in this regard, see M. Waibel et al., *The Backlash against Investment Arbitration* (Alphen aan den Rijn, Netherlands: Wolters Kluwer, 2010); see also A. van Aaken, 'Control Mechanisms in International Investment Law' in Z. Douglas, J. Pauwelyn and J. E. Viñuales (eds.), *The Foundations of International Investment Law* (Oxford University Press, 2014), 409, 415 *et seq.*

[34] Cf. K. Miles, *The Origins of International Investment Law* (Cambridge University Press, 2013), Chaps. 1 and 2 and p. 386, where she describes the history of international investment law to date as 'a story of "assertion of power and responses to power"'. I contend that such swinging back and forth of the pendulum has come to a halt because of the increasing double role of most Contracting Parties that are simultaneously capital exporters and capital importers; only compare the likes of China, the United States and the European Union: see UNCTAD, World Investment Report 2015, 5, 8, figs. I.3 and I.8, UNCTAD website: http://unctad.org/en/PublicationsLibrary/wir2015_en.pdf (accessed 22 September2016).

[35] According to UNCTAD, as of September 2016, Germany has concluded 135 BITs and 64 other IIAs that are still in force: see UNCTAD website: http://investmentpolicyhub.unctad.org/IIA/CountryBits/78#iiaInnerMenu (accessed 22 September 2016).

[36] See official position of the German government as stated on the website of the German Ministry for Economic Affairs and Energy: www.bmwi.de/EN/Topics/Foreign-trade/TTIP/faq.html (accessed 22 September 2016): 'It should only be possible to initiate investor-to-state dispute settlement as a last resort after exhausting the legal process before the national courts.'

[37] *Ibid.*: 'The German government would like to keep the arbitration procedures out of the TTIP negotiations. They are only needed where there is no functioning state based on the rule of law, and that does not pertain to the EU and the US.' Also note that Sigmar Gabriel,

different in policy approach to the likes of Ecuador or Argentina. Similarly, there is an ongoing discussion within the government of the Netherlands calling into question the established investment policy which led to a recent general impact study of investor-State dispute settlement.[38] I have already hinted at initiatives and considerations with regard to the EU investment policy – the most recent being the creation of a permanent investment court within a specific treaty regime, which has recently been included in the CETA and the EU–Vietnam Free Trade Agreement (FTA).[39]

The antagonism thus is not so much anymore one of 'developed' vs. 'developing' States, 'capital-exporting' vs. 'capital-importing' States or 'the West against the rest'[40] but rather Contracting Parties vs. investor and the investor-State tribunal. As has been foreshadowed in preceding paragraphs, this is most obvious – and will grow in trend in the near future – with regard to the conclusion of new IIAs. While it is true that there remain situations in which predominantly capital-importing States conclude IIAs with predominantly capital-exporting States that display the old power imbalance and thus one-sided pro-investment content of IIAs concluded between the 1960s and the early 2000s, these instances are becoming more the exception than the rule. This is not least due to the growing number of (mega-)regional

the German Minister for Trade and Energy, has recently declared that in his opinion the overall TTIP negotiations 'have failed'; see 'German minister says TTIP has failed', *Financial Times*, 28 August 2016, available at; www.ft.com/content/9603d94e-6d2f-11e6-a0c9-1365ce54b926 (accessed 22 September 2016).

38 See C. Tietje and F. Baetens, 'The Impact of Investor-State Dispute Settlement (ISDS) in the Transatlantic Trade and Investment Partnership', study prepared for the Minister for Foreign Trade and Development Cooperation, Ministry of Foreign Affairs, The Netherlands, dated 24 June 2014.

39 See Chapter 8; and Chapter II, Section 3, Sub-sections 4 and 5 of the EU-Vietnam Free Trade Agreement as of January 2016, available at http://trade.ec.europa.eu/doclib/press/index.cfm?id=1437 (accessed 22 September 2016); Chapter 8, Section F of the CETA as of 29 February 2016, available at http://trade.ec.europa.eu/doclib/docs/2016/february/tradoc_154329.pdf (accessed 22 September 2016); see also EU Commission, 'CETA: EU and Canada Agree on New Approach on Investment in Trade Agreement', press release of 29 February 2016, available at http://europa.eu/rapid/press-release_IP-16-399_en.htm (accessed 22 September 2016); and EU Commission, 'Concept Paper: Investment in TTIP and Beyond – The Path for Reform', 11–12, available at http://trade.ec.europa.eu/doclib/docs/2015/may/tradoc_153408.PDF (accessed 22 September 2016).

40 However, see Lauge Poulsen's interesting study on investment treaty negotiation dynamics between developed and developing countries: L. N. Skovgaard Poulsen, *Bounded Rationality and Economic Diplomacy: The Politics of Investment Treaties in Developing Countries* (Cambridge University Press, 2015).

FTAs[41] that display an amalgamation of various trade and investment interests of often several Contracting Parties and thereby considerably level any power imbalances. However, for the approximation of the Contracting Parties' interests, it should often suffice that the formerly capital exporters have become or are becoming also capital importers. Even with regard to an IIA where it is rather unlikely that capital flows in both directions, the capital-exporting Contracting Party will probably be unable or even reluctant to push for a liberal IIA of the old days. This is not only because of negotiation dynamics – if capital exporter A has concluded restrictive treaties with B, C, and D, in negotiation with capital importer E, it has little leverage to deviate considerably from the substance of those other treaties and maybe even its own rather restrictive Model IIA – but it is also because the pressure of public opinion to limit the reach of investor protection and investor-State dispute settlement is increasing.[42] Look again at Germany, which is still mainly a capital exporter and is unlikely to become a strong capital importer in the near future.[43] Nonetheless, the German government is considering abandoning its decades-old policy of strong investor protection and questions established standards of investment protection.[44]

Public opinion is also a factor in why all Contracting Parties, including the traditional capital exporters, will be more and more prone to push for a restrictive interpretation or overhaul of their old, liberal IIAs. Adding to this, of course, is the aforementioned increased likelihood that both Contracting Parties may find themselves in the respondent seat in an investor-State arbitration.[45] The quasi-precedential effect of investment

[41] See UNCTAD World Investment Report 2016, 101, UNCTAD website: http://unctad.org/en/PublicationsLibrary/wir2016_en.pdf (accessed 22 September 2016).

[42] I only refer again to the about 150,000 submissions to the EU consultation on investor-state dispute settlement; see the online public consultation on investment protection and investor-to-state dispute settlement (ISDS) in the Transatlantic Trade and Investment Partnership Agreement (TTIP), EU Commission website: http://trade.ec.europa.eu/consultations/index.cfm?consul_id=179 (accessed 22 September 2016).

[43] See UNCTAD, World Investment Report 2015, 5, 8, figs. I.3 and I.8, UNCTAD website: http://unctad.org/en/PublicationsLibrary/wir2015_en.pdf (accessed 22 September 2016).

[44] See nn. 36 and 37.

[45] E.g. according to the UNCTAD World Investment Report 2014, of the fifty-six investment arbitrations introduced in 2013, twenty-six were directed against high-income countries, while nineteen were introduced against lower-income countries and eleven against emerging economies; see UNCTAD World Investment Report 2014, 124, available at http://unctad.org/en/PublicationsLibrary/wir2014_en.pdf (accessed 8 September 2015); as for the year 2014, the UNCTAD World Investment Report 2015 (p. 112) claims

arbitration awards and decisions plays a significant role here. As is established practice in investor-State arbitration, tribunals frequently refer to prior decisions on other IIAs and the argumentation employed therein as persuasive authority.[46] Hence, only a change in case law will reduce the risk for the Contracting Parties to find themselves subject to awards that clash with fundamental domestic policies, including important public interest issues.[47]

B. Reassertion of Control and Its Implications

(1) A Bit of Crystal Ball Gazing

Assuming that the assessments made earlier are correct, they beg consideration of a more general nature. First of all, are we returning to a modified form of diplomatic protection? If the opponents of investor-State dispute

that '40 per cent of all cases were brought against developed countries.' See http://unctad.org/en/PublicationsLibrary/wir2015_en.pdf (accessed 16 March 2016). This trend persistent in 2015; see UNCTAD World Investment Report 2016, 105, available at http://unctad.org/en/PublicationsLibrary/wir2016_en.pdf (accessed 22 September 2016).

46 See C. Schreuer and M. Weiniger, 'Conversations Across Cases: Is There a Doctrine of Precedent in Investment Arbitration?', 5 January 2007, available at www.univie.ac.at/intlaw/conv_across_90.pdf (accessed 16 March 2016); I. M. Ten Cate, 'The Costs of Consistency: Precedent in Investment Treaty Arbitration', *Columbia Journal of Transnational Law*, 51 (2012–13), 418, 436–47; for an example from the case law, see *Impregilo S.p.A.* v. *Argentine Republic*, ICSID Case No. ARB/07/ 17, Award of 21 July 2011, para. 108: 'It is true that . . . the jurisprudence regarding the application of MFN clauses to dispute settlement provisions is not fully consistent. Nevertheless, in cases where the MFN clause has referred to "all matters" or "any matter" regulated in the BIT, there has been near-unanimity in finding that the clause covered the dispute settlement rules. On this basis, the majority of the Tribunal reaches the conclusion that Impregilo is entitled to rely, in this respect, on the dispute settlement rules of the Argentina-[United States] BIT and that the case cannot be dismissed for non-observance of the requirements in Article 8(2) and (3) of the Argentina-Italy BIT.' This is fuelled by what Stephan Schill termed the 'multilateralisation' of international investment law, that is, that many IIAs contain very similar language, which invites tribunals to cite decisions on similar clauses in other IIAs indiscriminately; see generally, S. W. Schill, *The Multilateralization of International Investment Law* (Cambridge University Press, 2009). However, as noted by many, such indiscriminate reference often brushes over subtle or not so subtle differences in treaty language and thus is prone to draw conclusions that cannot be drawn; see e.g. I. M. Ten Cate, 'The Costs of Consistency', 447 *et seq.*

47 Of note, this is an aspect of the quasi-precedential effect of investment arbitration case law, the dynamic of which is preferential to the Contracting Parties and is often overlooked in the strife for curbing such effect; see e.g. S. Hindelang, 'Part II: Study on Investor-State Dispute Settlement (ISDS) and Alternatives of Dispute Resolution in International Investment Law', European Parliament, Directorate-General for External Policies, Policy Department, *Investor-State Dispute Settlement (ISDS) Provisions in the EU's International Investment Agreements*, Vol. 2: *Studies*, 42, 56, 61, 66–9, 103, 114.

settlement have their way, this scenario is not as absurd as it may have sounded even a few years ago. Technically, Contracting Parties could make way with all IIAs in an afternoon: amend the various sunset clauses in the respective IIAs and jointly terminate all treaties subsequently.[48] And the public hostility towards a system of dispute settlement that is unfamiliar to most and based on private adjudication by a non-permanent panel of three old white men (with only a few, however notable,[49] exceptions) who have the authority to review all government action without any form of appeal, which is even likely to increase in the years to come, will possibly spark a significant response by policy makers.

However, I contend that we will not witness the end of investor-State dispute settlement any time soon.[50] Apart from the fact that an afternoon as the one just described may be possible but not at all probable, the alignment or at least approximation of the Contracting Parties' interests, in my opinion, will prevent the full demise of the system. As I mentioned earlier, the blurring of the line between capital importers and capital exporters means at the same time that one and the same Contracting Party may find itself more often in both roles – host State in one case, home State in another case. This is indeed one of the main factors of Contracting Parties' reassertion of control because the old home States are becoming respondents in investor-State arbitration. However, it also means that old host States experience a change in position as well and will increasingly find themselves in the roles of home States of investors bringing claims against the other Contracting Party.[51] With emerging economies investing into so-called developed economies and with

[48] As Martins Paparinskis illustrated so poignantly in his presentation ('International Investment Law: Analogy and Cohesiveness of International Law') at the CJICL Conference in Cambridge on 11 May 2014.

[49] I am thinking of Gabrielle Kaufmann Kohler and Brigitte Stern in particular. See Chapter 14 for further data in this respect.

[50] In my opinion, this assessment still stands if the EU Commission continues to pursue its recent agenda and successfully pushes for inclusion of its 'investment court system' in its future FTAs; see EU Commission, 'Concept Paper: Investment in TTIP and Beyond – The Path for Reform', 11–12, available at http://trade.ec.europa.eu/doclib/docs/2015/may/tradoc_153408.PDF (accessed 16 March 2016). While the judges of the 'tribunal of first instance' and 'appeal tribunal' are to be appointed by the TTIP Contracting Parties alone and the proposal introduces an appeals mechanism, the remaining architecture very much resembles the standard investor-state arbitration model and hence still presents many of the features that are the target of criticism; see Articles 9–30 of the EU Commission's draft TTIP investment chapter proposal, available at https://ustr.gov/sites/default/files/TPP-Final-Text-Investment.pdf (accessed 22 September 2016).

[51] According UNCTAD, in the last three years, about 40 per cent of the investment claims registered were introduced against developed states; see UNCTAD World Investment

emerging countries concluding IIAs among themselves, turning the tables will be a common scenario in the future. The effectiveness of an international arbitration system with a relatively well-working enforcement system will be appreciated by any Contracting Party that may find itself in the position of an investor's home State.

(2) *Some Preliminary Thoughts on the Implications with Regard to Investment Arbitration*

Furthermore, let me expound some general theoretical considerations on the implications of Contracting Parties' reassertion of control over IIAs and investment treaty arbitration. Such reassertion of control means an attempt to shift authority[52] back from the investor and the investor-State tribunal to the Contracting Parties. One of the motives for the intended authority shift is the perception, among the Contracting Parties themselves and among their civil societies, that a system that may adjudicate issues of public interest must take such public interest into account.[53] Depending on the level of intensity of reassertion,[54] if the Contracting Parties to IIAs take control over the agreements and/or the arbitration, the question arises as to whether Contracting Parties are the right and should be the only trustees of the public interest. In turn, on the answer to this question depends how much control the Contracting Parties are legitimately able to assert.

This introduction is not the right place to elaborate *in extenso* on these vexing matters – although I will say as much that I think that any model other than one that grants States[55] considerable discretion to pursue the public interest of their *polis* by some kind of trusteeship model is at odds with the present landscape of public international law that still places great weight on sovereignty.[56] However, I point to the intriguing questions that

Report 2016, 105, available at http://unctad.org/en/PublicationsLibrary/wir2016_en.pdf (accessed 22 September 2016).

52 Ingo Venzke explains very well the difference between power and authority: see I. Venzke, *How Interpretation Makes International Law* (Oxford University Press, 2012), 63: 'To have authority is distinct from having power in that it implies a certain degree of deferred judgement on [the] part of others. It feeds on social legitimacy – on the general belief of society, which upholds that one should not do what the authority says' (footnotes omitted).

53 See A. Kulick, *Global Public Interest in International Investment Law*, 151.

54 See Section C(3).

55 Or regional international organisations vested with sovereign authority in specific fields by their member states, such as the European Union with regard to trade and investment policy; cf. Article 207, TFEU.

56 See A. Kulick, *Global Public Interest in International Investment Law*, 85–94, 149–50; see also on the limits of hinging interpretive reasoning on democracy A. Kulick, 'Investment

follow. For example, is it a preferable alternative to further empower third, non-sovereign parties to pursue the public or their third-party interest, either in the form of enhanced amicus curiae briefs (e.g. for non-governmental organisations (NGOs)) or even of intervening party status in any way similar to Article 62 of the International Court of Justice (ICJ) Statute of interested third (non-sovereign) parties? It goes without saying that in particular the latter suggestion would be a game changer in investor-State dispute settlement. On the other side of the spectrum, if Contracting Parties are to be in control, in the most radical consequence this could serve as justification for making way with the entire system of investor-State dispute settlement that is based precisely on the idea that Contracting Parties abandon a certain level of control (i.e. sovereignty).[57]

However, without intending to anticipate any considerations in the contributions in this book, in particular, those of Martins Paparinskis (Chapter 2), Antonios Tzanakopoulos and Eleni Methymaki (Chapter 7), as well as myself (Chapter 6), as an introduction to the general theoretical *problematique*, I want to submit some preliminary thoughts on the relationship of the Contracting Parties and the investor-State and State-State tribunals with regard to matters of dispute settlement.

(a) The Paradox of the Public Law Model

One of the fundamental rationales of international investment law as we know it is precisely that Contracting Parties to a considerable degree abandon sovereignty (and thus control) by vesting an international tribunal with the authority to decide an investment dispute, which is intended to warrant a certain level of investment protection in order to promote investment and development.[58] The more Contracting Parties reassert control over the IIA and investment treaty arbitration, the more such rationale is undermined and the less international investment law serves its very purpose.

Law, Treaty Interpretation and Democracy', *Cambridge Journal of International and Comparative Law*, 5 (2015), 441–60.

57 As considerable parts of public opinion appear to call for.

58 See A. Roberts, 'Power and Persuasion in Investment Treaty Interpretation: The Dual Role of States', *American Journal of International Law*, 104 (2010), 179, 183; A. Lowenfeld, *International Economic Law*, 2nd edn. (Oxford University Press, 2008), 537 (with regard to the purpose of the ICSID Convention); W. Alschner and E. Tuerk, 'The Role of International Investment Agreements in Fostering Sustainable Development', in F. Baetens (ed.), *Investment Law within International Law: Integrationist Perspectives* (Cambridge University Press, 2013), 217.

This leads us to a paradox of the public law model.[59] International investment treaty arbitration resembles public law adjudication because it means judicial control of the exercise of public authority. However, international investment law exhibits a void in that it lacks proper responses to accommodate considerations of public interest – which are, by necessity, a defining feature of a public law dispute.[60] Now, if the reassertion of Contracting Parties' control over IIAs and investment arbitration is mainly based on the rationale to fill this void, it risks digging its own grave: the more Contracting Parties retain control over investor-State dispute settlement and the less an investor-State tribunal enjoys actual independence, the less the public law model is accurate to characterise the system and hence the less reassertion of control is necessary to re-balance it in the way just described. This is not to mean, to my mind, that the public law model is not a viable rationale for Contracting Parties' reassertion of control. Quite the contrary, it proves that the public interest and Contracting Parties' reassertion of control are connected. However, it demonstrates the viable limits of such reassertion and that abandoning the system of investor-State dispute settlement altogether would be a dubious option to choose.

(b) Agency and Trusteeship in Investor-State Arbitration

What now for the relationship of investment arbitration and IIA interpretation with regard to Contracting Parties' reassertion of control? International relations theory offers the ideal-type models of agency and trusteeship to explain why States delegate authority to international courts and tribunals.[61] Under a principal-agent model, States (principals) delegate authority to international courts and tribunals (agents) to resolve international disputes for reasons of efficiency, that is, because a tribunal is better placed to resolve a dispute than the parties to the dispute themselves.[62] The trusteeship model, by contrast, follows a different rationale, focusing on credibility and independence rather than efficiency. According to this model, States delegate authority to international judicial bodies because the decision of

[59] See Section A(1).

[60] See A. Kulick, *Global Public Interest in International Investment Law*, 151.

[61] See A. T. Guzman, 'Why LDCs Sign Treaties That Hurt Them', *Virginia Journal of International Law*, 38 (1997–8), 639; A. Roberts, 'Power and Persuasion in Investment Treaty Interpretation', 179, 186.

[62] See e.g. E. Posner and J. Yoo, 'Judicial Independence in International Tribunals', 1, 6–7, 14; T. Ginsburg, 'Bounded Discretion in International Judicial Lawmaking', *Virginia Journal of International Law*, 45 (2004–5), 631, 641–4.

a neutral third party increases the confidence in and credibility of their commitments and other obligations under public international law.[63] This entails an aspect of legitimacy because of the international control of national decision-making by ideally independent international judicial bodies.[64] The reach of agents' and trustees' authority is defined and thereby limited by their respective underlying rationales of efficiency (agency) and credibility (trusteeship). Under a trusteeship model, the permissible level of control to be exerted by the Contracting Parties to a treaty providing for international judicial dispute resolution is hence lower than under an agency model.[65]

I agree with Anthea Roberts' overall assessment that the present system of investment arbitration is a hybrid of trusteeship and agency models.[66] Investor-State tribunals are trustees of dispute resolution. As mentioned earlier,[67] one of the main purposes of the current system of investment law and arbitration is investment promotion through international legal standards and international adjudication beyond the unilateral control of the host State. Such legitimising function may only be achieved by a relatively independent judicial body that is entrusted with settling the dispute between the investor and the host State. Moreover, of note, with regard to investor-State dispute resolution, the principals are here one of the Contracting Parties (i.e. the host State), on

[63] See e.g. K. J. Alter, 'Agents or Trustees? International Courts in Their Political Context', *European Journal of International Relations*, 14 (2008), 33, 38–44; L. Helfer and A.-M. Slaughter, 'Why States Create International Tribunals: A Response to Professors Posner and Yoo', *California Law Review*, 93 (2005), 899, 917.

[64] See A. von Bogdandy and I. Venzke, *In Wessen Namen? Internationale Gerichte in Zeiten globalen Regierens* (Berlin: Suhrkamp, 2014), 26–7; see also in more general terms and with regard to state-state judicial dispute settlement Y. Shany, 'Assessing the Effectiveness of International Courts: A Goal-Based Approach', *American Journal of International Law*, 106 (2012), 225, 259–60.

[65] See A. Roberts, 'Power and Persuasion in Investment Treaty Interpretation', 179, 186–7; see also K. J. Alter, 'Agents or Trustees? International Courts in Their Political Context', *European Journal of International Relations*, 14 (2008), 33, 46, 55–6 (while Alter mainly discusses issues of independence from the influence of one powerful party to the dispute, her argument pertains to trustees' independence from principals generally (i.e. both parties to the dispute) as an alternative to the state consensus-based legitimacy of principal-agent theory).

[66] See A. Roberts, 'Power and Persuasion in Investment Treaty Interpretation', 179, 188; see also A. Stone Sweet and F. Grisel, 'Transnational Investment Arbitration: From Delegation to Constitutionalization', in P.-M. Dupuy, F. Francioni and E.-U. Petersmann (eds.), *Human Rights in International Investment Law and Arbitration* (Oxford University Press, 2009), 118, 124–6, who regard investor-state tribunals furthermore as agents of 'the greater community'.

[67] See Section B(2)(a).

the one hand, and the investor, on the other hand. To be more precise, the IIA makes investor-State arbitration possible and usually provides for the Contracting Parties' general consent to this form of dispute resolution. However, a specific dispute to be resolved can only be introduced by the investor against one Contracting Party.[68] Hence, an agency model based exclusively on the Contracting Parties' consent to dispute resolution would be inaccurate to capture the specific features of investment arbitration. This is not to say that there is no room for Contracting Parties' control, but trusteeship means that the possibilities for such control are narrower than under an agency model – and, naturally, the Contracting Parties would still be free to amend the IIA in order to limit or discard the tribunal's trusteeship function.

Nonetheless, some features of investment law and arbitration may not be fully explained by a trusteeship model either.[69] Dispute resolution proper is not the only task bestowed upon investment law and arbitration. Rather, the interpretation of IIAs – in other words, defining the scope of investors' rights and the limits of Contracting Parties' exercise of governmental authority – is a crucial feature that is usually intertwined with dispute resolution: when resolving a dispute, an investor-State tribunal must interpret the IIA in order to determine whether the investor's claims are founded or not. The investor-State tribunal shares the authority to interpret the terms of the IIA with the Contracting Parties – who can amend, terminate and interpret the treaty – and usually a State-State tribunal for which the IIA often specifically reserves the role to resolve disputes of interpretation between the Contracting Parties. Consequently, here the room for Contracting Parties' reassertion of control is wider. As a preliminary conclusion, these considerations suggest that Contracting Parties may enjoy more leeway reasserting their control when matters of treaty interpretation are at stake as compared to issues where the dispute resolution function is in the foreground.[70]

This may translate into responses to specific doctrinal questions. For example, with regard to the typology of instruments of reassertion

[68] This second hybrid aspect of investor-state arbitration does not find mention in Anthea Roberts' analysis; see A. Roberts, 'Power and Persuasion in Investment Treaty Interpretation', 179, 188.

[69] Cf. the notion of constrained independence advanced by Helfer and Slaughter in L. Helfer and A.-M. Slaughter, 'Why States Create International Tribunals', 899, 929–30.

[70] In my opinion, these considerations are also relevant in the relationship between state-state and investor-state arbitration; see Chapter 6.

according to their chronology submitted later,[71] these considerations may provide guidelines as to when in an investor-State dispute an instrument of reassertion of control (e.g. joint interpretation) may still be legitimately employed by one Contracting Party and when a tribunal may legitimately disregard it. Still staying with the example of joint interpretation, the guidelines developed here would suggest that such an interpretation would infringe upon the trusteeship bestowed upon an investor-State tribunal by the IIA in question with respect to dispute resolution if undertaken after the request for arbitration. In that case, the purpose of the specific joint interpretation is not so much to retain general control over how the terms of the respective IIA are to be interpreted but rather to influence the outcome of the particular dispute, that is, dispute resolution in favour of one Contracting Party rather than a genuine interest in preserving the true intension of both Contracting Parties with regard to the meaning of the treaty.[72] Again, this line of reasoning only applies to the form most IIAs take at present, that is, providing for general consent to investor-State dispute settlement without specific provisions on joint interpretations or other mechanism specifically designed by the Contracting Parties to reassert their control. The Contracting Parties are free to amend the IIA to include specific limitations on the investor-State tribunal's judicial – in particular, its dispute settlement – function or draft new treaties that grant the Contracting Parties greater authority to intervene in an ongoing dispute in the first place.

Finally, a word on the relationship of Contracting Parties' reassertion of control and judicial independence. Naturally, a reassertion of control that is intended to shift power back from the (investor-State) tribunal and the investor to the Contracting Parties inheres the danger of infringing upon judicial independence.[73] Of no mitigation is Eric Posner and John Yoo's suggestion that in public international law disputes, judicial dependence rather than judicial independence serves best the effectiveness of international adjudication.[74] Apart from concerns with such understanding of

[71] See Section C. [72] See also Chapter 6.

[73] 'Judicial independence' here meaning 'shielding of the decision-making power of judges [or arbitrators] from control and interference by other actors', including the judges' or arbitrators' discretion to decide the legal issue at hand exclusively according to their best understanding of the law; see Y. Shany, 'Assessing the Effectiveness of International Courts', 225, 256; L. Helfer and A.-M. Slaughter, 'Why States Create International Tribunals', 899, 901–2, 907–8.

[74] E. Posner and J. Yoo, 'Judicial Independence in International Tribunals', 1, 6–7.

(international) adjudication voiced elsewhere,[75] their assumptions are based on an agency model of international adjudication that serves the efficiency of dispute resolution between the parties to the treaty that grants access to the international court or tribunal.[76] By contrast, as argued here, international investment treaty arbitration rather follows a hybrid model, as the Contracting Parties are not identical to the disputing parties.[77] The thus persisting friction with judicial independence further indicates the necessity of striking a careful balance between Contracting Parties' reassertion of control and the overall purpose of investment law and arbitration.

C. Typologies of the Different Instruments of Reassertion

In addition to an inquiry into the theoretical implications of Contracting Parties' reassertion of control, another main aim of this book is to trace and discuss the different instruments IIA Contracting Parties may actually employ to reassert their control over the treaty or the dispute. For an overview of their variety as well as to facilitate categorisation and classification – which, however, may not be undertaken in a comprehensive fashion here – I offer three typologies of the instruments of reassertion[78]: chronology (instrument raised at what time and until what point in the dispute?), actor (joint or individual action of the Contracting Parties necessary?) and control and intensity (who has the last resort?).

(1) Chronology

The first, most obvious typology relates to chronology. In this regard, I suggest five sub-categories corresponding to five stages of a dispute: (1) the pre-dispute phase (in particular, treaty drafting), (2) the looming-dispute phase (before a concrete dispute has materialised), (3) the pre-trial phase (before the request for arbitration), (4) the trial phase (after the request for arbitration but before the issuance of the award) and (5) the post-trial phase (after issuance of the award).

75 See L. Helfer and A.-M. Slaughter, 'Why States Create International Tribunals', 899; see also Y. Shany, 'Assessing the Effectiveness of International Courts', 225, 256.
76 E. Posner and J. Yoo, 'Judicial Independence in International Tribunals', 1, 6–7, 14.
77 Also cf. the counter-arguments in Y. Shany, 'Assessing the Effectiveness of International Courts', 225, 258–61.
78 It goes without saying that this is not to contend that no other typologies or categories may be created nor that the lists are exhaustive.

In the pre-dispute phase, a specific dispute has neither materialised nor is it foreseeable. This will usually coincide with the treaty drafting process. In this phase, the Contracting Parties thus may consider introducing restrictive dispute settlement clauses such as 'fork-in-the-road clauses', enhanced mechanisms for counterclaims, specific mechanisms for early dismissal of claims[79] Chapter 4 or expressly defining a hierarchical relationship between State-State and investor-State arbitration[80]. Further, on the substantive side, general exceptions clauses or other mechanisms may be added to protect legitimate regulatory interests[81], or certain kinds of rights or assets may be excluded from the definition of investment, such as sovereign bonds.

When a dispute is looming but has not yet fully materialised – for example, when a Contracting Party is in the process of undertaking rescue measures in response to a financial crisis that affect investor rights – instruments of reassertion of control may be one or several of the following: termination of the IIA (if there is no sunset clause)[82] or even the ICSID Convention, amendments to the treaty text, joint interpretations of possibly pertinent treaty clauses[83], State-State arbitration for interpretation of these treaty clauses[84] or consent or waiver of one Contracting Party with regard to violation of a provision of the IIA by the other Contracting Party.[85]

The third, pre-trial stage is marked by two guideposts. This stage defines the time between the materialisation of a dispute – usually identifiable by appeals to governmental authorities or even by domestic litigation – and the request for arbitration. In this phase, the potential respondent Contracting Party may resort to negotiation, mediation or conciliation with the potential claimant investor. Also, an exhaustion of local remedies or fork-in-the-road clause in the IIA – adopted at stage 1 – may unfold its strength here, since the investor would either have to

[79] See Chapter 4. [80] See Chapter 6. [81] See Chapter 10.

[82] See Chapter 9. If there is a sunset clause, termination would rather fall somewhere between the first and the second stage because a looming dispute will probably already have materialised or even have been settled once the termination takes effect after ten, fifteen or twenty years.

[83] See Chapter 7. [84] See Chapter 6.

[85] Here it becomes most obvious that the viability of several of these instruments depends on which status one grants the rights enshrined in the IIA; see on this Z. Douglas, 'The Hybrid Foundations of Investment Treaty Arbitration', *British Yearbook of International Law*, 74 (2003), 151, 162–64; Z. Douglas, *The International Law of Investment Claims* (Cambridge University Press, 2009), 1–38; K. Partlett, *The Individual in the International Legal System* (Cambridge University Press, 2011), 108–18.

plough its way through domestic court procedures before submitting the request for arbitration or would be forced to make the important policy decision which of the two alternative paths (domestic litigation or international arbitration) to choose. However, Contracting Parties may also seek to reassert their control by way of the instruments applicable in the second phase, that is, termination, amendment, joint interpretation, State-State arbitration or consent. Whether and to what extent resort to those instruments is a licit option is open to discussion and would also depend on the language of the IIA in question.[86]

Once the investor submits the request for arbitration, until the tribunal issues its final award, that is, at the trial stage, treaty amendment and termination are usually foreclosed – unless the IIA permits taking such measures into account.[87] More controversial, however, is the question whether joint interpretations, a Contracting Party's consent (or waiver) or the interpretation decision of a State-State tribunal must be taken into account in an investor-State arbitration or are even binding on the tribunal.[88] Earlier, I already touched upon some of the matters relevant in this context.[89] In addition, again, depending on what the Contracting Parties have enshrined in the IIA at stage 1, the IIA may permit third non-sovereign parties to intervene or even may grant intervening party status to the investor's home State. Also, arbitrator selection and potential arbitrator challenges play a considerable role at this stage, as do procedural mechanisms such as applications for early dismissal or counterclaims.

At the fifth, post-trial stage, after the final award has been issued, the respondent Contracting Party may contest the award. It may either seek to halt enforcement of a non-ICSID award or even seek to nullify it,[90] or

[86] For a typology of state-state arbitration clauses, see A. Roberts, 'State-to-State Investment Arbitration: A Hybrid Theory of Interdependent Rights and Shared Interpretative Authority', *Harvard Journal of International Law*, 55 (2014), 1, 6–10. See also Chapter 6.

[87] Which is, admittedly, a very unlikely scenario.

[88] This is one of the intriguing matters to be discussed in Chapters 2, 6 and 7. See also A. Roberts, 'State-to-State Investment Arbitration', 1, 63–6; on the issue of parallel investor-state and state-state arbitration proceedings, *lis pendens* and *res judicata*. see C. Lo, 'Relations and Possible Interactions between State-State Dispute Settlement and Investor-State Arbitration under BITs', *Contemporary Asian Arbitration Journal*, 6 (2013), 1, 10–24.

[89] See Section B(2).

[90] See e.g. Article 34 of the UNCITRAL Model Law or Article V of the Convention on the Recognition and Enforcement of Foreign Arbitral Awards of 10 June 1958 (New York Convention); for the texts, see UNCITRAL website: www.uncitral.org/pdf/english/texts/arbitration/ml-arb/07-86998_Ebook.pdf and www.uncitral.org/pdf/english/texts/arbitration/NY-conv/XXII_1_e.pdf (accessed 22 September 2016).

it may initiate annulment proceedings before an ICSID ad hoc committee pursuant to Article 52 of the ICSID Convention. Further, way may even be open to file an appeal for full legal review of the award.

(2) *Actor*

The second typology categorises the instruments of reassertion according to whether they require joint action of both Contracting Parties or individual action by one Contracting Party is sufficient. Joint mechanisms are, *inter alia*, treaty drafting, treaty amendment, consensual termination of the IIA, joint interpretation and consensual resort to State-State arbitration. The latter may occur, for example, if the Contracting Parties agree that interpretation of a specific clause should not be left to an investor-State tribunal but if at the same time they cannot agree on a joint interpretation or amendment of the treaty.

Individual mechanisms, by contrast, are, for example, unilateral termination (of the IIA or of the ICSID Convention), frivolous claims applications, counterclaims and challenges of the award before domestic courts, annulment proceedings and possibly an appeal (if once provided for in the applicable IIA). Of note, consent to a breach of a treaty provision[91] or waiver of such claim,[92] if considered viable, stands somewhere between joint and individual mechanisms. Individual action by one Contracting Party suffices – the investor's home State. However, such consent (or waiver) is usually given following negotiations between both Contracting Parties upon the (individual) initiative of usually the investor's host State.

[91] International Law Commission, 'Articles on the Responsibility of States for Internationally Wrongful Acts', *ILC Yearbook 2001*, Vol. II, Part 2, 26, Article 20: 'Valid consent by a State to the commission of a given act by another State precludes the wrongfulness of that act in relation to the former State to the extent that the act remains within the limits of that consent'; see also the ILC Commentary, *ibid.*, 73: 'In the case of a bilateral treaty . . . States have the right to dispense with the performance of an obligation owed to them individually, or generally to permit conduct to occur which (absent such permission) would be unlawful so far as they are concerned.'

[92] Which applies, as will be often the case in investor-state arbitration, if consent is given only after the conduct breaching the treaty has occurred; see International Law Commission, *ILC Yearbook 2001*, Vol. II, Part 2, Commentary on Article 20, 73: 'Consent to the commission of otherwise wrongful conduct may be given by a State in advance or even at the time it is occurring. By contrast, cases of consent given after the conduct has occurred are a form of waiver or acquiescence, leading to loss of the right to invoke responsibility. This is dealt with in article 45'; J. Crawford, *State Responsibility: The General Part* (Cambridge University Press, 2013), 287; see also *ibid.*, 121–3; and Article 45 of the Vienna Convention on the Law of Treaties.

(3) *Ultimate Control and Intensity*

The third and final typology I submit is a categorisation of the instruments of reassertion according to whom the instrument grants the final word, the Contracting Parties jointly or individually or the tribunal. A high level of control lies undoubtedly with the Contracting Parties with regard to treaty drafting, amendment and termination. However, as long as a tribunal may interpret the IIA, drafting and amendment are no warranty that the tribunal follows exactly what the Contracting Parties had in mind. The same may apply to joint interpretations and consent. Even challenges to an arbitrator are usually to decide for the two remaining members of the arbitral panel.[93] In fact, any matter of interpretation, if not foreclosed for the tribunal to review, places ultimate control in the hands of the tribunal. This is true for interpretative guidelines, for example definitions of substantive provisions such as fair and equitable treatment or indirect expropriation as much as it is true for the insertion of general exceptions clauses, unless and only to the extent to which the IIA expressly grants the Contracting Parties a non-justiciable margin of appreciation.[94] It is this conundrum in particular, that is, that most instruments of reassertion still grant the tribunal at least a certain degree of final control, which fuels Contracting Parties' initiatives to insert appeal mechanisms into IIAs. A second instance vested with the power to overrule the findings of the first instance and possibly appointed exclusively by the Contracting Parties,[95] so the intention, may alleviate the concerns with the present model, where the tribunal in many

[93] See also generally on challenges to arbitrators in investment disputes, J. D. Fry and J. I. Stampalija, 'Forged Independence and Impartiality: Conflicts of Interest of International Arbitrators in Investment Disputes', *Arbitration International*, 30 (2014), 189. See also Chapter 15.

[94] Which, admittedly, is still quite unusual but might increase in number in future IIA provisions, for example, with regard to emergency measures taken in response to a national crisis.

[95] See e.g. the European Commission's proposal with regard to a permanent investment court: EU Commission, 'Concept Paper: Investment in TTIP and Beyond – The Path for Reform', 11–12, available at http://trade.ec.europa.eu/doclib/docs/2015/may/tradoc_153408.PDF (accessed 22 September 2016); see also the German initiative with respect to a permanent investment court: German Ministry for Economic Affairs and Energy, 'Modell-Investitionsschutzvertrag mit Investor-Staat-Schiedsverfahren für Industriestaaten unter Berücksichtigung der USA', 17 *et seq.*, available at www.bmwi.de/BMWi/Redaktion/PDF/M-O/modell-investitionsschutzvertrag-mit-investor-staat-schiedsverfahren-gutachten,property=pdf,bereich=bmwi2012,sprache=de,rwb=true.pdf (accessed 22 September 2016). See also Chapter 5.

respects enjoys the final word.[96] A similar consideration is behind explicit provisions on joint interpretations and the possibility to determine when the interpretation takes effect, which is envisaged in Article X.27 of CETA or Articles 9.24.3 and 27.2.2(f) of the Trans-Pacific Partnership Agreement (TPP), for example. Where the Contracting Parties clarify their intentions to curb the authority of the (investor-State) tribunal with regard to interpreting the IIA from the outset, the tribunal has no clout to second-guess such decision by the Contracting Parties if they clearly limit the scope within which the tribunal may exercise its judicial function.

D. Methodology, Structure and Contents of This Book

The aim of this edited volume is threefold. It seeks, firstly, to inquire into the theoretical foundations of IIAs and the rights and roles IIAs grant to investors, Contracting Parties, and the arbitral tribunal and to critically reflect on the purpose and desirability of investor-State dispute settlement. Martins Paparinskis[97] undertakes a theoretical inquiry into who plays the 'game of reassertion' of control in international investment law and how the rules of that game look like. The ultimate question of control – who are the masters of the IIA? – also features in Eleni Methymaki and Antonios Tzanakopoulos's piece on joint interpretations in Chapter 7. One is tempted to quickly respond to such a question: the Contracting Parties, naturally. However, in a complex system of dispute settlement that oscillates somewhere between agency and trusteeship, what roles does it hold, for example, for the investor-State and State-State tribunals, considering that at least in the former case the Contracting Parties and the parties to the dispute are not identical, as I will discuss, among other issues, in Chapter 6.

[96] See European Commission, DG Trade, 'Factsheet on Investor-State Dispute Settlement', 4–5, available at http://trade.ec.europa.eu/doclib/docs/2013/october/tradoc_151791.pdf (accessed 22 September 2016); European Commission, 'Concept Paper: Investment in TTIP and Beyond – The Path for Reform', 8–9, 11–12, available at http://trade.ec.europa.eu/doclib/docs/2015/may/tradoc_153408.PDF (accessed 22 September 2016). This is not to say, however, that there are no considerations that militate against the introduction of an appeals mechanism, see e.g. A. H. Qureshi, 'An Appellate System in International Investment Arbitration?', in P. Muchlinski, F. Ortino and C. Schreuer (eds.), *The Oxford Handbook of International Investment Law* (Oxford University Press, 2008), 1154.

[97] See Chapter 2.

Yet, despite all the recent media coverage and the enormous amounts awarded in cases such as *Occidental*[98] or *Yukos*,[99] Mavluda Sattorova's piece[100] presents case studies of States that do not seem to have realised the teeth international investment law possesses and, in turn, underestimate or even overlook the potential that a reassertion of control over the IIAs to which they are Parties may inhere. Her contribution's focus on domestic law responses to investor-State dispute settlement as a means of reassertion of control reveals an inspiring addition to the potential toolbox of reassertion of control by the Contracting Parties to IIAs, which we would usually mostly associate with responses on the international level.

Secondly, the contributions in Parts II and III will target procedural and substantive aspects and avenues for Contracting Parties to reassert control over IIAs and investment treaty arbitration. This is the core of this book, since little attention has been given in the literature so far to the questions arising from such reassertion of control for the actual solution of specific procedural and substantive matters in practice. What are the currently employed and potential avenues to reassert control over the IIAs or investment arbitration?

With regard to procedural aspects, discussed in Part II, the contribution of Friedrich Rosenfeld[101] looks at an increasingly important procedural instrument that Contracting Parties may attempt to employ in order to reassert control: procedures for early dismissal of claims, including and beyond Rule 41(5) of the ICSID Arbitration Rules. Freya Baetens[102] looks at the stage after the issuance of the award, including enforcement, annulment, challenge and (potential) appeal. Finally, as a lynchpin to Part III, discussing substantive aspects, State-State arbitration as a means of reassertion of control will be in the focus of my aforementioned contribution in Chapter 6.

This is where Antonios Tzanakopoulos and Eleni Methymaki in Chapter 7 on joint interpretations by the Contracting Parties pick up the thread, leading into the substantive matters in Part III, pertaining in particular to the law of treaties. As yet another aspect of treaty interpretation,

[98] See *Occidental Petroleum Corporation and Occidental Exploration and Production Company* v. *Republic of Ecuador*, ICSID Case No. ARB/06/11, Award of 5 October 2012.

[99] See *Yukos Universal Limited (Isle of Man)* v. *Russian Federation*, UNCITRAL, PCA Case No. AA 227, Final Award of 18 July 2014. However, note also the Judgment of The Hague District Court of 20 April 2016 (C/09/477160 / HA ZA 15-1) that set aside the Award of 18 July 2014.

[100] See Chapter 3. [101] See Chapter 4. [102] See Chapter 5.

Rumiana Yotova[103] will shed light on systemic integration in IIA interpretation as instrument for the Contracting Parties' reassertion of control. The very topical matter of IIA termination, with a specific nod to sunset clauses, is the target of Fernando Lusa Bordin's contribution[104]. Finally, Paul Barker[105] and Diane A. Desierto[106] will consider substantive matters beyond specific aspects of the law of treaties, that is, legitimate regulatory interests of Contracting Parties and remedies.

The third aim of this book is to spot and discuss future trends and current and future policies that are intended to reassert or capable of reasserting Contracting Parties' influence over IIAs and investment treaty arbitration. Part IV is dedicated to this latter endeavour. Eric de Brabandere[107] inquires how definitions of substantive standards such as fair and equitable treatment or indirect expropriation, which are to be included in future IIAs such as the investment chapters on CETA or TTIP or a future EU Model BIT, may serve as control mechanisms. Nikos Lavranos[108] traces wider developments of EU investment policy, regarding both within the EU and with third parties. Eventually, the final two chapters will look at the individuals who decide investment disputes. Michael Waibel will discuss current and future arbitrator selection procedures, including the new EU initiative as to the so-called 'investment court system' integrated in the CETA and the EU-Vietnam FTA[109]. Last but not least, Stephan Wilske's and Melanie Eckardt's contribution[110] will consider matters of arbitrator challenge, inspired by the observation that respondent States in particular challenge arbitrators based on their academic writings as a tactical means to take control over the investment arbitration.

Let me conclude with a few brief words on the methodological approach of this book. As mentioned earlier, international investment law is currently under attack. Confronted with the 'public interest challenge'[111] and faced with hostile public opinion, the question is increasingly being raised as to whether it is desirable and necessary to have a special regime of dispute settlement for foreign investors. This is, indeed, the existential question of international investment law and arbitration. This book takes this question seriously but approaches the issue of legitimacy crisis and public interest challenge from a different angle. The contributions in this book seek to observe the consequences and implications of the current

[103] See Chapter 8. [104] See Chapter 9. [105] See Chapter 10. [106] See Chapter 11.
[107] See Chapter 12. [108] See Chapter 13. [109] See Chapter 14. [110] See Chapter 15.
[111] See A. Kulick, *Global Public Interest in International Investment Law*, 50–2; and see Section A(1).

trend of reassertion of control by focusing on an inquiry into whether the current investment regime and the instruments of general public international law, particularly the law of treaties, has to offer are adequate to accommodate that trend. Hence, methodologically, the initial approach employed by this book is descriptive rather than prescriptive. As elaborated earlier, most contributions will, in a first step, look at procedural and substantive mechanisms – of international investment law and arbitration and/or general public international law – that Contracting Parties (1) are currently employing or (2) may employ in order to reassert control over investment treaties or investment treaty arbitration. Furthermore, the theoretical, empirical and policy perspectives mentioned before complement the picture.

However, this descriptive focus only seemingly lacks normative ambition. Firstly, while having been asked to present and discuss the avenues of how Contracting Parties do and may reassert control by using specific procedural or substantive means, the authors of the individual chapters enjoyed the freedom to evaluate the (potential) use of such instruments of reassertion, and all took the liberty of making use of this freedom. Secondly, it is not the purpose of this book to give a final verdict on the existential question of international investment law and arbitration as identified earlier. However, the book intends to offer insights into whether one of the foundational presumptions of those who view ISDS as an 'unjustified privilege'[112] can stand, that is, that the current regime, with the necessary reform and the public international law toolbox at hand, can be reformed so as to adequately meet the 'public interest challenge'. Hence, this volume is also supposed to offer guidance in addressing the question whether the still relatively young field of international investment treaty law and arbitration is an 'inherently dubious transitional phenomenon'[113] or whether – with the adequate reform and room for Contracting Parties' reassertion of control – it is here to stay.

[112] See, instead of many, M. Kumm, 'An Empire of Capital? Transatlantic Investment Protection as the Institutionalization of Unjustified Privilege', *European Society of International Law Reflection*, 4(3).

[113] *Ibid.*

2

Masters and Guardians of International Investment Law

How to Play the Game of Reassertion

MARTINS PAPARINSKIS

A. Introduction

Any discussion of reassertion of control by Contracting Parties over international investment law must proceed on the basis of certain assumptions about the nature of the legal order within which it takes place. The intellectual framework for this chapter is provided by the mainstream view of public international law, described by James Crawford in the following terms:

> [I]nternational law is the product of a process of claim and counterclaim, assertion and reaction, by Governments as representative of States and by other actors at the international level. This implies a diffuse judgment which may take time to arrive at, although where the judgment is widely shared or is formulated by a body recognised as authoritative in the matter, such as the Security Council acting under Chapter VII of the Charter or a competent regional organisation, or a competent court or tribunal, the judgment may be arrived at fairly rapidly and may stick. But it is always the process of articulation and assessment that occurs where rights or interests are engaged at the international level that matters. International law is a form of *praxis* involving diffuse, decentralised but nonetheless observably real authority. At the same time it is a process in which rights are asserted and duties relied on by reference to norms based on express agreement or custom. International law is both a process of assertion and reliance *and* a system of principles and rules: together they constitute the course of international law, confounding those critics who simplemindedly assert that it can be one (process) or the other (system) but not both.[1]

[1] J. Crawford, 'Chance, Order, Change: The Course of International Law', *RCADI*, 365 (2013), 9, 21–22 (emphasis in the original); also V. Lowe, *International Law* (Oxford University Press, 2007), chap. 2.

It goes without saying – but may go even better by being said – that international law is not the only frame of reference for discussion of international investment matters, nor is it necessarily a better frame than others. Much valuable work in the field is done by scholars with a background in international commercial arbitration, international commercial litigation and domestic public law; by scholars of critical-theoretical or inter-disciplinary persuasions; and by economists and political scientists. But the perspective of public international law, articulated with appropriate modesty and with no necessary claim to greater legitimacy, can at the very least usefully complement these voices.[2]

International investment law is public international law.[3] There is nothing conceptually different, innovatory or *sui generis* about it. All of its constituent elements flow from entirely unremarkable and well-known law-making techniques of international law and could constitute *sui generis* only if that concept were to be given a remarkably broad meaning, as including everything that is not identical to pre-existing blueprints. This point may sound like, but is not meant to be, a pejorative one. The manner in which investment protection law is built from its constitutive parts reflects perfectly decent workmanship on the part of treaty drafters, particularly in treaties concluded since 2014. But it is nevertheless the case that neither the particular elements nor the broader systemic structures present any conceptual or *sui generis* challenges to traditional canons of international legal reasoning.[4]

That legal questions posed regarding international investment law pose no conceptual challenges to traditional legal reasoning is a proposition that fully applies to inquiry in relation to reassertion. Assertion of control – whether met by acceptance, acquiescence, indifference or objection – is the usual process by which international law is made. But

[2] This is a fairly close paraphrase of R. O'Keefe, *International Criminal Law* (Oxford University Press, 2015), vii; see similarly I. Brownlie, *International Law and the Use of Force by States* (Oxford University Press, 1963), v–vii; R. Churchill and V. Lowe, *The Law of the Sea*, 3rd edn. (Manchester University Press, 1999), 2–3.

[3] J. Alvarez, 'The Public International Law Regime Governing International Investment', *RCADI*, 344 (2011); Eric de Brabandere, *Investment Treaty Arbitration as Public International Law: Procedural Aspects and Implications* (Cambridge University Press, 2014), 7 *et seq.*

[4] M. Paparinskis, 'Analogies and Other Regimes of International Law', in Z. Douglas, J. Pauwelyn and J. Viñuales (eds.), *The Foundations of International Investment Law: Bringing Theory into Practice* (Oxford University Press, 2014), 73, 73; also Y. Radi, 'In Defence of "Generalism" in International Legal Scholarship and Practice', *Leiden Journal of International Law*, 27 (2014), 303.

this does not mean that all questions will have easy and straightforward answers or that all challenges will easily fit within familiar patterns of discussion and resolution. Reassertion of control by Contracting Parties in relation to a regime of international law (perceived as) dominated by bodies of international dispute settlement is certainly not unique, and one might point to similar developments in other areas of international law. But it does appear to be in some ways a relatively recent phenomenon, borne out of reflections upon the merits of increased resort to and creation of various judicial and arbitral institutions since the early 1990s. Vaughan Lowe has described this perspective in the following terms:

> In the light of history, it may be that the past decade – epitomized by the remarkable focus on the legal aspects of the invasion of Iraq in 2003 and of the so-called 'War on Terror', by the crushing weight of the cases (now numbering around 160,000) piling on to the docket of the European Court of Human Rights, and by the emergence of international investment arbitration and international trade disputes as two of the most fecund and febrile areas of legal practice – will be seen as the high-water mark of the litigation of international disputes. It may be that there is an increasing perception that courts and tribunals are not at all well-equipped for dealing with certain kinds of international dispute.[5]

This chapter will explain how the 'game of reassertion' should be played and judged in the contemporary legal order.[6] The argument will be presented in four steps. Before properly engaging with the game of reassertion in investment law, it is useful to consider how similar games have been played in the past. The first part of this chapter therefore introduces examples of assertion in international law that provide a backdrop for the discussion regarding investment law (Section B). The second part will set out the rules of the reassertion game: benchmarks of international law regarding sources, responsibility, and dispute settlement (Section C). The third part introduces the players who seek to reassert: States and, more broadly, Parties (Section D). The fourth part deals with some players and bystanders who may be affected by reassertion, including investors, non-disputing parties and Tribunals (Section E). The overall and rather uninspiring

[5] V. Lowe, 'The Function of Litigation in International Society', *International and Comparative Law Quarterly*, 61 (2012), 209, 210.

[6] See, on international law and games, R. O'Keefe, 'Curriculum Vitae: A Prequel', *Current Legal Problems*, 69 (2016) (forthcoming); also A. Bianchi, D. Peat and M. Windsor (eds.), *Interpretation in International Law* (Oxford University Press, 2015), esp. chaps. 1, 2 and 17.

thesis is that these questions do not call for a re-examination of the conceptual underpinnings of the international legal order. What is needed is (only) a competent application of rules of the game to various situations that, while quite possibly very complex, are by no means unique in their complexity in the broader perspective of international law.

B. How the Game of Reassertion Is Played

Assertion, reaction and reassertion all contribute to making and developing international law. Assertion and contestation of control have provided an influential framework for discussing the relationship between States and international organisations.[7] Assertion and reassertion of authority by international law-makers over settlers of international disputes is a not uncommon element of this process. How has the game of reassertion been played in international law? By way of more or less random example, one way for that to happen is for international law-makers to assert their authority in line with the position taken by international courts. Significant parts of the law of treaties and State responsibility have been developed in just these terms.[8] Law-makers may adopt and grant seal-of-approval, through assertion, positions by international courts of questionable persuasiveness. The adoption by State practice of the position of the International Criminal Tribunal for Former Yugoslavia regarding war crimes in non-international armed conflicts may serve as an example for that proposition.[9] In these and other comparable cases, law-makers and dispute settlers are nudging rules in the same direction. In another example, in relation to the law of the sea and maritime delimitation, Judge Peter Tomka has observed that 'there is every indication that the lockstep march and practice of States and international judicial and arbitral bodies will continue onward, and

[7] D. Sarooshi, *International Organizations and Their Exercise of Sovereign Powers* (Oxford University Press, 2006).

[8] V. Gowlland-Debbas, 'The Role of the International Court of Justice in the Development of the Contemporary Law of Treaties', in C. Tams and J. Sloan (eds.), *The Development of International Law by the International Court of Justice* (Oxford University Press, 2013), 25; J. Crawford, 'The International Court of Justice and the Law of State Responsibility', *ibid.*, 71.

[9] R. Cryer, 'International Criminal Tribunals and the Sources of International Law', *Journal of International Criminal Justice*, 10 (2012), 1045, 1051; O'Keefe, *International Criminal Law*, 126–8.

towards greater unity and coherence in the application and interpretation of legal principles'.[10]

But lockstep march is not the only possible form that the response by States may take. States may make the decision not to adopt questionable positions taken by courts by way of positive assertion. This may very well happen regarding the customary definition of terrorism suggested by the Special Tribunal for Lebanon.[11] States may successfully reassert authority so as to displace or even supersede the position of courts. The reversal of position expressed by the Permanent Court of International Justice regarding flag State jurisdiction in the *SS Lotus* case, first through treaty law and then probably through customary law, is an example of this.[12] States may attempt to reassert authority over positions taken by competent international courts, with the result that reasonable people will disagree about what the best legal position is; certain aspects of use of force[13] and belligerent reprisals demonstrate how this can happen.[14] States can also direct their disapproval at the particular adjudicator through various means: terminate consent to pending adjudication,[15] refuse to participate in proceedings,[16] withdraw from proceedings and refuse to comply with *res judicata*,[17] criticise the adjudicator and the

[10] P. Tomka, 'The Contribution of the International Court of Justice to the Law of the Sea', in D. Attard et al. (eds.), *The IMLI Manual on International Maritime Law*, Vol. I: *The Law of the Sea* (Oxford University Press, 2014), 618, 642.

[11] B. Saul, 'Amicus Curiae Brief on the Notion of Terrorist Acts Submitted to the Appeals Chamber of the Special Tribunal for Lebanon Pursuant to Rule 131 of the Rules of Procedure and Evidence', *Criminal Law Forum*, 22 (2011), 365; O'Keefe, *International Criminal Law*, 160.

[12] V. Lowe and A. Tzanakopoulos, 'The Development of the Law of the Sea by the International Court of Justice', in Tams and Sloan, *The Development of International Law*, 183–4.

[13] E. Wilmshurst, 'The Chatham House Principles of International Law on the Use of Force in Self-Defence', *International and Comparative Law Quarterly*, 55 (2006), 963, 966, 967, 969–70; D. Bethlehem, 'Principles of Self-Defense – A Brief Response', *American Journal of International Law*, 107 (2013), 579, 581, 583.

[14] Cryer, 'International Criminal Tribunals', 1052–4.

[15] PCA, 'Press Release: Arbitration between the Republic of Croatia and the Republic of Slovenia', 5 August 2015, available at: www.pcacases.com/web/sendAttach/1389 (accessed 24 February 2016).

[16] *Arctic Sunrise Arbitration (Netherlands* v. *Russia)*, PCA Case No. 2014-02, Note Verbale from the Russian Federation to the PCA of 27 February 2014, available at: www.pcacases.com/web/sendAttach/1315 (accessed 24 February 2016).

[17] M. Nash (Leigh), *Cumulative Digest of United States Practice in International Law 1981–1988*, Book III (Washington, DC: Office of the Legal Adviser, Department of State, 1995), 3326–56.

validity of its decisions,[18] withdraw consent to adjudication of future cases,[19] dismantle the adjudicator[20] or even physically attack individual adjudicators.[21] And, of course, States may reassert authority in a more constructive manner, strengthening rather than weakening adjudicators. The creation of the Appellate Body of the World Trade Organisation (WTO AB) may be read along these lines, and finessing rules of appointments to ensure a higher quality of individual adjudicators provides a narrower example in the European context.[22]

In short, the game of reassertion of authority by international law-makers over settlers of international disputes does take place in practice. It will not necessarily be always played when a colourable excuse exists – a degree of tolerable dissatisfaction is built into the act of consent to formalised dispute settlement – and players attempting reassertion need not be successful when the game is played. But if it does happen, a prediction regarding the 'diffuse judgment which may take time to arrive at'[23] will be difficult to make, particularly if reassertion has just begun or is in the process of being articulated or evaluated. The story of development of the law of the continental shelf may give some sense of the necessary modesty with which an international lawyer on a given day should speculate about future developments.[24] The proclamation by US President Truman of 28 September 1945 is usually taken as the starting point of

[18] M. du Plessi, T. Maluwa and A. O'Reilly, 'Africa and the International Criminal Court', Chatham House International Law, January 2013, available at: www.chathamhouse.org/sites/files/chathamhouse/public/Research/International%20Law/0713pp_iccafrica.pdf (accessed 24 February 2016).

[19] *Request for Interpretation of Judgment of 31 March 2004 in the Case Concerning Avena and Other Mexican Nationals (Mexico* v. *United States of America)*, Judgment of 19 January 2009, ICJ Reports 2009, 3, para. 15.

[20] E. de Wet, 'The Rise and Fall of the Tribunal of the Southern African Development Community: Implications for Dispute Settlement in Southern Africa', *ICSID Review*, 28 (2013), 45.

[21] Less common now than in days past, V. V. Veeder, 'The *Lena* Goldfields Arbitration: The Historical Roots of Three Ideas', *International and Comparative Law Quarterly*, 47 (1998), 747, 781, although a few instances of factually contested unpleasant doings do come to mind; D. Caron and L. Caplan (eds.), *The UNCITRAL Arbitration Rules: A Commentary*, 2nd edn. (Oxford University Press, 2013), 225; 'Priyatna Abdurrasyid 1930–2015', Global Arbitration Review of 17 June 2015.

[22] M. Bobek, *Selecting Europe's Judges: A Critical Review of the Appointment Procedures to the European Courts* (Oxford University Press, 2015).

[23] Crawford, 'Chance, Order, Change', 21.

[24] J. Crawford and T. Viles, 'International Law on a Given Day', in K. Ginther et al. (eds.), *Völkerrecht zwischen normativem Anspruch und politischer Realität. Festschrift für Karl Zemanek zum 65. Geburtstag* (Berlin: Duncker & Humblot, 1994).

the process, with contributions from claims by other States, work of the International Law Commission, treaty practice through multilateral law of the sea treaties, treaty delimitation practice, judgments by various international courts and arbitral tribunals and practice of other institutions shaping the law.[25] What could one reasonably expect from an international lawyer who was asked to prepare a brief memorandum on issues and developments to be presented in the early morning of Monday 1 October?

A summary of rules on rules would be a good starting point, to know the benchmarks against which developments will be evaluated, with main participants in the law-making process elaborated in greater detail, and educated guesses about their likely conduct ventured (even if they might be better provided by advisers with expertise other than, or additional to law). But the results of the game – structure and content of the regime and particular rules that could emerge – would depend on many considerations: choices by players and non-players of the particular game and related games, (changing) conditions for entry and participation in the game, (changing) powers of players and possible changes in the rules of the game themselves, as well as events and developments in areas outside the game.[26] Even if developments are discussed in a short- to midterm perspective, much depends on the underlying and necessarily speculative assumptions about the extent of systemic changes.[27] It is extraordinarily hard to get the results right, particularly over an extended period of time. It is not impossible: Eli Lauterpacht's paper on drafting investment treaties from 1962 identified with remarkable perceptiveness many of the key issues that investment law was to face in the next half-century, from technical points such as the definition of investment and ambiguity of some obligations to systemic questions such as obligations of investors and links between legal protection and development.[28] But the

[25] Churchill and Lowe, *The Law of the Sea*, chap. 8.

[26] D. Roughton and C. Trehearne, 'The Continental Shelf', in D. Attard et al. (eds.), *The IMLI Manual on International Maritime Law*, Vol. I: *The Law of the Sea* (Oxford University Press, 2014), 137.

[27] Cf. two recent explorations of the crystal ball, with titles that suggest markedly different assumptions about the extent of change, J. Kalicki and A. Joubin-Bret (eds.), *Reshaping the Investor-State Dispute Settlement System* (Leiden, Netherlands: Brill, 2015); St Hindelang and M. Krajewski (eds.), *Shifting Paradigms in International Investment Law* (Cambridge University Press, 2016).

[28] E. Lauterpacht, 'The Drafting of Treaties for the Protection of Investment', *International and Comparative Law Quarterly Supplementary Publication*, 3 (1962), 18.

law of unintended consequences makes this hard,[29] so an international lawyer may very well prefer to play it safe and limit herself to setting out the rules of the game, powers of players seeking to reassert and powers of other players. The next sections will proceed to do exactly that.

C. Rules of the Game of Reassertion

The rules of the game of reassertion are the same as for the general game of international law. For the purposes of convenience, they will be discussed along the three cross-cutting categories of sources, responsibility and dispute settlement. Sources of international law include treaties, customary law, general principles of international law and possibly unilateral acts. Secondary rules of recognition of customary law are mostly set out in judicial decisions and at the moment are being synthesised by the International Law Commission (ILC).[30] Rules of recognition of the law of treaties are mostly set out in the 1969 Vienna Convention on the Law of Treaties (VCLT) (and, when international organisations are involved, its sister convention of the 1986 vintage) and are to a considerable extent (treated as) reflective of customary law. General principles are usually read as involving two different types of legal argument: general principles of *international* law proper[31] and general principles of *domestic* law, which may be synthesised from commonalities in leading domestic legal systems and *mutatis mutandis* transposed to the international level.[32] There is support for the proposition that unilateral acts may

[29] In a 1996 paper, Lauterpacht noted that 'while it is possible to contemplate the changes in standards, it is difficult to foresee the denial to individuals of the procedural competence that has now been so widely conferred on them': E. Lauterpacht, 'International Law and Private Foreign Investment, *Indiana Journal of Global Legal Studies*, 4 (1996–1997), 259, 275–6. In 1997, he was appointed as President of a Tribunal, the award of which, with the benefit of hindsight, was the starting point for the now commonplace critical discussion of investment law; *Metalclad Corporation* v. *Mexico*, ICSID Additional Facility Case No. ARB(AF)/97/1, Award of 30 August 2000.

[30] See the ILC website at: http://legal.un.org/ilc/guide/1_13.htm (accessed 24 February 2016); and P. Dumberry, *The Formation and Identification of Rules of Customary International Law in International Investment Law* (Cambridge University Press, 2016).

[31] Bin Cheng, *General Principles of Law as Applied by International Courts and Tribunals* (Cambridge, UK: Grotius, 1953); A. Mitchell et al. (eds.), *Good Faith and International Economic Law* (Oxford University Press, 2015).

[32] H. Lauterpacht, *Private Law Sources and Analogies of International Law* (Harlow, UK: Longmans, Green & Co., 1927). A study group of the ILA on the use of domestic law principles for the development of international law is considering these matters; see ILA website at: www.ila-hq.org/en/committees/study_groups.cfm/cid/1033 (accessed 24 February 2016).

impose international obligations.[33] Judicial and arbitral decisions, while important in elaborating the content of rules of international law, are not sources of international law (unless law-makers adopt them into treaty or customary law, or special procedural rules exist to such effect). Sources of law are closely related to responsibility for breach of obligations, the rules on which are set out in the 2001 ILC Articles on State responsibility (2001 ILC Articles) (and, when international organisations are involved, its sister Articles from 2011 or perhaps even special secondary rules for certain organisations) and are again to considerable extent, if lesser for the latter Articles, (treated as) reflective of customary law.[34] Finally, the basic structural underpinning of international dispute settlement is the necessity for opt-in by disputing parties.[35]

I would not want to overstate the certainty with which these basic rules may be articulated and applied. The law of State responsibility, set out with considerable authority in the 2001 ILC Articles,[36] provides a convenient example for the different shades that uncertainty over rules may cast over the game. Does its essentially inter-State structure affect the manner in which the Articles, or particular parts of the Articles, can be applied to international investment law?[37] Is it appropriate to analogise between the position of third States and the position of investors in relation to, say, counter-measures?[38] Are rules on attribution of conduct of State-owned corporations accurate and satisfactory for the purposes of

[33] *Nuclear Tests (Australia* v. *France)*, Judgment of 20 December 1974, ICJ Report No. 1974, 253, paras. 46–9; 2006 ILC Guiding Principles applicable to Unilateral Declarations of States Capable of Creating Legal Obligations, see ILC website at: http://legal.un.org/ilc/texts/instruments/english/commentaries/9_9_2006.pdf (accessed 24 February 2016).

[34] S. Olleson, *State Responsibility before International and Domestic Courts* (Oxford University Press, 2017).

[35] A. Steingruber, *Consent in International Arbitration* (Oxford University Press, 2012); G. Hernández, *The International Court of Justice and the Judicial Function* (Oxford University Press, 2014), 47–50; Y. Shany, *Questions of Jurisdiction and Admissibility before International Courts* (Cambridge University Press, 2015).

[36] J. Crawford, *State Responsibility: The General Part* (Cambridge University Press, 2013), 42–4.

[37] *Yukos Universal Limited (Isle of Man)* v. *Russian Federation*, UNCITRAL, PCA Case No. AA 227, Final Award of 18 July 2014, fn. 10; *Gold Reserves* v. *Venezuela*, ICSID Case No. ARB(AF)/09/1, Award of 22 September 2014, para. 679; *Quiborax SA and Non Metallic Minerals SA* v. *Bolivia*, ICSID Case No. ARB/06/2, Award of 16 September 2015, paras. 554–61; J. Crawford, 'Investment Arbitration and the ILC Articles on State Responsibility', *ICSID Review*, 25 (2010), 127.

[38] K. Parlett, 'The Application of the Rules on Countermeasures in Investment Claims', in C. Chinkin and F. Baetens (eds.), *Sovereignty, Statehood and State Responsibility* (Cambridge University Press, 2015), 389.

investment arbitration?[39] Is not there a slight systemic oddity when the seemingly least elaborate rules on reparations, relating to contribution to damage, end up having the greatest effect on quantum in the largest damages awards?[40] And would responsibility of States and international organisations be subject to special rules when the European Union is in some sense implicated?[41] These are not trivial questions capable of straightforward answers.

Questions of similar complexity may be raised relating to sources and dispute settlement. If the scope of a primary obligation and the criteria for determining its breach are not affected by the nature of the entity invoking responsibility, is it possible for a State to oppose to an investor such interpretative materials that satisfy the criteria of Article 32 VCLT, but that investor could not have had access to?[42] How is customary law identified in a procedural setting structured so as to preclude the usual method of generation of customary law through inter-State opposition of claims? Is the law of indirect expropriation set out in the Trans-Pacific Partnership (TPP) a codification of customary law, a crystallisation of customary law, an emerging general customary rule, a rule of special custom or nothing more than a (misleadingly described) treaty rule?[43] Does one interpret consent expressed in domestic law by reference to (general principles of) statutory interpretation, principles of treaty interpretation, principles of interpretation of unilateral declarations or principles developed relating to comparable regimes of international dispute settlement?[44] There is ground for reasonable disagreement on what the best answers to these questions are. But the important point is that default

[39] Cf. Crawford, *State Responsibility*, 161–6; A. Badia, *Piercing the Veil of State Enterprise in International Arbitration* (Alphen aan Den Rijn, Netherlands: Kluwer Law, 2014); J. Dereje, *Staatsnahe Unternehmen* (Baden-Baden, Germany: Nomos, 2016).

[40] *Yukos*, paras. 1594–637; J. Gill and R. Gupta, 'The Principle of Contributory Fault after *Yukos*', *Dispute Resolution International*, 9 (2015), 93.

[41] Cf. P. Eeckhout, *EU External Relations Law*, 2nd edn. (Oxford University Press, 2011), 262–4, with F. Hoffmeister, 'Litigating against the European Union and Its Member States – Who Responds under the ILC's Draft Articles on International Responsibility of International Organisations?', *European Journal of International Law*, 21 (2010), 723; P. J. Kuijper and E. Paasivirta, 'EU International Responsibility and Its Attribution: From the Inside Looking Out', in M. Evans and P. Koutrakos (eds.), *The International Responsibility of the European Union* (Oxford, UK: Hart, 2013).

[42] See *HICEE B.V.* v. *Slovakia*, PCA Case No. 2009–11, Partial Award of 23 May 2011, paras. 128–40.

[43] See 2015 Trans-Pacific Partnership, Annex 9-B, available at: https://ustr.gov/sites/default/files/TPP-Final-Text-Investment.pdf (accessed 24 February 2016).

[44] See *PNG Sustainable Development Program Ltd.* v. *Papua New Guinea*, ICSID Case No. ARB/13/33, Award of 5 May 2015, paras. 259–69.

assumptions about formation and implementation of international law will provide the vocabulary for discussing and answering them.

The final page in the rule book must contain an index of similar games. International investment law is becoming increasingly sophisticated both in its law-making and adjudicative capacities, but on many issues its pedigree is more modest than that of other similar regimes. Flicking through rules for similar games may be at the very least instructive and possibly also legally relevant for filling particular gaps. Reasonable people may disagree about what games are the most similar to international investment law.[45] The starting point should be that international investment law is part of public international law. Therefore, rules for public law and international commercial arbitration, while descriptively similar in some ways, would not be commonly included in this index (unless particular elements of those games are brought directly into investment law). Once the inquiry is located firmly within public international law, three similar games suggest themselves: the law of human rights, the law of treaties on third parties and the law of inter-State regimes – historically diplomatic protection but increasingly also trade law.[46] Of course, these are different games with sometimes very different rules, and nothing can replace a careful examination of the particular issue. And comparative reasoning must always try to capture the elusive essence of other regimes without unduly simplifying them.[47] But casting a glance towards contiguous legal regimes will provide a sense of whether or not there is a trend in international law in relation to resolving particular issues in a particular manner.

[45] A. Roberts, 'Clash of Paradigms: Actors and Analogies Shaping the Investment Treaty System', *American Journal of International Law*, 107 (2013), 45; V. Vadi, *Analogies in International Investment Law and Arbitration* (Cambridge University Press, 2015).

[46] Paparinskis, 'Analogies and Other Regimes of International Law', 73; J. Kurtz, *The WTO and International Investment Law* (Cambridge University Press, 2016). A possibly unappreciated regime of international economic law that provides for a right of an individual to submit a case against a State to arbitration is international tax law; see 2014 OECD Model Tax Convention, Art. 25(5), available at: www.oecd.org/ctp/treaties/2014-model-tax-convention-articles.pdf (accessed 24 February 2016).

[47] E.g. arguments for proportionality in international investment law that draw upon human rights experience: G. Bucheler, *Proportionality in Investor-State Arbitration* (Oxford University Press, 2015); C. Henckels, *Proportionality and Deference in Investor-State Arbitration* (Cambridge University Press, 2015), should acknowledge the extent of contestation of proportionality in human rights literature; see chapters by Letsas and Verdirame in R. Cruft et al. (eds.), *Philosophical Foundations of Human Rights* (Oxford University Press, 2015); also G. Husctoft et al. (eds.), *Proportionality and the Rule of Law* (Cambridge University Press, 2014).

D. Playing for the Reasserting Team

Contracting Parties – mostly but not exclusively States – will play for the reasserting team. Contracting Parties can do almost everything as law-makers. They can create treaty rules with any content whatsoever, agree on special customary rules among themselves or contribute to general customary law, create special rules of treaty law and State responsibility and create international courts and tribunals. There may be policy arguments for making particular rules, and making such rules may well have broader implications in terms of treaty and responsibility law. But this does not affect the law-making discretion, which is only limited by peremptory rules and third-party rights under international law, issues not usually perceived as being a great concern for investment law. In short, Contracting Parties can draft the rules of the games with great discretion, almost unlimited in principle and almost entirely unlimited in practice.

Their powers to tinker with the rules during the game cannot be stated in such categorical terms. Two opinions on the contested question of interpretation by Contracting Parties of treaty rules at issue in pending disputes[48] may serve as an illustration of this. James Crawford took the view that

> the parties to the treaty . . . own the treaty. It is their treaty. It is not anyone else's treaty. In the context of investment treaty arbitration there is a tendency to believe that investors own bilateral investment treaties, not the states parties to them. So, for example, when the NAFTA provides for interpretation of its provisions by a Commission of states parties, this is regarded as somehow an infringement on the inherent rights of investors under the NAFTA. That is not what international law says. International law says that the parties to a treaty own the treaty and can interpret it. One might say within reason, but one might not question the application of reason as they see fit.[49]

Conversely, one of Crawford's academic and curial predecessors thought that

> [t]his is surely against the most elementary rules of the due process of justice . . . It is very sad to see this present betrayal of principles of which the United States has long been the revered author and practitioner.[50]

[48] See a recent discussion in *Mesa Power Group, LLC* v. *Canada*, PCA Case No. 2012–17, Award of 24 March 2016, paras. 467–83.

[49] J. Crawford, 'A Consensualist Interpretation of Article 31(3) of the Vienna Convention', in G. Nolte (ed.), *Treaties and Subsequent Practice* (Oxford University Press, 2013), 29, 31.

[50] *Methanex Corp.* v. *US*, UNCITRAL Arbitration, Second Expert Opinion of Sir Robert Jennings of 6 September 2001, 6–7.

That the mere presence of procedural rights for non-State actors will not suspend normal law-making processes under international law must be right. But the feeling of normative unease about an international legal order that would never question the reason of reshaping rules in pending cases is also present. Since both these views cannot be held simultaneously, the interplay of rules, principles and rules on rules should provide a framework for elaborating a compromise solution (perhaps, in the particular instance, drawing a distinction between existence and opposability of particular rules or materials). Once the rules are created, the powers and responsibilities of Contracting Parties will fall to be determined through the interplay of rules on sources, responsibility and particular primary obligations. There are certain things that Contracting Parties may do on their own and more things that they can do collectively, but the precise contours and manner of these things can no longer be determined by a general reference to law-making capacities and instead have to be articulated and implemented through the technical vocabulary of particular rules.

Contracting Parties do not have to but are likely to be States, and this has certain implications. As Vaughan Lowe has put it,

> BITs [bilateral investment treaties] do not exist in isolation. They are rooted in the rich compost of municipal and international legal systems; and they can only properly be understood in that context . . . the treaties [should be] considered not as self-sufficient monads but as components in a legal process that moves through overlapping legal orders, national, regional and international.[51]

One consequence lies at the plane of domestic law: the persistence of the regulatory powers of the State through the permanent sovereignty over natural resources.[52] Another one flows from the interaction of investment law and domestic law. There is considerable support for the view that 'contribution and risk assumption form part of the core elements which characterize an investment'.[53] It is not unusual for

[51] V. Lowe, 'Book Review of *Commentaries on Selected Model Investment Treaties / edited by Chester Brown*', *ICSID Review*, 30 (2015), 275, 276.

[52] V. Lowe, 'Regulation or Expropriation', *Current Legal Problems*, 55 (2002), 447, 450.

[53] *Caratube International Oil Company* v. *Kazakhstan*, ICSID Case No. ARB/08/12, Decision on the Annulment Application of 21 February 2014, para. 235; also *KT Asia* v. *Kazakhstan*, ICSID Case No. ARB/09/8, Award of 17 October 2013, paras. 188–223; *Nova Scotia Incorporated (Canada)* v. *Venezuela*, ICSID Case No. ARB(AF)/11/1, Award of 30 April 2014, paras. 90–7, 105–13; *Poštová Banka, AS and Istrokapital SE* v. *Greece*, ICSID Case No. ARB/13/8, Award of 9 April 2015, paras. 360–71; *İçkale İnşaat Limited Şirket* v. *Turkmenistan*, ICSID Case No. ARB/10/24, Award of 8 March 2016,

domestic and international legal orders to interact in various ways.[54] But the deep, perhaps even *sine qua non* enmeshing of domestic law and the particular regime of international law may be worthy of a particular note. The third point relates to international law. International investment law is not clinically isolated from other regimes of international law, which may have consequences on the rights, powers and responsibilities of Contracting Parties both as a matter of international law and on the domestic plane.[55] These regimes may also provide a procedural, policy and political framework for articulating arguments of reassertion. The fourth point is a rather pedestrian one. Contracting Parties may *ex officio* have access to various institutions, through which they may formally and informally affect how the game is played, be that the United Nations Commission on International Trade Law (UNCITRAL), the Organisation for Economic Co-operation and Development (OECD), the United Nations Conference on Trade and Development (UNCTAD), or the ILC.

Analogies from other regimes of international law are, as analogies must be, both similar and different. The richness of other debates should probably caution against excessive simplification of lessons for Contracting Parties of investment treaties. A procedural example is provided by attempts by certain States to reassert authority over the European Court of Human Rights. Is the lesson to take away from, say, the 2012 Brighton Declaration that Strasbourg is nudged in the direction of tightening its rules on jurisdiction and admissibility and getting better

paras. 289–91; *MNSS BV and Recupero Credito Acciaio NV* v. *Montenegro*, ICSID Additional Facility Case No. ARB(AF)/12/8, Award of 4 May 2016, paras. 189–90; TPP, Art. 9(1), 9-2.

[54] D. Bethlehem, 'International Law, European Community Law and National Law: Three Systems in Search of a Framework – Systemic Relativity in the Interaction of Law in the European Union', in M. Koskenniemi (ed.), *Legal Aspects of the European Union* (Leiden, Netherlands: Brill, 1997); A. Roberts, 'Comparative International Law: The Role of National Courts in Creating and Enforcing International Law', *International and Comparative Law Quarterly*, 60 (2011), 57; A. Tzanakopoulos and C. Tams, 'Introduction: Domestic Courts as Agents of Development of International Law', *Leiden Journal of International Law*, 26 (2013), 531.

[55] P.-M. Dupuy et al. (eds.), *Human Rights in International Investment Law and Arbitration* (Oxford University Press, 2009); J. Viñuales, *Foreign Investment and the Environment in International Law* (Cambridge University Press, 2012); F. Baetens (ed.), *Investment Law within International Law* (Cambridge University Press, 2013); V. Vadi, *Cultural Heritage in International Investment Law and Arbitration* (Cambridge University Press, 2014); D. Desierto, *Public Policy in International Economic Law: The ICESCR in Trade, Finance, and Investment* (Oxford University Press, 2015).

judges, just as international investment arbitration?[56] Or is the structural difference relating to exhaustion of domestic remedies too significant for any analogies to be drawn? Or does it suggest that the proper way for States to reassert authority over international courts would be to introduce domestic remedies or other forms of interaction with domestic courts into investment law? Or, conversely, is the lesson that excessive integration of domestic and international rules and adjudicators is precisely the problem that needs to be addressed?[57] Or is the analogy missing the crucial teleological point that it is a very different matter for a Contracting Party to reassert control over a regime justified on utilitarian grounds than over one founded on normative considerations?[58] But does not such a dichotomy considerably simplify the heated debates about teleology both within investment law and within human rights?[59] And so on. Such glimpses from contiguous legal regimes should reinforce the modesty with which lawyers draw lessons about the likely dynamic of

[56] See Council of Europe website at: www.echr.coe.int/Documents/2012_Brighton_FinalDeclaration_ENG.pdf (accessed 24 February 2016). Indeed, NAFTA Federal Trade Commission's (FTC) practice of re-interpretation has been invoked as a possible way for Contracting Parties to reassert control: A. Speaight, 'An Aspect of Strasbourg Court Reform', in Commission on a Bill of Rights, *A UK Bill of Rights? The Choice before Us*, Vol. 1 (2012), 234, 238–42, available at: http://webarchive.nationalarchives.gov.uk/20130128112038/http://www.justice.gov.uk/downloads/about/cbr/uk-bill-rights-vol-1.pdf (accessed 24 February 2016).

[57] P. Sands, 'The Government Is Playing a Dangerous Game Trying to Scrap the Human Rights Act', *The Guardian*, 21 October 2015; BIICL, 'Meeting Report: The Death of the Human Rights Act, the Birth of a New Constitutional Settlement?', 2 February 2016, available at: www.biicl.org/documents/882_full_meeting_report_02-02-16__human_rights_-_appg_rol_draft_meeting_2_february_2016_final.pdf?showdocument=1 (accessed 1 May 2016); 'Sub-Committee Publishes Report on British Bill of Rights Proposal', 9 May 2016, available at: www.parliament.uk/business/committees/committees-a-z/lords-select/eu-justice-subcommittee/news-parliament-2015/hra-report-published/ (accessed 9 May 2016).

[58] L. Poulsen et al., 'Costs and Benefits of an EU-USA Investment Protection Treaty', April 2013, available at: www.gov.uk/government/uploads/system/uploads/attachment_data/file/260380/bis-13-1284-costs-and-benefits-of-an-eu-usa-investment-protection-treaty.pdf (accessed 24 February 2016).

[59] See an argument about rule of law and foreign direct investment: BIICL et al., *Risk and Return: Foreign Direct Investment and the Rule of Law*, available at: www.biicl.org/documents/625_d4_fdi_main_report.pdf (accessed 24 February 2016), and a discussion of variety of approaches to foundations of human rights: Cruft, *Philosophical Foundations of Human Rights*. Causes and effects of international investment law are themselves debated in increasingly rich and sophisticated literature; see C. Dupont and T. Schultz, 'Towards a New Heuristic Model: Investment Arbitration as a Political System', *Journal of International Dispute Settlement*, 7 (2016), 3.

future developments and sources of inspiration that law-makers would rely upon. For example, who would have predicted that the European Commission's proposal of a new Investment Court System[60] would entirely ignore rich European experience regarding selection of judges[61] and instead emulate the structure of the Iran–US Claims Tribunal? It may be banal to say that the power to create includes the power to create odd and surprising things, but it is nevertheless true.

E. Not Playing for the Reasserting Team

The first player not playing for the reasserting team is one with considerable powers within the status quo: the investor. As far as contestation of control goes, the starting point is that investors have to take the rough with the smooth. A reflection upon various regimes of international dispute settlement will show that there is a great diversity of approaches to procedural rights (using that term in the loosest sense) of non-State actors.[62] There are many regimes that address non-State actors, whether the emphasis is for setting up a framework for their conduct (international humanitarian law and law of the sea), providing benefits (international trade law) or viewing a beneficial state of their affairs as a goal in itself (international criminal law, to some extent environmental law) yet without obviously expressing these rules in terms of procedural rights by non-State actors at the level of international law.[63] Even if we live in an

[60] 'Commission Proposes New Investment Court System for TTIP and Other EU Trade and Investment Negotiations', available at: http://europa.eu/rapid/press-release_IP-15-5651_en.htm (accessed 24 February 2016).

[61] Bobek, *Selecting Europe's Judges*.

[62] See generally K. Parlett, *The Individual in the International Legal System* (Cambridge University Press, 2011).

[63] This is a sweeping statement in which much hangs on the word 'obviously'. There may be some authority for viewing (some aspects of) trade and humanitarian law as giving rise to individual rights, whether at the domestic or international level: Kurtz, *The WTO and International Investment Law*, chap. 6; C. Evans, *The Right to Reparation in International Law for Victims of Armed Conflict* (Cambridge University Press, 2012); international criminal procedure has developed rights in relation to victims: C. McCarthy, *Reparations and Victim Support in the International Criminal Court* (Cambridge University Press, 2014), and litigation may play a role in international environmental law: J. Peel and H. Osofsky (eds.), *Climate Change Litigation* (Cambridge University Press, 2015); P. Sands, 'Climate Change and the Rule of Law: Adjudicating the Future in International Law', *Journal of Environmental Law*, 28 (2016), 19. But even if defensible and increasingly important, the procedural rights of non-State actors are not central to these regimes.

age of adjudication,[64] there is little practice that would suggest that interpretation of legal rules that affect non-State actors, once established, is (increasingly) entrusted to judicial bodies that can hear their claims.

Even regimes most comparable to investment law suggest no obvious systemic tilt or pattern. In the post–First World War international law, States sometimes emphasised the inter-State perspective and created institutions like the US–Germany Mixed Claims Commission, where individuals had no role at all and 'the Government of the United States is the actual claimant.'[65] Articulating instead the individual-State perspective, States created the Upper Silesia Arbitral Tribunal, where individuals directly brought claims even against their own States of nationality with no interference by any other actor.[66] Other adjudicative bodies that address injuries to individuals fall somewhere between these extremes, explicitly formulating and qualifying individual rights, usually without prejudice to broader issues of principle. Examples include the (never-operating) International Prize Court, which would have provided rights to States to suppress some but not all claims by their nationals[67]; the Iran–US Claims Tribunal, where 'small claims' were presented by States[68]; the OECD Draft Convention on the Protection of Foreign Property, where individual claims would have been suspended during their State's claims[69]; ICSID Convention, where the opposite rule operates[70] and many more examples in other tribunals (including at least one case of explicit agency in the United Nations Convention on the Law of the Sea (UNCLOS) rules on prompt release[71]). These are different policy choices for different circumstances rather than an elaboration of or contribution to a more general legal proposition.

Once access to international courts has been provided, non-State actors would, of course, be able to operate within a sophisticated framework of international procedural law (where powers to fulfil judicial functions may, but not necessarily will, include inherent powers, whether or not codified in the relevant documents[72]). But there is not much that

[64] C. Greenwood, 'International Law in the Age of Adjudication', available at: http://legal.un.org/avl/ls/Greenwood_CT.html (accessed 1 May 2016).

[65] (1923) 7 RIIA 23, 26. [66] (1928) 4 ILR 291.

[67] Convention (XII) relative to the Creation of International Prize Court, signed at The Hague, 18 October 1907, Article 4.

[68] Iran–US Claims Tribunal, Claims Settlement Declaration of 19 January 1981, Article III(3).

[69] Article 7(d). [70] Article 27(1). [71] Article 292(2).

[72] *ConocoPhillips Petrozuata BV and Others* v. *Venezuela*, ICSID Case No. ARB/07/30, Decision on Respondent's Request for Reconsideration of the Tribunal's Decision of 10 March 2014 of 9 February 2016, paras. 20–38.

non-State actors could influence otherwise. As a matter of *lex lata*, whether and what courts to provide is a discretionary decision by law-makers, and the legal toolbox provides sophisticated instruments and policy arguments for a great variety of solutions. It is therefore perfectly justifiable for treaty-makers to reassert their authority through changes in treaty language that would impose particular limitations or conditions on investors' right to bring the claim, as well as to elaborate on or change treaty obligations or include particular exceptions, carve-outs or reservations. If adjudicative bodies have already been created, technical rules of investment law and other regimes of law, as well as certain general principles, could be pressed to crystallise the status quo, but it is uncertain to what extent this would be effective. The analogous regimes only reinforce the point about lack of systemic grain. One might be forgiven for thinking that the normative appeal of human rights would provide a strong argument in contestation. But the correctness of this proposition may be more obvious in debates in some States than in others,[73] and the winding down of the individual-State elements of the Southern African Development Community (SADC) Tribunal was ultimately effective, even if not entirely elegant.[74] Indeed, the arguments for return to diplomatic protection,[75] or some analogies drawn from international trade law, view formal isolation of non-State actors from international legal process as a worthy goal.[76]

Non-disputing parties (which may include non-disputing Parties) are to some extent like investors as disputing parties, similarly reliant

[73] See the separate opinions to the Report of the Commission on a Bill of Rights, in which the opinion entitled 'In Defence of Rights' was signed by a minority of two who voted against the conclusions, available at: http://webarchive.nationalarchives.gov.uk/20130128112038/http:/www.justice.gov.uk/downloads/about/cbr/uk-bill-rights-vol-1.pdf (accessed 24 February 2016).

[74] See SADC website at: www.sadc.int/about-sadc/sadc-institutions/tribun/ (accessed 24 February 2016); K. Alter et al., 'Backlash against International Courts in West, East and Southern Africa: Causes and Consequences', *European Journal of International Law*, 27 (2016), 293; J. Sarkin, 'A Critique of the Decision of the African Commission on Human and Peoples' Rights Permitting the Demolition of the SADC Tribunal: Politics versus Economics and Human Rights', *African Journal of International and Comparative Law*, 24 (2016), 215.

[75] 2015 Brazil–Mozambique BIT, available at: www.itamaraty.gov.br/index.php?option=com_content&view=article&id=8511&catid=42&Itemid=280&lang=pt-BR (accessed 24 February 2016).

[76] Whether informality limits the power of non-State actors or rather removes any formalised limitations is an open question, e.g. the apparent acknowledgement by Ukraine that its tobacco labelling-related claim against Australia was made at the request of the American Chamber of Commerce, see Interfax website at: http://en.interfax.com.ua/news/general/270076.html (accessed 24 February 2016).

on the existence of particular international courts and tribunals, and to some extent not alike. Their position within the structure of international dispute settlement is articulated upon the basis of policy considerations, which have been predominantly conceived as relating to public interest. Vaughan Lowe described the development of practice in the following terms, by using the NAFTA case of *Methanex* v. *US* (where a decision by California on limitations of production and sale of methyl tertiary-butyl ether, adopted on health grounds, was challenged) as a starting point:

> [T]he question here is: how should we accommodate the public interest in such cases? It would be unthinkable for the government of the UK or the European Community to be able to adopt measures such as those in question in *Methanex*, and for a legal challenge to them to be heard and decided *in camera*, and for the decision to remain 'confidential'. Should the position be any different where such measures are the focus of an investment dispute heard by an international arbitration tribunal? ... [W]hat kinds of public interest are appropriate to be put before international tribunals, and who should decide that question? Who should be permitted to make representations in the public interest? ... And how should the public interest be presented and represented in the proceedings? ... [D]evelopments in investment tribunals, in the NAFTA and investment treaties, and in the WTO, are part of a clear trend towards increasing what might, somewhat tendentiously, be called 'public participation' in private dispute settlement ... [T]he trend is clear, and is clearly borne out of the concern to promote transparency and what is termed the legitimacy (which seems often to mean little more than the ability to fend off authoritative or organised criticism) of decisions taken by tribunals adjudicating upon disputes which implicate questions of serious public concern.[77]

In one sense, the trend is indeed clear – and reflected in the procedural rules and most of the recent treaty instruments[78] – this suggests that non-disputing parties could be an important element of reassertion. But, as Lowe himself recognises, '[t]he trend is by no means universal.'[79] In other regimes of international dispute settlement, such access either does not

[77] V. Lowe, 'Private Disputes and the Public Interest in International Law', in D. French et al. (eds.), *International Law and Dispute Settlement: New Problems and Techniques* (Oxford, UK: Hart, 2010), 8–11; also A. Rigo Sureda, *Investment Treaty Arbitration: Judging under Uncertainty* (Cambridge University Press, 2012), 124–7.

[78] Y. Ronen and Y. Naggan, 'Third Parties', in C. Romano et al. (eds.), *The Oxford Handbook of International Adjudication* (Oxford University Press, 2014), 806, 821–5.

[79] Lowe, 'Private Disputes and the Public Interest in International Law', 11.

exist at all (the International Court of Justice (ICJ)[80] and inter-State arbitration) or is apparently applied without overwhelming enthusiasm (Iran–US Claims Tribunal,[81] WTO AB,[82] and UNCLOS Annex VII[83]). This may be read as suggesting that the trend in support of public participation in investor-State arbitration is systemically anomalous, and the support that Contracting Parties bestow upon non-disputing parties may be less significant than public declarations suggest (as reflected in the single ratification of the 2014 Mauritius Convention in mid-2016[84]).

The final player of importance in the game of reassertion is in many ways the central one under the status quo: the investment arbitration tribunal. A starting point for thinking about the issue is that international investment arbitration operates as if it were a regime of international dispute settlement and therefore has to be debated in that perspective. International investment arbitration is part and parcel of the contemporary international law of dispute settlement. Cases are often decided by the same individuals who have sat (or may still be sitting) on the bench of ICJ, WTO AB, UNCLOS Annex VII Tribunals, European Court of Human Rights, or the Court of Justice of the European Union.[85] Counsels are often the same members of *barreau invisible* and use the same vocabulary and precedents.[86] When tribunals are faced with reassertion, the small print of relevant instruments would guide the engagement, assisted by the comparative backdrop of international dispute settlement.

80 P.-M. Dupuy, 'Article 34', in A. Zimmermann et al. (eds.), *The Statute of the International Court of Justice*, 2nd edn. (Oxford University Press, 2012), 585, 603–4.

81 D. Caron and L. Caplan, *The UNCITRAL Arbitration Rules: A Commentary*, 2nd edn. (Oxford University Press, 2013), 40.

82 E.g. *EC-Measures Prohibiting the Importation and Marketing of Seal Products*, WT/DS400/AB/R and WT/DS401/AB/R, Report of the Appellate Body of 22 May 2014, para. 1.15; *US-Measures Concerning the Importation, Marketing and Sale of Tuna and Tuna Products*, WT/DS381/AB/RW, Report of the Appellate Body of 20 November 2015, fn. 68.

83 *Netherlands* v. *Russia*, PCA Case No. 2014-02, Procedural Order No. 3 (Greenpeace International's Request to File *Amicus Curiae* Submission) of 8 October 2014, available at: www.pcacases.com/web/sendAttach/1320 (accessed 24 February 2016).

84 See UNCITRAL website at: www.uncitral.org/uncitral/en/uncitral_texts/arbitration/2014Transparency_Convention_status.html (accessed 24 February 2016).

85 L. Swigart and D. Terris, 'Who Are International Judges?', in K. Alter et al. (eds.), *The Oxford Handbook of International Adjudication* (Oxford University Press, 2014), 619.

86 E. Sthoeger and M. Wood, 'The International Bar', in K. Alter et al. (eds.), *The Oxford Handbook of International Adjudication* (Oxford University Press, 2014), 639.

When questions of systemic importance arise, they will often turn on different readings of the function of tribunals[87]: is it to settle the particular disputes? Contribute to friendly relations between parties (or Parties)? Develop law in a particular (presumably progressive) direction? Defend a non-State actor against the arbitrary power of the State (or States, or international organisation(s))? Enlighten the curious reader on all matters on arbitrators' (or arbitrator's) mind? Or something entirely different? These are, of course, questions that fall neatly within the respected pedigree of discussion of the international judicial functions in various international courts and tribunals, which has taken place, with only slight exaggeration, since the beginning of international dispute settlement.[88] It may be that a generalist international lawyer's perspective could be adopted, taking a step back to reflect upon the function that international law and dispute settlement could be expected to fulfil within this legal regime. Such an examination could possibly lead to modest conclusions about the role of this manner of adjudication. But reasonable people may disagree with this conclusion, and reassertion through creation of stronger international adjudicators – even courts with appellate bodies – will affect the functions that they could be expected to fulfil (with perhaps paradoxical implications for the supporters of these efforts).

F. Conclusion

It is appropriate to conclude this unabashedly black-letter chapter with a modestly conceptual point drawing upon two statements by Christian Tomuschat. First, he suggests that

> the ideal of the rule of law, a precept which belongs to the core elements of today's system of international law [means that] the interpretation of legal rules, once they have been established, should be entrusted to judicial bodies, without any interference by political bodies ... Judicial bodies should not be put under political control. Their findings may not be

[87] J. Alvarez, 'What Are International Judges For? The Main Functions of International Adjudication', in K. Alter et al. (eds.), *The Oxford Handbook of International Adjudication* (Oxford University Press, 2014), 158.

[88] O. Spiermann, *International Legal Argument in the Permanent Court of International Justice* (Cambridge University Press, 2005), part 3; H. Lauterpacht, *The Function of Law in the International Community* (Oxford University Press, 2011, first published 1933); V. Lowe, 'The Function of Litigation in International Society', *International and Comparative Law Quarterly*, 61 (2012), 209; G. Hernández, *The International Court of Justice and the Judicial Function* (Oxford University Press, 2014).

> disregarded as soon as they do not correspond to expectations nurtured at the time when the rules concerned where issued.[89]

Secondly,

> This does not detract from the power of the legislative authorities concerned to alter the law if they come to the conclusion that some judicial pronouncements have erred in trying to identify the true meaning of a given legal rule. Judges are not the masters of the law they are called upon to interpret.[90]

There is much to approve of in both points that Tomuschat makes, but to follow them simultaneously could lead to an ultimately un-resolvable tension. Is a particular reassertion an inappropriate example of judicial bodies being put under political control? Or is it a praiseworthy case of correction of an error in a judicial pronouncement by the true masters of the law? In legal terms, the answer will be provided by the process and system of international law. But the perspective of the rule of law, itself a much[91] – perhaps even essentially – contested concept,[92] provides a sense of the manner in which the game of reassertion will be played in international investment law. Questions about the proper relationship between those who make rules and those who settle disputes about rules go to the core of international investment law, as well as international law – and law more broadly.[93] Significantly different answers to these

89 *Ecuador* v. *US*, UNCITRAL Arbitration, Expert Opinion of Professor Tomuschat of 24 April 2012, 28.

90 *Ibid.*, 29.

91 Cf. the variety of approaches: 'Declaration of the High-Level Meeting of the General Assembly on the Rule of Law at the National and International Levels', UNGA Res. 67/1, adopted 30 November 2012, UN Doc. A/RES/67/1; and G. Fitzmaurice, 'The General Principles of International Law Considered from the Standpoint of the Rule of Law', *RCADI*, 92 (1957), 1; A. Watts, 'International Law and the Rule of Law', *German Yearbook of International Law*, 36 (1993), 15; I. Brownlie, *The Rule of Law in International Affairs* (Alphen aan Den Rijn, Netherlands: Kluwer, 1998); J. Crawford, 'International Law and the Rule of Law', *Adelaide Law Review*, 24 (2003), 3; A. Nollkaemper, *National Courts and the International Rule of Law* (Oxford University Press, 2011); 'Symposium: Are Sovereigns Entitled to the Benefit of International Rule of Law', *European Journal of International Law*, 22 (2012), 313; 'Roundtable: The International Rule of Law', *Ethics in International Affairs*, 28 (2014), 39; R. McCorquodale, 'Defining the International Rule of Law: Defying Gravity?', *International and Comparative Law Quarterly* (2016), 277.

92 J. Waldron, 'Is the Rule of Law an Essentially Contested Concept (in Florida)?', *Law and Philosophy*, 21 (2002), 137; D. Collier et al., 'Essentially Contested Concepts: Debates and Applications', *Journal Political Ideologies*, 11 (2006), 211, 228–33.

93 See recently J. Finnis, 'Judicial Power: Past, Present and Future', 21 October 2015, available at: http://judicialpowerproject.org.uk/wp-content/uploads/2015/10/John-Finnis-lecture-20102015.pdf, and responses thereto, available at: http://judicialpowerproject.org.uk/category/debates/finnis-responses/ (both accessed 24 February 2016).

complex, diversely describable and open concepts may be given even by perfectly reasonable debaters – should one be able to find them[94] – and one can only hope that through progressive competition of ideas, a greater coherence of systemic values and refinement of institutions could be achieved.

[94] Cf. on the one hand, EFILA, website at: www.efila.org, and on the other hand, Corporate Europe Observatory, website at: www.corporateeurope.org (both accessed 24 February 2016).

3

Reassertion of Control and Contracting Parties' Domestic Law Responses to Investment Treaty Arbitration

Between Reform, Reticence and Resistance

MAVLUDA SATTOROVA

A. Introduction

History shows that attempts by States to reassert control over international investment law and dispute settlement are a cyclical phenomenon, which manifests itself in various forms. Resistance is one of them. The foremost and oft-cited example of resistance towards the internationalisation of investment protection is the Calvo Doctrine, which underpinned an historical opposition by Latin American States to diplomatic protection and the notion of international minimum standard. The doctrine has exerted considerable influence on the subsequent development of international norms on investment protection, from the ground breaking resolutions by the UN General Assembly (which purported to replace the idea of internationalisation of investment disputes with the principle of national treatment) to more recent calls to reinstate the local remedies rule in investment arbitration.[1] Although the practical significance of the UN resolutions was subsequently obliterated by an en masse treatification of international investment law, whereby even the staunchest detractors of internationalisation signed investment treaties and joined the ICSID Convention, the echoes of Calvo's influence on national approaches can still be traced in existing investment protection instruments.[2]

[1] E.g. Australia has recently voiced its support for reinstating the local remedies rule to protect national adjudicatory powers over investment disputes. See L. Trakman 'Choosing Domestic Courts over Investor-State Arbitration: Australia's Repudiation of The Status Quo', *UNSW Law Journal*, 35 (2012), 979.

[2] Notable examples are the Commonwealth of Independent States investment protection instruments which establish the primacy of national laws and remedies. See M. Sattorova,

More recently, reassertion of control through resistance to the internationalisation of investment protection and dispute settlement has manifested in a withdrawal by States (mostly developing countries) from the investment protection regime. To mention a few, in 2007, Bolivia submitted a written notice of its denunciation of the ICSID Convention, and a similar step was later taken by Ecuador in 2009. Furthermore, the Ecuadorian Constitution has been amended to expressly prohibit international arbitration of investor-State disputes.[3] In 2009, Russia officially announced its decision to withdraw from the Energy Charter Treaty.[4] Indonesia, too, has recently confirmed its intention to terminate and renegotiate more than sixty bilateral investment treaties.[5]

The current trend towards reassertion of control over investment protection and dispute settlement has not been limited to developing countries alone. As observed by the editor in Chapter 1, for the first time in the history of international investment law the interests of States parties, both developed and developing, are becoming approximated in the sense of their shared dissatisfaction with the drafting patterns on which the bulk of existing investment treaties are modelled. Faced with a growing number of investment claims and at the same time cognizant of the important gains bestowed by investment treaty instruments on their own businesses abroad, the governments of developed economies – most notably Canada and the United States – were forced to adopt a long-term review of their investment treaty policies. The reformed treaty models feature a number of significant changes symbolising an almost paradigmatic even if inchoate shift in the perceptions of investment treaty law and its principal functions. These innovations include references to the promotion of sustainable development as one of the

'International Investment Law in Central Asia: The Making, Implementation and Change of Investment Rules from a Regionalist Perspective', *Journal of World Investment & Trade*, 16 (2015), 1089, 1094–5.

3 D. Ma, 'A BIT Unfair? An Illustration of the Backlash against International Arbitration in Latin America', *Journal of Dispute Resolution* (2012), 571.

4 See generally A. Kaushal, 'Revisiting History: How the Past Matters for the Present Backlash against the Foreign Investment Regime', *Harvard International Law Journal*, 50 (2009), 491, 493; also A van Aaken, 'Perils of Success? The Case of International Investment Protection', *European Business Organisation Law Review*, 9 (2008), 1.

5 See an official notice at http://indonesia.nlembassy.org/organisation/departments/economic-affairs/termination-bilateral-investment-treaty.html; see also recently Grace D. Amianti, 'Govt Revises Investment Treaties', *The Jakarta Post*, 12 May 2015, available at www.thejakartapost.com/news/2015/05/12/govt-revises-investment-treaties.html (accessed 29 February 2016).

overarching treaty objectives alongside investment protection, more detailed and elaborate provisions on expropriation and the guarantee of fair and equitable treatment and public policy exceptions – all aimed at alleviating concerns over the growing exposure of States to investor claims.

Both resistance and reform have already received some attention in international legal scholarship.[6] However, what remains unexplored is the existence of variation in the ways host States reassert control over international investment law. A significant number of States have so far refrained from any significant overhaul of their investment treaties. Others have attempted to reassert control over investment protection and dispute settlement through changes in domestic legal frameworks. Furthermore, existing scholarship has so far been preoccupied with patterns of State behaviour in the international scene, such as treaty reform, thus leaving unaddressed the reassertion by States of control over investment treaty law through changes in national laws and policies. The aim of this chapter is to analyse the hitherto less visible and underexplored patterns of State behaviour such as reticence (or selective adjustment), preservation of the status quo (or passivity), dispute prevention and domestic contestation (or grassroots resistance).

This chapter seeks to fill the gap in investment treaty scholarship by moving away from currently prevailing emphasis on the international dimension of State behaviour and towards the domestic dimension. In doing so, it intends to make a novel contribution to the debate by (1) examining the ways host States reassert control and exposing a variety of the actual rather than abstractly imagined patterns of State behaviour as emerging from recent empirical studies, (2) casting light on responses by developing States (rather than focusing exclusively on their developed treaty counterparts) and highlighting a significant variation in how States have behaved so far, and (3) forsaking the currently prevailing State-centric narratives of international investment law in favour of an approach which enables one to identify some of the important actors and factors underpinning the emerging variety of ways in which host States seek to reassert control over investment treaty law and its arbitration mechanism.

[6] See e.g. M. Waibel et al. (eds.), *The Backlash against Investment Arbitration: Perceptions and Reality* (Alphen aan den Rijn, Netherlands: Kluwer Law International, 2010); J. McIlroy, 'Canada's New Foreign Investment Protection and Promotion Agreement: Two Steps Forward, One Step Back?', *Journal of World Investment & Trade*, 5 (2004), 621.

This chapter will proceed as follows. Part B will juxtapose treaty reforms on the one hand and reticence and preservation of status quo on the other. It will question why the initial encounter with investor-State arbitration in a respondent capacity appears to have prompted a revision of investment treaties by countries such as Canada and the US, while other countries have shown a degree of reticence even after having become targeted by investment claims. In addressing this question, fresh empirical insights from developing countries will be analysed. Part C will critically examine the presently under-explored form of reassertion of control by host States – the creation of domestic mechanisms for dispute prevention and management. Even this form of reassertion of control by States manifests itself differently, with some States adopting a full-fledged dispute prevention mechanisms and others confining themselves to dispute management only. This, in turn, prompts an inquiry into factors underlying host State choices. Part D will draw attention to the recent political contestation of investment treaty rules in domestic settings, including through grassroots opposition to new investment and trade agreements. It will examine how host State responses to developments in international investment law might be influenced by domestic political process and what implications this entails for the existing conceptualisation of investment treaty-making. Part E will conclude by identifying some of the common factors that appear to underpin all four forms of reassertion of control by host States and propose a re-orientation of existing narratives towards less State-centric and more pluralist understanding of host State behaviour in the investment treaty context.

B. Between Reticence and Preservation of the Status Quo: Why Are States Reluctant to Launch Comprehensive Treaty Reform?

Although treaty reform manifests primarily through changes to international commitments of Contracting State parties, it offers a useful backdrop against which domestic approaches to reasserting control over investment treaty law could be analysed. Investment treaty reform is frequently a reflection of a shift in the Contracting State's perception of international investment law, at times influenced by domestic political discourse and often accompanied by relevant changes in national laws and policies on investment. Such shifts in domestic attitudes are often prompted by the Contracting State's exposure to investment arbitration claims. As evidenced by the recent history of international investment law, the first significant wave of reform was precipitated by the proliferation of investment disputes and the invocation of investment treaty rules against countries such as Canada and the United States. Until then, it was deemed somewhat inconceivable that international investment treaties could be deployed against the very States that championed them. Once exposed to actual investment treaty claims, the erstwhile advocates of international investment protection had to revisit their stance so as to avoid having to pay significant damages awards in future arbitrations.

The reformist impulse, however, has not manifested itself uniformly. Unlike Canada and the United States, many governments have remained somewhat reticent about changing their investment treaty practice. Amended model treaties of other investment protection champions – including the United Kingdom, the Netherlands and Switzerland – continue to follow the traditional drafting patterns and do not feature changes of the kind embraced in the revised Canadian and US treaty models. This is despite the fact that many of these countries – long known as strong advocates of investment treaty protection – had an experience of being targeted or threatened by investment disputes, with their governments being prompted to take a fresh look at their investment treaties. A similar inclination to preserve the status quo – or a considerable degree of reticence in reasserting control over investment treaty protection and dispute settlement – can also be discerned among many developing countries. The question arises as to why, despite having been drawn into investment arbitration in a respondent capacity, some States have not made significant changes in their investment treaty practice, while others responded to their encounter with investment claims by revisiting their treaty rules. Recent empirical insights from developing countries, including Turkey and Uzbekistan, provide a useful background to address this question.[7]

Both Turkey and Uzbekistan have a significant number of investment treaties (seventy-six and forty-six, respectively) and have been exposed to investment arbitration on a number of occasions. Both countries have experienced the financial implications of investor-State arbitration. For instance, even in a case where the investor claims were dismissed, Turkey's expenses amounted to US$35,702,417.76. Similarly, although

[7] M. Sattorova, M. Erkan and O. Omiunu, 'How Do Host States Respond to Investment Treaty Law? Some Empirical Observations', *European Yearbook of International Economic Law* (forthcoming 2016).

no damages awards have so far been issued against Uzbekistan, in defending its interests in one case alone – *Metal-Tech* v. *Uzbekistan* – the government incurred arbitration costs in the amount of US$7,985,954.95.[8] Despite having actually experienced the financial bite of investor-State arbitration, both Turkey and Uzbekistan have so far refrained from systemic reform of their investment treaties. The important question that these examples prompt is why, notwithstanding the lessons about investment treaties and their liability implications, so many countries continue to be reticent about their investment treaties.

To begin with, the government of Turkey has not revised its investment-protection commitments on a scale comparable to changes introduced in treaties of the United States and Canada. Although the government proclaimed itself to be on a path towards the so-called selective adjustment[9] of its treaties, even a brief glance at its most recent treaties reveals limited and sporadic changes. Turkey's opting for making selective (and currently very piecemeal) modifications can arguably be explained by its desire to prioritise 'low-hanging fruit' and to address most pressing and immediate concerns while postponing an overhaul of treaty core commitments.[10] According to the United Nations Conference on Trade and Development (UNCTAD), selective adjustments may also reflect the State's preference for tailoring treaty modifications to individual negotiating State parties 'in order to accommodate particular economic relationships'.[11] Furthermore, the incremental approach may appeal to certain countries because it 'makes it less likely that the change will be perceived as a reduction of the agreement's protective value'.[12]

Recent studies involving interviews with Turkish government officials offer further insights into the factors underpinning the reticence with which Turkey has approached its investment treaties in the years following its involvement in investor-State disputes.[13] Firstly, it transpires that prior to Turkey's first encounter with investor-State arbitration, government officials had been largely unaware of the scope and implications of such treaties. The interviews reveal that some learning occurred after the

[8] *Metal-Tech Ltd.* v. *Republic of Uzbekistan*, ICSID Case No. ARB/10/3, Award of 4 October 2013, para. 414.

[9] UNCTAD, *Transformation of the International Investment Agreement Regime*, TD/B/C.II/EM.4/2, 12–14, available at http://unctad.org/meetings/en/SessionalDocuments/ciiem4d2_en.pdf (accessed 29 February 2016). The recent Turkish BITs feature such innovations as a note on regulatory expropriation and, in some treaties, public policy exceptions. These changes are not made consistently in the recent treaty stock.

[10] *Ibid.*, 14. [11] *Ibid.* [12] *Ibid.*

[13] M. Sattorova, M. Erkan and O. Omiunu, 'How Do Host States Respond'.

country was first hit by investment treaty claims. However, they also suggest that learning has been confined to those who were involved, in one way or another, in the process of defending the government in investment arbitration. Officials in other tiers of the government showed very limited or no awareness of investment treaties even after the government had to defend itself in investment arbitration on more than one occasion. Secondly, even after Turkish officials became increasingly aware of investment treaties and their financial implications, no concrete steps were undertaken to prevent or delimit the State's exposure to investment treaty arbitration and its sanction mechanism. On some occasions, the government ignored its previous experience in evaluating future implications of investment treaties. For instance, respondents to interviews recalled a situation in which the government proceeded with a ratification of an investment treaty without a proper legal screening, notwithstanding the country having been earlier exposed to a number of high-profile investment arbitration claims which, in turn, offered an opportunity to reflect on the scope of investment treaty commitments.[14] This 'partial' learning and an 'incomplete' translation of the lessons learnt into concrete changes in law and policy may be relevant in explaining Turkey's current choice of selective and minor adjustment of its investment treaties. The emerging empirical evidence suggests that reticence over reforming investment treaties is not always a reflection of the State's fear about diminishing protective value of treaties or its desire to tailor treaty commitments to individual treaty partners. State behaviour in signing and amending treaties is not always perfectly rational,[15] and the government's choice to make only minor changes to its treaty commitments can be a product of incomplete learning caused by a lack of awareness and insufficient coordination between various agencies and officials within the government.

Interviews and a historical analysis of national statutory material in Uzbekistan also suggest a degree of reticence and a tendency towards preserving the status quo with regard to the country's investment treaty commitments. An initial encounter with investor-State arbitration raised the level of awareness about the reach of investment treaties and their financial implications for the government.[16] Just as in Turkey, however, the increasing levels of awareness were confined to government officials

[14] *Ibid.*

[15] See L. Poulsen and E. Aisbett, 'When the Claims Hit: Bilateral Investment Treaties and Bounded Rational Learning', *World Politics*, 65 (2013), 273.

[16] M. Sattorova, M. Erkan and O. Omiunu, 'How Do Host States Respond'.

directly involved in defending the State in investment arbitration cases. This 'partial learning' has not been translated into a concerted effort to prevent or mitigate future exposure of the government to investment claims – Uzbekistan has continued to sign and ratify investment treaties, and there is no evidence of the government's intention to amend its existing treaties. What is noteworthy is the fact that the government did make an attempt to prevent its exposure to future investment claims by making relevant changes in domestic legislation. For instance, one such attempt was made in 2006 when following a number of claims brought against the State by foreign investors,[17] the central ministerial body initiated proceedings in the constitutional court requesting an interpretation of a dispute settlement provision in the law which provided for investors' access to arbitration.[18] The constitutional court held that certain investors 'mistakenly construed' the provision concerning the settlement of an investment dispute by means of arbitration as an expression of State consent to refer disputes to ICSID in line with the Washington Convention. Having acknowledged that generally recognised principles of international law take precedence over national laws, the constitutional court stressed the supremacy of the national constitution and pointed to a provision therein which vested the competent State courts with jurisdiction over the adjudication of disputes involving governmental bodies. It thus concluded that the contentious provision could not be relied upon as an expression of consent to ICSID arbitration and that express and written consent to arbitration ought to be obtained in each individual case.[19] Despite having resorted to constitutional review in an attempt to regain control over investor-State dispute settlement, the government of Uzbekistan did not amend the

[17] The decision of the constitutional court does not specify which foreign investor claims prompted a request for the interpretation of the relevant provisions in national law. The existing data on investment arbitration claims brought against Uzbekistan suggests that the request for interpretation might have been the consequence of arbitral proceedings initiated in PCA Case No. AA280 between *Romak S.A. (Switzerland)* v. *Republic of Uzbekistan* and *Newmont USA Limited and Newmont (Uzbekistan) Limited* v. *Republic of Uzbekistan*, ICSID Case No. ARB/06/20. See M. Sattorova, 'International Investment Law in Central Asia: The Making, Implementation and Change of Investment Rules from a Regionalist Perspective', *Journal of World Investment & Trade*, 16 (2015), 1089, 1113.

[18] Decision of the Constitutional Court of the Republic of Uzbekistan 'On Interpretation of Part 1 of Article 10 of the Law of the Republic of Uzbekistan on Guarantees and Measures of Protection of Foreign Investor Rights', translated by the author; a version in Russian is available at www.lex.uz/pages/getpage.aspx?lact_id=1267669 (accessed 29 February 2016).

[19] *Ibid.*

relevant provisions in either the national statutes or its subsequent investment treaties.[20]

These case studies indicate that even though, as some scholars have suggested, the country may initiate a revision of its investment treaties after experiencing their bite[21], host State responses may vary significantly. In contrast with Canada and the United States, developing countries such as Turkey and Uzbekistan have so far been reluctant to launch a comprehensive revision of their investment treaties. The empirical insights also call for an inquiry into the causes of such variation. One, perhaps too obvious an explanation, can be found in a hegemony narrative of international investment law. The reluctance on the part of developing States to embrace treaty reform at the same pace as that of Canada and the United States could be attributed to the fact that 'BITs [bilateral investment treaties], and the terms within them, are particularly susceptible to global power dynamics. For one, most treaties are signed by pairs of States in which one State is to some degree more powerful than the other.'[22] The qualitative insights referred to earlier also point to internal capacity (or the lack thereof) as a potentially significant factor underlying the host State's choice to refrain from any significant changes in its investment treaty policy. Lack of awareness of the true implications of investment treaty law, insufficient coordination between various agencies and officials within the government and inability to translate lessons learnt into concrete legal changes appear to play a part in the host government's decision to preserve the status quo or make only minor changes to its investment treaty policy.

Another hypothesis is that the current reticence with regard to modifying investment treaties can be attributed to the fact that both Turkey and Uzbekistan perceived their experience of investment arbitration as overall positive. Some respondents in the Turkish case study pointed to the fact that a number of unmeritorious claims against the country were dismissed, thus leaving the government with an impression that the investment arbitration regime is overall balanced, and hence it would be in Turkey's interests to remain committed to its investment protection promises.[23] Respondents also referred to the use of investment arbitration by Turkish

[20] *Ibid.* See also M. Sattorova, 'International Investment Law in Central Asia', 1113–4.

[21] L. Poulsen and E. Aisbett, 'When the Claims Hit', 273, 282.

[22] T. Allee and C. Peinhardt, 'Evaluating Three Explanations for the Design of Bilateral Investment Treaties', *World Politics*, 47 (2014), 62.

[23] This echoes explanations for the selective adjustment strategies and reticence towards reform; see UNCTAD, *Transformation of the International Investment Agreement*

investors abroad, which the respondents believed to contribute to the perception of the regime as being useful for Turkey.[24] It can be inferred that the government of Uzbekistan have so far been reticent in its stance on investment arbitration (even despite announcing its intentions to change national laws on investment protection in the past) because no damages or arbitration costs award has so far been rendered against it. Yet, again, notwithstanding the small scale of interviews, the emerging empirical data suggest that host State reticence in reasserting control over investment protection disciplines, including State reluctance to launch a comprehensive revision of its investment treaties, is driven by a number of factors and not limited to the State's desire to preserve the protective value of treaties.

At the same time, while both the bargaining power of a host State and the extent of its exposure to financial consequences of investment arbitration (and its rate of success in defending itself in investment disputes) may be significant factors, they do not quite explain the variation in the ways many host States, in particular, developing countries, have acted – or attempted to reassert control – after their encounter with arbitration and its sanctions mechanism. A brief look at how other developing countries responded to their encounter with investment treaty law and arbitration suggests that other factors might be at play in motivating States to reassert control over international investment law in one or another way.

Kazakhstan, for instance, has experienced the full bite of investment treaty law, with significant sums in damages awarded to investor-claimants in a number of cases.[25] The extent of Kazakhstan's liabilities under investment arbitration awards to date arguably should have prompted the government to scale back its investment treaty commitments. Although no empirical data are currently available to evaluate the perceptions of the investment treaty regime among government officials in Kazakhstan, an overview of national laws relating on investment protection and dispute settlement to date show no signs of the government's intention to modify its existing investment treaties or incorporate relevant safeguards into new treaties so as to delimit the State's exposure to financial consequences of defending itself in investor-State disputes. Instead, the government responded by creating domestic mechanisms

Regime, 14, available at http://unctad.org/meetings/en/SessionalDocuments/ciiem4d2_en.pdf 12–4 (accessed 29 February 2016).

[24] *Ibid.*

[25] A brief look at the awards rendered against Kazakhstan indicates that its liabilities thereunder exceed US$640 million.

for defending State interests in investor-State arbitration and, importantly, for the prevention of investment disputes. Similar developments can be discerned in other developing countries, including Colombia and Peru, both of which introduced domestic legal frameworks for the prevention and management of investment disputes. The following section will critically evaluate this form of reassertion of control by host States over investment treaty law, namely, reassertion of control through changes in domestic, not international, legal commitments.

C. Dispute Prevention and Management: What For and at Whose Behest?

(1) Re-asserting Control by Establishing Domestic Frameworks for Dispute Prevention

While developed States appear to have reacted to the first wave of investment disputes and the prospect of being targeted by investor claims by expressing disbelief and, in some cases, a degree of incredulous consternation, for many developing countries the primary concern has been the costs of liability and of defending against investor claims.[26] For instance, Kazakhstan's liabilities under recent investor-State arbitration awards exceed the sum of US$640 million.[27] After being drawn into investor-State arbitration, many developing States realised that no adequate domestic institutional frameworks were in place to detect and solve disputes with investors at early stages, resulting in the general lack of preparedness for investment arbitration. To address these concerns, a number of countries have been reported to be 'proactively implementing policies aimed at preventing international investor-State arbitration, where possible.'[28]

The creation of dispute prevention mechanisms is arguably the most predictable response by a State to being placed in a respondent's seat.

[26] See UNCTAD, *Best Practices in Investment for Development. How to Prevent and Manage Investor-State Disputes: Lessons from Peru*, Investment Advisory Series B, No. 10 (United Nations, 2011).

[27] This is a total of sums awarded against Kazakhstan in the following cases: *Stati, Ascom Group SA, Terra Raf Trans Traiding, Ltd.* v. *Republic of Kazakhstan*, SCC Arbitration V (116/2010), Award of 19 December 2013; *AIG Capital Partners, Inc. and CJSC Tema Real Estate Company* v. *Republic of Kazakhstan*, ICSID Case No. ARB/01/6, Award of 7 October 2003; *Biedermann International, Inc.* v. *Republic of Kazakhstan and the Association for Social and Economic Development of Western Kazakhstan 'Intercaspian'*, SCC Case No. 97/1996, Award of 1999 (not public, exact date of award unknown).

[28] UNCTAD, *Best Practices in Investment for Development*, 10.

Many traditional justifications of international investment law and its arbitration mechanism have argued that damages as a remedy would sufficiently pressure host States into complying with and incorporating the normative standards prescribed by investment treaties into their domestic laws.[29] In other words, holding a host State liable for an investment treaty breach would prompt the State to reassert effectively control over investment dispute settlement by creating a governmental agency responsible for detecting, identifying and controlling risk-increasing activities in which its government agencies and officials may engage.[30] Here a host State is able to reclaim control over the outcomes of investor-State arbitration not through changes to its investment treaty commitments or modalities of its participation in the investment arbitration regime but rather through focusing on the behaviour of its government officials and agencies that interact with foreign investors and whose acts can result in investor-State arbitration disputes. In order to prevent the detrimental financial impact of investment treaty sanctions while also maintaining its own favourable reputation as a treaty partner and a recipient of investments, a host State would need to create an internal loss-allocation regime to ensure that monetary losses incurred as a result of damages awards are shifted to a governmental agency which has managerial, supervisory and budgetary authority and political power over bureaucrats whose activities lead to State liability.[31] Since investor-State disputes originate in problems which investors encounter in their dealings with host government organs, a monitoring and response mechanism should target all stages of government decision-making. It is essential that 'all levels of government and agencies that interact with foreign investors understand the scope and consequence of the commitments under IIAs [international investment agreements] and the practical implications for their day-to-day activities'.[32]

Just as is the case with the reformist trends at the international level, however, reassertion of control through focusing on domestic mechanisms of investment dispute management and prevention has different modalities. Again, there is considerable variation in the ways the notions of dispute prevention and management have been embraced among host States. Some countries have responded to their encounter with

[29] S. W. Schill, *The Multilateralization of International Investment Law* (Cambridge University Press, 2009), 373.

[30] D. Cohen, 'Regulating Regulators: The Legal Environment of the State', *University of Toronto Law Journal*, 40 (1990), 245.

[31] *Ibid.*, 213. [32] UNCTAD, *Best Practices in Investment for Development*, 11.

investment arbitration and its liability mechanism by putting in place a full-fledged dispute prevention and management framework. Others have only created an agency responsible for defending government interests in investor-State arbitration. There are also examples of host States which have not created any such mechanism even after their involvement in investor-State arbitration incurred significant expenses for the State budget. This variation is currently underexplored, and so are the factors underpinning State motivations to adopt one or another form of dispute management and prevention. Are the emerging domestic strategies adequate and effective enough to allow States to regain control over investor-State dispute settlement? What lies beneath the fact that some States have in place a comprehensive dispute prevention strategy, while others confined themselves to optimising defence in investment disputes, thus focusing only on dispute management?

An overview, albeit cursory, of the existing domestic mechanisms of dispute prevention and management points to an inchoate but probably paradigmatic shift from the historically prevalent emphasis on internationalisation of investment protection towards an emerging recognition of how important domestic structures are in both settling and preventing investor-State disputes. The following discussion also seeks to identify some possible explanations for host State choice of reasserting control over investment protection by making changes in domestic legal orders. To this end, the analysis will differentiate between the two principal responses by host States discernible in recent practice: (1) the creation of a full-fledged dispute *prevention* framework and (2) the creation or reform of the existing dispute *management* mechanisms.

(2) Dispute Prevention as a Means of Reducing Host State Exposure to Investment Arbitration

One of the most well known models of proactive domestic response to investment arbitration is that which Peru adopted after having faced first investment claims and realising that 'the institutional framework required to optimally defend the State in ISDS [investor-State dispute settlement] cases was not in place.'[33] To address this shortcoming, in 2006, Peru adopted Law No. 28933, followed by a number of regulatory decrees in 2008 and 2009 that created the International Investment Disputes State Coordination and Response System (hereinafter the

[33] *Ibid.*, 19.

Response System).[34] The Response System has brought together the different State agencies that are involved in creating the international investment legal framework.[35] The three crucial pillars of the system are (1) a direct link enabling investors to register their concerns or investment problems so that they can be addressed before escalating into an investment arbitration dispute;[36] (2) government agencies' obligation to promptly report to the Response System Coordinator any investment disagreement or dispute that may result in an investment arbitration case;[37] and (3) the allocation of responsibility for financial costs of Peru's involvement in an investment dispute on the agency that took measures which triggered the dispute.[38] The framework also incorporates a training component to ensure that government agencies at all levels and tiers are aware of Peru's investment obligations and their consequences.

While aimed at facilitating an amicable settlement of investor-State disagreements and enabling the State to prepare a strong defence in arbitration, the imposition of responsibility on the agency whose actions led to the dispute aims to enhance accountability of government bodies for breaching Peru's investment treaty commitments.[39] An overarching aim of the policy is to serve as a deterrent of measures not compatible with treaty standards.[40]

Peru's model of the Response System is notable in that it goes beyond the immediate concerns relating to optimal defence of the State interests in investment arbitration and acknowledges the importance of raising the awareness among, and ensuring accountability of, public officials in different tiers and branches of government. The UNCTAD report has stressed the importance of awareness when noting that 'disputes that reach the stage of arbitration can originate with measures taken by agencies or entities that at times do not have full understanding or knowledge of the commitments undertaken by central governments in IIAs.'[41] As mentioned earlier, recent case studies support this finding – the awareness of investment treaty law and its liability implications for host States is particularly low among government officials in local and regional executive bodies and the judiciary.[42] As a consequence, such decision-makers are unlikely 'to internalise the constraints of investment treaty protections'[43] not only when evaluating the adoption of new

[34] *Ibid.*, 20. [35] *Ibid.*, 22. [36] *Ibid.*, 25. [37] *Ibid.*, 30. [38] *Ibid.*, 31. [39] *Ibid.*, 31.
[40] *Ibid.*, 46. [41] *Ibid.*, 12.
[42] See M. Sattorova, M. Erkan and O. Omiunu, 'How Do Host States Respond'.
[43] J. Bonnitcha, *Substantive Protection under Investment Treaties: A Legal and Economic Analysis* (Oxford University Press, 2014), 122.

governmental measures but also in exercising their day-to-day decision-making powers vis-à-vis foreign investors. The empirical data suggest that even after the respective governments became exposed to a number of investment treaty arbitrations, many government officials in the executive and judicial organs have remained unaware of both the very existence of investment treaty law and the fact that their acts or omissions affecting foreign investors may lead to investment arbitration claims.[44] Peru's model addresses these concerns: its function is not limited to creating financial deterrents against illegal behaviour by bureaucrats but also importantly includes a training component to raise the levels of awareness about investment treaty law and its liability implications, such awareness being a prerequisite to effective dispute prevention.

Peru's is an example of the State reasserting control through a full-fledged dispute management and prevention framework. Other broadly similar examples can be found in Kazakhstan. In Kazakhstan, for instance, the initial exposure to investment arbitration has led to the creation of a department vested with the task of dealing with investor claims. Representing and protecting Kazakhstan's interests in investment disputes are not the only functions of the department; its other objective is to prevent investment disputes. What is interesting is how the notion of prevention is described in the agency's mandate: it comprises legal expertise of investment contracts and international agreements as well as analysis of the matters relating to harmonisation and implementation of international norms into national legislation.[45] However, beyond the references to dispute prevention and implementation of international norms in the national sphere, there is no evidence of how learning from its involvement in investment arbitration is to be translated into concrete changes in the legal environment, the shortcomings of which are often seen as an impediment to doing business in the country.[46]

At the same time, analysis of developments in the national legislation reveals some evidence of changes aimed at the improvement of an investment climate in general, thus alluding to the government's

[44] See notes 17–20 and accompanying text.

[45] The outline of the department's mandate in Russian language is available on the website of the Ministry of Justice of the Republic of Kazakhstan: http://kapital.kz/details/27535/ne-tolko-zacshicshatsya-no-i-vnimatelnee-chitat-kontrakty.html (accessed 29 February 2016). See also http://tengrinews.kz/kazakhstan_news/kazahstan-otstoyal-iski-3-milliarda-dollarov-mejdunarodnyih-arbitrajah-2013-godu-250785/ (accessed 29 February 2016).

[46] See e.g. US Department of State, Bureau of Economic and Business Affairs, 2013 Investment Climate Statement – Kazakhstan, February 2013, available at www.state.gov/e/eb/rls/othr/ics/2013/204668.htm (accessed 29 February 2016).

recognition of the importance of dispute prevention. For instance, the most recent amendment to the Law on Investments has created an investment ombudsman.[47] One of the principal functions of the ombudsman is to provide a rapid response system for difficulties which foreign investors may encounter in their dealings with various government agencies in Kazakhstan. Some of its key responsibilities include (1) solving issues related to the rights and interests of foreign investments during implementation of investment projects; (2) mediating settlement of disputes between investors and State authorities; (3) offering support in legal proceedings; and (4) where problems cannot be solved under the existing legislation, designing and recommending proposals on the improvement of the legislation to the competent legislative organs of the Republic of Kazakhstan.[48] It is not clear from the official statements accompanying this legal development whether creation of the ombudsman was linked to concerns emanating from Kazakhstan's experience of acting as a respondent in a number of investment treaty arbitrations. The media briefs suggest that the ombudsman was modelled on the South Korean experience, where the eponymous institution played a central part in the State's investment promotion strategy (as opposed to being designed to prevent investment disputes).[49]

(3) Dispute Management: A Minimalist Approach

Reassertion of control through emphasis on domestic prevention and management of investment disputes is not representative of how most developing countries have responded to their involvement in investment arbitration. As is the case with the investment treaty reform trend, at one end of the spectrum are the countries such as Peru where dissatisfaction with their experience of investment arbitration has prompted the creation of domestic legal solutions aimed at reducing the State's future exposure to liability towards foreign investors. At the other end of the spectrum are the countries which have opted to make only minor domestic legal changes and those where the encounter with investment treaty arbitration has not led to the adoption of any concrete dispute

[47] See www.invest.gov.kz/?option=news&itemid=136 (accessed 29 February 2016).

[48] See Article 12-1 of the Law No. 373-II on Investments, 8 January 2003, as amended 12 June 2014.

[49] See e.g. http://trevianinternational.com/kazakhstan-investors-monitor-july-16-2013/ (accessed 29 February 2016). See M. Sattorova, M. Erkan and O. Omiunu, 'How Do Host States Respond'.

prevention strategy. This section will seek to uncover the relative reticence on the part of some countries in embracing full-fledged dispute prevention mechanisms and analyse the factors which may explain such patterns of reassertion of control by host States.

Consider, for example, Turkey. In the aftermath of the first wave of investment claims against the government, Executive Decree No. 659 regulating the provision of legal services for government departments put the legal department of the prime minister's office in charge of defending Turkey's interests in international disputes, including in investment arbitration cases.[50] The department may handle the claim by itself or coordinate actions of the government authorities involved in the dispute. The decree does not expressly mention dispute prevention or accountability of government agencies in cases where their actions result in Turkey's international responsibility. Turkey's response has thus been confined to optimising the defence of the State's interests in investment arbitration, with the questions of investment dispute prevention left largely unaddressed.

Contrastingly, Uzbekistan's experience of defending itself in a number of investment arbitration cases has not elicited any notable institutional changes with regard to either dispute prevention or management. The Ministry of Justice remains responsible for representation of the government's interests in investment arbitration, and no special unit or department has been created to prevent and manage investment disputes. Neither have there been any formal changes to the existing legal framework on the payment of awards and judgments rendered against government organs and/or their officials.[51] As mentioned earlier, an attempt was made to change the interpretation of the provisions granting foreign investors access to international arbitration; despite the fact that government representatives expressed an intention to remove the State consent to arbitration from the law, the subsequent amendments to the law left the relevant provision intact. The question arises as to the factors underlying this variation in domestic law responses: why have some States taken a more comprehensive approach to investment dispute prevention than others?

[50] Law No 659 of 29 September 2011. The Turkish-language version is available at http://mevzuat.basbakanlik.gov.tr/ (accessed 29 February 2016).

[51] The Russian-language version of the rules governing the payment of judgments and awards of compensation for damages caused by government bodies and officials is available at www.lex.uz (accessed 29 February 2016).

(4) *Reassertion by Whom? Domestic Reforms and Their (External) Champions*

A comparative assessment of Peru's and Kazakhstan's responses with those of Turkey and Uzbekistan offers some potentially useful insights and raises some novel questions. Firstly, contrary to the assumption that an exposure to investment arbitration is likely to compel the host State to set up a mechanism to prevent future disputes, it appears that States can differ significantly in the way they respond to investment treaty disputes and, in particular, to the costs of arbitration and the imposition or threat of monetary liability. Even though both Turkey and Uzbekistan incurred significant financial costs in defending themselves in investment arbitration cases, neither has translated its 'learning' experience into concrete steps towards preventing investment claims and, particularly, towards addressing the causes of investment disputes. One possible explanation for this is that due to a degree of success with defending their interests, the two countries perceived their experience of investment arbitration to be overall positive and thus did not see any reason to query and address the underlying causes of investment disputes. However, Peru could be said to be in a comparable position with regard to a high proportion of cases where investors failed to succeed in their claims against it; nonetheless, the government of Peru did put in place a mechanism to prevent and manage investment disputes. Other examples of countries which introduced a formal dispute prevention and management system include Colombia, which, despite having never faced an investment arbitration claim, nevertheless established a formal legal framework with the aim of reducing the risks of non-compliance with the international commitments it assumed under investment treaties.[52] Thus, the fact that Turkey and Uzbekistan did not create similar dispute prevention mechanisms may not necessarily be attributable to their satisfaction with the outcome of the investment disputes brought against them; a more complex chain of causative events is likely to be at work.

Another possible explanation for the fact that no formal dispute prevention mechanisms were created in Turkey and Uzbekistan could be found in the involvement of international organisations, including the

[52] USAID/APEC, *Investor-State Dispute Prevention Strategies: Selected Case Studies*, 2013, 13, available at www.apec.org/Groups/Committee-on-Trade-and-Investment/~/media /Files/Groups/IEG/20130625_IEG-DisputePrevention.pdf (accessed 29 February 2016).

providers of technical assistance, in devising the relevant rules and their implementation. A brief look at the genesis of the dispute prevention systems adopted in Peru and Colombia shows a key role played by external entities such as UNCTAD and the European Union.[53] During the first years after the dispute prevention systems were launched, both governments received support from UNCTAD and the European Union to organise training of government officials.[54] While it is not clear whether the idea for the formal prevention mechanism also came from the external actors, it seems that the availability of capacity-building support frequently plays a decisive role in government decision-making. Conceptually, the variation in the ways developing host States responded to investment treaty arbitration – and the emergence of domestic mechanisms for dispute prevention through which States can mediate their participation in the investment treaty regime – reveal the importance of peering behind the notion of State as a unitary actor and identifying domestic factors that shape international legal behaviour of States. As Chayes and Chayes argued in their management theory of State compliance with international law, '[i]n modern times, the sovereign is no longer a unitary actor who can bind the domain by his own will. Power in modern States is recognised as being distributed along formal and informal networks, and legitimacy is compromised unless consent to international commitments is elicited through internal procedures, formal or informal.'[55]

That dispute prevention and management frameworks in Peru and Colombia have been created with the aid of international organisations brings to the fore international relations theories which link changes in government behaviour with the availability of resources. Long before investment arbitration has captured the attention of the international scholarly community, Chayes and Chayes argued that the process of facilitating State compliance with international rules should involve *informing* States of international laws and building State capacity to comply.[56] When analysed through this lens, the fact that some developing States (such as Turkey and Uzbekistan) have not adopted formal

[53] *Ibid.*, 16 (noting the support Colombia received from the European Union to implement its dispute prevention strategy); also UNCTAD, *Best Practices in Investment for Development*, 37.

[54] *Ibid.*, 37–8.

[55] A. Chayes and A. Chayes, *The New Sovereignty: Compliance with International Regulatory Agreements* (Cambridge, MA: Harvard University Press, 1995), 128.

[56] *Ibid.*, 25.

measures on the prevention of investment disputes need not necessarily be regarded as either their satisfaction with the regime or their deliberate defiance to act. Rather, such behaviour of Contracting States parties can be a result of ambiguities surrounding investment treaties and of their implications for host States, as well as a lack of host State capacity to reassert control by making relevant changes in domestic laws. As the qualitative studies referred to earlier indicate, the ways developing countries respond to investment arbitration can be significantly influenced by a lack of awareness about international investment law and a lack of capacity to effectively 'learn' and to translate lessons from their involvement in investor-State arbitration into concrete changes. If host States are expected to respond to investment arbitration by refraining from behaviour that leads to investment disputes, it is essential that '[t]he issue of the party's capacity to carry out its obligations is examined and addressed, perhaps by some form of technical assistance or other resources if available'[57] – so as to raise the levels of awareness and to help put in place effective dispute prevention mechanisms at a domestic level.

The fact that international organisations may have played a significant part in the creation of domestic dispute prevention frameworks in developing countries also raises an important question: is this a reassertion of control by host States or by international organisations? Does the involvement of international organisations carry an enabling effect, or is it effectively an exercise of control by external actors over developing governments preventing the latter from making their own choices with regard various modalities of participation in the investment treaty regime? Might externally imposed models hamper the emergence of 'internally felt' norms and the production of new, innovative ways of interaction between developing States and the global investment protection regime? While answering these questions falls outside the scope of this chapter, it is fitting to stress the need for less State-centric and more pluralistic analyses of developments in investment treaty law. A steadfast adherence to the unitary conception of States conceals the variety of domestic and external factors which underpin choices made by host governments in deciding how to regain control over the formation and interpretation of investment protection rules.

[57] *Ibid.*, 110.

D. Domestic Contestation: Towards Pluralist Explanations of Host State Approaches to Investment Treaties and Arbitration

Peering beyond the unitary conception of State is also a useful analytical exercise inasmuch it allows one to differentiate yet another form of reassertion of control over international investment law – domestic contestation of investment treaties and investment arbitration – and to identify some of the forces that have precipitated related developments in the international investment law regime. Recent debates over mega-regional investment agreements have cast into a sharp relief the presently underexplored role of domestic groups – and of domestic political process – in shaping host State behaviour and modalities of its participation in the investment treaty regime.

In the European Union, the debate was sparked in 2013, after the European Commission was issued with a mandate to negotiate a free trade agreement with an investment chapter between the United States and the European Union – the Transatlantic Trade and Investment Partnership (TTIP). In what was an unprecedented step in the history of international investment agreements, the Commission opened up public consultation, inviting the general public to express its position on the inclusion of provisions on investment arbitration in the proposed agreement. Although the Commission subsequently declined to register the European Citizens' Initiative STOP TTIP launched by non-governmental organisations (NGOs) and supported by the Greens,[58] the debate about investment treaty protection and arbitration has received considerable attention in political discourse. The European Economic and Social Committee voiced its opposition to the inclusion of investor-State arbitration provisions in the TTIP or in the EU-Canada Comprehensive Economic Trade Agreement (CETA).[59] As stated by the rapporteur, '[t]his is not an opinion against investor protection but an opinion that opposes ISDS which is not a form of dispute settlement acceptable to a large majority of civil society'.[60] While the draft opinion of the Legal Affairs Committee of the European Parliament initially favoured investor-State arbitration

[58] The European Citizens' Initiative (ECI) provides a platform for citizens to present a legislative proposal to the Commission if they collect over a million signatures.

[59] On issues of reassertion policy regarding TTIP and CETA in the European Union context, see also Chapter 13.

[60] See www.eesc.europa.eu/?i=portal.en.press-releases.35910 (accessed 29 February 2016).

provisions, it subsequently changed its tenor as a result of amendments from the Greens and the radical left (GUE).[61] Six of the fourteen parliamentary committees – including the committees on Economic and Monetary Affairs, Legal Affairs, Employment, Environment, Petitions and Constitutional Affairs – expressed their opposition to the investor-State arbitration mechanism and its inclusion in the TTIP.[62] In France, the website of the Socialist Party has reported that the European social-democratic heads of States and of governments agreed on a common position to block the inclusion of provisions on investor-State arbitration. The opposition to ISDS has also escalated in Germany, with the leader of a parliamentary group for the Left party expressing concerns over the lack of transparency,[63] and the German Environment Minister, Barbara Hendricks, dismissing the investment arbitration mechanism as 'simply not necessary'.[64]

Interest-group politics and the heightened public attention to TTIP negotiations and the matters of investment treaty protection have most certainly influenced the European Union's evolving position on investment treaty protection. As evidenced by the Commission's statement following the analysis of the public consultation submissions, the European Union had to acknowledge the existence of considerable scepticism against investment arbitration.[65] The Commission has responded by stressing its commitment to the reforms aimed at designing 'more balanced investment chapters' in EU agreements.[66] One example of such reform is the incorporation of 'a set of modern provisions which rebalance the rights of the State and the investor in favour of the State, and its

[61] See Euractive, 'Parliament's Opposition to TTIP Arbitration on the Rise', available at www.euractiv.com/sections/trade-society/parliaments-opposition-ttip-arbitration-rise-313935 (accessed 29 February 2016).

[62] See www.euractiv.com/sections/trade-society/parliaments-opposition-ttip-arbitration-rise-313935 (accessed 29 February 2016).

[63] 'Berlin anti-TTIP Trade Deal Protest Attracts Hundreds of Thousands', available at www.theguardian.com/world/2015/oct/10/berlin-anti-ttip-trade-deal-rally-hundreds-thousands-protesters (accessed 29 February 2016).

[64] Euractiv, 'France and Germany to Form United Front against ISDS', available at www.euractiv.com/sections/trade-society/france-and-germany-form-united-front-against-isds-311267 (accessed 29 February 2016). See also Chapter 1.

[65] The European Commission, 'Online Public Consultation on Investment Protection and Investor-to-State Dispute Settlement (ISDS) in the Transatlantic Trade and Investment Partnership Agreement', Brussels, 13.1.2015 SWD(2015) 3 final, available at http://trade.ec.europa.eu/doclib/docs/2015/january/tradoc_153044.pdf (accessed 29 February 2016).

[66] See the statement by the Commissioner Cecilia Malmström, available at http://ec.europa.eu/commission/2014–2019/malmstrom/blog/investments-ttip-and-beyond-towards-international-investment-court_en (accessed 29 February 2016).

right to regulate in the public interest' in EU-Canada CETA.[67] Other proposed reforms include measures to increase transparency of arbitral proceedings,[68] creating a code of conduct for arbitrators, access to an appeal system and a medium-term goal, working towards the establishment of a permanent multilateral investment court.[69]

A similar agitation over investment treaties and investment arbitration has been a feature of the domestic political process surrounding the negotiation of TTIP, the Transpacific Trade Partnership (TPP) and CETA in the United States and Canada, respectively. In the United States, the matters relating to investment protection made a significant issue in the political discourse in 1992 when one candidate in the presidential election campaigned against North American Free Trade Agreement (NAFTA).[70] The influence of domestic political actors on the process of formation and change of US investment treaties is particularly discernible when viewed in the context of fast-track authority. Fast-track legislation, also known as 'trade promotion authority' (TPA), was first adopted in the Trade Act of 1974. It was designed to strike a balance between presidential and congressional authority: although the US Constitution grants Congress a final say on trade matters, the 'fast track' approval now enables the president to negotiate trade agreements and bring them back to the Congress for an up-or-down vote only. To renew the expired fast-track authority in 2002, the Bush administration had to establish some support within Congress, including by addressing concerns increasingly voiced by environmental and other groups over the implications of investment protection for public-policy regulations.[71] As a consequence, the Bush administration negotiated a binding interpretation of the NAFTA Chapter 11 clarifying the scope of certain substantive investment obligations.[72] From a broader political

[67] *Ibid.*

[68] See e.g. 'European Commission Pushes for Full Transparency for ISDS in Current Investment Treaties', available at http://europa.eu/rapid/press-release_IP-15-3881_en.htm(accessed 29 February 2016).

[69] See C. Malmström, 'Investments in TTIP and Beyond: Towards an International Investment Court', available at http://ec.europa.eu/commission/2014-2019/malmstrom/blog/investments-ttip-and-beyond-towards-international-investment-court_en (accessed 29 February 2016).

[70] See J. E. Mendenhall, 'The Evolving US Position on International Investment Protection and Its Impact on the US Position in the Trans-Pacific Partnership Negotiations' in N. J. Calamita and M. Sattorova, *The Regionalization of International Investment Treaty Arrangements* (London: BIICL, 2015), 255.

[71] *Ibid.* [72] *Ibid.*, 265.

perspective, the binding interpretation – a first significant step in investment treaty reform – was a product of the government's political strategy to prevent members of Congress from using the contentious investment rules as a reason to oppose future trade agreements.

Recently, the TTIP/TPP negotiations have caused division within the Democratic Party and proved to be a bone of contention in the political discourse over the fate of the proposed trade promotion authority (replacing the fast-track authority that expired in 2007). An open letter to the US Senate and House initiated by Alliance for Justice, an NGO, and endorsed by prominent US figures, including Professor Joseph Stiglitz and leading academics from Yale, Harvard and the University of California, urged the US government not to include investment arbitration provisions in the TPP.[73] Anti-TPP/TTIP groups rallied against the renewal of fast-track authority.[74] In a letter addressed to Ambassador Froman, US-based labour, environmental, health, consumer, business, family farm, faith-based and other interest groups commended on the creation of a public consultation process for the European civil society and requested that the same opportunity be provided to stakeholders and NGOs in the United States.[75] Although unions succeeded in pressuring House Democrats to vote against Obama's trade agenda in order to derail the renewal of TPA[76] (which would make it easier for the US government to conclude the TPP deal), only two weeks later the fast-track bill did receive US Senate approval and was signed into law on 29 June 2015.[77] However, the prospects of TPP ratification still remain questionable as the fate of the trade deal has turned into one of the hotly contested issues taken up by the 2016 presidential election campaign. While negotiation of the TPP has been concluded and the text released in November 2015,[78]

[73] See www.washingtonpost.com/r/2010-2019/WashingtonPost/2015/04/30/Editorial-Opinion/Graphics/oppose_ISDS_Letter.pdf (accessed 29 February 2016).

[74] See 'Labor Groups Rally against Trade Promotion Authority', available at http://thehill.com/policy/finance/238956-labor-groups-rally-against-trade-promotion-authority (accessed 29 February 2016).

[75] The letter is available at www.etuc.org/sites/www.etuc.org/files/press-release/files/letter_to_amb._froman_requesting_public_consultation_on_investment_2014.pdf (accessed 29 February 2016).

[76] See Trade Promotion Authority (TPA), 'Frequently Asked Questions', at https://fas.org/sgp/crs/misc/R43491.pdf (accessed 29 February 2016).

[77] Reuters, 'Obama Signs Trade Bills into Law, Says Tough Battle Still Ahead', 29 June 2015, available at www.reuters.com/article/us-usa-trade-obama-idUSKCN0P92GP20150629#qMeQYbHfz0FkB8ze.97 (accessed 29 February 2016).

[78] See https://ustr.gov/trade-agreements/free-trade-agreements/trans-pacific-partnership/tpp-full-text (accessed 29 February 2016).

the text may still undergo further legal review, and the domestic political dynamic may yet precipitate other developments in the substance and scope of the agreement's investment protection commitments.

Even a brief glance at the political dynamic underpinning the negotiation of new trans-Atlantic and trans-Pacific agreements reveals that the formation (and change of) international investment agreements is becoming increasingly influenced by domestic politics – a factor that has been somewhat neglected in existing investment treaty scholarship. Domestic political structures and preferences appear to play a significant part in shaping the ways in which host States have responded to developments in international investment law. The importance of viewing State behaviour not just as a set of strategic calculations by a unitary actor but rather as a product of complex interactions between political players at the domestic level has been acknowledged in the more recent theories of compliance with international law. Notable among them is Joel Trachtman's domestic coalitions–based theory which seeks to explain and predict State behaviour by uncovering 'the black box of the state in order to see the internal workings of the domestic political process' and focusing on the individuals and groups that influence governments through political institutions and social practices.'[79] Trachtman exposes the cracks in the explanations based on the unitary model of the State – including their ignorance of the domestic political dynamic, which underpins the State's decision to comply, modify or withdraw from international legal regimes.[80] He argues that 'there is no unified, *ex ante* national interest. The national interest is the result of a domestic political process, taking into account opportunities and risks in the international market.'[81] Indeed, as the recent developments in investment treaty practice demonstrate, the unitary model of the State may have been a reasonable heuristic device where investment treaty rules were predominantly matters of foreign policy determined independently of domestic constituents' interests and preferences. It can still be used as an effective analytical tool in explaining treaty practice of States where domestic political input is stifled or non-existent. However, as investment treaty reform in the United States and the European Union has revealed so far, international investment law has been increasingly moving from the realm of 'beyond the border' to 'inside the border' issues.[82]

[79] J. P. Trachtman, 'International Law and Domestic Political Coalitions: The Grand Theory of Compliance with International Law', *Chicago Journal of International Law*, 11 (2010), 128–9.

[80] *Ibid.*, 130. [81] *Ibid.*, 130–1. [82] *Ibid.*, 131.

It is important to remain cognizant of the limits of explanatory and predictive powers of the domestic coalitions-based theory in the particular context of international investment law. As Trachtman acknowledges, where decisions are made by administrative agencies and the judiciary, 'both at some distance from the full brunt of legislative lobbying',[83] a different theoretical model would be required. As the preceding discussion suggests, Trachtman's theory is more suitable for explaining State behaviour in the international scene, that is, the formation and reform of investment treaties. It is certainly less suited for explaining the reassertion of control over international investment law by developing States by making changes in national legislation, including in countries where national constitutional arrangements and political conditions militate against the emergence and effective functioning of sufficiently robust domestic constituencies.

Yet, just as is the case with the management of compliance theory by Chayes and Chayes, application of the domestic coalitions-based theory would make an important contribution to legal discourse by moving away from the prevailing State-centric narratives of international investment law towards deconstructing the notion of State and identifying other actors and factors which determine the ways in which host States respond to the rapid developments in investment treaty practice and arbitral case law. It can also be useful in predicting State behaviour in the international investment policy scene. With domestic constituencies becoming increasingly vocal in the debate over international investment agreements, the shape of the latter is likely to be correspondingly influenced by the domestic political configuration within host States. In particular, much will depend on how a particular host State accommodates the interaction between various stakeholders and how its laws enable the formation of communities willing to expend political capital in support of one or another policy stance on international investment protection. For instance, the EU laws on citizens' initiative – a platform allowing citizens to initiate legislative proposals by making a collective submission to the Commission – provide a useful illustration of how national (or in the case of the European Union, supranational) law can influence the outcome of international treaty reform by enabling or preventing domestic interest groups and individuals from having a say in the political debate. Put differently, national laws mediating the relationship between individuals and the

[83] *Ibid.*, 134.

State may play a pivotal role in shaping international outcomes, that is, the ways in which host States reassert control over international investment law.

E. Conclusion

This chapter has sought to explore the domestic dimension of the reassertion of control by States parties. Drawing on recent empirical insights from developing countries, it has highlighted the variation in the ways host States have responded to the fast-paced changes in international investment law and attempted to uncover some of the factors behind such variation. It transpires that whether host States have shown reticence, embarked on domestic reform of dispute prevention and management mechanisms or grappled with domestic contestation of investment treaty rules, all of these forms of reassertion of control hinge on socio-economic, political and legal capacity of host States. Developing countries in particular appear to have been influenced by the lack of awareness of true implications of investment treaty law, insufficient co-ordination between various agencies and officials within the government and an inability to translate lessons learnt into concrete legal changes. Although the amount of empirical data is currently limited and further longitudinal studies on a broader geographical scale are necessary, the emerging findings point to the growing importance of peering behind the unitary conception of State and identifying the factors which shape host State engagement with international norms on investment protection and dispute settlement. This chapter also makes a case for a greater focus on the perceptions and reality in developing countries, whose patterns of participation in the making and implementation of investment treaty norms still remain under-analysed.

This chapter has also drawn attention to the currently under-explored role of international organisations in influencing host States' choices in reasserting control over international investment law. Given the evidence of the involvement of international organisations in constructing recent dispute management and prevention mechanisms in developing States, the overarching question is: reassertion of control by whom? This chapter has also sought to cast light on grassroots opposition as a form of domestic response to international investment law. Just as is the case with the emerging evidence regarding the role of international organisations in motivating States to act in one of another way, the recent examples of domestic political contestation of investment treaty norms point to the importance of constructing a more nuanced portrayal of international investment law so that a plurality of external and domestic influences is identified in elucidating the ways host States realign their international investment protection commitments.

PART II

Procedural Aspects and Avenues of Reassertion

4

Early Dismissal of Claims in Investment Arbitration

FRIEDRICH ROSENFELD

A. Introduction

In the last two decades, there has been a significant increase of investment arbitrations. According to statistics of the International Centre for Settlement of Investment Disputes (ICSID), the number of cases registered under the ICSID Convention and the Additional Facility Rules until 31 December 2015 amounted to 549, out of which 517 cases date from 1996 onwards.[1] At the same time, the statistics show that States still win in more than half the cases decided by arbitral tribunals under the ICSID Convention and the Additional Facility Rules.[2]

Despite this high success rate, a number of States have criticised the time and costs needed to defend their position in investment proceedings. The criticism has been particularly sharp in situations where the underlying claim of the investor had from its outset no prospects of success.[3] Why conduct lengthy and expensive proceedings if arbitration is doomed to fail?

It is against this background that various initiatives have been taken to create mechanisms for the early dismissal of claims. Some of these mechanisms have only recently been applied in case law.[4] Others are

[1] The ICSID Caseload: Statistics (Issue 2016–1), 7, available at https://icsid.worldbank.org/apps/ICSIDWEB/resources/Documents/ICSID%20Web%20Stats%202016-1%20(English)%20final.pdf (accessed 24 February 2016).

[2] *Ibid.*, 14.

[3] Cf. S. Puig and C. Brown, 'The Power of ICSID Tribunals to Dismiss Proceedings Summarily: An Analysis of Rule 41(5) of the ICSID Arbitration Rules', Sydney Law School, Legal Studies Research Paper No. 11/33, 2011, 3; Eric de Brabandare, 'The ICSID Rule on Early Dismissal of Unmeritorious Treaty Claims: Preserving the Integrity of ICSID Arbitration', *Manchester Journal of International Economic Law* 9(1) (2012), 23 *et seq.*

[4] Jurisprudence on ICSID Arbitration Rule 41(5) includes *MOL Hungarian Oil and Gas Company PLC* v. *Republic of Croatia*, ICSID Case No. ARB/13/32, Decision on

yet to be tested in practice.[5] As we are venturing into largely unchartered legal territory,[6] this chapter takes a closer look at these different instruments, which include a procedural mechanism for early dismissal under the ICSID Arbitration Rules (see Section B) as well as treaty mechanisms under certain investment agreements (see Section C).

It is submitted that most of the mechanisms for early dismissal provide for a rather weak form of control by States. While increasing codificatory efforts have limited the flexibility of arbitral tribunals to conduct the proceedings as they deem appropriate, States are not in a position to control the ultimate outcome of cases. The situation is different under the

Respondent's Application under ICSID Arbitration Rule 41(5) of 2 December 2014; *PNG Sustainable Development Program, Ltd.* v. *Independent State of Papua New Guinea*, ICSID Case No. ARB/13/33, Tribunal's Decision on the Respondent's Objections under Rule 41(5) of the ICSID Arbitration Rules of 28 October 2014; *Elsamex S.A.* v. *República de Honduras*, Decisión sobre la Excepción de Elsamex S.A. contra la Solicitud de Anulación del Laudo presentada por la República de Honduras, ICSID Case No. ARB/09/4, Decision of 7 January 2014; *Emmis International Holding B.V., Emmis Radio Operating, B.V., Mem Magyar Electronic Media Kereskedelmi És Szolgáltató KFT* v. *Hungary*, ICSID Case No. ARB/12/2, Decision on Respondent's Objection under ICSID Arbitration Rule 41(5) of 11 March 2013; *Accession Mezzanine Capital L.P. and Danubius Kereskedöház Vagyonkezelö Zrt* v. *Hungary*, ICSID Case No. ARB/12/3, Decision on Respondent's Objection under Arbitration Rule 41(5) of 16 January 2013; *Vattenfall AB and Others* v. *Federal Republic of Germany*, ICISD Case No. ARB/12/12, Decision of 2 July 2013, reported in *IA Reporter*, 4 July 2013; *Rafat Ali Rizvi* v. *Republic of Indonesia*, ICSID Case No. ARB/11/13, Award on Jurisdiction of 16 July 2013, para. 20; *Global Trading Resource Corp. and Global International, Inc.* v. *Ukraine*, ICSID Case No. ARB/09/11, Award of 1 December 2010; *Brandes Investment Partners, LP* v. *Bolivarian Republic of Venezuela*, ICSID Case No. ARB/08/3, Decision on the Respondent's Objection under Rule 41(5) of the ICSID Arbitration Rules of 2 February 2009; *Trans-Global Petroleum, Inc.* v. *Hashemite Kingdom of Jordan*, ICSID Case No. ARB/07/25, Tribunal's Decision on the Respondent's Objection under Rule 41(5) of the ICSID Arbitration Rules of 12 May 2008; *Rachel S. Grynberg, Stephen M. Grynberg, Miriam Z. Grynberg, and RSM Production Corporation* v. *Grenada*, ICSID Case No. ARB/10/6, Award of 10 December 2010. Additional cases without public decision include *CEAC Holdings Limited* v. *Montenegro*, ICSID Case No. ARB/14/8, Decision of 27 January 2015; *Transglobal Green Energy, LLC and Transglobal Green Panama, S.A.* v. *Republic of Panama*, Decision of 17 March 2015; *Edenred S.A.* v. *Hungary*, ICSID Case No. ARB/13/21, Decision of 6 June 2014.

5 See Section C(3).

6 Some of the early decisions on ICSID Arbitration Rule 41(5) have been discussed in M. Potesta and M. Sobat, 'Frivolous Claims in International Adjudication: A Study of ICSID Rule 41(5) and of Procedures of Other Courts and Tribunals to Dismiss Claims Summarily', *Journal of International Dispute Settlement*, 3 (2012), 137 *et seq.*; A. Goldsmith, 'Trans-Global Petroleum: "Rare Bird" or Significant Step in the Development of Early Merits-Based Claim-Vetting?', *ASA Bulletin*, 26 (2008), 667 *et seq.*; L. Markert, 'Preliminary Objections Pursuant to ICSID Arbitration Rule 41(5): Soon to Become the Preliminary Objection of Choice?', *Transnational Dispute Management*, 9 (2012), 1 *et seq.*

Comprehensive Economic and Trade Agreement (CETA), which includes a non-judicial mechanism for the early dismissal of certain claims relating to financial services. In this limited field, States have gained control over the ultimate outcome of the proceedings, and the law-based paradigm of investment protection appears to have given way to a policy-based paradigm of investment protection (see Section D).

B. The Procedure for Early Dismissal under the ICSID Arbitration Rules

Under the ICSID Arbitration Rules, a formal procedure for the early dismissal of claims exists as of 2006, when ICSID Arbitration Rule 41(5) was created. The rationale of this provision was to establish a procedure for the expedited dismissal of certain claims at an early stage of the case.[7] As such, it was intended to compensate the limited screening powers of the secretary-general at the date of registration.[8]

ICSID Arbitration Rule 41(5) requires an application from a party (see Section B(1)) that is made within a limited time frame (see Section B(2)) and sets forth that a claim is manifestly without legal merit (see Section B(3)). Once these three requirements are fulfilled, and provided that no other expedited procedure has been agreed upon, the tribunal shall give the parties the opportunity to present their observations (see Section B(4)) and notify its decision at an early stage of the proceedings (see Section B(5)). In what follows, each of these elements will be examined in greater detail.

(1) Application from a Party

The procedure for early dismissal under ICSID Arbitration Rule 41(5) cannot be initiated *ex officio* by an arbitral tribunal. Instead, it requires an application from a party. As was correctly observed by the arbitral tribunal in *Global Trading* v. *Ukraine*, this party is always the respondent.[9] A claimant which has initiated investment arbitration

[7] A. Antonietti, 'The 2006 Amendments to the ICSID Rules and Regulations and the Additional Facility Rules', *ICSID Review*, 21 (2006), 427, 439.

[8] 'Possible Improvements of the Framework for ICSID Arbitration', ICSID Secretariat Discussion Paper, 22 October 2004, available at https://icsid.worldbank.org/apps/ICSIDWEB/resources/Documents/Possible%20Improvements%20of%20the%20Framework%20of%20ICSID%20Arbitration.pdf (accessed 24 February 2016).

[9] *Global Trading Resource Corp. and Global International, Inc.* v. *Ukraine*, footnote 1.

proceedings obviously has no interest in having its own case dismissed. And the prospects of using ICSID Arbitration Rule 41(5) in response to a counterclaim are not very likely to become relevant in practice. This is due in part to the simple fact that counterclaims are still the exception in investment arbitration proceedings. Besides, the application under ICSID Arbitration Rule 41(5) has to be filed at a very early stage of the proceedings and, hence, at a time when no potential counterclaim has typically been asserted.[10] In this regard, it may be observed that ICSID Arbitration Rule 41(5) benefits States more than investors.

Notwithstanding the aforesaid, it would be incorrect to conclude that ICSID Arbitration Rule 41(5) is a mere instrument for the reassertion of control by States. Instead, ICSID Arbitration Rule 41(5) may also benefit the investor in annulment proceedings initiated by a State. The case of *Elsamex S.A.* v. *República de Honduras* illustrates this.[11] This case arose from an investment dispute between the Spanish company Elsamex S.A. and the Republic of Honduras in connection with a highway repair contract. After Elsamex S.A. had obtained an award in its favour, the Republic of Honduras initiated annulment proceedings. In response, Elsamex S.A. filed an application under ICSID Arbitration Rule 41(5) and contended that the application was manifestly without legal merit. The Annulment Committee confirmed that Elsamex S.A. was entitled to file such application. It based its decision upon ICSID Arbitration Rule 53 pursuant to which the arbitration rules – and hence also ICSID Arbitration Rule 41(5) – apply *mutatis mutandis* to annulment proceedings.[12] The conclusion to be drawn is that both States and investors may profit from ICSID Arbitration Rule 41(5).

(2) *Timing*

An application pursuant to ICSID Arbitration Rule 41(5) has to be filed no later than thirty days after the constitution of the arbitral tribunal and in any event before the first session of the arbitral tribunal. It is important to note in this regard that the respondent receives the claimant's request for arbitration at the time of its registration.[13] Based on this information, the respondent can start preparing its application under ICSID

[10] Potesta and Sobat, 'Frivolous Claims in International Adjudication', 13. See also ICSID Arbitration Rule 40(2).

[11] *Elsamex S.A.* v. *República de Honduras.*

[12] *Elsamex S.A.* v. *República de Honduras*, paras. 89 *et seq.*

[13] Article 36 of the ICSID Convention.

Arbitration Rule 41(5) even before the arbitral tribunal has been constituted.[14] Strategically, this may be beneficial for the respondent: by submitting an application under ICSID Arbitration Rule 41(5), a respondent may present its view on a case at a very early stage of the proceedings. This may help to shape the tribunal's perception of a case even before the claimant has submitted its full memorial.[15]

The failure to file an application under ICSID Arbitration Rule 41(5) does not preclude a respondent from raising identical objections in the further course of the proceedings. The arbitral tribunal in *Cementownia 'Nowa Huta' S.A.* v. *Republic of Turkey* confirmed this with respect to ICSID Arbitration (AF) Rule 45(6), which has the same wording as ICSID Arbitration Rule 41(5).[16] In *Cementownia 'Nowa Huta' S.A.* v. *Republic of Turkey*, respondent contended during the course of the proceedings that claimant's claims were manifestly without merit. Claimant objected to this and asserted that respondent should have immediately filed an application for early dismissal pursuant to ICSID Arbitration (AF) Rule 45(6) at an early stage of the proceedings. The arbitral tribunal did not endorse claimant's argument. It held that claimant's position was inconsistent with the express wording of ICSID Arbitration (AF) Rule 45, which allows a respondent to assert objections up until the filing of its counter-memorial.[17] Accordingly, the failure to file an application for early dismissal does not have a preclusionary effect. This makes perfect sense. In light of the high standards that apply in proceedings for early dismissal and the risk that many applications will ultimately fail, a respondent may well have an interest not to make use of this mechanism and to bring the same arguments in the normal course of proceedings.

(3) Objection That a Claim Is Manifestly without Legal Merit

An application under ICSID Arbitration Rule 41(5) further requires an objection that a claim is manifestly without legal merit. Such objection

[14] Cf. Markert, 'Preliminary Objections Pursuant to ICSID Arbitration Rule 41(5)', 9 and Annex 1.

[15] As of today, most cases in which applications under ICSID Arbitration Rule 41(5) have been filed are still pending. Accordingly, there are no reliable data that would allow a final assessment of the impact of ICSID Arbitration Rule 41(5) applications on the outcome of the proceedings.

[16] *Cementownia 'Nowa Huta' S.A.* v. *Republic of Turkey*, ICSID Case No. ARB(AF)06/2, Award of 17 September 2009.

[17] *Ibid.*, para. 110. The arbitral tribunal found that claimant's claim was manifestly ill founded. *Ibid.*, paras. 157, 163.

has to be specified as precisely as possible. As will be shown later, arbitral tribunals have observed high standards in interpreting these requirements, that is, the existence of a claim (see Section B(3)(a)), that has no legal merit (see Section B(3)(b)) and passes the threshold of manifestness (see Section B(3)(c)). An even higher standard has been applied in annulment proceedings (see Section B(3)(d)).

(a) Claim

The object of an application under ICSID Arbitration Rule 41(5) is a claim. The use of the singular 'claim' as opposed to 'claims' indicates that an application under ICSID Arbitration Rule 41(5) may well be initiated with respect to one out of several claims. If successful, the proceedings will be dismissed with regard to this particular claim but continue with regard to the remaining claims.[18]

In practice, such a dismissal of isolated claims has been treated with particular caution. The Annulment Committee in *Elsamex* v. *Honduras*, for example, warned to exercise judicial prudence when dismissing one of several claims. It explained that claims are often related and that such interdependencies may not always be detected with ease at an early stage of the proceedings.[19] In line with this jurisprudence, it is recommendable to file applications under ICSID Arbitration Rule 41(5) against isolated claims only if these are clearly unrelated to the remaining parts of the claims. Efficiency considerations further support this proposition. The goal of reducing time and costs would not be achieved if, despite the early dismissal, the proceedings have to be continued with regard to related claims raising similar issues.

(b) Without Legal Merit

The claim must be without legal merit. According to settled jurisprudence of investment tribunals, the notion of 'merit' must be interpreted as covering both objections to jurisdiction and objections to the merits of a claim (see Section B(3)(b)(i)). There is no similar consensus regarding the interpretation of the adjective 'legal' (see Section B(3)(b)(ii)).

(i) The Notion of 'Merit' Arbitral tribunals have consistently interpreted the notion of 'merit' as covering both objections to jurisdiction

[18] See e.g. *Emmis International Holding B.V., Emmis Radio Operating, B.V., Mem Magyar Electronic Media Kereskedelmi És Szolgáltató KFT* v. *Hungary*.

[19] *Elsamex S.A.* v. *República de Honduras*, para. 139.

and objections to the merits of a claim. The authority most frequently invoked in this regard is the decision of the arbitral tribunal in *Brandes* v. *Venezuela*. In this decision, the arbitral tribunal held:

> There exist no objective reasons why the intent not to burden the parties with a possibly long and costly proceeding when dealing with such unmeritorious claims should be limited to an evaluation of the merits of the case and should not also englobe an examination of the jurisdictional basis on which the tribunal's powers to decide the case rest.[20]

Until today, tribunals have confirmed this.[21] At first glance, such an interpretation is not compelling as ICSID Arbitration Rule 41(5) makes no reference to jurisdictional objections. Its wording 'without legal merit' is at best ambiguous. Moreover, the preparatory works of ICSID Arbitration Rule 41(5) show that this provision had originally been designed to facilitate the dismissal of 'all or part of a claim on the merits' in an expedited procedure.[22] It was only the writings of ICSID Counsel Aurélia Antonietti[23] and former ICSID Secretary-General Antonio Parra[24] which revealed that even the ICSID Secretariat finally considered ICSID Arbitration Rule 41(5) to be applicable to objections on jurisdiction. This change in the conceptualisation of ICSID Arbitration Rule 41(5) makes sense in view of its object and purpose: The rationale to prevent lengthy and costly proceedings applies for objections to jurisdiction and objections to the merits alike. Admittedly, Article 36 of the ICSID Convention already allows for a first screening by the secretary-general, who shall not register requests where the dispute is manifestly outside the jurisdiction of the Centre. Yet the screening powers of the secretary-general are extremely narrow and based on the limited information contained in a request for arbitration. In an application under

20 *Brandes Investment Partners, LP* v. *Bolivarian Republic of Venezuela*, para. 52.

21 *PNG Sustainable Development Program, Ltd.* v. *Independent State of Papua New Guinea*, para. 91; *Global Trading Resource Corp. and Global International, Inc.* v. *Ukraine*, para. 30; *Brandes Investment Partners, LP* v. *Bolivarian Republic of Venezuela*, para. 50.

22 'Suggested Changes to the ICSID Rules and Regulations', Working Paper of the ICSID Secretariat dated 12 May 2005, available at https://icsid.worldbank.org/apps/ICSIDWEB/resources/Documents/Suggested%20Changes%20to%20the%20ICSID%20Rules%20and%20Regulations.pdf (accessed 24 February 2016).

23 Antonietti, '2006 Amendments to the ICSID Rules and Regulations', 440 *et seq.*

24 A. Parra, 'The Development of the Regulations and Rules of the International Centre for Settlement of Investment Disputes', *International Law*, 41 (2007), 47 *et seq.* Note that even Parra referred to ICSID Arbitration Rule 41(5) as a mechanism for dismissal of 'patently unmeritorious claims', which is, again, ambiguous wording.

ICSID Arbitration Rule 41(5), a respondent may adduce additional facts to support its contention that a dispute is manifestly outside the jurisdiction of ICSID.[25] In sum, ICSID Arbitration Rule 41(5) therefore must be applied for objections to jurisdiction and objections to the merits alike.

(ii) **The Notion of 'Legal'** There is no similar consensus regarding the interpretation of the adjective 'legal'. The dilemma is the following: on the one hand, it has correctly been observed that the strict timetable imposed by ICSID Arbitration Rule 41(5) does not allow testing factual allegations by taking evidence.[26] On the other hand, the legal merits of a claim may hardly be assessed in isolation from the facts upon which a claim rests.[27] Accordingly, one may have difficulties in answering the question of which facts an arbitral tribunal shall consider in rendering its application under ICSID Arbitration Rule 41(5). Two approaches can be distinguished.

The first approach consists in looking solely at the facts alleged by claimant and deciding whether, on this basis, a claim may be dismissed for lack of legal merit. The idea behind this is the following: if on the basis of the best factual presumption for claimant its claims are still manifestly without legal merit, then there is simply no need to take any evidence. The arbitral tribunals in *Brandes* v. *Venezuela*[28] and *PNG* v. *Papua New Guinea*[29] rendered their decisions on the basis of such considerations.

The second approach also takes the facts adduced by the claimant as the starting point but filters out a certain number of factual allegations that are a priori not acceptable for an arbitral tribunal. The decision in *Trans-Global Petroleum, Inc.* v. *Hashemite Kingdom of Jordan* evidences this approach. While the arbitral tribunal in this case was in principle also

[25] *Trans-Global Petroleum, Inc.* v. *Hashemite Kingdom of Jordan*, paras. 45, 79; A. Diop, 'Objections under Rule 41(5) of the ICSID Arbitration Rules', *ICSID Review* 25 (2005), 312 (319).

[26] *Trans-Global Petroleum, Inc.* v. *Hashemite Kingdom of Jordan*, para. 91.

[27] *Ibid.*, para. 97.

[28] *Brandes Investment Partners, LP* v. *Bolivarian Republic of Venezuela*, para. 61. This recalls the test developed by Judge Higgins in the *Oil Platforms* case. See *Case Concerning Oil Platforms* (*Islamic Republic of Iran* v. *United States of America*), Preliminary Objection, Judgement, Separate Opinion of Judge Higgins, ICJ Reports 1996, 803, para. 32. For a different view, see *Trans-Global Petroleum, Inc.* v. *Hashemite Kingdom of Jordan*, para. 103.

[29] *PNG Sustainable Development Program, Ltd.* v. *Independent State of Papua New Guinea*, para. 90. Note, however, that this Arbitral Tribunal referred in a footnote to the later-mentioned decision in *Trans-Global Petroleum Inc.* v. *Hashemite Kingdom of Jordan*.

committed not to weigh the credibility or plausibility of the claimant's submissions, it held that it would not accept at face value 'any factual allegation which the tribunal regards as (manifestly) incredible, frivolous, vexatious or inaccurate or made in bad faith'. In a similar vein, it would not accept any legal submissions that are presented as 'factual allegations'.[30] The decision may have been motivated by the wish not to unduly limit the scope of ICSID Arbitration Rule 41(5) applications.[31] Yet, it prevents a claimant from submitting potentially relevant facts. This can only be justified in exceptional cases.

The question of which facts may be considered by an arbitral tribunal in ruling upon an application under ICSID Arbitration Rule 41(5) has to be distinguished from the question of how many facts are required to render such decision. In this respect, the arbitral tribunal in *Global Trading* v. *Ukraine* observed that a balance would need to be struck between the right of the objecting party to have patently unmeritorious claims disposed of at an early stage and the duty of the tribunal to meet the requirements of due process.[32] The tribunal held that in case of doubt, a tribunal should decide not to dismiss a case summarily. This limits the potential for the reassertion of control.

(c) Manifestly

ICSID Arbitration Rule 41(5) further specifies that a claim needs to be 'manifestly' without legal merit. The requirement of 'manifestness' sets forth a high threshold. The most authoritative statement on the interpretation of the term 'manifestly' stems from the arbitral tribunal in *Trans-Global Petroleum, Inc.* v. *Hashemite Kingdom of Jordan*, which held:

> [T]he ordinary meaning of the word requires the respondent to establish its objection clearly and obviously, with relative ease and dispatch. The standard is thus set high. Given the nature of investment disputes generally, the Tribunal nonetheless recognises that this exercise may not always be simple, requiring (as in this case) successive rounds of written and oral submissions by the parties, together with questions addressed by the tribunal to those parties. The exercise may thus be complicated; but it should never be difficult.[33]

[30] *Trans-Global Petroleum, Inc.* v. *Hashemite Kingdom of Jordan*, para. 105.

[31] This approach has also been endorsed by the tribunal in *Rachel S. Grynberg, Stephen M. Grynberg, Miriam Z. Grynberg, and RSM Production Corporation* v. *Grenada*, para. 6.1.2.

[32] *Global Trading Resource Corp. and Global International, Inc.* v. *Ukraine*, para. 34.

[33] *Trans-Global Petroleum, Inc.* v. *Hashemite Kingdom of Jordan*, para. 88.

The arbitral tribunal reached this conclusion by having regard to the ordinary meaning of the term 'manifestly' as well as its meaning under Articles 36(6), (1)(b) and 57 of the ICSID Convention. The arbitral tribunal found further support for its interpretation in the short time limits set forth in ICSID Arbitration Rule 41(5). According to the arbitral tribunal, a written and reasoned award 'at the first session or promptly thereafter' would only be feasible in clear and obvious cases.[34]

Various tribunals have confirmed this interpretation.[35] As a result, an application under ICSID Arbitration Rule 41(5) may only be successful under limited circumstances. Essentially, it presupposes that a claim is not even conclusive and that the legal issues are – to put it in the terms of the arbitral tribunal in *PNG* v. *Papua New Guinea* – 'undisputed or genuinely undisputable'.[36] In support of its view, the arbitral tribunal in *PNG* v. *Papua New Guinea* explained that it would be inappropriate to resolve novel issues of law in a manner that limits the parties' right to be heard and the tribunal's opportunity to reflect.[37] This limits the potential to use ICSID Rule 41(5) as a mechanism to reassert control.

(d) Standard Applicable in Annulment Proceedings

According to the Annulment Committee in *Elsamex* v. *Honduras*, an even higher standard applies when a decision under ICSID Arbitration Rule 41(5) is rendered in annulment proceedings. The Annulment Committee based its decision on ICSID Arbitration Rule 53, pursuant to which ICSID Arbitration Rule 41(5) only applies *mutatis mutandis*, that is, with the necessary adaptations.[38]

In deciding which necessary adaptations would need to be made, the Annulment Committee noted two key differences between the original arbitration proceedings and annulment proceedings. First, it observed that more information is available in annulment proceedings. Thus, the object of an annulment proceeding is an arbitral award which is supposed to have

[34] *Ibid.*, para. 90. See also *Brandes Investment Partners, LP* v. *Bolivarian Republic of Venezuela*, para. 54.

[35] *Global Trading Resource Corp. and Global International, Inc.* v. *Ukraine*, para. 35; *Brandes Investment Partners, LP* v. *Bolivarian Republic of Venezuela*, para. 63; *Rachel S. Grynberg, Stephen M. Grynberg, Miriam Z. Grynberg, and RSM Production Corporation* v. *Grenada*, para. 6.1.2; *MOL Hungarian Oil and Gas Company PLC* v. *Republic of Croatia*, para. 45.

[36] *PNG Sustainable Development Program, Ltd.* v. *Independent State of Papua New Guinea*, para. 89.

[37] *PNG Sustainable Development Program, Ltd.* v. *Independent State of Papua New Guinea*, para. 94.

[38] *Elsamex S.A.* v. *República de Honduras*, paras. 115 *et seq.*

covered all relevant aspects of the dispute.[39] According to the Annulment Committee, this difference does not help to render the assessment less complex and difficult. Second, the Annulment Committee noted that there are no remedies against an award rendered by the Annulment Committee. Notably, the decision under ICSID Arbitration Rule 41(5) in conjunction with ICSID Arbitration Rule 53 is not subject to a further annulment proceeding. Instead, it is final.[40] On account of the foregoing, the Annulment Committee concluded that a higher standard of conviction would need to be fulfilled when applying ICSID Arbitration Rule 41(5) in annulment proceedings.[41] Possible reasons to dismiss an annulment application under ICSID Arbitration Rule 41(5) would include the non-existence of grounds of annulment or the misuse of the annulment proceedings as an appeals mechanism.[42]

(4) *Opportunity for the Parties to Present Their Observations*

Once the aforementioned requirements are fulfilled, and provided that no other expedited procedure has been agreed upon,[43] the tribunal shall give the parties the opportunity to present their observations. Arbitral tribunals have encountered difficulties in deciding how to comply with this requirement. This is due to the following dilemma: ICSID Arbitration Rule 41(5) does not envisage lengthy rounds of written or oral submissions by the parties. It provides that the arbitral tribunal shall render its decision in the first session or shortly thereafter.[44] At the same time, however, arbitral tribunals have correctly observed that a claimant should not be denied access to justice without the opportunity to be heard both in writing and orally.[45]

Arbitral tribunals have solved this dilemma by organising what may be designated as a mini case management conference. This approach was followed, for example, by the arbitral tribunal in *Global Trading* v. *Ukraine*, which held a preliminary consultation in the form of

[39] *Ibid.*, para. 122. [40] *Ibid.*, para. 123. [41] *Ibid.*, para. 125.

[42] *Ibid.*, paras. 130 *et seq.*

[43] In this respect, see the passages below on treaty mechanisms for early dismissal.

[44] *Trans-Global Petroleum, Inc.* v. *Hashemite Kingdom of Jordan*, para. 90.

[45] *Global Trading Resource Corp. and Global International, Inc.* v. *Ukraine*, para. 33. In an *obiter dictum*, the tribunal held that a mere written procedure could suffice in situations where the application is not granted. In these cases, the tribunal held that the rights of the objection party would remain intact, as the preliminary objection would not preclude the reassertion of the objection in the further proceedings. See also *Trans-Global Petroleum, Inc.* v. *Hashemite Kingdom of Jordan*, para. 92.

a conference call to determine the procedure under ICSID Arbitration Rule 41(5).[46] On this occasion, the parties agreed to have two rounds of written argument as well as an oral phase to be held in conjunction with the first session of the tribunal.[47] The deadlines were subsequently extended upon agreement, and the first session was rescheduled.[48] In a similar vein, the parties in *Mol* v. *Croatia* agreed to have within a period of four months two rounds of full written submissions and two rounds of oral argument on respondent's application under ICSID Arbitration Rule 41(5).[49]

While this approach appears convincing from the perspective of due process considerations, it risks defeating the goal of ICSID Arbitration Rule 41(5) to establish a summary procedure that saves time and costs. This will be examined in greater detail later (see Section D).

(5) Decision

ICSID Arbitration Rule 41(5) envisages that the arbitral tribunal renders its decision in the first session or shortly thereafter. In line with the applicable high standards, most of the hitherto applications under ICSID Arbitration Rule 41(5) have been unsuccessful.[50] Exceptions include situations where a claimant presented a contractual claim as a treaty claim[51] or cases where the consent to arbitrate only covered

[46] *Global Trading Resource Corp. and Global International, Inc.* v. *Ukraine*, para. 18.

[47] *Ibid.* [48] *Ibid.*, para. 20.

[49] *MOL Hungarian Oil and Gas Company PLC* v. *Republic of Croatia*, para. 12.

[50] Unsuccessful applications include *MOL Hungarian Oil and Gas Company PLC* v. *Republic of Croatia*, para. 52; *PNG Sustainable Development Program, Ltd.* v. *Independent State of Papua New Guinea*, para. 99; *Elsamex S.A.* v. *República de Honduras*, para. 147; *Rafat Ali Rizvi* v. *Republic of Indonesia*, para. 20; *Brandes Investment Partners, LP* v. *Bolivarian Republic of Venezuela*, para. 73. The following applications have been granted in part: *Accession Mezzanine Capital L.P. and Danubius Kereskedöház Vagyonkezelö Zrt* v. *Hungary*, para. 78; *Emmis International Holding B.V., Emmis Radio Operating, B.V., Mem Magyar Electronic Media Kereskedelmi És Szolgáltató KFT* v. *Hungary*, para. 71; *Trans-Global Petroleum, Inc.* v. *Hashemite Kingdom of Jordan*, para. 124. The following non-public cases continued after the decision on ICSID Rule 41(5): *Vattenfall AB and Others* v. *Federal Republic of Germany; CEAC Holdings Limited* v. *Montenegro; Transglobal Green Energy, LLC and Transglobal Green Panama, S.A.* v. *Republic of Panama*; and *Edenred S.A.* v. *Hungary.* It therefore appears that the applications were at least in part unsuccessful.

[51] *Rachel S. Grynberg, Stephen M. Grynberg, Miriam Z. Grynberg, and RSM Production Corporation* v. *Grenada*, para. 7.3.7.

expropriation claims so that the non-expropriation claims were dismissed for lack of jurisdiction.[52]

As regards the decision on costs, a number of arbitral tribunals have applied the rule 'cost follows the event'.[53] The case of *Mol* v. *Croatia* illustrates this. Here the arbitral tribunal noted that the object and purpose of ICSID Arbitration Rule 41(5) is to reduce the time and costs of investment arbitration proceedings. As an unsuccessful application would defeat this object and purpose, it would be incumbent upon the unsuccessful party to bear the cost of the ICSID Arbitration Rule 41(5) procedure. Based on such reasoning, there is hence effective protection against an undue reassertion of control by States to the detriment of investors.

C. Treaty Mechanisms for the Early Dismissal of Claims

While most international investment treaties contain no separate mechanism for the early dismissal of claims, there are a number of notable exceptions. An early example can be found in the 1967 Organisation for Economic Co-operation and Development (OECD) Draft Convention on the Protection of Foreign Property, which never came into force (see Section C(1)). Existing treaty mechanisms for the early dismissal of claims include Article 10.20.4 *et seq.* of the Dominican Republic–Central American Free Trade Agreement (DR-CAFTA) as well as similarly worded provisions contained in certain bilateral treaties (see Section C(2)). Finally, the current drafts of European investment treaties give an account of future mechanisms for the early dismissal of claims (see Section C(3)).

(1) An Early Example

The OECD prepared its Draft Convention on the Protection of Foreign Property in 1967.[54] It was an attempt to create a multi-lateral framework

[52] *Emmis International Holding B.V., Emmis Radio Operating, B.V., Mem Magyar Electronic Media Kereskedelmi És Szolgáltató KFT* v. *Hungary*, para. 71.

[53] *MOL Hungarian Oil and Gas Company PLC* v. *Republic of Croatia*, para. 54. For a similar approach, see *Rachel S. Grynberg, Stephen M. Grynberg, Miriam Z. Grynberg, and RSM Production Corporation* v. *Grenada*, para. 8.3.4. See also *Trans-Global Petroleum, Inc.* v. *Hashemite Kingdom of Jordan*, para. 123. In this case, the parties had agreed on such cost allocation.

[54] 'OECD Draft Convention on the Protection of Foreign Property', available at http://acts.oecd.org/Instruments/ShowInstrumentView.aspx?InstrumentID=242&InstrumentPID=237&Lang=en&Book= (accessed 24 February 2016).

for the protection of foreign investment. While the project ultimately failed, it is evidence of how investor-State arbitration was conceptualised at that time. In this regard, it is interesting to note that the OECD Draft Convention on the Protection of Foreign Property already foresaw a mechanism for the early dismissal of claims. Thus, the Convention contained an 'Annex Relating to the Statute of the Arbitral Tribunal', whose Article 6 lit. c (ii) provided:

> The Arbitral Tribunal may also, in the case of proceedings instituted by a national of a Party to the Convention and upon preliminary application by the respondent: . . . (ii) Dismiss the claim if, from the statements made by that national to the Tribunal, the institution of the proceedings appears frivolous or vexatious.

At a time when the ICSID Convention had just entered into force – and long before the wave of investor-State dispute resolution began to materialise – a predecessor of the current mechanisms for early dismissal of frivolous or vexatious claims hence already existed.

(2) *Current Examples*

Since 1967, the legal framework on international investment protection has changed considerably, resulting in a network of more than 3,000 international investment treaties being currently in force. And still, most of these international investment agreements (IIAs) do not contain a treaty mechanism for the early dismissal of claims. Exceptions include Article 10.20.4 *et seq.* of the DR-CAFTA and similarly worded provisions in certain investment treaties.[55]

Pursuant to Article 10.20.4 of the DR-CAFTA, an arbitral tribunal may address as a preliminary matter the objection that 'as a matter of law, a claim submitted is not a claim for which an award in favor of the claimant may be made under Article 10.26.' According to Article 10.20.5

[55] Examples include Article 10.19.4 of the United States–Morocco Free Trade Agreement; Article 10.19.4 of the United States–Oman Free Trade Agreement; Article 10.20.4 of the United States–Peru Free Trade Agreement; Article 10.20.4 of the United States–Colombia Free Trade Agreement; Article 10.20.4 of the United States–Panama Free Trade Agreement; Article 11.20.6 of the United States–Korea Free Trade Agreement. See also Article 28.4 of the US Model BIT 2012. These treaties are available at https://ustr.gov/trade-agreements/free-trade-agreements (accessed 24 February 2016). Apart from US treaties, Article 10.20.6 of the Korea-Australia Free Trade Agreement (KAFTA) contains a similar provision. KAFTA is available at http://dfat.gov.au/trade/agreements/kafta/official-documents/Pages/chapter-11-investment.aspx (accessed 24 February 2016).

of the DR-CATFA, an arbitral tribunal shall decide on an expedited basis such objection as well as any objection that it lacks jurisdiction to decide the case.

Article 10.20.4 *et seq.* of the DR-CAFTA have several structural similarities with ICSID Arbitration Rule 41(5): in both cases the provisions set a legal basis for early dismissal of cases. Moreover, each procedure is subject to tight procedural timetables and deadlines, which shall ensure the efficiency of the proceedings.[56]

And yet, the arbitral tribunal in *Pac Rim* v. *El Salvador* correctly observed that the provisions should not be treated interchangeably.[57] The main difference between Article 10.20.4 *et seq.* of the DR-CAFTA and ICSID Arbitration Rule 41(5) lies in the distinctive standard for the dismissal of claims. While ICSID Arbitration Rule 41(5) requires that a claim is 'manifestly without legal merit', Article 10.20.4 *et seq.* of the DR-CAFTA are broader and allow dismissing claims that are unfounded 'as a matter of law'. The arbitral tribunal in *Pac Rim* v. *El Salvador* correctly observed that Article 10.20.4 of the DR-CAFTA is not limited to 'frivolous' claims.[58] A comparable observation has been made with regard to the similarly worded provision of Article 10.20.4 of the US–Peru FTA by the arbitral tribunal in *Renco* v. *Peru.*[59]

A further difference between Article 10.20.4 of the DR-CATFA and ICSID Arbitration Rule 41(5) lies in the fact that Article 10.20.4 of the DR-CAFTA explicitly mandates arbitral tribunals to consider in addition to all undisputed facts the relevant factual allegations made by the claimant in its notice (or amended notice) of arbitration which shall be assumed to be true.[60]

Thirdly, Articles 10.20.4 and 10.20.5 of the DR-CAFTA contain more guidance on various aspects of the procedure, including

1. Deadlines for hearings to be held,
2. The timing for the decision to be rendered by the arbitral tribunal,

[56] *Pac Rim Cayman LLC* v. *Republic of El Salvador*, ICSID Case No. ARB/09/12, Decision on the Respondent's Preliminary Objections under CAFTA Articles 10.20.4 and 10.20.5 of 2 August 2010, para. 112.

[57] *Ibid.*, para. 118. [58] *Ibid.*, para. 108.

[59] *In the Matter of an Arbitration Proceeding under Chapter 10 of the United States–Peru Trade Promotion Agreement and the UNCITRAL Arbitration Rules (2010) in the Arbitration Proceeding between The Renco Group, Inc.* v. *Republic of Peru*, UNCT/13/1, Decision as to the Scope of the Respondent's Preliminary Objections under Article 10.20.4 of 18 December 2014, para. 237.

[60] *Pac Rim Cayman, LLC* v. *Republic of El Salvador*, para. 87.

3. A mandatory suspension of any proceedings on the merits and
4. Considerations to be taken into account when rendering the decision on costs.

In sum, the treaty mechanism for the early dismissal of claims under Articles 10.20.4 and 10.20.5 of the DR-CAFTA has structural similarities with the procedural mechanism for the early dismissal of claims under ICSID Arbitration Rule 41(5). Yet, ICSID Arbitration Rule 41(5) grants more flexibility to tribunals and less control to States over the procedure. Vice versa, Articles 10.20.4 and 10.20.5 of the DR-CAFTA grant less flexibility to tribunals and more control to States over the procedure.

(3) *Future Examples*

If one looks at the future mechanisms for early dismissal of claims, it appears that negotiators have taken efforts to create even more avenues to end proceedings right at their outset. The example of the Comprehensive Economic and Trade Agreement (CETA) illustrates this.

To begin with, CETA includes a mechanism for the early dismissal of claims that are manifestly without legal merit. According to Article 8.32 of the CETA, a respondent may, no later than thirty days after the constitution of the arbitral tribunal and before the first session of the arbitral tribunal, file an objection that a claim is manifestly without legal merit. On receipt of such objection, the arbitral tribunal shall suspend the proceedings on the merits and establish a schedule for considering any objections consistent with its schedule for considering any other preliminary question.[61] The arbitral tribunal shall, after giving the disputing parties an opportunity to present their observations, at its first session or promptly thereafter issue a decision or award stating the grounds therefore. In so doing, it shall assume the alleged facts to be true. Being a provision for the early dismissal of claims that are 'manifestly without legal merit', Article 8.32 of the CETA has considerable parallels with ICSID Arbitration Rule 41(5).[62]

[61] 'Consolidated CETA Text', Article 8.32, final text of February 2016, available at http://trade.ec.europa.eu/doclib/docs/2016/february/tradoc_154329.pdf (accessed 23 October 2016).

[62] A difference between the two provisions lies in the fact that ICSID Arbitration Rule 41(5) provides more flexibility on the decision as to whether or not to suspend the decision on the merits. Moreover, as shown earlier, ICSID Arbitration Rule 41(5) is silent on the question of whether or not the facts adduced by the claimant shall be assumed to be true. See Section B(3)(b)(ii).

Besides, CETA includes in Article 8.33 a mechanism to decide – as a preliminary matter – objections that, as a matter of law, a claim is not a claim for which an award in favour of the claimant may be made even if the facts alleged were assumed to be true. As such, Article 8.33 of the CETA has many commonalities with the treaty mechanisms discussed earlier.[63] As regards the interplay between Articles 8.32 and 8.33 of the CETA, Article X.29 provides that an application under Article 8.32 may not be filed if the respondent has filed an objection under Article 8.33 of the CETA. Beyond this, neither CETA nor the preparatory works contain further guidance on the exact interplay between Articles 8.32 and 8.33 of the CETA.

Finally, CETA includes a filter mechanism to dismiss claims based on measures taken for prudential reasons. This has the following background: according to Article 13.16 of the CETA, parties are entitled to adopt or maintain reasonable measures for prudential reasons, such as measures for the maintenance of the safety, soundness, integrity or financial responsibility of a financial institution. Article 13.18 of the CETA establishes a Financial Services Committee, which shall include representatives of authorities in charge of financial services policy. According to Article 13.21 of the CETA, the responsibilities of the Financial Services Committee include the decision as to whether and, if so, to what extent a respondent may validly invoke the prudential reasons under Article 13.16 of the CETA in defence of a claim. Such a determination, which may in certain cases be made jointly with the CETA Trade Committee, shall be binding on an arbitral tribunal. Taken together, Articles 13.16, 13.18 and 13.21 of the CETA hence create a mechanism for the early dismissal of claims in a non-judicial procedure. The Financial Service Committee is a political body and not an arbitral tribunal. It takes decisions in a procedure that is not subject to any procedural guarantees such as obligations of fair trial and due process.

D. Assessment

The preceding observations give rise to the question of whether we are already experiencing a trend back from the law-based paradigm of investment protection towards a power-based paradigm of investment protection, where political stakeholders decide upon the investors' fate. Do we have to be concerned about the proliferation of mechanisms for the early dismissal of claims? In answering these questions, a distinction

[63] See Section C(2).

needs to be made between the judicial mechanisms for early dismissal under ICSID Arbitration Rule 41(5) and certain investment treaties, on the one hand (see Section D(1)), and the non-judicial mechanism for early dismissal under Articles 13.16, 13.18 and 13.21 of the CETA, that is, the determination by the Financial Services Committee, on the other (see Section D(2)).

(1) Judicial Mechanisms: Limited Control over the Procedure

As regards the judicial mechanisms for early dismissal, States have not regained control over the outcome of investment arbitrations, and the law-based paradigm of investment protection has remained unaffected. The introduction of provisions such as ICSID Arbitration Rule 41(5) or Article 10.20.4 *et seq.* of the DR-CAFTA does not mean that the position of States is improved to the detriment of investors, let alone that States win more often. This is confirmed by the fact that (1) most applications for early dismissal have failed and (2) investors may at least to some extent also make use of these mechanisms in annulment proceedings.

If at all, States have gained limited control over the procedure. There are now clear specifications as to when an application for early dismissal has to be filed, which standard applies and when the decision has to be taken. Similar to the trend from standards to rules in substantive investment law,[64] the procedure of international investment law is hence subject to increasing codification.

While this may bring about more predictability and offer the strategic advantage of shaping a tribunal's perception of a case at an early stage of the proceedings, it also limits the flexibility of arbitral tribunals. One should not forget that even in the absence of a provision such as ICSID Arbitration Rule 41(5), arbitral tribunals were already in a position to render decisions on early dismissal under their inherent powers. Arguably, the increasing regulation of the procedure limits these powers so that it is, for example, more difficult, if not impossible, for an arbitral tribunal to render a decision on early dismissal after the deadlines mentioned in ICSID Arbitration Rule 41(5) or a similar treaty provision have elapsed.

In addition to the aforesaid, the use of mechanisms for early dismissal is no guarantee for more efficiency. Indeed, an early dismissal is only

64 Cf. F. Rosenfeld, 'The Trend from Standards to Rules in International Investment Law and Its Impact upon the Interpretive Power of Arbitral Tribunals', *Proceedings of the American Society of International Law*, 107 (2013), 191 *et seq.*

legitimate if it is restricted to claims that are on their face without chance of success and provided that guarantees of due process are observed. However, if one accepts such high standards, many applications will ultimately fail, and the result is the exact the opposite from what was originally intended. The proceedings risk becoming longer and even more costly. The arbitral tribunal in *Mol* v. *Croatia* correctly recognised this dilemma when it held that successive rounds of written and oral submissions together with questions addressed by the arbitral tribunal would carry a tribunal into a 'hybrid territory somewhere between Rule 41(5) and Rule 41(1)'.[65] Against this background, all actors involved should exercise caution when conducting proceedings for early dismissal: Parties should carefully examine whether to initiate such application at all and should not misuse the proceedings as a pretext for an additional round of extensive submissions. Arbitral tribunals, in turn, should take the opportunity to shape the further conduct of the proceedings in case that an application for early dismissal is not successful.

(2) Non-Judicial Mechanisms: Control over the Outcome

As regards the non-judicial mechanism for early dismissal under Articles 13.16, 13.18 and 13.21 of the CETA, that is, the determination by the Financial Services Committee of whether a State may validly rely upon prudential measures in defence of a claim, things look different. In this respect, States have regained control over the outcome of investment proceedings.

From the vantage point of States, one may try to justify this as a necessary means to align international investment law with the legitimate interest to keep certain regulatory freedom. One may also be tempted to draw parallels to other instruments such as joint binding interpretation mechanisms through which States exercise their function as masters of the treaties.[66]

And yet, these analogies are not compelling. It is one thing to acknowledge the role of States as masters of the treaties and to endorse their right to determine the meaning of abstract norms of international investment law through a joint binding interpretation. Such joint binding interpretation is a hermeneutic process that has its normative foundation in Article 31 para. 2 lit. a of the Vienna Convention on the Law of Treaties.

[65] *MOL Hungarian Oil and Gas Company, PLC* v. *Republic of Croatia*, para. 45.

[66] On the issue of joint interpretations by the Conctrating Parties, see Chapter 7.

It is doctrinally a different thing to accord States the position as masters of the dispute. Such a non-judicial mechanism of dispute resolution risks being perceived as a step backwards in the system of investment protection. In a limited field, the law-based paradigm of investment protection appears to have given way to a policy-based paradigm of investment protection.

5

Keeping the Status Quo or Embarking on a New Course?

Setting Aside, Refusal of Enforcement, Annulment and Appeal

FREYA BAETENS*

A. Introduction

In 2014, the European Commission engaged in a public consultation over the Transatlantic Trade and Investment Partnership (TTIP), which is being negotiated between the European Union and the United States.[1] Some of the strongest concerns regarding foreign investment protection which became evident related to the proposed system of investor-State dispute settlement (ISDS). These concerns are not isolated: other States and stakeholders have raised similar objections against the ISDS mechanisms incorporated in over 3,000 international investment agreements (IIAs).[2] Some States have withdrawn from procedural ISDS treaties, such as the Convention on the Settlement of Investment Disputes

* I thank the organiser (Dr Andreas Kulick) and the participants at the Workshop 'Contracting Parties' Reassertion of Control over International Investment Agreements and International Investment Treaty Dispute Settlement' in Tübingen (26–28 June 2015) for their useful feedback, as well as my research assistant, Theodora N. Valkanou. Errors and omissions remain, of course, my own.

1 European Commission, 'Report: Online Public Consultation on Investment Protection and Investor-to-State Dispute Settlement (ISDS) in the Transatlantic Trade and Investment Partnership Agreement (TTIP)', SWD (2015) 3 final, 13 January 2015.

2 See e.g. The Australian Greens, Green MPs, 'Fair Deal or No Deal: The Dangers of the TPP and ISDS', available at: http://greensmps.org.au/campaigns/tpp; Public Citizen, 'TPP Leak Reveals Extraordinary New Powers for Thousands of Foreign Firms to Challenge US Policies and Demand Taxpayer Compensation: Unveiling of Parallel Legal System for Foreign Corporations Will Fuel TPP Controversy, Further Complicate Obama's Push for Fast Track', available at www.citizen.org/documents/tpp-investment-leak-2015-release.pdf; Australian Fair Trade and Investment Network, Ltd, 'Campaign against Inclusion of ISDS in the Korea-Australia Agreement', available at http://aftinet.org.au/cms/patricia-ranald-report-korea-australia-free-trade-agreement-12-1013 (both accessed 13 March 2016).

between States and Nationals of Other States (ICSID Convention),[3] and renegotiated or terminated their substantive IIAs.[4] Most fears seem to relate to the arbitral process (bringing claims, running proceedings and adjudicating cases), but one worry deals with 'an old sore' in international dispute settlement: the lack of appellate mechanisms which would allow for a fresh and independent look at allegedly wrongly decided cases.

In turn, the call for an appeal mechanism is located within a broader debate concerning finality and judicial review of international adjudicatory decisions in many subfields of international law. While virtually all domestic legal systems anticipate the possibility that a first-instance judge 'got it wrong', international courts and tribunals may seem to aspire to decisional infallibility. The situation is not so clear-cut, however, as there are ways open to States seeking to resist unpalatable awards. These are seeking to have the award set aside, opposing enforcement, and, in the case of ICSID awards, applying for annulment. This chapter addresses each of these status quo mechanisms in turn before analysing the establishment of a new appellate mechanism.

A final preliminary remark: 'reassertion of control' could be seen as a misnomer in the context of these various ways to review arbitral awards. States can (and should) exercise control over the international obligations they undertake as well as the dispute settlement mechanisms to which they subject themselves. This ex ante control takes place during the drafting stage of a treaty as well as through constitutionally required approval processes. However, it seems much less appropriate for a State which (through a process to which it consented) has been alleged or duly found to be in breach of its international obligations to produce a 'get out of jail free' card post factum as a means of 'reasserting control'. Such State control over an adjudicatory body would hardly comply with the principle of fair trial or the independent exercise of the judicial function. Hence, in the context of this chapter, the neutral term 'judicial review' is used instead, on the basis that the purpose is to reassert a balance

3 Convention on the Settlement of Investment Disputes between States and Nationals of Other States (International Centre for Settlement of Investment Disputes [ICSID]) (opened for signature 18 March 1965, entered into force 14 October 1966), 575 UNTS 159.

4 Withdrawal from the ICSID Convention: e.g. Bolivia, Ecuador and Venezuela (UNCTAD, 'Denunciation of the ICSID Convention and BITs: Impact on Investor-State Claims', IIA Issues Note No. 2, December 2010, available at: http://unctad.org/en/Docs/webdiaeia20106_en.pdf; termination and/or renegotiation of BITs: e.g. Ecuador and Indonesia (see e.g. termination of Indonesia–Netherlands BIT: http://indonesia.nlembassy.org/organization/departments/economic-affairs/termination-bilateral-investment-treaty.html (both accessed 13 March 2016)).

between public and private interests while enhancing the coherency, consistency and predictability of ISDS – to the presumed benefit of all parties involved.

B. The Status Quo: Post-Award Recourse

Under the current system, litigants who disagree with an award that has been rendered in an investor-State dispute settlement procedure have three options to challenge this decision: they can actively seek to have the award set aside by the courts of the seat of the arbitration (Section A), they can oppose any enforcement action hoping that the courts of third States will refuse to enforce (Section B) or, in ICSID cases, they can apply for annulment (Section C). Each of these options is examined in this chapter in three respects: (1) their legal effect, (2) the applicable scope and standard of review and (3) their potential to reassert a balance of interests.

(1) Setting Aside by Courts of the Seat of Arbitration

In non-ICSID arbitrations,[5] the parties must adhere to the applicable law at the place of arbitration, the *lex arbitri*, which contains mandatory rules concerning for example the grounds for challenging an award through a 'setting-aside' application. The UN Commission on International Trade Law (UNCITRAL) Model Law seeks to harmonise domestic arbitration laws in this regard.[6] Many countries such as Australia, Canada and Nigeria have incorporated the UNCITRAL Model Law in their legislation with only minor modifications,[7] although the rules of the *lex arbitri* may still differ. This chapter mainly focuses on the UNCITRAL

[5] It is not possible for a State to challenge an ICSID award before national courts at the seat of the arbitration on the basis of *lex arbitri* on the basis of Article 54(1) of the ICSID Convention. However, Article 54(1) of the ICSID Convention applies to the pecuniary obligations solely – with regard to non-pecuniary damages which may be awarded by a tribunal, such as specific performance, the ICSID enforcement rules do not apply. Furthermore, Article 54(1) does not apply to awards which are made under the ICSID Additional Facility rules (ICSID Arbitration (Additional Facility) Rules, 1 *ICSID Report* 249 (as amended with effect from 10 April 2006), 15 *ICSID Report* 656).

[6] UNCITRAL, 'Model Law on International Commercial Arbitration' (1985), *GAOR* 40th Session Supp. 17 (A/40/17), Annex I, with amendments (2006), *GAOR* 61st Session, Supp. No. 17 (A/61/17) (hereafter UNCITRAL Model Law): this Model Law may also apply to investor-State arbitrations (footnote 2 to Article 1(1)).

[7] Commonwealth Secretariat, 'UNCITRAL Model Law on International Commercial Arbitration: Explanatory Documentation Prepared for Commonwealth Jurisdictions'

Model Law, with occasional reference to domestic *lex arbitri* when relevant in specific cases.

(a) Legal Effect of a Successful Application to Set Aside

If an application to set aside an award is successful before the courts of the seat of arbitration, the award is usually considered to be invalid and unenforceable by other national courts as well. The important difference with successful opposition to enforcement is that a setting-aside cancels the award in much the same manner as a successful annulment or appeal procedure. However, this legal effect is not universally accepted: in a number of (controversial) cases, awards which had been set aside by a court under the *lex arbitri* were nevertheless enforced by a court in another State.[8]

(b) Applicable Scope and Standard of Review

In Chapter VII ('Recourse against Award'), the UNCITRAL Model Law outlines, in an exhaustive manner, two groups of grounds under which an arbitral award can be set aside or challenged by a 'court or other authority for certain functions of arbitration assistance and supervision'.[9] The first group applies to formal flaws in the arbitration process, for example, if the party making the application was unable to present its case or if composition of the arbitral tribunal was not in accordance with the arbitration agreement.[10] The second group allows for an award to be set aside in cases where the court finds that '(i) the subject-matter of the dispute is not capable of settlement by arbitration under the law of this State; or (ii) the award is in conflict with the public policy of this State'.[11] A setting-aside application has to be submitted within three months after which the award has been received or after which the request for

(1991), 3–4, available at www.uncitral.org/pdf/english/texts/arbitration/ml-arb/Model-Law-Arbitration-Commonwealth.pdf (accessed 13 March 2016).

[8] *Hilmarton Limited* v. *Omnium de Traitement et de Valorisation*, Decision No. 484, French Cour de Cassation, First Civil Chamber (1994); US District Court for the District of Columbia in the case *Chromalloy Aeroservices, Inc* v. *Arab Republic of Egypt*, 939 F., Supp. 907 (D.D.C. 1996); *Corporación Mexicana de Matenimiento Integral, S. de R.L. de C.V.* v. *Pemex-Exploración y Producción*, No. 10 Civ. 206 (AKH), 2013 WL 4517225 (S.D.N.Y. 2013). See also the *travaux préparatoires* of Article 34 of the UNCITRAL Model Law, available at www.uncitral.org/uncitral/en/uncitral_texts/arbitration/1985Model_arbitration_travaux.html (accessed 13 March 2016).

[9] Article 6 of the UNCITRAL Model Law: 'Each State enacting this model law specifies the court, courts or, where referred to therein, other authority competent to perform these functions.'

[10] Article 34(2) of the UNCITRAL Model Law (emphasis added).

[11] *Ibid.*

correction or interpretation of the original award has been disposed of by the arbitral tribunal.[12] Most States have implemented legislation that limits the grounds on which an award may be set aside along the lines of the UNCITRAL conditions.[13] However, some domestic courts have decided to allow reopening of the merits of a case on the basis of more broadly defined conditions in their arbitration law.[14]

(c) Potential to Reassert a Balance of Interests

The conditions for setting aside an award under the UNCITRAL Model Law essentially mirror the grounds for refusing recognition or enforcement, though with one important difference: an application for setting aside an arbitral award can only be submitted to a court in the State which served as the seat of arbitration and only within three months after the final award has been rendered.[15] The main advantage of the set-aside option is that it allows for the removal of an award from the legal order forthwith after the award has been rendered (provided that the domestic courts of the *forum lex arbitri* act sufficiently quickly).

However, the setting-aside option has significant disadvantages. Firstly, the invalidity and non-enforceability of set-aside awards are not universally recognised. For example, the fact that an award has been set aside forms a ground upon which a domestic court 'may' (not 'must') refuse recognition and enforcement under the Convention on the Recognition and Enforcement of Foreign Arbitral Awards (the New York Convention).[16] Secondly, the possibility to set aside an award only applies to non-ICSID awards, whereas ICSID awards make up the vast majority (about 70 per cent) of all investor-State arbitral awards.[17] Thirdly, the mere submission of an application to set aside an award will only entail an adjournment of the enforcement decision if it is

[12] Article 34(3) of the UNCITRAL Model Law.

[13] See e.g. *Société PT Putrabali Adyamulia* v. *Société Rena Holding and Société Mnogutia Est Epices*, Decision No. 121, French Cour de Cassation, First Civil Chamber (2007); *Aloe Vera of America, Inc* v. *Asianic Food (S) Pte, Ltd.*, 3 SLR(R) 174 (2006).

[14] See e.g. *AJT* v. *AJU*, Court of Appeal, Singapore, SGCA 41 (2011); *SNF* v. *Cytec*, French Cour de Cassation, First Civil Chamber (2008); *Société PT Putrabali Adyamulia* v. *Société Rena Holding and Société Mnogutia Est Epices*, Decision No. 121, French Cour de Cassation, First Civil Chamber (2007).

[15] Article 34(3) of the UNCITRAL Model Law.

[16] Article V(1)(e) of the Convention on the Recognition and Enforcement of Foreign Arbitral Awards (done 10 June 1958, entered into force 7 June 1959), 330 *UNTS* 38.

[17] UNCTAD, 'World Investment Report 2015: Reforming International Investment Governance' (2015), 112–14, available at http://unctad.org/en/PublicationsLibrary/wir2015_en.pdf (accessed 13 March 2016).

considered 'proper', and the State may be ordered 'to give suitable security'.[18] Fourthly, the grounds upon which a domestic court may conduct a judicial review are limited to formal requirements and public order reasons. Fifthly, in practice, domestic courts have rarely been willing to set aside awards,[19] as demonstrated in, for example, *Ecuador* v. *Occidental*,[20] *Dallah Real Estate* v. *Pakistan*[21] and *Ecuador* v. *Chevron*.[22]

(2) Refusal of Enforcement by the Courts of Third States

If the State's application to set aside the award is unsuccessful, or if the State has opted not to apply for a setting aside, or if the three months' time period has lapsed and the award has not been complied with, the investor will likely resort to judicial enforcement of the award by a national court. In this case, the defending State may ask the court to refuse enforcement on the basis of the New York Convention. By contrast, under the ICSID Convention (pecuniary), obligations resulting from an ICSID award may be enforced within any State party[23] as if it were a final judgment of a court of that State: no grounds are open for opposing enforcement, except for immunity from execution.[24]

(a) Legal Effect of Successful Opposition to Enforcement

Unlike setting aside, the legal effect of successful opposition to enforcement only applies to enforcement in that particular State; the award is not annulled or invalidated as such. As States may have assets in several countries, the investor may be able to bring another case on the

[18] Article VI of the New York Convention.

[19] L. Markert and C. Titi, 'States Strike Back: Old and New Ways for Host States to Defend against Investment Arbitrations', in A. K. Bjorklund (ed.), *Yearbook on International Investment Law and Policy 2013–2014* (Oxford University Press, 2015), 401, 418–20; See also S. W. Schill, 'System-Building in Investment Treaty Arbitration and Lawmaking', in A. von Bogdandy and I. Venzke (eds.), *International Judicial Lawmaking* (New York: Springer, 2012), 133, 147–8.

[20] *Ecuador* v. *Occidental Exploration & Production Co.*, APP.L.R. 03/02 (2006).

[21] *Dallah Real Estate & Tourism Holding Company* v. *Ministry of Religious Affairs, Government of Pakistan*, UKSC 46 (2010).

[22] *Republiek Ecuador* v. *Chevron Corporation (USA) en Texaco Petroleum Company*, Hoge Raad, ECLI:NL:HR:2014:2837, Judgment (2014).

[23] Provided that the State is a member of the ICSID Convention. As of 9 November 2015, 159 States were party to the ICSID Convention.

[24] Article 54 of the ICSID Convention.

basis of the same arbitral award before the domestic courts of another State.[25]

(b) Applicable Scope and Standard of Review

Enforcement is regulated by several legal instruments, international and national. The most widely accepted international treaty in this regard,[26] the New York Convention, stipulates that State parties are under an obligation to recognise foreign arbitral awards as binding and to enforce them in accordance with their rules of procedure.[27] Enforcement of an award can be objected to by a party against whom enforcement is sought by reliance upon the exhaustive grounds for refusal laid out in Article V, which are virtually identical to the formal grounds upon which an award can be set aside under the UNCITRAL Model Law, such as requirements concerning the arbitration agreement, proper notice, the scope of the submission to arbitration and the composition of the arbitral authority or the arbitral procedure.[28] Only one ground is different from its counterparts discussed in the preceding section: '[t]he award has not yet become binding on the parties, or has been set aside or suspended by a competent authority of the country in which, or under the law of which, that award was made.'[29] Refusal of the enforcement or recognition of an award may also be allowed for reasons of public order.[30] Similar grounds for opposition to enforcement are listed in the UNCITRAL Model Law as well as in numerous regional treaties and domestic laws.[31]

(c) Potential to Reassert a Balance of Interests

Local review by a competent authority with the power to refuse recognition and enforcement under the New York Convention can be envisaged as a way in which Contracting Parties can reassert a balance between

[25] See, in general, A. S. Alexandroff and I. A. Laird, 'Compliance and Enforcement', in P. Muchlinski, F. Ortino and C. Schreuer (eds.), *The Oxford Handbook of International Investment Law* (Oxford University Press, 2008), 1171; D. Bishop, *Enforcement of Arbitral Awards against Sovereigns* (JurisNet, LLC, 2009).

[26] As of 9 November 2015, 156 States were party to the New York Convention.

[27] Article III of the New York Convention.

[28] Article V(1) of the New York Convention.

[29] Article V(1)(e) of the New York Convention.

[30] Article V(2) of the New York Convention.

[31] See e.g. Article 36 of the UNCITRAL Model Law; Article IX of the European Convention on International Commercial Arbitration; Article 5 of the Inter-American Convention on International Commercial Arbitration.

public and private interests in investment disputes. For this purpose, public policy grounds as referred to in Article V(2) of the New York Convention would seem most relevant. Opposition to enforcement has, however, two major disadvantages. Firstly, the respondent State can only oppose the enforcement of non-ICSID awards, which make up about 30 per cent of all investor-State arbitral awards. Public policy grounds as the basis for a refusal to enforce or recognise an award are, in the traditional view, excluded in the context of arbitration under the ICSID Convention. However, sparse case law to the contrary exists. In *Jose Cartellone Construcciones Civiles, S.A.* v. *Hidroelectrica Norpatagonia, S.A.*, for example, the Argentine Supreme Court held that notwithstanding the fact that the award was rendered under procedures that prohibited any appeal, a determination as to whether the award contradicted *ordre public* was within the scope of the domestic court's competence.[32] These decisions have been rejected by most commentators based on the view that the ICSID drafters did not adopt the New York Convention formula because they intended recognition and enforcement under the ICSID Convention to be categorical.[33] Secondly, even though opposition to enforcement has a moderately higher success rate than applications to set aside,[34] successful opposition may turn out to be a pyrrhic victory. The award remains in existence, and the claimant may decide to launch procedures in other countries where the respondent State has assets, resulting in protracted and expensive litigation.

(3) ICSID Annulment

States which wish to set aside ICSID arbitral awards or oppose their enforcement cannot rely on the *lex arbitri*, the New York Convention or any other similar regional or domestic rules. What they can do is to initiate annulment proceedings.

[32] *Jose Cartellone Construcciones Civiles, S.A.* v. *Hidroelectrica Norpatagonia, S.A.*, Supreme Court of the Argentinean Republic, Decision (2004), para. 19.

[33] C. H. Schreuer, L. Malintoppi, A. Reinisch and A. Sinclair, *The ICSID Convention: A Commentary*, 2nd ed. (Cambridge University Press, 2009), 1139–41.

[34] Opposition to enforcement is more likely to be successful than set-aside because enforcement proceedings are more likely to be brought in a forum favourable to the defendant (e.g. the defendant's home State), and in case of enforcement against the State, State immunity is likely to apply to enforcement, whereas it will not normally apply to a set-aside procedure.

(a) Legal Effect of a Successful Annulment Application

There is a fundamental difference between a successful appeal and an annulment: an ad hoc annulment committee cannot substitute its own judgment on the merits for the decision of the original tribunal, and moreover, 'annulment is concerned only with the legitimacy of the process of decision. It is not concerned with the substantive correctness of the decision. Appeal is concerned with both.'[35] Thus, if an ad hoc committee annuls an award, the latter is effectively (totally or partially) removed from the legal order. To this extent, either party may submit the dispute to a new ICSID tribunal.[36]

(b) Applicable Scope and Standard of Review

All ICSID awards are final and binding, but awards can be annulled for the exhaustively enumerated reasons under Article 52 of the ICSID Convention: (a) improper constitution of the tribunal; (b) manifest excess of powers by the tribunal; (c) corruption of a tribunal member; (d) serious departure from a fundamental rule of procedure and; (f) failure to state reasons by the tribunal. Parties have primarily invoked the grounds of manifest excess powers, failure to state reasons, and serious departure from a fundamental rule of procedure.[37] Frequently, all three grounds, or two out of the three, have been invoked together. In recent decades, increasing numbers of losing parties have filed annulment applications. After the first application in 1984, only five applications were registered between 1985 and 1999; ten applications in the next five years (2000–4), twenty-one between 2005 and 2009, followed by no less than forty applications between 2010 and 2014. Adding the twelve annulment proceedings brought by November 2015, this brings the total tally up to eighty-nine applications (concluding and pending) for annulment over the course of thirty-five years, with over 90 per cent being brought in the last fifteen years. Investors submitted thirty-nine annulment applications versus forty-seven applications by States; three cases were initiated by both parties. Twenty-one annulment proceedings have been discontinued,

[35] C. H. Schreuer, L. Malintoppi, A. Reinisch and A. Sinclair, *The ICSID Convention*, 901.

[36] Article 52(6) of the ICSID Convention.

[37] V. Balaš, 'Review of Awards', in P. Muchlinski, F. Ortino and C. Schreuer (eds.), *The Oxford Handbook of International Investment Law* (Oxford University Press, 2008), 1125, 1146–50; C. Knahr, 'Annulment and Its Role in the Context of Conflicting Awards', in M. Waibel, A. Kaushal, K-H. L. Chung and C. Balchin (eds.), *The Backlash against Investment Arbitration: Perceptions and Reality* (Alphen aan den Rijn, Netherlands: Kluwer Law International, 2010), 151, 153–60.

Table 5.1 *Overview of ICSID Annulment Applications*

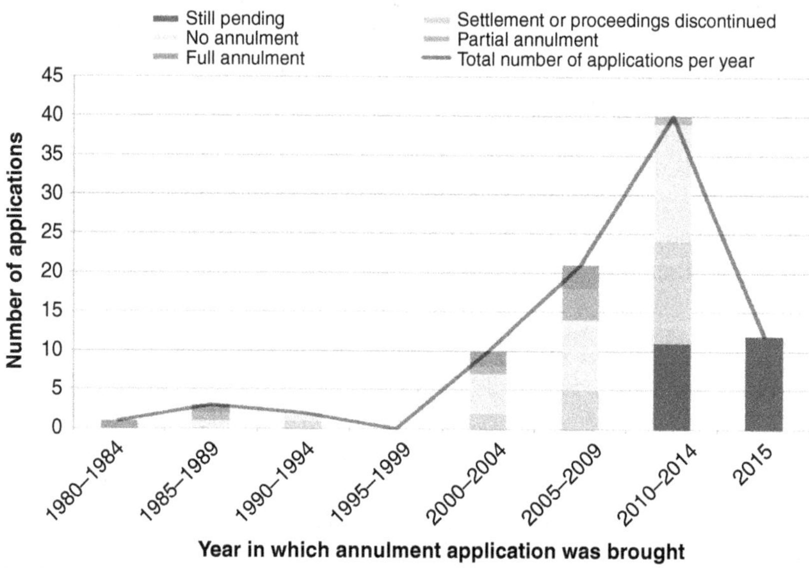

and twenty-three are pending. Of the remaining forty-five decisions, thirty-one entirely dismissed the application (of which fourteen were brought by investors, fifteen by States, and two by both), seven decisions partially annulled the challenged award (two by investors and five by States) and seven decisions annulled the challenged award in its entirety (three by investors, three by States and one by both) (Table 5.1).

In sum: respondent States have filed the majority of annulment applications (55 per cent of all applications), and they have also been slightly more successful (57 per cent of all annulments) than investors. Furthermore, statistics show that, discounting pending and discontinued cases, about 31 per cent of these proceedings have resulted in a partial or full annulment, although the number of successful annulments seems to be decreasing: between 2011 and 2015, only two awards were partially annulled (both as a result of an application for annulment submitted by the defending State): *Occidental* v. *Ecuador*[38] and *Pey Casado et al.* v. *Chile.*[39]

[38] *Occidental Petroleum Corporation and Occidental Exploration and Production Company* v. *Republic of Ecuador*, ICSID Case No. ARB/06/11, Decision on Annulment of the Award of 2 November 2015.

[39] *Victor Pey Casado and President Allende Foundation* v. *Republic of Chile*, ICSID Case No. ARB/98/2, Decision on Annulment of the Award of 18 December 2012.

(c) Potential to Reassert a Balance of Interests

The annulment system has been increasingly criticised for a number of reasons. Firstly, it has been suggested that several ad hoc committees overstepped the boundaries of their mandate so as to 'improperly re-examine the merits of a case, thereby effectively transforming an annulment proceeding into an appeal'.[40] It is not desirable from the viewpoint of creating a stable and predictable legal environment that some ad hoc committees seem willing to point out errors in the application of the law, while others refuse to annul even when concluding the original tribunal applied the law wrongly.[41] Secondly, in view of the fact that annulment applications have led to a (wholly or partially) different decision in about a third of the cases, question marks can be placed on decisions that cannot withstand even a restricted review.[42] The unwillingness of the State to comply with awards that are apparently open to serious criticism is understandable.[43]

(4) Preliminary Conclusion

Based on the preceding analysis, it appears that the existing means to challenge arbitral awards are insufficient to reassert a balance of interests, should this balance be allegedly negatively affected by an arbitral award. The very limited grounds upon which an award can be set aside, opposed or annulled do not allow for a review on the merits, but this is precisely where the interests need to be balanced. The question thus becomes: should an appeal mechanism be established by way of remedy?

[40] M. Burgstaller and C. B. Rosenberg, 'Challenging International Arbitral Awards: To ICSID or not to ICSID?', *Arbitration International*, 27 (2011), 91, 96; See also T. W. Waelde, 'ICSID 'Annulment Committee'', *Transnational Dispute Management*, 1(1) (February 2004); E. Gaillard, 'A Black Year for ICSID', *Transnational Dispute Management*, 4(5) (September 2007); C. Schreuer, 'Three Generations of ICSID Annulment Procedures', in E. Gaillard and Y. Banifatemi (eds.), *Annulment of ICSID Awards* (Oxford, UK: Juris Publishing, 2004), 17.

[41] F. Baetens, 'To ICSID or not to ICSID is not the Question', in I. A. Laird and T. J. Weiler (eds.), *Investment Treaty Arbitration and International Law* (Oxford, UK: Juris Publishing, 2012), 211, 215–16.

[42] Y. Ngangjoh-Hodu and C. C. Ajibo, 'ICSID Annulment Procedure and the WTO Appellate System: The Case for an Appellate System for Investment Arbitration', *Journal of International Dispute Settlement*, 6 (2015), 1.

[43] See, in general, C. Alfons, *Recognition and Enforcement of Annulled Foreign Arbitral Awards: An Analysis of the Legal Framework and Its Interpretation in Case Law and Literature* (Bern, Switzerland: Peter Lang, 2010).

C. Establishing an Appeal Mechanism?

Domestic dispute settlement usually offers parties a possibility to appeal against a judgment of a court of first instance before a court of appeal, possibly even to challenge that decision before a supreme court. In international adjudication, appeal possibilities were for a long time the exception: arbitral awards, such as those of the Permanent Court of Arbitration (PCA) or the Iran-US Claims Tribunal, like judgments of the International Court of Justice (ICJ), are final – no appeal is possible, although there is limited provision for revision. More recently established forms of international adjudication, however, do contain the possibility of appeal: for example, the proceedings before the World Trade Organisation (WTO), the International Criminal Court or the Court of Justice of the European Union (the latter two, perhaps not incidentally, dealing also with public/private claims).

Critics lament the fact that whereas arbitral tribunals in ISDS proceedings often decide on the legality of sensitive national measures, there is no general possibility for the State (or for that matter the investor) to lodge an appeal against such decisions, even though those tribunals may have ignored relevant elements or misapplied the law.[44] Another point of critique is the perceived lack of consistency between awards rendered by arbitral tribunals established under various arbitration institutions and rules (e.g. ICSID, UNCITRAL, PCA, International Chamber of Commerce (ICC) and Stockholm Chamber of Commerce (SCC)).[45] One proposed solution, advocated by the European Commission, among others, is to replace the current ad hoc arbitration system with a standing court for international investment

[44] See K. Miles, *The Origins of International Investment Law: Empire, Environment and the Safeguarding of Capital* (Cambridge University Press, 2013), 349–50, 381–2; C. J. Tams, *An Appealing Option? The Debate about an ICSID Appellate Structure* (Bern, Switzerland: Institut für Wirtschaftsrecht, 2006); D. A. Gantz, 'An Appellate Mechanism for Review of Arbitral Decisions in Investor-State Disputes: Prospects and Challenges', *Vanderbilt Journal of Transnational Law*, 39 (2006), 39.

[45] UNCTAD, 'Reform of Investor-State Dispute Settlement: In Search of a Roadmap', IIA Issues Note No. 2, June 2013, available at http://unctad.org/en/PublicationsLibrary/webdiaepcb2013d4_en.pdf (accessed 13 March 2016): J. Zhan, 'International Investment Law and Development', in M.-C. Cordonier Segger, M. W. Gehring and A. Newcombe (eds.), *Sustainable Development in World Investment Law* (Alphen aan den Rijn, Netherlands: Kluwer Law International, 2011), 13, 18–19; A. K. Bjorklund, 'Investment Treaty Arbitral Decisions as Jurisprudence Constante', in C. B. Picker, I. D. Bunn and D. W. Arner (eds.) *International Economic Law: The State and Future of the Discipline* (Oxford, UK: Hart Publishing, 2008), 265, 266.

matters.[46] Another (possibly complementary) solution would be to establish an appellate mechanism that would guard the balance between public and private interests while enhancing the coherency, consistency and predictability of investment jurisprudence. An analogy is drawn with the Appellate Body system under the WTO as this regime is in terms of subject matter and balancing exercise between economic and other objectives most like the investment regime (A), followed by an examination of the current proposals for an appellate tribunal in an international investment context (B). Each of these mechanisms is scrutinised in light of the characteristics discussed earlier (legal effect, applicable scope and standard of review and potential to reassert a balance of interests) as well as two additional features (nature and composition and time and cost limits). Finally, the last section (Section C) addresses the relation of a new appeal process to the existing review mechanisms as well as the push towards a multilateral appellate mechanism.

(1) The WTO Appellate Body

(a) Legal Effect of a Successful Appeal

The WTO Appellate Body, established by the Dispute Settlement Body (DSB), is established to 'hear appeals from panel cases'.[47] While the appeal is pending, the panel report does not need to be implemented.[48] The Appellate Body may uphold, modify or reverse the legal findings and conclusions of the panel.[49] The DSB and the parties are considered to have accepted the report by the Appellate Body without amendment

[46] European Commission, 'Concept Paper: Investment in TTIP and Beyond – The Path for Reform: Enhancing the Right to Regulate and Moving from Current Ad Hoc Arbitration towards an Investment Court', 5 May 2015, available at http://trade.ec.europa.eu/doclib/docs/2015/may/tradoc_153408.PDF; European Commission, press release, 'Commission Proposes New Investment Court System for TTIP and Other EU Trade and Investment Negotiations', 16 September 2015, available at http://europa.eu/rapid/press-release_IP-15-5651_en.htm (accessed 13 March 2016).

[47] Marrakesh Agreement Establishing the World Trade Organization (opened for signature 15 April 1994, entered into force 1 January 1995), 1867 UNTS 3, Annex 2 (Understanding on Rules and Procedures Governing the Settlement of Disputes), 1869 UNTS 401.

[48] Congressional Research Service (United States), 'Dispute Settlement in the World Trade Organization (WTO): An Overview', 26 November 2012, 10, available at www.fas.org/sgp/crs/misc/RS20088.pdf (accessed 13 March 2016); Y. Guohua, B. C. Mercurio and L. Yongjie, *WTO Dispute Settlement Understanding: A Detailed Interpretation* (Alphen aan den Rijn, Netherlands: Kluwer Law International, 2005), 191.

[49] Article 17(13) of the DSU.

unless the DSB decides by consensus not to adopt it.[50] Once the report has been accepted, it becomes binding upon the parties to the dispute, replaces the original panel's report and has to be implemented within a reasonable time period.[51]

(b) Applicable Scope and Standard of Review

According to the Dispute Settlement Understanding (DSU), an appeal is limited to issues of law covered in the panel report and legal interpretations developed by the panel.[52] After two decades of jurisprudential practice, the common view is that the Appellate Body has remained within this mandate: allegations concerning *ultra vires* rulings are rare.[53]

(c) Nature and Composition

The Appellate Body is composed of seven members with demonstrated expertise in law, international trade and the subject matter of the covered agreements generally who are appointed for a term of four years (with possible reappointment for another four-year term).[54] The Appellate Body sits on each case in a division of three members. The members of each division are randomly selected, and there is no prohibition against Appellate Body members sitting on cases involving the State of which they are a national.[55] Most importantly, after the oral hearing, which is attended only by the three members of the division, the written pleadings in each case are discussed among *all* members of the Appellate Body, although the final decision is to be made by the three-member division. This practice, known as 'collegiality', aims at ensuring that regional or legal culture differences in a particular case are fully understood.[56]

[50] Article 17(14) of the DSU.

[51] P. Van den Bossche and W. Zdouc, *The Law and Policy of the World Trade Organization: Text, Cases and Materials*, 3rd edn. (Cambridge University Press, 2013), 291–2.

[52] Article 17(6) of the DSU.

[53] Van den Bossche and Zdouc, *The Law and Policy of the World Trade Organization*, 235–41.

[54] Article 17(3) of the DSU.

[55] Rule 6(2) of the WTO Working Procedures for Appellate Review; J. Hillman, 'Moving Towards an International Rule of Law? The Role of the GATT and the WTO in Its Development', in G. Marceau (ed.), *A History of Law and Lawyers in the GATT/WTO: The Development of the Rule of Law in the Multilateral Trading System* (Cambridge University Press, 2015), 60, 70.

[56] Rule 4 of the WTO Working Procedures for Appellate Review; P. Delimatsis, 'Institutional Transparency in the WTO', in A. Bianchi and A. Peters (eds.), *Transparency in International Law* (Cambridge University Press, 2013), 112, 122–3; A. Alvarez-Jimenez, 'The WTO Appellate Body's Decision-Making Process: A Perfect Model for International

(d) Time and Cost Limits

The disputing party must notify the DSB of its decision to appeal before the adoption of the panel report (which may take place between the twentieth and the sixtieth day after circulation of the panel report).[57] The Appellate Body, in turn, delivers its report within sixty days (or, exceptionally, ninety days) from the date a party to the dispute formally notifies its decision to appeal.[58] Following circulation of the Appellate Body report, the DSB has thirty days to decide by consensus *not* to adopt it.[59] The DSU does not contain any specific provisions to limit the additional costs which an appeal entails: disputing parties carry their own legal representation costs, but there is no fee for initiating or participating in appeals. The costs of the Appellate Body are borne by the WTO Members, its budget amounting to approximately 2 percent of the overall WTO Secretariat budget.[60]

(e) Potential to Reassert a Balance of Interests

Unlike ISDS, the WTO dispute settlement system, including its Appellate Body, does not need to (re)assert a balance between public and private interests because, *stricto sensu*, it only deals with disputes between States, without private parties being involved. Often, however, private interests will play an indirect role. Moreover, WTO panels and the Appellate Body have to balance economic and other public interests while maintaining the coherence, consistency and predictability of its jurisprudence. This is explicitly recognised in the DSU, which provides that

> [t]he dispute settlement system of the WTO is a central element in providing security and predictability to the multilateral trading system. The Members recognize that it serves to preserve the rights and obligations of Members under the covered agreements, and to clarify the existing provisions of those agreements in accordance with customary rules of interpretation of public international law. Recommendations and rulings of the DSB cannot add to or diminish the rights and obligations provided in the covered agreements.[61]

Adjudication?', *Journal of International Economic Law*, 12 (2009), 289, 301 *et seq.*; D. P. Steger, 'Improvements and Reforms of the WTO Appellate Body', in F. Ortino (ed.) *The WTO Dispute Settlement System, 1995–2003* (Alphen aan den Rijn, Netherlands: Kluwer Law International, 2004), 40, 43–4.

57 Article 16 of the DSU. 58 Article 17(5) of the DSU. 59 Article 17(14) of the DSU.

60 P. F. A Macrory, A. E. Appleton, and M. G. Plummer, *The World Trade Organization: Legal, Economic and Political Analysis*, Vol. I (New York: Springer, 2005), 1289.

61 Article 3(2) of the DSU.

In terms of assessing the potential of the Appellate Body to reassert any balance of interests, the focus of its jurisprudence lies strongly, and understandably, on the application and interpretation of the WTO covered agreements, sometimes allegedly to the disadvantage of other public interests.[62]

(2) *Current Models for Appellate Mechanisms in an International Investment Context*

(a) Anticipatory Model: *Rendez-Vous* Clause

Allowing for the creation of an appellate mechanism is not an entirely new development in the context of ISDS. Several free trade agreements (FTAs) concluded by the United States contemplate the establishment of a standing body to hear appeals from investor-State arbitral panels, but this has not yet materialised in practice. The drafters of the US–Chile FTA (2003) were the first to follow this 'anticipatory model' when they adopted a clause stating that an appellate mechanism could be inserted in the future, provided that this were to be established under a separate multilateral agreement.[63] The Dominican Republic–Central America–US FTA (CAFTA) (2004) went slightly further through the inclusion of a *rendez-vous* clause requiring the establishment of a Negotiating Group to develop an appellate body or similar mechanism,[64] considering, among other things, the nature and composition of an appellate mechanism, the applicable scope and standard of review, transparency, the legal effect of decisions on appeal and the relationship of the appellate review with other applicable rules. Notwithstanding these provisions, there has been no announcement of any such negotiations, and no draft text regarding the establishment of any such appellate mechanism has ever been made public.

The first EU FTAs with an investment chapter, that is, the Comprehensive Economic and Trade Agreement between Canada and the European Union (CETA) and the EU–Singapore FTA, also follow the anticipatory model. According to the text that resulted from the CETA negotiations, the

[62] See e.g. D. Nicol, 'Business Rights as Human Rights', in T. Campbell, K. D. Ewing and A. Tomkins (eds.), *The Legal Protection of Human Rights: Sceptical Essays* (Oxford University Press, 2011), 229, 238–9; H. Grosse Ruse-Khan, 'Assessing the Need for a General Public Interest Exception in the TRIPS Agreement', in A. Kur and M. Levin (eds.), *Intellectual Property Rights in a Fair World Trade System: Proposals for Reform of TRIPS* (London: Edward Elgar, 2011), 167, 203–4.

[63] Article 10.19(10) of the US–Chile FTA.

[64] Annex F of the CAFTA.

Committee on Services and Investment has to provide a forum for the parties to consult on a list of matters virtually identical to the points of consideration of the Negotiating Committee under CAFTA.[65] In the FTA with Singapore, a *rendez-vous* clause has been incorporated committing the Contracting Parties to look into the possibility of establishing an appellate mechanism.[66] As these treaties have yet to enter into force and, moreover, merely anticipate the establishment of an appellate review process, it would be premature to attempt to examine their potential to reassert the balance of public/private interests or any of the other elements identified in previous sections.

(b) European Commission Model: A Standing Appellate Body

The creation of a standing Appellate Body for investment matters, as envisaged by the European Commission, would 'ensure consistency and increase the legitimacy of the system by subjecting awards to review'.[67] Although the only examples of such an Appellate Body are to be found in the draft texts of the TTIP and the EU–Vietnam FTA,[68] it is possible to engage in a brief preliminary analysis of the characteristics of the appellate mechanism identified earlier. By way of caveat: these texts have been proposed by the European Commission and are being discussed with the EU Member States and the European Parliament, after which they still need to be signed and ratified by the EU's negotiating partners. What, if anything, will emerge remains to be seen, and the following paragraphs merely briefly discuss the model as it stands.[69]

[65] Article X.42 of the Consolidated CETA Text, published on 26 September 2014, available at http://trade.ec.europa.eu/doclib/docs/2014/september/tradoc_152806.pdf (accessed 13 March 2016).

[66] Article 9.30 of the EU-Singapore Free Trade Agreement, authentic text as of May 2015, available at http://trade.ec.europa.eu/doclib/press/index.cfm?id=961 (accessed 13 March 2016).

[67] European Commission, Fact Sheet: 'Investment Protection and Investor-to-State Dispute Settlement in EU Agreements', November 2013, 9, available at http://trade.ec.europa.eu/doclib/docs/2013/november/tradoc_151916.pdf (accessed 13 March 2016).

[68] Draft text TTIP, 'Trade in Services, Investment, E-Commerce', published on 12 November 2015, available at http://trade.ec.europa.eu/doclib/docs/2015/november/tradoc_153955.pdf (hereafter Draft TTIP Investment Chapter); EU-Vietnam Free Trade Agreement, agreed text as of January 2016, available at http://trade.ec.europa.eu/doclib/press/index.cfm?id=1437 (both accessed 13 March 2016).

[69] A more extensive analysis of the EU's proposed Investment Court System (ICS) can be found in: Baetens, F., 'The European Union's Proposed Investment Court System: Addressing Criticisms of Investor-State Arbitration While Raising New Challenges', 43 Legal Issues of Economic Integration 4 (2016).

(i) Legal Effect of a Successful Appeal When an appeal procedure is initiated, the Appeal Tribunal has three possible courses of action. Firstly, it may 'dismiss the appeal on an expedited basis where it is clear that the appeal is manifestly unfounded'.[70] Secondly, it may reject the appeal, in which case the 'provisional award' becomes final.[71] Thirdly, if the appeal is well founded, it may modify or reverse the provisional award in whole or in part, specifying 'precisely how it has modified or reversed the relevant findings and conclusions of the Tribunal'.[72] Notwithstanding such specification, the case will then be referred back to the original Tribunal, which, after hearing the parties if appropriate, must revise its provisional award to reflect the findings and conclusions of the Appeal Tribunal, which are binding upon the original Tribunal.[73]

Under the ICSID annulment rules, a similar system already exists: if an award is annulled, either party can request for the dispute to be submitted to a new tribunal.[74] As the jurisprudence shows, this may pave the way towards increased interpretative discord and, potentially, even a second annulment procedure.[75] Hence, it would be better if the Appeal Tribunal had the mandate to replace the original award with its own decision, as is the prerogative of the WTO Appellate Body and virtually every domestic court of appeal in the world.

(ii) Applicable Scope and Standard of Review A permanent Appeal Tribunal is to be established to hear appeals from the awards issued by the Tribunal[76] on the grounds

(a) that the Tribunal has erred in the interpretation or application of the applicable law;
(b) that the Tribunal has manifestly erred in the appreciation of the facts, including the appreciation of relevant domestic law; or
(c) those provided for in Article 52 of the ICSID Convention, in so far as they are not covered by (a) and (b).[77]

[70] Article 29(2), Section 3 of the Draft TTIP Investment Chapter. [71] *Ibid.* [72] *Ibid.*
[73] Article 28(7), Section 3 of the Draft TTIP Investment Chapter.
[74] Article 52(6) of the ICSID Convention.
[75] See e.g. *Amco Asia Corporation* v. *Republic of Indonesia*, ICSID Case No. ARB/81/1, Decision on Annulment of 16 May 1986; Decision on Annulment of 17 December 1992; *Compañía de Aguas del Aconquija S.A. and Vivendi Universal S.A.* v. *Argentine Republic*, ICSID Case No. ARB/97/3, Decision on Annulment of 3 July 2002; Decision on Annulment of 10 August 2010; *Klöckner Industrie-Anlagen GmbH and others* v. *United Republic of Cameroon and Société Camerounaise des Engrais*, ICSID Case No. ARB/81/2, Decision on Annulment of 3 May 1985; Decision on Annulment of 17 May 1990.
[76] Article 10(1), Section 3, of the Draft TTIP Investment Chapter.
[77] Article 29(1), Section 3, of the Draft TTIP Investment Chapter.

The formulation of the second ground, that is, manifest error in appreciation of the facts, raises new questions: how is 'manifest' to be interpreted? Should the erroneous appreciation have been in itself determinative of the outcome of the decision, or is it sufficient that it was one of the contributing elements? If the former, this risks severely limiting the scope of appeal since virtually every decision will be based on multiple grounds, which are unlikely to be all erroneous. For this reason, the latter interpretation would seem preferable, but in that case the question becomes: what distinguishes manifest from non-manifest contributing factors? Furthermore, as the Appeal Tribunal can also hear appeals on the grounds provided for in Article 52 of the ICSID Convention,[78] it would be useful to clarify how exactly 'manifest excess of powers by the tribunal' and 'serious departure from a fundamental rule of procedure' are to be understood as the existing case law is divergent in this regard.[79]

More generally, the proposed scope of review seems to be broader than that of the WTO Appellate Body ('issues of law covered in the panel report and legal interpretations developed by the panel') as this system does not refer to, for example, improper constitution of the tribunal, manifest excess of powers, corruption or serious departure from procedural rules.

(iii) Nature and Composition The Appeal Tribunal is to be composed of six members: the Contracting Parties are to each propose three candidates, two nationals and one non-national.[80] A committee would be empowered to 'increase the number of the Members of the Appeal Tribunal by multiples of three', to be appointed on the same (2:1) basis.[81] The Appeal Tribunal members are to be appointed for a six-year term, renewable once.[82]

Extensive limitations apply to the composition of the ad hoc committee in the ICSID annulment system, excluding, among others, nationals

[78] Article 52(b) of the ICSID Convention.

[79] For a detailed discussion on case law, see L. J. E. Timmer, 'Manifest Excess of Powers as a Ground for the Annulment of ICSID Awards', *Journal of World Investment & Trade*, 14 (2013), 775; R. Doak Bishop and S. M. Marchili, *Annulment under the ICSID Convention* (Oxford University Press, 2012); M. Scherer, 'ICSID Annulment Proceedings Based on Serious Departure from a Fundamental Rule of Procedure (Article 52(1)(d) of the ICSID Convention)', in A. J. Bělohlávek and N. Rozehnalová (eds.), *The Relationship between Constitutional Values, Human Rights and Arbitration* (Huntington, NY: Juris, 2011), 211.

[80] Article 10(3), Section 3 of the Draft TTIP Investment Chapter.

[81] Article 10(4), Section 3 of the Draft TTIP Investment Chapter.

[82] Article 10(5), Section 3 of the Draft TTIP Investment Chapter.

of either the home or host State of the investor as well as the States of nationality of the original Tribunal members.[83] If such limitations had applied to an appellate body established under the new investment agreements, this would have entailed that the large majority of people with relevant expertise would have been prohibited from serving. Instead, the Commission has wisely followed the DSU provision, which allows members of the Appellate Body to sit on cases involving the State of which they are a national.

A valid point of critique of the current ISDS system is that the pool of regularly appointed arbitrators is too limited and not sufficiently diverse. When detailing how the roster of (Appeal) Tribunal members will be compiled, the Commission has regrettably omitted any specification as to whether and how adequate gender and geographical distribution (e.g. representation of the smaller EU Member States) will be ensured. This consideration is equally absent from the provisions on composition of the WTO Appellate Body (although members should be 'broadly representative of membership in the WTO').[84]

Members of the Appeal Tribunal are to be available at all times, on short notice, and be abreast of other dispute settlement activities under the TTIP.[85] An almost identical formulation can be found in the DSU regarding the duties of Appellate Body members.[86] Members have to refrain from taking on work 'as counsel or as party-appointed expert or witness in any pending or new investment protection dispute under this or any other agreement or domestic law'[87] and comply with the Code of Conduct.[88] Like WTO Appellate Body members,[89] members of the Appeal Tribunal 'shall not be affiliated with any government' and 'shall not take instructions from any government or organisation with regard to matters related to the dispute'.[90] However, as a *contradictio in terminis*, a footnote is added stating that 'this does not imply that persons who are government officials or receive an income from the government, but who are otherwise independent of the government, are ineligible.'[91] It would seem impossible to view 'government officials' and those paid by

[83] Article 52(3) of the ICSID Convention. [84] Article 17(3) of the DSU.
[85] Article 10(11), Section 3 of the Draft TTIP Investment Chapter.
[86] Article 17(3) of the DSU.
[87] Article 11(1), Section 3 of the Draft TTIP Investment Chapter.
[88] Annex II (Code of Conduct for Members of the Tribunal, the Appeal Tribunal and Mediators), Section 3 of the Draft TTIP Investment Chapter.
[89] Article 17(3) of the WTO DSU.
[90] Article 11(1), Section 3 of the Draft TTIP Investment Chapter.
[91] Footnote 6 to Article 11(1), Section 3 of the Draft TTIP Investment Chapter.

a government as 'not affiliated with any government'. In order to ensure (the perception of) impartiality, such persons ought to be excluded from serving on the Appeal Tribunal bench.

As an alternative solution, a roster of unpaid 'available and qualified arbitrators' could be compiled from which the persons serving on the Appeal Tribunal bench could be drawn if/when a dispute arises. This would suffice to handle the workload and be most cost-effective.

(iv) Time and Cost Limits The proposal puts forward strict time limits: the original Tribunal has to issue its provisional award within eighteen months of the submission of the claim or adopt a decision specifying the reasons for the delay.[92] Either disputing party 'may appeal before the Appeal Tribunal a provisional award, within 90 days of its issuance'.[93] The appeal proceedings are not to exceed 180 days from the date of formal notification of the appeal unless the Appeal Tribunal informs the disputing parties of the reasons for the delay together with an estimate of the period within which it will issue its decision.[94] In no case should the proceedings exceed 270 days. If the Appeal Tribunal modifies or reverses the original decision, the case is remanded to the Tribunal, which 'shall seek to issue its revised award within 90 days of receiving the report of the Appeal Tribunal'.[95] This would, in principle, mean that any procedure could last at most thirty months from the date of submission of the claim.

In comparison: an application for ICSID annulment must be made within 120 days of the rendering of the original award.[96] Yet, time limits on the process of annulment and the submission of the claim to a new tribunal are not set out in the ICSID Convention, but between mid-2007 and mid-2012, the average annulment proceeding that resulted in a decision on the merits took twenty-six months from the registration to the issuance of the decision.[97] WTO appeal procedures should not last more than sixty days, with an absolute maximum of

92 Article 28(6), Section 3 of the Draft TTIP Investment Chapter.
93 Article 29(1), Section 3 of the Draft TTIP Investment Chapter.
94 Article 29(3), Section 3 of the Draft TTIP Investment Chapter.
95 Article 28(6), Section 3 of the Draft TTIP Investment Chapter.
96 Article 52(2) of the ICSID Convention.
97 ICSID Secretariat, 'Background Paper on Annulment for the Administrative Council of ICSID', *ICSID Review*, 27 (2012), 443, 463–4, para. 62; see also A. Raviv, 'Achieving a Faster ICSID', in Special Issue: *Reform of Investor-State Dispute Settlement: In Search of A Roadmap, Transnational Dispute Management*, 11(1) (January 2014).

ninety days – a deadline which is respected in almost 90 per cent of cases.[98]

Costs for the proposed Appeal Tribunal are strictly delimited as well: its members are to be paid a monthly retainer fee and a fee for each day worked as a member, about the same as for WTO Appellate Body members (being a retainer fee of around €7,000 per month).[99] Similar to the WTO system, the retainer fee of members as well as expenses for support from a secretariat are to be paid by the Contracting Parties to the treaty. Unclarity exists as to whether the fees of Appellate Tribunal members for days worked on a dispute and the legal fees of the winning party to a dispute may be shared by the parties to the dispute or born by the losing party.[100] In most ICSID annulment proceedings to date, the ad hoc committee also ordered the parties to share equally costs incurred by the centre (including fees and expenses of the ad hoc committee) and to bear their own expenses.[101]

(v) Potential to Reassert a Balance of Interests Although it is very speculative to assess an as-of-yet-non-existent Appeal Tribunal's potential to reassert a balance of interests, some brief preliminary remarks can be made: clearly, the Commission has attempted to alleviate public fears and reassert a public/private interests balance in the drafting of the new Investment Court System in general and the Appeal Tribunal in particular. The broad scope of review, the selection of members and the strict time limits are steps in the right direction. More work needs to be done, for example, concerning the competence of the Appeal Tribunal to replace the original award with its own decision, the clarification of the grounds for review and the compliance with gender and geographical distribution standards.

(1) Linking Existing Review Mechanisms to Future Appeal Structures

(a) Relation of a New Appeal Process to Existing Review Mechanisms

One issue that merits attention is the relationship between the future appeal mechanism and the existing review mechanisms (setting aside,

98 Y. Shany, *Assessing the Effectiveness of International Courts* (Oxford University Press, 2014), 218.

99 Article 10(12), Section 3 of the Draft TTIP Investment Chapter.

100 Article 10(13) and (15), Section 3 of the Draft TTIP Investment Chapter.

101 To the contrary: *CDC Group plc* v. *Republic of Seychelles*, ICSID Case No. ARB/02/14, Decision on Annulment of 29 June 2005, para. 89; *Repsol YPF Ecuador S.A.* v. *Empresa Estatal Petróleos del Ecuador (Petroecuador)*, ICSID Case No. ARB/01/10, Decision on Annulment of 8 January 2007, paras. 86–8.

refusal to enforce and annulment). Would it be possible, for example, for a State to simultaneously appeal and seek to have the original decision set aside by the domestic courts in the place of arbitration? Could the appeal decision itself form the object of setting aside, refusal to enforce or annulment? From a procedural economy perspective, this would be undesirable – as has been recognised, for example, by the European Commission, which proposes that final awards cannot be subject to further 'appeal, review, set aside, annulment or any other remedy'.[102] Any Contracting Party has to recognise these awards rendered as binding and 'enforce the pecuniary obligation within its territory as if it were a final judgement of a court in that Party',[103] but execution remains governed by the domestic laws concerning the execution of judgments in force where such execution is sought.[104]

For the benefit of all parties involved, a solution ought to be worked out to prevent extensive litigation at the enforcement stage before domestic courts: after an independent and impartial body in first instance and on appeal has found a State in breach of its obligations, the judicial process would turn into a mockery if such State would nevertheless be able to lawfully refuse to comply.

(b) Towards a Multilateral Appellate Mechanism?

An appellate mechanism should preferably be developed at the multilateral level in co-operation with UNCITRAL, ICSID and ICC because a situation in which each IIA has its own appeal mechanism would lead to even greater unpredictability. However, in view of the failure of the Multilateral Agreement on Investment (MAI) negotiations[105] and the lukewarm reactions of most of the European Union's negotiating partners about having an appeal mechanism even in a bilateral treaty,[106] a multilateral institution seems currently still politically

[102] Article 30(1), Section 3 of the Draft TTIP Investment Chapter.

[103] Article 30(2), Section 3 of the Draft TTIP Investment Chapter.

[104] Article 30(3), Section 3 of the Draft TTIP Investment Chapter.

[105] For an overview of the negotiation history, see J. Karl, 'The Negotiations on the OECD Multilateral Agreement on Investment', in M. Bungenberg, J. Griebel, S. Hobe and A. Reinisch (eds.), *International Investment Law* (Oxford, UK: Hart Publishing, 2015), 342.

[106] Negative reaction from the United States, 29 October 2015: http://www.reuters.com/article/2015/10/29/us-trade-ttip-idUSKCN0SN2LH20151029; negative reaction from Canada, 9 December 2015: www.theglobeandmail.com/report-on-business/economy/canada-warns-ceta-could-collapse-if-european-union-reopens-negotiations/article27663715/; on the contrary, positive reaction from Vietnam, 2 December 2015: http://trade.ec.europa.eu/doclib/press/index.cfm?id=1409 (all accessed 13 March 2016).

unfeasible. Bearing in mind that more than half the world's IIAs currently in force involve EU Member States, the European Union would seem ideally placed to launch the initiative by creating an appeal mechanism that is common to all EU treaties. As the EU Member States bilateral investment treaties (BITs) are being gradually replaced by EU IIAs, the new appellate system could be progressively expanded in bilateral negotiations by adding names to the roster of Appeal Tribunal members.

D. Conclusion

The creation of an appeal mechanism, which would allow appeals against all investment arbitration awards and which would result in binding, authoritative decisions, could increase the consistency of arbitral awards. Whereas the legal effect of a setting aside may be disputed, where non-enforcement may have to be won in each and every State in which enforcement is sought, and where annulment may require parties to re-argue their case before a new tribunal, the establishment of an arbitral mechanism could ensure an efficient and expeditious re-examination.

The creation of an appellate mechanism in investment disputes has its opponents. Under the Commission's public consultation, the proposal for an appeal mechanism produced divergent views. A number of respondents questioned 'whether the proposed approach will achieve the objectives (of both NGOs and companies)'.[107] An appellate mechanism indeed risks compromising the finality of arbitration, undermining a core characteristic of international arbitration. One often-heard concern is that losing parties will appeal as a matter of course. The WTO experience demonstrates that this may indeed be the case in the first years but that as soon as a 'predictable' jurisprudence emerges, the number of appeals decreases.[108] In any case, such increased 'appeals' already take place in the form of ICSID annulment applications. In order to prevent frivolous appeals that simply aim at prolonging the proceedings and increase the costs, it could be considered to put in place a 'loser pays'

[107] European Commission Staff working document, 'Online Public Consultation on Investment Protection and Investor-to-State Dispute Settlement (ISDS) in the Transatlantic Trade and Investment Partnership Agreement', SWD(2015) 3 final, 13 January 2015, 24.

[108] A. Mitchell, *Challenges and Prospects for the WTO* (London: Cameron May Ltd., 2005), 26.

system at the appellate level.[109] But it remains to be seen whether this system will ever see the light of day and, if so, whether it will much resemble the proposal that is currently on the table.

International courts and tribunals are no more infallible than their domestic counterparts, and particularly in areas where the effects of a 'wrong decision' may be so disastrous, the need for coherence, legal certainty and predictability which can be obtained through judicial review arguably trumps the time/cost advantage of finality after a first-instance procedure. The status quo mechanisms of setting aside, refusal of enforcement or annulment offer very little help in this regard as they generally do not extend to the merits of awards and, in the case of ICSID, not even to all issues of jurisdiction. A preferably multilateral appellate system could create a *jurisprudence constante* among arbitral awards, thereby reasserting a public/private interests balance and improving the predictability of the law, consolidating the acceptability of ISDS (whether in the form of ad hoc arbitration, a fixed roster of arbitrators/judges or a permanent court) and contributing towards greater public trust in the legitimacy of the resulting decisions.

[109] C. Tietje and F. Baetens, 'The Impact of Investor-State Dispute Settlement (ISDS) in the Transatlantic Trade and Investment Partnership', study prepared for the Minister for Foreign Trade and Development Cooperation, Ministry of Foreign Affairs, The Netherlands, Reference: MINBUZA-2014.78850, 24 June 2014, para. 199.

6

State-State Investment Arbitration as a Means of Reassertion of Control

From Antagonism to Dialogue

ANDREAS KULICK

A. Introduction

International investment agreements (IIAs) usually provide for both investor-State and State-State arbitration without any further indication as to the relationship between the two. Standard State-State arbitration clauses permit any Contracting Party to seize a tribunal to settle any 'dispute' with another Contracting Party as to the 'application or interpretation' of the respective IIA. Such broad wording opens various possibilities for conflict with investor-State arbitration, for example, if the investor's home State introduces a parallel diplomatic protection claim[1] or if the investor's host State and respondent in the investor-State arbitration resorts to State-State arbitration in order to settle a matter of interpretation that is pertinent in the investor-State dispute. Beyond the issue of parallel proceedings, questions arise as to the effect of a State-State award, particularly pertaining to interpretation of the IIA in subsequent investor-State arbitrations where the interpretation of the same IIA clause is relevant for resolving the investor-State dispute. Are State-State interpretation awards binding on investor-State tribunals operating under the same IIA, do they only have to consider them or can they even completely ignore them? Depending on the answer to this and similar questions, State-State arbitration inheres a considerable potential for the Contracting Parties to reassert control over the IIA and/or investor-State arbitration – usually rather unilaterally than jointly.[2]

[1] Which, however, is only possible if the parallel investor-State arbitration is not an ICSID proceeding; see Article 27(1) of the ICSID Convention and Section B(2).

[2] On multiple ways of unilateral and joint ways of reassertion of control, see Chapter 1. A joint reassertion of control would usually amount to a joint interpretation. On the latter, see Chapter 7.

This chapter first sets out a typology of State-State claims based on their potential for a Contracting Party's reassertion of control (Section B). Thereinafter, Section C will lay the groundwork for developing principles governing the relationship between State-State and investor-State arbitration by presenting five premises defining the architecture of such relationship. Section D first sets out and elaborates on the five principles that, to my mind, govern the interaction between the two different forms of arbitral dispute settlement that most IIAs offer (Section D(1)). Second, the chapter presents the consequences that in my opinion should emanate from such principles and that should crystallise, so I contend, into a judicial dialogue between State-State and investor-State tribunals operating under the same IIA (Section D(2)).

B. A Typology of State-State Claims

A Contracting Party to an IIA that introduces State-State arbitration proceedings may do so for a number of different reasons and in pursuit of a number of different purposes. These may range from, for example, settling a dispute over the effect of the unilateral termination of the IIA by one Contracting Party, to settling a dispute over a diplomatic protection claim in espousal of an investor of the claimant State party, to seeking an interpretation of a specific IIA clause that is a matter of dispute also in a parallel investor-State arbitration under the same IIA. Some of these, such as the first one mentioned, usually do not coincide with and thus have only an indirect relation, if any, to investor-State arbitration. Others, such as the third one mentioned, particularly if the respondent State in an investor-State arbitration introduces a State-State arbitration under the same treaty after the investor-State proceedings have commenced, may be employed deliberately by such State as an instrument to influence the outcome of the investor-State arbitration.

In the following, I will flesh out a typology of State-State claims according to their potential for reassertion of control and – which is a central factor with regard to the intensity of reassertion – their relationship to investor-State claims. The typology will present what I identify as four[3] different types of State-State claims under IIAs in

[3] Anthea Roberts submits a further category which she calls 'declaratory claims'. These pertain to situations where '[a] home state ... seek[s] a declaration that the host state has violated the treaty, without identifying particular investors that have been harmed or seeking compensation on their behalf ... [or] more controversially [where] a host state ... seek[s] declaration that it did not violate the treaty' (A. Roberts, 'State-to-State Investment

ascending order of their potential to serve as a means of reassertion of control over the interpretation of the treaty and the outcome of dispute settlement. As indicated earlier, in the most prominent instances of reassertion potential, that is, where State-State and investor-State arbitrations are being introduced under the same IIA and pertaining to overlapping issues, the timeline for when which arbitration proceedings have been introduced (and when which proceedings have concluded) is of particular importance for differentiating the intensity of reassertion.

This section will start with more detailed analyses of what I may call 'inter-State treaty violation claims' (Section B(1)), 'diplomatic protection claims' (Section B(2)) and 'abstract interpretation claims' (Section B(3)). With regard to the fourth category, 'concrete interpretation claims' in my terminology, in this section I will limit myself to presenting the typology of its individual sub-categories and a brief account of their tentative reassertion potential (Section B(4)). However, the subsequent sections (Sections C and D) will – as part of a broader discussion of the relationship between State-State and investor-State dispute settlement – contain a more elaborate analysis of the implications of such latter category with regard to the potential for Contracting Parties' reassertion of control over IIA interpretation and dispute settlement.

(1) *Inter-State Treaty Violation Claims*

As mentioned earlier, most IIAs contain a clause that opens access to State-State arbitration in case of a dispute between the Contracting Parties[4] over the 'interpretation or application' of the treaty, albeit a clinical distinction of 'interpretation' and 'application' issues may not always be possible. The categories of this typology discussed in Sections B(3) and B(4) pertain mainly to the IIA interpretation, while the categories discussed in this sub-section and Section B(2) deal predominantly with issues of application of the respective IIA.

Arbitration: A Hybrid Theory of Interdependent Rights and Shared Interpretative Authority', *Harvard International Law Journal*, 55 (2014), 1, 67). However, as these instances should in any case be rare, do only marginally pertain to issues of reassertion and mostly will overlap with my first ('inter-state treaty violation claims') or fourth category, I decided not to include them as a self-standing fifth category. However, see note 79.

4 That is, between two of the Contracting Parties, if the IIA has more than two Contracting Parties. For the implications of whether the IIA is bilateral or plurilateral, see also Section D(1).

Diplomatic protection claims relate to a specific dispute of an investor of one Contracting Party with another Contracting Party in which the investor's home State espouses the investor's claim. By contrast, what I term 'inter-State treaty violation claims' are abstract application claims. Here again, two sub-categories exist. Firstly, there are such claims not linked to a specific dispute between the investor and its host State but which concern a dispute that arose out of and remains exclusively within the inter-State realm. Such disputes may arise with regard to the termination or denunciation of the treaty or any other issues in dispute between the Contracting Parties as to the validity of the treaty as such, if such dispute cannot be resolved through negotiations. Secondly, inter-State treaty violation claims may concern issues arising in the aftermath of an investor-State dispute, that is, when the latter has already been settled through investor-State dispute settlement but when the host State refuses to honour the award, particularly if it refuses enforcement.[5]

Hence, this category pertains to claims that may only be resolved in the inter-State realm.[6] Overlap with investor-State dispute settlement is not an issue – even in the second sub-category, as the dispute over treaty violation for failure to comply with the investor-State award necessarily arises after the investor-State proceedings have concluded. Consequently, the potential for reassertion of control is rather limited. Due to the lack of overlap with investor-State arbitration, this category of State-State claims cannot be employed to assert any sort of influence over specific investor-State arbitration proceedings. However, these kinds of claims serve the purposes of clarification and stabilisation of the treaty frame in that they resolve a dispute as to the existence and validity of the treaty or the compliance of a host State with its obligations arising out of an investor-State award. In the first instance, the exertion of control by the Contracting Parties is limited to ascertaining that or whether the treaty frame still exists; in the second instance, the investor's home State ensures compliance of the host State's treaty obligations with regard to an investor-State award.

[5] See also Roberts, 'State-to-State Investment Arbitration', 1, 12; *Republic of Ecuador* v. *United States* (PCA Case 2012–05), Expert Opinion with Respect to Jurisdiction of Professor Michael W. Reisman of 4 April 2012, 17, 22–3.

[6] As also discussed in Section C, for that reason, Michael Reisman, in his expert opinion in the *Ecuador* v. *US* arbitration, argues that State-State arbitration under IIAs should be limited to disputes that fall under category (1); see *Republic of Ecuador* v. *United States*, 17, 22–3.

(2) Diplomatic Protection Claims

The second category of State-State investment arbitration claims involves concrete application claims. As mentioned earlier, they pertain to issues of diplomatic protection, that is, where the investor's home State introduces State-State arbitration on behalf of the investor for violation of the treaty. Here the potential for reassertion is considerably higher than in the first category, since the merits of the claim are identical to those which would be at issue if the investor introduced an investor-State arbitration against the host State. Hence, the 'dispute' referred to in the State-State arbitration clause is identical in substance with the 'dispute' under the investor-State arbitration clause, except for the parties to the dispute. This means that State-State and investor-State arbitration proceedings may coincide and overlap under the second category of claims.

In International Centre for Settlement of Investment Disputes (ICSID) arbitrations, Article 27(1) of the ICSID Convention excludes resort to diplomatic protection during ongoing ICSID investor-State proceedings:

> No Contracting State shall give diplomatic protection, or bring an international claim, in respect of a dispute which one of its nationals and another Contracting State shall have consented to submit or shall have submitted to arbitration under this Convention, unless such other Contracting State shall have failed to abide by and comply with the award rendered in such dispute.[7]

Therefore, from the date when an investor accepts the host State's general consent to ICSID arbitration usually given in IIAs until the conclusion of the ICSID proceedings (by award, settlement or conclusion of the annulment proceedings), diplomatic protection is excluded by Article 27(1) of the ICSID Convention. After the conclusion of the proceedings, considering the said provision's wording, a claim espousing the investor's claim is limited to a compliance claim under the second sub-category of 'inter-State treaty violation claims' discussed earlier.[8]

However, is the rule enshrined in Article 27(1) of the ICSID Convention also applicable in non-ICSID proceedings? If the applicable IIA contains a clause similar or identical to Article 27 of the ICSID Convention that

[7] Convention on the Settlement of Investment Disputes between States and Nationals of Other States, entered into force on 14 October 1966 (hereinafter ICSID Convention), Article 27(1).

[8] See Section B(1). See also C. Trevino, 'State-to-State Investment Treaty Arbitration and the Interplay with Investor-State Arbitration under the Same Treaty', *Journal of International Dispute Settlement*, 3 (2013), 1, 22.

applies to all investor-State disputes,[9] a Contracting Party is equally prevented from introducing a diplomatic protection claim under the IIA's State-State arbitration clause.[10] The more complicated situation arises if there is no such provision in the IIA. The tribunal in the *Italy-Cuba* case[11] considered this question. Italy initiated State-State arbitration proceedings under the Italy–Cuba bilateral investment treaty (BIT) due to a dispute over alleged breaches of the BIT by Cuba with regard to the treatment of sixteen Italian investors. Italy argued that it enjoyed 'double standing' ('*double légitimation*'), that is, that it could bring its claim both in its own right and on behalf of its investors.[12] While the tribunal rejected Cuba's contention[13] that the mere existence of an investor-State arbitration clause, such as Article 9 of the Italy–Cuba BIT, prevented the investor's host State from bringing a diplomatic protection claim, it considered, in an *obiter dictum* and without any further explanation, that the rule enshrined in Article 27 of the ICSID Convention might be applied 'by analogy' ('*n'empêche pas l'application de ce principe par analogie*').[14] Similarly, Chittharanjan Amerasinghe appears to insist that there exists a customary rule of international law excluding State-State diplomatic protection claims once investor-State proceedings have been introduced.[15] While one may consider existence of such a rule useful for matters of policy and legal security, I would be very hesitant to argue that this is the result of the correct application of the *lex lata*. Rather, it appears that at the time of its conclusion the ICSID Contracting Parties deemed it necessary to include an explicit rule to that effect in Article 27 of the ICSID Convention, and there is no conclusive evidence for sufficient State practice and *opinio iuris* that would support emergence of a customary rule since then.[16]

[9] As does e.g. Article 34(3) of the ASEAN Comprehensive Investment Agreement.

[10] For further examples of IIAs containing such Article 27–type clauses, see M. Potesta, 'State-to-State Dispute Settlement Pursuant to Bilateral Investment Treaties: Is There Potential?', in N. Boschiero, T. Scovazzi, C. Ragni and C. Pitea (eds.), *International Courts and the Development of International Law: Essays in Honour of Tullio Treves* (The Hague: T.M.C. Asser Press, 2013), 753, 765, n. 57.

[11] *Republic of Italy* v. *Republic of Cuba*, Ad Hoc Arbitration, Interim Award of 15 March 2005, Final Award of 1 January 2008.

[12] See *ibid.*, Interim Award of 15 March 2005, paras. 24–5. [13] See *ibid.*, para. 47.

[14] See *ibid.*, para. 65.

[15] C. F. Amerasinghe, *Diplomatic Protection* (Oxford University Press, 2008), 341.

[16] For further support on this issue, on which I cannot dwell here, see Trevino, 'State-to-State Investment Treaty Arbitration', 1, 20–1; see also M. Paparinskis, 'Investment Arbitration and the Law of Countermeasures', *British Yearbook of International Law*, 79 (2008), 264, 281–7; M. Potesta, 'International Decisions: *Republic of Italy* v. *Republic of Cuba*', *American Journal of International Law*, 106 (2012), 341, 345–6.

Furthermore, if an IIA Contracting Party pursues a diplomatic protection claim under the State-State arbitration clause of the treaty, such latter clause does not tacitly derogate from the customary exhaustion of the local remedies rule. As the ruling of the International Court of Justice (ICJ) in the *ELSI* case,[17] as well as the *Italy* v. *Cuba* interim award,[18] confirms, such rule of customary international law[19] does apply with regard to any diplomatic protection claim, whether pursued through State-State arbitration under an IIA or otherwise, unless the respective treaty explicitly excludes such a requirement. Hence, absent such a provision, an IIA Contracting Party is excluded from bringing a State-State arbitration on behalf of its investor as long as the latter has not pursued all remedies available before the domestic courts of the host State.[20]

Therefore, the potential for Contracting Parties' reassertion of control via a diplomatic protection claim remains rather limited. Firstly, resort to State-State arbitration for such a purpose is closed in all ICSID cases where the investor has consented to ICSID arbitration. Secondly, in the remaining cases, the investor will usually not exhaust local remedies before introducing an investor-State dispute, which, at least in my view, bars access to State-State arbitration. Thirdly, even in those quite rare circumstances that remain, it is the investor's home State that claims, on substance, the same violations and may seek the same relief as the investor in a parallel investor-State arbitration. While the investor might view this as a rather paternalistic initiative, whereby the home State may argue differently and less investor-friendly than the investor in the parallel investor-State claim, the incentive for the home State to employ a diplomatic protection claim as a means of reassertion of control is low.

(3) *Abstract Interpretation Claims*

Moving from (primarily) 'application claims' to 'interpretation claims', the third category of State-State claims in view of their potential for

[17] *Elettronica Sicula SpA (ELSI) (United States of America* v. *Italy)*, Judgment of 20 July 1989, ICJ Reports 1989, 15, 42.

[18] *Republic of Italy* v. *Republic of Cuba*, Interim Award of 15 March 2005, paras. 86–91.

[19] See e.g. *Interhandel (Switzerland* v. *United States of America)*, Judgment of 21 March 1959, ICJ Reports 1959, 6, 27.

[20] See also Trevino, 'State-to-State Investment Treaty Arbitration', 1, 11–12; Potesta, 'State-to-State Dispute Settlement Pursuant to Bilateral Investment Treaties', 753, 756–61; for a different opinion, albeit rather with a view to political desirability than based on the *lex lata*, see Roberts, 'State-to-State Investment Arbitration', 1, 42.

reassertion of control is what I may term an 'abstract interpretation claim'.[21] Under this scenario, which has not yet arisen in practice, one Contracting Party, usually the one likely to be the respondent party in tentative, albeit not yet looming future investor-State arbitrations, would resort to State-State arbitration under the applicable IIA to receive an interpretation of a specific treaty clause. While it is true that 'interpretive disputes are unlikely to be purely abstract',[22] it is nonetheless perceivable that a State might want to clarify a matter of interpretation in dispute between the Contracting Parties – also in order to anticipate any subsequent investor-State arbitrations where such issue might arise. For example, when its 2001–2 crisis materialised, Argentina could have submitted the interpretation of Article XI of the US–Argentina BIT,[23] which later became contentious in a high number of investor-State disputes, to State-State arbitration with the United States – provided that the requirements of a 'dispute' between the Contracting Parties had been met. Michael Reisman has recently argued that this form of recourse to IIA State-State arbitration resembles advisory procedures available before a number of international courts[24] in that it determines a matter of law, that is, interpretation of a specific clause of the respective IIA, not (necessarily) related to a specific contentious issue.[25] However, the value of such comparison is limited, mainly for two reasons. Firstly, the same IIA Contracting Party may be party to both investor-State and State-State proceedings, whereas in advisory opinion procedures parties to contentious disputes usually do not have standing.[26] Secondly, the ultimate aim of an abstract interpretation claim would most likely be to prejudge or authoritatively determine an interpretation issue that may come up before future investor-State tribunals under the same or similarly worded IIA(s), whereas advisory

[21] Similar terminology used by Roberts, 'State-to-State Investment Arbitration', 1, 54.

[22] *Ibid.*

[23] Treaty between the United States of America and the Argentine Republic Concerning the Reciprocal Encouragement and Protection of Investment, entered into force on 20 October 1994. Article XI reads: 'This Treaty shall not preclude the application by either Party of measures necessary for the maintenance of public order, the fulfillment of its obligations with respect to the maintenance or restoration of international peace or security, or the Protection of its own essential security interests.'

[24] See *Republic of Ecuador* v. *United States*, (PCA Case 2012 -05), Expert Opinion with Respect to Jurisdiction of Professor Michael W. Reisman of 4 April 2012, 15, 18.

[25] E.g. Article 96 of the UN Charter and Articles 65–8 of the ICJ Statute or Articles 47–9 of the European Convention on Human Rights.

[26] E.g. Article 96 of the UN Charter and Article 47 of the European Convention on Human Rights do not allow States to seize the ICJ or the European Court of Human Rights (ECtHR), respectively, for an advisory opinion.

opinions often are resorted to where no other avenue for judicial determination of the legal matter is available.[27] Hence, to my mind, one fares better in understanding the aim and reach of abstract interpretation claims without drawing such comparisons.

However, the target behind Professor Reisman's comparison of interpretation claims with advisory opinions was the requirement of a 'dispute' in most State-State arbitration clauses.[28] Indeed, a central *problématique* of any interpretation claim under a State-State arbitration clause of an IIA, be it abstract or concrete, is what constitutes a 'dispute over the interpretation' of the treaty between the Contracting Parties. This matter was at the heart of the *Ecuador* v. *US* arbitration,[29] which, however, pertained to a concrete interpretation claim.[30] In this arbitration, the United States – apparently successfully[31] – argued that the existence of a 'dispute' pursuant to Article VII of the US-Ecuador BIT required a 'positive opposition' of views regarding the interpretation of a treaty clause,[32] which was absent in the case at hand. In fact, disagreeing with the tribunal's interpretation of a treaty provision in the *Chevron* v. *Ecuador* partial award on the merits,[33] Ecuador subsequently sought an interpretive agreement with the United States. However, the United States did not respond to the request. Thereupon, Ecuador introduced State-State arbitration proceedings under Article VII of the US-Ecuador

[27] See also R. Higgins, 'A Comment on the Current Health of Advisory Opinions', in V. Lowe and M. Fitzmaurice (eds.), *Fifty Years of the International Court of Justice: Essays in Honour of Sir Robert Jennings* (Cambridge University Press, 1996), 567; see also S. Rosenne, *The Law and Practice of the International Court*, Vol. III: *Procedure*, 2nd edn. (Leiden, Netherlands: Martinus Nijhoff, 2006), 1671–83.

[28] Such as Article VII of the US-Ecuador BIT, on which Professor Reisman commented in his expert report on behalf of the United States in the *Ecuador* v. *US* arbitration; see *Republic of Ecuador* v. *United States* (PCA Case 2012–05), Expert Opinion with Respect to Jurisdiction of Professor Michael W. Reisman of 4 April 2012, 13–21.

[29] *Republic of Ecuador* v. *United States*, PCA Case No. 2012-05.

[30] On concrete interpretation claims, see Section B(4).

[31] The award in the *Ecuador* v. *US* arbitration remains unpublished to date, but according to news reports, the majority of the tribunal mainly endorsed the view of the United States; see 'US-Ecuador Inter-State Investment Treaty Award Released to Parties; Tribunal Members Part Ways on Key Issues', *IA Reporter*, 30 October 2012, available at www.iareporter.com/articles/us-ecuador-inter-state-investment-treaty-award-released-to-parties-tribunal-members-part-ways-on-key-issues/ (accessed 25 September 2016).

[32] See *Republic of Ecuador* v. *United States* (PCA Case 2012–05), Respondent's Memorial on Jurisdiction of 25 April 2012, 29–33.

[33] *Chevron Corporation (USA) and Texaco Petroleum Company (USA)* v. *Republic of Ecuador*, UNCITRAL, PCA Case No. 34877, Partial Award on the Merits of 30 March 2010.

BIT, arguing, *inter alia*, that the refusal of the United States to respond to its request was sufficient for a 'dispute' under the said arbitration clause.

International case law does not offer an unequivocal answer as to how to set the threshold for a 'dispute' in international litigation or arbitration. Definitions range from 'disagreement on a point of law or fact, a conflict of legal views or interests between two persons'[34] or even 'present divergence of interest and opposition of legal views'[35] to the requirement that 'it must be shown that the claim of one party is positively opposed by the other.'[36] Further, in *Georgia* v. *Russia* the ICJ determined that 'the existence of a dispute may be inferred from the failure of a State to respond to a claim in circumstances where a response is called for.'[37] In addition, in an award of 20 May 2014, an investor-State tribunal confronted with the question of what constituted a 'dispute' pursuant to Article 8 of the Netherlands–Slovakia BIT held that 'the existence of a dispute is readily acknowledged where a claimant submits specific and argued claims, which are denied by a respondent. Hence, for the Tribunal to have jurisdiction, it suffices if it is established that there is a conflict of legal views between the Parties.'[38]

According to a news report summarising the gist of the arguments of the majority and dissenting opinions in the *Ecuador* v. *US* arbitration, the majority held that the mere silence of the United States in response to Ecuador's request for a joint interpretation could not be viewed as meeting the requirements of a 'dispute'. In the eyes of the majority, hence, there must be a middle ground for the investor's host State in such a situation, that is, remaining silent in order not to interfere with the investor-State tribunal's decision. By contrast, the dissenting arbitrator,

[34] *Mavrommatis Palestine Concessions (Greece* v. *United Kingdom)*, Judgment of 30 August 1924, PCIJ Series A No. 2, 11.

[35] *Texaco Overseas Petroleum Co. and California Asiatic Oil Co.* v. *Libyan Arab Republic*, Preliminary Award of 27 November 1975, 53 I.L.R. 389, 416.

[36] *South West Africa (Ethiopia* v. *South Africa)*, Preliminary Objections, Judgment of 21 December 1962, ICJ Reports 1962, 317, 328; see also *Republic of Philippines* v. *People's Republic of China*, PCA Case No. 2013–19, Award on Jurisdiction and Admissibility of 29 October 2015, para. 149 (however, see para. 152, where the arbitral tribunal effectively inferred such dispute from the statements of the Philippines and China's rather 'non-statement'). See also the most recent ICJ decision in *Obligations concerning Negotiations relating to Cessation of the Nuclear Arms Race and to Nuclear Disarmament (Marshall Islands* v. *United Kingdom)*, Preliminary Objections, Judgment of 5 October 2016, para. 41, where the Court added the additional requirement of 'objective awareness' with regard to the 'positive opposition'. For criticism see the numerous dissents to the judgment.

[37] *Application of the International Convention on the Elimination of All Forms of Racial Discrimination (Georgia* v. *Russian Federation)*, Preliminary Objections, Judgment of 1 April 2011, ICJ Reports 2011, 70, 84; see also to the same effect the tribunal's findings in the *Philippines* v. *China* arbitration referenced in the previous footnote.

[38] *Achmea B.V.* v. *Slovak Republic*, UNCITRAL, PCA Case No. 2013–12 (Number 2), Award on Jurisdiction and Admissibility of 20 May 2014, para. 168.

Professor Viñuesa, took a binary approach, arguing that there was no possibility for the United States not to take sides and still avoid a 'dispute' with Ecuador over interpretation of the treaty provision in question.[39]

These positions and the aforementioned case law on the requirements of a dispute indicate that a well-balanced understanding of what constitutes a 'dispute' in State-State arbitrations based on clauses similar to Article VII of the US–Ecuador BIT ideally should prevent both of the following. On the one hand, it should prevent the one Contracting Party from conjuring up a dispute just by contending that it exists, and on the other hand, it should prevent the other Contracting Party from avoiding a dispute by denying that it exits.[40] For reasons that I will further elaborate on later,[41] I think that an IIA providing for both investor-State and State-State dispute settlement and opening access to the latter with regard to a dispute over the 'application or interpretation' of the IIA without any further qualification must be read such as to make such access effectively available to any Contracting Party. Therefore, the general reference to the prevalence of investor-State arbitration over State-State arbitration by the United States[42] did not constitute a legitimate ground for remaining silent on the issue of interpretation of Article II(7) of the US–Ecuador BIT. If it were otherwise, a Contracting Party's mere contention that it has no view on the matter and that hence, due to the lack of a 'dispute', State-State arbitration is not available, would enable this Contracting Party to bar the other Contracting Party, unilaterally and in any instance, from access to State-State arbitration. Thus, while this is not the place to discuss the details of how to define a 'dispute' in international adjudication in general or in IIA State-State arbitration in particular, I opine that one should abandon the 'positive opposition' requirement.[43]

[39] See 'US-Ecuador inter-state investment treaty award released to parties; tribunal members part ways on key issues', IA Reporter of 30 October 2012, available at http://www.iareporter.com/articles/us-ecuador-inter-state-investment-treaty-award-released-to-parties-tribunal-members-part-ways-on-key-issues/ (accessed 25 September 2016).

[40] See also *South West Africa (Ethiopia* v. *South Africa)*, Preliminary Objections, Judgment of 21 December 1962, ICJ Reports 1962, 317, 328: 'A mere assertion is not sufficient to prove the existence of a dispute any more than a mere denial of the existence of the dispute proves its non-existence'; Roberts, 'State-to-State Investment Arbitration', 1, 56; Trevino, 'State-to-State Investment Treaty Arbitration', 1, 5–6.

[41] See Sections C and D(1).

[42] See 'US-Ecuador Inter-State Investment Treaty Award Released to Parties; Tribunal Members Part Ways on Key Issues', *IA Reporter*, 30 October 2012, available at www.iareporter.com/articles/us-ecuador-inter-state-investment-treaty-award-released-to-parties-tribunal-members-part-ways-on-key-issues/ (accessed 25 September 2016); see also *Republic of Ecuador* v. *United States*, 59–62.

[43] Although it seems that at least the ICJ steers in the opposite direction, see *Marshall Islands* v. *United Kingdom*, para. 41 and above at note 36.

(4) *Concrete Interpretation Claims*

This leaves the final and most pertinent category regarding the potential for reassertion of control, that is, concrete interpretation claims, where the dispute[44] over the interpretation of a specific IIA clause is related to a specific dispute between one Contracting Party and the investor of another Contracting Party. As mentioned earlier,[45] since Sections C and D will focus on discussing legal problems pertaining primarily to such claims, in this sub-section I will merely present the different sub-categories – here chronology is particularly pertinent – and evaluate their different potential for reassertion of control.

What is common to all three sub-categories that I will develop subsequently, State-State arbitration will most likely be commenced by the investor's host State alone. Therefore, Article 27(1) of the ICSID Convention that concerns only diplomatic protection claims of the home State is inapplicable in those circumstances. Usually, for the host State, the purpose of resorting to a concrete interpretation claim is to influence the outcome of a looming or ongoing investor-State dispute or to assert control over its enforcement, including challenges to the finality or validity of the award. The intensity of potential reassertion is linked to the point in time when the State-State arbitration is introduced in relation to parallel investor-State arbitration where the same interpretation is at stake. Therefore, the first sub-category pertains to situations where State-State proceedings conclude before the investor introduces proceedings against the host State. Due to the relatively tight schedule that IIAs often set for State-State arbitration proceedings to conclude,[46] it is possible that a host State may consider anticipating a looming but not yet materialised investor-State arbitration by resorting to a concrete interpretation claim if it is foreseeable that the interpretation of one or several clauses of the IIA most likely will be of relevance in the investor-State arbitration.

[44] As mentioned earlier, here again the issue may arise as to what constitutes a 'dispute' between the parties under the applicable IIA's State-State arbitration clause. I refer to my comments on this matter in Section B(3).

[45] See Section B(1).

[46] E.g. Article VII(2) and (3) of the US–Ecuador BIT applicable in the *Ecuador v. US* arbitration leaves merely ten months in total from the submission of request to arbitrate to the delivery of the award; see Treaty between the United States of America and the Republic of Ecuador Concerning the Encouragement and Reciprocal Protection of Investment.

Similarly, a host State may consider introducing State-State arbitration after investor-State proceedings have concluded.[47] Here the host State may pursue a twofold purpose. Firstly, it will usually seek to question the outcome of the investment arbitration and thereby challenge the finality of the investor-State arbitral award.[48] Secondly, cumulatively or alternatively to the first purpose, the host State may seek to influence the interpretation of the clause in question for future disputes under the same treaty – whether looming or not – by offering an alternative or – depending on the viewpoint[49] – even authoritative interpretation to the one adopted by the preceding investor-State tribunal. The latter situation resembles either the first sub-category (if other disputes are looming) or the third, 'abstract interpretation claims' category (if no other disputes are looming). What distinguishes this situation from those two other scenarios mentioned, however, is that here an interpretation by an investor-State tribunal already exists. Such interpretation may serve as persuasive precedent for future investor-State arbitrations under the same treaty or under other treaties containing similarly worded clauses. Thus, there is a specific incentive for the host State to seek a second chance for an alternative finding and reasoning that either questions the persuasiveness of the former award and/or itself may persuade other subsequent tribunals to follow the same line of argument.

With regard to both the first and the second sub-categories, the potential for reassertion is considerable in that the host State may employ concrete interpretation claims to prejudge interpretation issues of the same or similar clauses in future investor-State arbitrations under the same or similarly worded treaties. In the case of the second sub-category, a State-State award adopting a different interpretation than the previous investor-State award may even serve as basis for domestic or international annulment proceedings, which indicates the second sub-category's higher potential for reassertion of control of the two.

However, both sub-categories do not directly interfere with the outcome of the specific investment arbitration, as is the case with the third and most reassertion-intense sub-category of parallel State-State and investor-State arbitration proceedings. Here again, the timeline is of importance, that is, whether the State-State arbitration or the investor-State arbitration proceedings have been introduced first and in the latter

[47] This second sub-category was the situation present in the *Ecuador* v. *US* arbitration; see *Republic of Ecuador* v. *United States*.

[48] See also Trevino, 'State-to-State Investment Treaty Arbitration', 1, 8, 33.

[49] See also Section D(1).

case whether or not the State-State proceedings conclude before the investor-State proceedings.[50] An example of a parallel State-State arbitration being introduced after the commencement of investor-State proceedings is the *Peru* v. *Chile* arbitration. In *Lucchetti* v. *Peru*,[51] a Chilean investor resorted to ICSID arbitration in 2002 under the Peru–Chile BIT.[52] Thereupon, according to what is known of the non-public State-State proceedings, Peru filed a concrete interpretation claim for lack of jurisdiction of the investor-State claim and asked the *Lucchetti* tribunal to stay the proceedings until the conclusion of the State-State arbitration proceedings. The latter refused, which, in turn, led Peru to abandon its State-State claim.[53]

Clearly, the purpose of such third sub-category of concrete interpretation claims is to influence the outcome of the already ongoing investor-State arbitration. If Peru had not abandoned its claim after the State-State tribunal refused the stay of proceedings and had obtained a State-State award finding that there was no jurisdiction for *Lucchetti*[54] under the Peru–Chile BIT, and if that award had been rendered before the *Lucchetti* tribunal closed the proceedings, it would have had two avenues of reassertion. Firstly, Peru could have argued in the investor-State proceedings that the *Lucchetti* tribunal was bound by the finding of the 'authoritative' interpretation of the State-State arbitration. Secondly, if the *Lucchetti* tribunal rejected such submission and granted *Lucchetti*

[50] Considering that State-State arbitrations in most instances conclude much faster than investor-State proceedings, see note 45; usually the State-State tribunal will be the first one to reach an award.

[51] *Empresas Lucchetti, S.A. and Lucchetti Peru, S.A.* v. *Republic of Peru*, ICSID Case No. ARB/03/4 (also known as *Industria Nacional de Alimentos, A.S. and Indalsa Perú S.A.* v. *Republic of Peru*).

[52] Entered into force on 11 August 2001, subsequently terminated.

[53] See *Empresas Lucchetti, S.A. and Lucchetti Peru, S.A.* v. *Republic of Peru*, Award of 7 February 2005, paras. 7, 9, 25–37; see also M. J. Luque Macías, 'Reliance on Alternative Methods for Investment Protection through National Laws, Investment Contracts, and Regional Institutions in Latin America', in S. Hindelang and M. Krajewski (eds.), *Shifting Paradigms in International Investment Law: More Balanced, Less Isolated, Increasingly Diversified* (Oxford University Press 2015), 291, 308, 312; J. Wong, 'The Subversion of State-to-State Investment Treaty Arbitration', *Columbia Journal of Transnational Law*, 53 (2014–15), 6, 22–3.

[54] Since little is known of the *Peru* v. *Chile* arbitration, one can only speculate how Peru framed its application for interpretation. Naturally, Peru could not ask the State-State tribunal to find that *Lucchetti* had no standing because the latter was not a party to the arbitration. Instead, it is likely that Peru seized the State-State tribunal for an interpretation of the treaty as to whether an investor in the same situation as *Lucchetti* fulfilled the requirements of jurisdiction under the Peru–Chile BIT.

jurisdiction nonetheless, the State-State arbitration tribunal's findings could have served as a basis of Peru's annulment claim. Or if this had been non-ICSID proceedings, the host State could have sought annulment before domestic courts. In both instances, ICSID and domestic annulment procedures, the host State again would have had two lines of argument: firstly, contending that the investor-State tribunal's finding was flawed because it did not consider itself bound by the State-State award, although the latter was actually binding and, secondly, suggesting that the investor-State tribunal had misinterpreted the applicable BIT, pointing to the State-State tribunal's interpretation as evidence for the correct interpretation.

Finally, the State-State arbitration for a concrete interpretation claim introduced by the host State may be the first one to commence, before the start of the then-parallel investor-State proceedings. Naturally, this situation would only materialise if investor-State proceedings appear inevitable, as the host State would otherwise not risk introduction of concrete interpretation proceedings that might well result in an unfavourable award. Here, given that State-State arbitrations are supposed to conclude within a short period of time according to many IIA clauses,[55] the State-State arbitral award might come at an early stage of the investor-State arbitration. Therefore, and because the State-State arbitration – usually – would look less like a deliberate obstruction of the parallel investor-State proceedings since it was the first one to commence, an investor-State tribunal might be more inclined to consider itself bound or at least be persuaded by the State-State award.

C. Five Premises Regarding the Relationship between State-State and Investor-State Arbitration

Taking the aforementioned challenges and implications of reassertion of control vis-à-vis State-State arbitration into account, Sections C and D will seek to develop principles of how to balance the relationship between State-State and investor-State arbitration within a regime that provides for both. For this purpose, Section C will set out five premises which I deem characteristic of the current regime and which, to my mind, lay the foundation on which principles shall be developed in Section D.

Firstly, apart from the rare cases of specific treaty language to such effect, IIAs do not determine the relationship between State-State and

[55] See also note 45.

investor-State arbitration, lest a clear-cut hierarchy. Instead, most IIAs contain both State-State and investor-State dispute settlement clauses, indicating that Contracting Parties may introduce State-State arbitration in case of a dispute over the 'application or interpretation' of the treaty and may resort to investor-State arbitration with regard to their 'investments' in the host State as defined by the treaty[56] or with respect to the breach of a treaty obligation.[57] Since disputes regarding investments or breaches of the treaty or similar language naturally involve issues of application and/or interpretation of the treaty, there is potential for considerable overlap between what an investor-State tribunal and a State-State tribunal may rule on based on the treaty text. Hence, I find it utterly unconvincing to purport, as some commentators do,[58] that State-State arbitration should be limited to inter-State treaty violations – the first category of my earlier typology.[59] The treaty language is clear in giving State-State tribunals rather broad competences to settle any dispute between the Contracting Parties regarding 'application or interpretation' of the treaty, be those disputes abstract or concrete.[60] If the Contracting Parties had intended to limit the jurisdiction of the State-State tribunal, they could have chosen more restrictive treaty language and/or defined a clear-cut hierarchy giving preference to investor-State dispute settlement. Reading such strong limitations into IIAs not only defies logic but also cripples the text of standard IIA arbitration clauses and thereby disregards the maxim *ut res magis valeat quam pereat*.[61]

Secondly, the Contracting Parties are the masters of the treaty. This may sound like a truism, but sometimes enthusiasm over the force and reach of investor-State arbitration seems to sink this into oblivion. Treaty interpretation must start with the text that the Contracting Parties deliberately enshrined in order to pursue the purposes intended by the conclusion of the respective treaty. If the Contracting Parties, despite signing up to the revolution of investor-State arbitration, included and

[56] See Article 10(1) of the German Model BIT (2009).

[57] See Article 24(1) of the US Model BIT (2012).

[58] See J. Wong, 'The Subversion of State-to-State Investment Treaty Arbitration', *Columbia Journal of Transnational Law*, 53 (2014–15), 6, 34–4; *Republic of Ecuador* v. *United States* (PCA Case 2012–05), Expert Opinion with Respect to Jurisdiction of Professor Michael W. Reisman of 4 April 2012, 14–21, 22–3.

[59] See Section B(1). [60] See Section B(1)–(4).

[61] See *Fisheries Jurisdiction (Spain* v. *Canada)*, Judgment of 4 December 1998, ICJ Reports 1998, 432, 455 ('important role in the law of treaties); M. N. Shaw, *International Law*, 7th edn. (Cambridge University Press, 2014), 678–9.

constantly are continuing to include broadly worded State-State arbitration clauses in IIAs that allow seizing a tribunal for any dispute over the 'application or interpretation' of the treaty, it must be assumed that this is no accident. Rather, to my mind, this indicates that they wanted to retain a certain amount of control over the interpretation (and application) of the treaty in that both abstract and concrete disputes could also be settled in the inter-State realm.

Thirdly, and as a consequence of the second premise, the third-party rights that IIAs grant to investors eventually derive from the inter-State realm, that is, the agreement of the Contracting Parties in the form of the IIA.[62] Hence, the Contracting Parties define the scope of such rights and may jointly expand or limit such scope. Sometimes they may be in dispute over how far stretches such scope they agreed upon. For that purpose, *inter alia*, they created a mechanism to resolve such disputes over interpretation among themselves: State-State arbitration. Naturally, such disputes between the Contracting Parties may arise in relation to or absent a specific dispute with an investor.

However, fourthly, the Contracting Parties also usually give their general consent to investor-State arbitration with regard to any dispute between the investor of one Contracting Party and another Contracting Party. In other words, they agree to limit their sovereignty and hence considerably limit their influence over the standards of treatment of an investor once such investor accepts the general consent given and seizes an investor-State tribunal to settle a specific dispute of the investor with its host State.[63] Therefore, as long as the Contracting Parties do not limit such transfer of sovereignty or authority by amending the treaty, they cannot completely make way with the binding force of an investor-State arbitral award.

Fifthly and most pertinently, developing principles regarding the relationship between State-State and investor-State arbitration requires account of the role bestowed on State-State and investor-State tribunals by the IIA Contracting Parties. As discussed in Chapter 1,[64] international relations theory offers the ideal-type models of agency and trusteeship to explain why States delegate authority to international courts and

[62] On the various theories of the nature of the rights enshrined in IIAs, see K. Parlett, *The Individual in International Law* (Cambridge University Press, 2011), 109–19.

[63] See also Chapter 1 and A. Kulick, 'Investment Arbitration, Investment Treaty Interpretation, and Democracy', *Cambridge Journal of International and Comparative Law*, 4 (2015), 441–460.

[64] See Chapter 1.

tribunals.[65] Under a principal-agent model, States (principals) delegate authority to international courts and tribunals (agents) to resolve international disputes for reasons of efficiency, that is, because a tribunal is better placed to resolve a dispute than the parties to the dispute themselves.[66] The trusteeship model, by contrast, follows a different rationale, focusing on credibility and independence rather than efficiency. According to this model, States delegate authority to international judicial bodies because the decision of a neutral third party increases the confidence in and credibility of their commitments and other obligations under public international law.[67] This entails an aspect of legitimacy due to the international control of national decision-making by ideally independent international judicial bodies.[68] The reach of agents' and trustees' authority is defined and thereby limited by their respective underlying rationales of efficiency (agency) and credibility (trusteeship). Under a trusteeship model, the permissible level of control to be exerted by the Contracting Parties to a treaty providing for international judicial dispute resolution is hence lower than under an agency model.[69]

[65] See for investment law literature applying agency and trusteeship models e.g. A. T. Guzman, 'Why LDCs Sign Treaties That Hurt Them', *Virginia Journal of International Law*, 38 (1998), 639; A. Roberts, 'Power and Persuasion in Investment Treaty Interpretation: The Dual Role of States', *American Journal of International Law*, 104 (2010), 179, 186; A. van Aaken, 'Control Mechanisms in International Investment Law' in Z. Douglas, J. Pauwelyn and J. E. Viñuales (eds.), *The Foundations of International Investment Law* (Oxford University Press, 2014), 409, 413–15.

[66] See e.g. E. Posner and J. Yoo, 'Judicial Independence in International Tribunals', *California Law Review*, 92 (2005), 1, 6–7, 14; T. Ginsburg, 'Bounded Discretion in International Judicial Lawmaking', *Virginia Journal of International Law*, 45 (2005), 631, 641–4.

[67] See e.g. K. J. Alter, 'Agents or Trustees? International Courts in Their Political Context', *European Journal of International Relations*, 14 (2008), 33, 38–44; L. Helfer and A.-M. Slaughter, 'Why States Create International Tribunals: A Response to Professors Posner and Yoo', *California Law Review*, 93 (2005), 899, 917.

[68] See A. von Bogdandy and I. Venzke, *In Wessen Namen? Internationale Gerichte in Zeiten globalen Regierens* (Frankfurt am Main: Suhrkamp, 2014), 26–7; see also in more general terms and with regard to State-State judicial dispute settlement Y. Shany, 'Assessing the Effectiveness of International Courts: A Goal-Based Approach', *American Journal of International Law*, 106 (2012), 225, 259–60.

[69] *See* A. Roberts, 'Power and Persuasion in Investment Treaty Interpretation', 179, 186–7; see also K. J. Alter, 'Agents or Trustees? International Courts in Their Political Context', *European Journal of International Relations*, 14 (2008), 33, 46, 55–6. While Alter mainly discusses issues of independence from the influence of one powerful party to the dispute, her argument pertains to trustee's independence from principals generally (i.e. both parties to the dispute) as an alternative to the State consensus-based legitimacy of principal-agent theory.

In the introductory chapter[70] I contended that the present system of investment arbitration is a hybrid of trusteeship and agency models.[71] Investor-State tribunals enjoy a trusteeship role with regard to the settlement of specific disputes between investors and States. However, for example, with regard to treaty interpretation – that is, the role of clarifying the scope of investors' rights and the limits of Contracting Parties' exercise of governmental authority – investor-State tribunals share this role with State-State tribunals and the Contracting Parties. In fact, other than standard IIA State-State dispute settlement clauses that explicitly bestow State-State tribunals with a competence to interpret the treaty, typical investor-State dispute settlement clauses do not expressly refer to treaty interpretation.

D. Judicial Dialogue: Fleshing Out Principles

Based on the preceding five premises, in this final section I flesh out principles that in my opinion should govern the relationship of State-State and investor-State arbitration. For the sake of conciseness, I choose to focus on the 'interpretation' role of investment arbitration tribunals under IIAs and thereby leave aside the interplay of State-State and investor-State arbitration with respect to the first two categories presented in Sections B(1) and B(2). Three factors will frame and influence the subsequent development of principles: the timeline of when which arbitration was introduced in the particular case, the intensity of the specific issue's potential of Contracting Parties' reassertion of control and whether the matter at hand pertains rather to the respective tribunals' agency or to its trusteeship functions as conferred by the respective IIA. Overarching these principles and further developed with respect to their consequences (see Section D(2)) is what I refer to as 'judicial dialogue', the solution I offer to resolve issues of parallel and potentially conflicting State-State and investor-State proceedings over the same or similar matters.

[70] See Chapter 1.

[71] See also Roberts, 'Power and Persuasion in Investment Treaty Interpretation'. 179, 188; A. Stone Sweet and F. Grisel, 'Transnational Investment Arbitration: From Delegation to Constitutionalization', in P.-M. Dupuy, F. Francioni and E.-U. Petersmann (eds.), *Human Rights in International Investment Law and Arbitration* (Oxford University Press, 2009), 118, 124–6, who regard investor-State tribunals moreover as agents of 'the greater community'. Further, note the notion of constrained independence advanced by Helfer and Slaughter in L. Helfer and A.-M. Slaughter, 'Why States Create International Tribunals: A Response to Professors Posner and Yoo', *California Law Review*, 93 (2005), 899, 929–30.

(1) *Five Principles*

The preceding considerations crystallise into five principles governing the relationship of State-State and investor-State arbitration in interpretation disputes. Firstly, Contracting Parties may legitimately resort to State-State arbitration regarding the interpretation of IIAs in both abstract and concrete[72] interpretation disputes. Absent explicit treaty language to such effect, no hierarchical order generally bars State-State arbitration on an issue of interpretation, be it linked to or detached from a specific dispute between an investor of one Contracting Party and another Contracting Party.[73]

Therefore, parallel State-State and investor-State arbitration proceedings – pertaining, at least *inter alia*, to the same interpretation issue – are possible. Thus, secondly, the relationship between the one and the other and particularly the effect of interpretation awards of a State-State tribunal should depend on the function the State-State and investor-State tribunals perform in the specific instance, based on agency and trusteeship models of delegation. Therefore, one should differentiate according to whether in the specific instance in which the interpretation issue arises the respective tribunal rather acts as trustee or as agent of the Contracting Parties in question and according to whether its primary function is the interpretation of a treaty clause or the settlement of a specific dispute. Consequently, two scenarios arise that entail principles three and four: if the State-State arbitration has been introduced before the specific investor-State arbitration proceedings have commenced and the reverse situation, that is, investor-State proceedings preceding State-State proceedings.

Thus, thirdly, the State-State tribunal's interpretation decision must prevail if State-State proceedings were the first introduced. As mentioned earlier,[74] the standard IIA State-State arbitration clause grants a specific role to the State-State tribunal with respect to disputes over, *inter alia*, IIA 'interpretation'. By contrast, investor-State dispute settlement clauses make no specific reference to treaty interpretation, which is only an incidental task for the tribunal to perform in pursuit of its primary function, that is, settling the dispute between the investor and the host State over the specific treatment with regard to the specific investment protected under the IIA in question.

Furthermore, in case of a bilateral IIA, an interpretation dispute between the Contracting Parties with respect to a specific interpretive

[72] For the terminology, see Section B(3) and (4). [73] See also Section C.
[74] See Section C.

issue can only be litigated once in State-State arbitration under one and the same IIA. The principle of *res judicata* would bar a second State-State proceeding over the very same issue.[75] These observations indicate that the purpose of State-State arbitration in interpretation disputes is to clarify how, generally, a specific IIA clause should be interpreted. By contrast, in investor-State arbitration, the very same interpretation issue under the very same treaty may arise again and again and again in various separate claims by various investors, but the findings of an investor-State tribunal in one case is not binding on other tribunals – again, due to the primary task of investor-State arbitration being the settlement of a specific investor-State dispute. Instead, State-State interpretation claims, as presently understood, provide consistency with regard to interpretation of the same IIA.[76]

Moreover, a State-State interpretation award under a bilateral IIA, eventually, is an expression of the Contracting Parties' agreement on how the IIA is to be interpreted and therefore should enjoy the same effect as a joint interpretation of the Contracting Parties.[77] This may sound counter-intuitive, considering that it is precisely the Contracting Parties' *dis*agreement which is the prerequisite for the State-State tribunal's jurisdiction.[78] However, to my mind, the Contracting Parties, by consent to State-State arbitration, have delegated authority to the State-State tribunal to resolve their dispute over interpretation of the IIA. Therefore, the tribunal's interpretation is the functional equivalent to a joint interpretation by the Contracting Parties: the Contracting Parties agreed that in case they cannot come to an agreement on what they intended with the treaty provision, the tribunal as an independent third party should decide. In both cases, the decision as to what the treaty provision should mean roots in the Contracting Parties' agreement, not in their disagreement. The disagreement in this case is no more than the switch point that opens the path to State-State arbitration and hence to

[75] On the principle of *res judicata* in international law in general, see A. Kulick, 'Article 60 ICJ Statute, Interpretation Proceedings, and the Competing Concepts of Res Judicata', *Leiden Journal of International Law*, 28 (2015), 73, 79–89.

[76] See also, similarly, Roberts, 'State-to-State Investment Arbitration', 1, 29, 63 ('interpretive awards can approximate a preliminary reference procedure'). For the differences, see later in this section and also Section D(2).

[77] On joint interpretations, see also Chapter 7.

[78] See Roberts, 'State-to-State Investment Arbitration', 1, 63: '[A] state-to-state award is less persuasive than an interpretative agreement because it involves a disagreement, rather than an agreement, between the masters of the treaty.'

the subsequent authoritative decision as to what the treaty provision should mean, which roots in the consensus of the Contracting Parties.

Moving to the fourth principle, the investor-State tribunal's incidental interpretation decision must prevail with regard to a specific dispute between an investor and an IIA Contracting Party if the State-State arbitration has been introduced after the investor-State proceedings have commenced.[79] This is so because, with regard to the settlement of a specific dispute between an investor of one Contracting Party and another Contracting Party, IIAs grant investor-State tribunals a trusteeship role.[80] The wording of standard IIA investor-State dispute settlement clauses pertains to the settlement of specific disputes over specific treatment with regard to specific investments under the specific IIA, which incidentally and necessarily involves the interpretation of one or several IIA provisions for the purpose of resolving the dispute at hand. If, at this juncture, the respondent State in the investor-State arbitration subsequently resorts to State-State arbitration to influence the outcome of the investor-State arbitration, to influence the annulment proceedings or to otherwise undermine the authority of the investor-State award, this is a bad-faith intervention that amounts to an abuse of process.[81] I submit that in such circumstances, as occurred in *Peru* v. *Chile* and *Ecuador* v. *United States*,[82] the respondent State in the investor-State arbitration/claimant State in the State-State arbitration does not primarily aim at resolving a matter of treaty interpretation – the legitimate purpose of a State-State claim – but rather at interfering with the settlement of a specific investor-State dispute, albeit it has unequivocally transferred such latter authority to the investor-State tribunal. However, by their general consent to investor-State arbitration, the Contracting Parties have entrusted the investor-State tribunal with the primary authority to settle specific disputes between specific investors and the host State regarding specific investments. Such is not the function of IIA State-State arbitration with regard to disputes pertaining to interpretation of an IIA. The fact that State-State arbitration permits diplomatic protection claims – under certain

[79] This includes instances of Anthea Robert's category of 'declaratory claims', where the host State seeks a declaration from the State-State tribunal that its particular conduct vis-à-vis the investor did not violate the IIA; see also note 3.

[80] See Section C and Chapter 1.

[81] See also Trevino, 'State-to-State Investment Treaty Arbitration', 1, 27, 29–30, 34; C. Lo, 'Relations and Possible Interactions between State-State Dispute Settlement and Investor-State Arbitration under BITs', *Contemporary Asia Arbitration Journal*, 6 (2013), 1, 23–4.

[82] See Section B(3) and (4).

conditions[83] – does not undermine this line of argument. Only the investor's home State could possibly introduce such a dispute (primarily) over the 'application', whereas the scenario discussed here pertains to State-State claims by the host State that is the respondent in a parallel investor-State arbitration.

Fifthly and finally, the aforementioned principles have less thrust if the IIA is not bilateral but rather pluri- or multilateral and/or if the IIA contains an appeals mechanism. In both instances, the architecture of State-State and investor-State dispute settlement as fleshed out before changes. In the case of a non-bilateral IIA, State-State arbitration does not involve all IIA Contracting Parties, and thus the interpretation award does not necessarily reflect the will of all Contracting Parties. Conversely, an appeal mechanism usually would intend to provide consistency of interpretation of the same IIA and thus would usurp such function.

(2) Consequences: Judicial Dialogue

What are the consequences of these five principles? On an abstract and more general level, these five principles amount to a form of coordination between State-State and investor-State tribunals operating under the same IIA that requires a judicial dialogue. While the term 'judicial dialogue' or '*dialogue des juges*' may evoke certain preconceptions from the comparative constitutional law literature,[84] I submit that with respect to the relationship of State-State and investor-State tribunals such dialogue faces far fewer obstacles than are usually attributed to a judicial dialogue between constitutional courts. Most importantly, the substantive law in question is identical, and both tribunals derive from the very same legal source, the same IIA. Further, a form of judicial dialogue has been practiced in investment treaty arbitration ever since its inception, the most prominent evidence being the frequent reference to earlier investor-State arbitration case law, even pertaining to a different IIA

[83] See Section B(2).

[84] See M. P. Maduro, 'Courts and Pluralism: Essay on a Theory of Judicial Adjudication in the Context of Legal and Constitutional Pluralism', in J. L. Dunoff and J. P. Trachtman (eds.), *Ruling the World? Constitutionalism, International Law, and Global Governance* (Cambridge University Press, 2009), 356, 371–9; M. S. Kuo, 'Discovering Sovereignty in Dialogue: Is Judicial Dialogue the Answer to Constitutional Conflict in the Pluralist Legal Landscape?', *Canadian Journal of Law and Jurisprudence*, 26 (2013), 341; O. Lepsius, 'Grundrechtspluralismus in Europa', in J. Masing, M. Jestaedt, David Capitant and A. Le Divellec, *Strukturfragen des Grundrechtsschutzes in Europa* (Tübingen: Mohr Siebeck, 2015), 45.

with non-identical wording, as well as to the jurisprudence of other international courts and tribunals, most notably the ICJ.[85] Taking into account the preceding five principles when State-State and investor-State arbitration either coincide or otherwise relate to each other, so I contend, will provide guidelines as to how such dialogue should look.

Following the preceding considerations (Section D(1)), I again differentiate between two scenarios: (1) if State-State arbitration was introduced first with regard to the specific interpretation issue and (2) if investor-State arbitration was introduced first. Under the first scenario, the State-State tribunal's interpretation is binding on all subsequent investor-State tribunals, regardless of whether the State-State arbitration pertained to an abstract or a concrete interpretation claim. Therefore, if the investor resorts to investor-State arbitration after the State-State arbitration has commenced but before it has concluded, the judicial dialogue should amount to the investor-State tribunal ordering a stay of proceedings until the State-State tribunal issues its interpretation award.[86]

Under the second scenario, that is, if the investor-State arbitration precedes the State-State arbitration, as states the fourth principle from earlier, introduction of a parallel State-State arbitration in order to influence the outcome of the particular investor-State arbitration amounts to bad faith and arguably an abuse of process. Consequently, judicial dialogue should lead the State-State tribunal either to refuse jurisdiction (for abuse of process)[87] or at least to stay the proceedings until the conclusion of the investor-State proceedings, including annulment and enforcement procedures. If the State-State tribunal refuses to acknowledge the consequences of judicial dialogue, the investor-State tribunal in any event would not be bound by the State-State tribunal's

[85] However, see for the pitfalls, particularly with regard to fragmentation, A. Bjorklund, 'Private Rights and Public International Law: Why Competition among International Economic Law Tribunals Is Not Working', *Hastings Law Journal*, 59 (2007–8), 241.

[86] I acknowledge that in case of a looming investor-State dispute this may lead to a race between the host State and the investor who is the first one to introduce the respective State-State/investor-State proceedings.

[87] See e.g. *Northern Cameroons (Cameroon* v. *United Kingdom)*, Preliminary Objections, Judgment of 2 December 1963, ICJ Reports 1963, 15, 29: 'There are inherent limitations on the exercise of the judicial function which the Court, as a court of justice, can never ignore. There may thus be an incompatibility between the desires of an applicant, or, indeed, of both parties to a case, on the one hand, and on the other hand the duty of the Court to maintain its judicial character. The Court itself, and not the parties, must be the guardian of the Court's judicial integrity'; see also *Nuclear Tests (Australia* v. *France)*, Judgment of 20 December 1974, ICJ Reports 1974, 253, 259–60.

interpretation award under such circumstances. Moreover, the judicial dialogue also involves international and domestic courts and tribunals at the annulment or enforcement stage. Therefore, I further submit that in international or domestic annulment proceedings, a State-State interpretation award rendered under the circumstances just described should be treated as a *nullum* by the ad hoc annulment committee or the domestic courts seized in the annulment or enforcement proceedings relating to the specific investor-State dispute at hand.

However, if, for example, the State-State tribunal stayed the proceedings until the conclusion of the investor-State dispute – including annulment and/or enforcement proceedings – and thereinafter continued its proceedings and rendered an interpretation award, such award would fall under scenario (1)[88] and hence would be binding on subsequent investor-State tribunals under the same IIA. This would even be the case if these investor-State disputes resembled the previous investor-State dispute with regard to facts and/or law but involved different investors. Hence, a host State that illegitimately intervenes in an investor-State dispute by seizing a State-state tribunal while investor-State proceedings are pending would still be able to achieve consistency and legal certainty with regard to interpretation issues that frequently come up in similarly situated but separate investor-State disputes under the same IIA.

[88] See earlier in this section.

PART III

Substantive Aspects and Avenues of Reassertion

7

Masters of Puppets?

Reassertion of Control through Joint Investment Treaty Interpretation

ELENI METHYMAKI AND ANTONIOS TZANAKOPOULOS*

A. Introduction

The explosion of international investment arbitration under international investment agreements (IIAs), whether bilateral or multilateral, in the last two decades has given birth to a new and purportedly distinct 'specialisation' in international law, that of international investment law. But it also eventually caused a significant 'backlash'[1] against investment arbitration and IIAs in general. This has led not solely to a new generation of IIAs[2] but also to a movement towards the reassertion of control over the operation of 'previous generations' of IIAs by their States parties. This reassertion of control is the attempt of States parties to IIAs to wrestle back control over their international obligations and regulatory authority from what they see as investment tribunals occasionally running amok.[3]

* Thanks to Dapo Akande, Andreas Kulick, Sotirios-Ioannis Lekkas, Christian J. Tams and all the participants of the Tübingen Workshop in June 2015. We retain responsibility for all errors. Eleni is grateful to the A. G. Leventis Foundation and the Foundation of Education and European Culture for supporting her studies at the University of Cambridge while work on this chapter was undertaken.

[1] For the term and relevant contributions, see M. Waibel et al. (eds.), *The Backlash against Investment Arbitration: Perceptions and Reality* (Alphen aan den Rijn, Netherlands: Kluwer, 2010). See also A. Kulick, 'Investment Arbitration, Investment Treaty Interpretation and Democracy', *CJICL* 4 (2015), 441–460 and Chapter 1.

[2] With the term 'new generation of IIAs' we mean agreements that have been adopted or renegotiated partly as a response to the extensive exposure to negative arbitral awards.

[3] See Chapter 1. Cf. also Kulick, 'Investment Arbitration, Investment Treaty Interpretation and Democracy', 445–6; N. Hachez and J. Wouters, 'International Investment Dispute Settlement in the Twenty-First Century: Does the Preservation of the Public Interest Require an Alternative to the Arbitral Model?' in F. Baetens (ed.), *Investment Law within*

The reasons for States parties seeking to reassert control over their IIAs may in part lie in the fact that States had not really realised what they were getting themselves into when they negotiated and concluded many of these agreements. The drafters of the agreements were not necessarily aware at the time of the implications that the structure and language of the treaty provisions would have in practice.[4] Indeed, many States were rushed into signing template agreements with little negotiation or advice, the Attorney-General of Ecuador admitting that it was as much akin to an accession contract as signing an agreement to be issued a credit card.[5] This may indeed explain the 'remarkable uniformity of language' used in many IIAs.[6]

Nor could the States have foreseen that the 'practice' would be a burgeoning practice of investment arbitration, now occupying most of the time of major public international law firms and practitioners, pouring over the mostly vague[7] clauses in the IIAs. Only recently, and mainly during the current century, has there been enough jurisprudence on investment disputes for States to realise in what far-reaching manner some of the provisions they agreed to could be construed[8] as a result of the 'combination of imprecise, ambiguous standards and ad hoc arbitral resolution'.[9] And indeed it is quite curious that it is arbitral jurisprudence (with each tribunal becoming *functus officio* and dissolving into thin air after each case) that has come to dominate the interpretative process in international investment law.

International Law: Integrationist Perspectives (Cambridge University Press, 2013) 417, 421 *et seq*.

4 See T. Wälde, 'Interpreting Investment Treaties: Experiences and Examples' in C. Binder et al. (eds.), *International Investment Law for the 21st Century: Essays in Honour of Christopher Schreuer* (Oxford University Press, 2009), 724, 737.

5 During Q&A following a speech on the *Chevron* case at the Oxford Public International Law Discussion Group in Michaelmas Term 2015. See also Hachez and Wouters, 'International Investment Dispute Settlement in the Twenty-First Century', 420; and cf. L. Poulsen, *Bounded Rationality and Economic Diplomacy* (Cambridge University Press, 2015).

6 N. J. Calamita, 'International Human Rights and the Interpretation of International Investment Treaties: Constitutional Considerations', in Baetens, *Investment Law within International Law*, 164, 167.

7 See, among others, M. Ewing-Chow and J. J. Losari, 'Which Is to Be the Master? Extra-Arbitral Interpretative Procedures for IIAs', *TDM*, 11 (2014), 2.

8 Wälde, 'Interpreting Investment Treaties', 737; see also F. M. Lavopa et al., 'How to Kill a BIT and Not Die Trying: Legal and Political Challenges of Denouncing or Renegotiating Bilateral Investment Treaties', *JIEL*, 16 (2013), 869, 872.

9 Calamita, 'International Human Rights and the Interpretation of International Investment Treaties', 167.

Finally, the current forceful trend of reassertion would not have materialised without the developed States, the ones who originally sought to establish the system, weighing in to change it[10] – not because they changed their minds about the system, of course, but simply because they were actually made to taste their own medicine, with claims being brought against them. The imperial/colonial foundations of the investment law regime ('we will teach you what the rule of law is' etc.) had not prepared developed States for the fact that these agreements were not a one-way street and that they could find themselves on the receiving end of claims. The figures corroborate this assumption, with almost half of all investment disputes introduced against high-income countries in recent years.[11]

But whatever the underlying reasons, there is no doubt as to what effectively launched the struggle of States parties to reassert control over their IIAs and investment arbitration. This is the fact that arbitral tribunals deciding investment disputes have at times (*many* times) approached their interpretative function very liberally with respect to both jurisdiction and the substantive standards of protection under the agreements.[12] At times, certain tribunals seemed not solely to simply assume that IIAs were concluded exclusively to protect investors[13] but also to make this assumption their ultimate guide to the interpretation of agreements, establishing the peculiar presumption *in dubio pro investore*.[14] Combined with the significant impact that such interpretations had on the regulatory authority of States, whether in terms of social welfare, protection of the environment, regulation of labour relations, taxation, and so forth, it is not surprising that reaction ensued, hence the need for a chapter discussing the attempt of States parties to reassert control over the interpretation and application of their investment agreements by imposing their own interpretation of the terms of their treaty as authoritative. In Section B, we set out the first

[10] See also Chapter 1. [11] *Ibid.*

[12] See Lavopa et al., 'How to Kill a BIT', 870 and nn. 4 and 5; M. Valenti, 'Restricting the Scope of International Investment Agreements as a Means to Set Limits to the Extent of Arbitral Jurisdiction' *TDM*, 11 (2014), 2; T. Ishikawa, 'Keeping Interpretation in Investment Treaty Arbitration "On Track": The Role of States Parties', *TDM*, 11 (2014), 2.

[13] In part due to States parties leaving 'the object and purpose of their agreements unexpressed or with a singular focus on investment protection': Calamita, 'International Human Rights and the Interpretation of International Investment Treaties', 183.

[14] For the term, see *Noble Ventures, Inc.* v. *Romania*, ICSID Case No ARB/01/11, Final Award of 12 October 2005, para. 52; see also M. Waibel, 'International Investment Law and Treaty Interpretation', in R. Hofmann and C. J. Tams (eds.), *International Investment Law and General International Law: From Clinical Isolation to Systemic Integration* (Baden-Baden, Germany: Nomos, 2011), 29, 39 *et seq.*

principles regarding the function of interpretation and the role of interpreters. In Section C, we seek to confirm these first principles by looking at the rules of international law positioning States as the masters of their treaties and to tease out objections to them as indicated by the practice of arbitral tribunals. We consider these and other potential objections to our approach in Section D, before we offer some brief concluding observations in Section E.

B. The Battle over Interpretative Authority

It is infinitely easier to contract out (or confer[15]) power to someone than it is to wrestle it back. A brief look at the attempts of the United Kingdom – before the Referendum of 23 June 2016 set it on a path that will most likely lead it to leave the European Union altogether – to wrestle back powers from the European Union against the wishes of the other Member States of the organisation is instructive in this respect.[16] But there may not be any need to wrestle powers back if you still have them: what is dealt with in this chapter is not the question of a State unilaterally asserting control over an agreement; rather, it is the question of the States parties to an agreement acting together to reassert control through the agreement's joint interpretation. This brings us promptly to the matter of authentic, and therefore also authoritative, interpretation.[17]

Every legal provision (norm) allows a range of plausible interpretations; that is, every legal norm has an interpretative radius which circumscribes the range of possible meanings attributable to it.[18] The law-maker determines

[15] See generally for the term in the context of international organisations D. Sarooshi, *International Organisations and Their Exercise of Sovereign Powers* (Oxford University Press, 2005).

[16] Cf., for example, the latest negotiations between the United Kingdom and the other European Union Member States before the 23 June 2016 Referendum: the United Kingdom managed to secure a 'deal' with respect to its 'special status' in the European Union with the consent of all Member States of the Union. See European Council meeting of 18 and 19 February 2016, Conclusions, Doc. EUCO 1/16, available at www.consilium.europa.eu/en/meetings/european-council/2016/02/EUCO-Conclusions_pdf/ (accessed 2 March 2016).

[17] According to the ninth edition of Oppenheim, 'authentic interpretations [of a treaty] given by the parties override general rules of interpretation'. R. Jennings and A. Watts (eds.), *Oppenheim's International Law*, Vol. 1: *Peace*, 9th edn. (Harlow, UK: Longman, 1996), para. 630. In what follows, the terms 'authentic' and 'authoritative' will be used interchangeably.

[18] See E. P. Hexner, 'Teleological Interpretation of Basic Instruments of Public International Organizations', in S. Engel (ed.), *Law, State, and International Legal Order: Essays in Honor of Hans Kelsen* (Knoxville: University of Tennessee Press, 1964), 119, 123.

who (i.e. which organ of the legal system) it is that will select among the possible meanings within the interpretative range in any given case.[19] The selection among the possible meanings (interpretations) within the interpretative range so made is a political decision.[20] The crucial question then becomes to which organ of the legal system has the law-maker given the power to make this political decision. Some caution is advised, however: we must differentiate between interpretation in the context of a dispute as opposed to general interpretation, and we must all the while keep in mind the peculiarities of the decentralised international legal order.

In the context of a specific dispute, a domestic legal order will most usually entrust the political decision of selecting among the possible meanings of a norm to a court. This is so because domestic legal orders provide for compulsory jurisdiction, which the international legal order, of course, does not. The international legal order (the States as law-makers) entrusts the selection among possible meanings of a norm by default to the peculiar organ formed by the two (or potentially more) States that are parties to the dispute. The dispute will be resolved when the States parties to it agree as to the authoritative interpretation of the legal norm in its application to the specific case. Exceptionally, international law-makers may entrust this political decision to another organ, less peculiar: an international court or tribunal. In such a case, it will be the international court or tribunal that will select among the possible interpretations that will make law for the specific case.[21]

Even in the circumstances where a court has been given the power to make law for the specific case, however, the law-maker (the States) has the power to override it, at least for the future, by reacting to the court's selection.[22] The reaction of States to the International Court of Justice's (ICJ's) decision in the *SS Lotus* case regarding exclusive flag State jurisdiction on the high seas bears witness to this power.[23] Similarly, Argentina and Chile agreed to set aside the arbitral award in the *Beagle*

[19] See H. Kelsen, *Reine Rechtslehre – Mit einem Anhang: Das Problem der Gerechtigkeit*, 2nd edn. (Vienna: Franz Deuticke, 1960), 242 *et seq*.

[20] *Ibid*. See also H. Kelsen, *The Law of the United Nations: A Critical Analysis of Its Fundamental Problems* (New York: Praeger, 1950).

[21] See Kelsen, *Reine Rechtslehre*, 242 *et seq*.

[22] See also R. K. Gardiner, *Treaty Interpretation*, 2nd edn. (Oxford University Press, 2015), 124.

[23] See International Convention for the Unification of Certain Rules Relating to Penal Jurisdiction in Matters of Collision or Other Incidents of Navigation, 439 UNTS 233, Article 1; Convention on the High Seas, 450 UNTS 11, Article 11.

Channel case following Papal mediation,[24] but in such a case we are no longer talking about the power to select among possible meanings of a norm in the context of a specific dispute: we are rather in the realm of selecting an authoritative interpretation once and for all for all cases. Or, to put it more precisely, we are in the realm of the law-maker *restricting the range of possible meanings of a norm once and for all* by selecting one of them to control indefinitely rather than selecting one among them to apply to a specific case.

While here the line between interpretation and amendment may become very thin indeed,[25] ultimately the power of authoritative interpretation of a norm (which is really what we are talking about) rests with the organ which promulgated the norm and which has the power to revoke it.[26] In the context of a treaty, the organ that has this power is the peculiar organ formed by *all* the States parties to it.[27] The international customary law of treaties as reflected in the Vienna Convention on the Law of Treaties (VCLT) confirms the position. This is not only (in fact, not at all) on the basis of the rules of interpretation reflected in Articles 31 and 32 of the VCLT[28] but rather on the basis of the rules regarding modification and termination reflected in Articles 30(3), 39 and 54.

First principles then confirm that States parties, acting together, are the masters of the treaties they make.[29] This is no less so for international

[24] See *Dispute between Argentina and Chile Concerning the Beagle Channel* (1977), XXI *UNRIAA*, 53.

[25] Cf. M. Akehurst, 'The Hierarchy of the Sources of International Law' *BYbIL*, 47 (1975), 273, 275–7.

[26] Cf. *Question of Jaworzina (Polish-Czechoslovakian Frontier)*, Advisory Opinion, [1923] PCIJ Series B, No. 8, 37: '[T]he right of giving an authoritative interpretation of a legal rule belongs solely to the person or body who has the power to modify or suppress it.'

[27] N. Kaasik, *Le contrôle en droit international* (Pedone, 1933), 297–8: 'Toute convention bi- ou multilatérale implique ... un transfert de chacun des États participants *à la communauté de droit que forment des ce moment ces États*' (emphasis added).

[28] Though see M. E. Villiger, *Commentary on the 1969 Vienna Convention on the Law of Treaties* (The Hague, Netherlands: Martinus Nijhoff, 2009), 429: 'It has been argued above that Article 31, para. 1 does not permit the interpreter to legislate or to revise the treaty. Authentic interpretation presents a different situation, since the parties to the treaty are their own masters. Thus, the parties may by means of the instruments, agreements or practice mentioned in para. 2 and subparas. 3(a) and (b) not only give a special meaning to the term at issue but also amend, extend or delete a text.'

[29] See the general position in Kaasik, *Le contrôle en droit international*, 295: 'Les États, tout en s'inclinant, en principe, devant le droit international, *restaient encore maîtres d'en interpréter les termes*, sans qu'aucun pouvoir central pût contrôler ni leur activité ni l'application par eux des normes du droit international' (emphasis added).

investment agreements.[30] As Crawford puts it, '[i]n the context of investment treaty arbitration there is a certain tendency to believe that investors own bilateral investment treaties, not the States parties to them ... That is not what international law says. International law says that the parties to a treaty own the treaty and can interpret it. One might say within reason, but one might not question their application of reason as they see fit.'[31] We turn now specifically to the issue of how States parties may reassert control over the content and application of their investment agreements by means of joint interpretation.

C. The Masters of the Treaty in Action

A treaty may well be 'a disagreement reduced to writing'.[32] As the product of compromise between States, it will inevitably contain vague and ambiguous provisions[33]; how could it not? After all, even the most competent negotiators cannot produce a text completely free of ambiguity; language itself does not permit this,[34] not to mention life in general (to quote Sir Humphrey Applebee: 'I foresee all sorts of unforeseen problems'). There is no *acte clair* in international law.[35] There will always be a range of possible (and thus plausible) interpretations, however narrow the interpretative radius of any norm (or act). But, in particular, in the context of negotiated agreements it is common for the parties to resort to some degree of 'constructive ambiguity'[36] lest the possibility of

[30] See e.g. UNCTAD IIA Issues Note, No. 4 (June 2013), 2, available at http://unctad.org/en/PublicationsLibrary/webdiaepcb2013d9_en.pdf (accessed 2 March 2016); and cf. Wälde, 'Interpreting Investment Treaties', 765, who uses the term 'owners'.

[31] J. R. Crawford, 'A Consensualist Interpretation of Article 31(3) of the Vienna Convention on the Law of Treaties', in G. Nolte (ed.), *Treaties and Subsequent Practice* (Oxford University Press, 2013), 29, 31.

[32] P. Allott, 'The Concept of International Law', *EJIL*, 10 (1999), 31, 43.

[33] See, among others, Wälde, 'Interpreting Investment Treaties', 735.

[34] See also A. van Aaken, 'Delegating Interpretative Authority in Investment Treaties: The Case of Joint Commissions', *TDM*, 11 (2014), 4, on the impossibility of drafting 'complete' contracts. The same applies generally to legal drafting: all rules of law will necessarily be both over-inclusive and under-inclusive, that is, will include within their scope circumstances which the drafters would not have intended to include (especially if they could foresee them) and vice versa. See M. Koskenniemi, 'The Fate of Public International Law: Between Technique and Politics', *MLR*, 70 (2007), 1, 9.

[35] According to the ninth edition of Oppenheim (Jennings and Watts (eds.), *Oppenheim's International Law*, para. 629), '[T]he finding whether a treaty is clear or not is not the starting point but the result of the process of interpretation.'

[36] See G. Hafner, 'Subsequent Agreements and Practice: Between Interpretation, Informal Modification and Formal Amendment', in Nolte, *Treaties and Subsequent Practice*, 105, 107.

a deal be blown out of the water. However, interpretation by the parties remains as an important safeguard so that they will not end up being bound by obligations they did not really (mean to) assume.[37]

(1) *Explicit Clauses on Binding Joint Interpretation*

Some agreements may include explicit clauses providing that States parties may issue a joint binding interpretation of provisions of the treaty. Such interpretation may be general or relating to a specific dispute and usually will be made explicitly binding upon a tribunal called upon to interpret and apply the treaty in the context of a specific dispute. The percentage of IIAs containing such provisions has gradually increased, and currently, most of the 'mega-regionals',[38] as well as many model bilateral investment treaties (BITs)[39] or newly concluded BITs and free trade agreements (FTAs)[40] contain them.[41]

One of the first and most prominent examples of an investment agreement containing an explicit provision on joint interpretation is

[37] See also Ewing-Chow and Losari, 'Which Is to Be the Master?', 1.

[38] See US CAFTA-DR, Articles 10.22 (3) and 19.1(3), available at https://ustr.gov/trade-agreements/free-trade-agreements/cafta-dr-dominican-republic-central-america-fta/final-text; ASEAN–Australia–New Zealand FTA, 2672 UNTS 3, Article 27(2) and (3); EU-Canada Comprehensive Economic and Trade Agreement (CETA), Articles X.27 and X.42, consolidated text available at http://trade.ec.europa.eu/doclib/docs/2014/september/tradoc_152806.pdf; Trans-Pacific Partnership Agreement (TPP), Articles 9.24(3) and 27.2(2), available at https://ustr.gov/tpp/; ASEAN Comprehensive Investment Agreement, Article 40(2) and (3), available at http://agreement.asean.org/; EU Proposal for the Investment Chapter in TTIP, Article 13, available at http://trade.ec.europa.eu/doclib/docs/2015/november/tradoc_153955.pdf (all accessed 2 March 2016).

[39] See 2012 US Model BIT, Article 30, available at https://ustr.gov/sites/default/files/BIT%20text%20for%20ACIEP%20Meeting.pdf; Indian Model BIT 2015, Article 14.9(iv), available at https://mygov.in/sites/default/files/master_image/Model%20Text%20for%20the%20Indian%20Bilateral%20Investment%20Treaty.pdf; Canadian Model BIT 2004, available at www.international.gc.ca/trade-agreements-accords-commerciaux/agr-acc/fipa-apie/fipa-purpose.aspx?lang=en (all accessed 2 March 2016).

[40] See Agreement between Canada–Peru BIT, Article 40, available at www.treaty-accord.gc.ca/text-texte.aspx?id=105078&lang=eng; Japan-Mexico EPA, Article 84(2), available at www.mofa.go.jp/region/latin/mexico/agreement/agreement.pdf; US–Rwanda BIT, Article 30(3), available at www.state.gov/documents/organization/101735.pdf; Canada–Jordan FTA, available at www.international.gc.ca/trade-agreements-accords-commerciaux/agr-acc/jordan-jordanie/index.aspx?lang=eng (all accessed 2 March 2016).

[41] G. Kaufmann-Kohler, 'Interpretive Powers of the Free Trade Commission and the Rule of Law', in *Fifteen Years of NAFTA Chapter 11 Arbitration* (JurisNet, 2011), 175, 176–80; D. Gaukrodger, 'The Legal Framework Applicable to Joint Interpretive Agreements of Investment Treaties' (10 February 2016), OECD Working Papers on International Investment Law, No. 2016/01, 5.

the North American Free Trade Agreement (NAFTA).[42] NAFTA provides for a special mechanism of joint interpretation through the Free Trade Commission (FTC), an organ comprising cabinet-level representatives of the three States parties and given the power to resolve disputes regarding the interpretation or application of NAFTA in accordance with Article 2001. In the context of NAFTA's investment chapter (Chapter 11), FTC Notes of Interpretation issued in accordance with Article 2001 are binding on any tribunal established under that chapter.[43]

Notably, some IIAs (or at least their templates, e.g. the 2004 Canadian Foreign Investment Protection Agreement (FIPA) and the 2012 US Model BIT) may opt for entrusting the evaluation of financial market and taxation measures taken by a host State to joint commissions of host and home State agencies, thereby allowing them to maintain control of the relevant provisions of the treaty.[44]

Two points should be made in this respect. Firstly, there are clauses that provide for a joint interpretation to be made by agreement between the States parties, with the form and means of the agreement left undetermined.[45] Other clauses provide for a specific mechanism or an institution that is entrusted with the authority to issue such binding interpretations.[46] In either case, the parties issue binding interpretations of the agreements. The only difference is essentially that in the latter case the peculiar organ formed by the parties to the agreement, explained in Section B, is given some semblance of separate existence (e.g. the FTC in NAFTA), while in the former case the peculiar organ is left in its original, not-in-any-way-institutionalised form.

Secondly, whereas some relevant treaty clauses provide for the competence of the parties to the treaty to issue a general interpretation,[47] others seem to allow such interpretation even with respect to pending

[42] NAFTA, Articles. 2001 and 1131(2), available at www.nafta-sec-alena.org/Home/Legal-Texts (accessed 2 March 2016).

[43] Article 1131(2) of the NAFTA.

[44] See van Aaken, 'Delegating Interpretative Authority in Investment Treaties', 2.

[45] See Article 27(2) of the ASEAN–Australia–New Zealand FTA; Article 40(2) of the ASEAN Comprehensive Investment Agreement.

[46] See Article 2001 of the NAFTA; Article X.42 of the CETA; Article 27.2(2) of the TPP; Article 19.1(3) of the US CAFTA-DR; Article 50 of the Canada–Peru BIT; Article 165 of the Japan-Mexico EPA.

[47] See Article 2001 of the NAFTA; Article 14.9(iv) of the India Model BIT 2015; Article 10.22(3) of the US CAFTA-DR; Article 9.24(3) of the TPP.

arbitral proceedings.[48] In the latter case, issues arise as to whether the parties *to the treaty* are in any way bound by their interpretation of a specific treaty standard against the background of a pending arbitral proceeding for all future instances where the same provision will be in dispute,[49] as well as to how such interpretation may affect equality of arms between the parties *to the dispute.*[50]

Interestingly, the Brazilian Cooperation and Facilitation of Investments Agreements (CFIAs) concluded in 2015 with a number of States establish joint committees that are entrusted with the overall administration of the agreements.[51] However, they do not provide either for an investor-State dispute settlement (ISDS) mechanism or for binding joint interpretation. In case an investor wishes to bring a complaint, the State of his or her nationality may take such complaint before the Committee, which will issue a final report on what is the position of the parties to the CFIA regarding the complaint.[52] The States parties will thus, acting through the Committee, decide in any given case what the content of the relevant provisions of the agreement is and whether there has been any infringement by the measure in question or whether the relevant State party has failed in implementing the agreement properly. Essentially this constitutes de facto joint interpretation of the agreement, taking the partially relevant process with respect to financial market and taxation measures contained in the 2004 Canadian FIPA and the 2012 US Model BIT a significant step further.[53]

Arbitral tribunals have had the opportunity to react to the adoption of joint interpretations, mainly in the context of NAFTA. A series of

[48] See Article 27(2) and (3) of the ASEAN–Australia–New Zealand FTA; Article 40(2) and (3) of the ASEAN Comprehensive Investment Agreement; Article 30 of the US Model BIT 2012. See further D. Desierto, 'Joint Decisions by State Parties: Fair Control of Tribunal Interpretations?' Kluwer Arbitration Blog, 8 June 2012, available at http://kluwerarbitrationblog.com/2012/06/08/joint-decisions-by-state-parties-fair-control-of-tribunal-interpretations/ (accessed 2 March 2016).

[49] Desierto, 'Joint Decisions by State Parties'.

[50] Kaufmann-Kohler, 'Interpretive Powers of the Free Trade Commission', 189. This matter is dealt further in Sections D(3) and(4).

[51] See e.g. 2015 Brazil-Mozambique CFIA, Articles 4, 15, 17; 2015 Angola-Brazil CFIA, Articles 4, 15, 17; 2015 Brazil-Malawi CFIA, Articles 3, 13, 14; 2015 Brazil-Chile CFIA, Articles 18, 24, 27; 2015 Brazil-Columbia CFIA, Articles 16, 22, 25; 2015 Brazil-Mexico CFIA, Articles 14, 18, 21. All available at http://investmentpolicyhub.unctad.org/IIA/CountryOtherIias/27#iiaInnerMenu (accessed 2 March 2016).

[52] Article 15 of the Brazil-Mozambique CFIA; Article 15 of the Angola-Brazil CFIA; Article 13 of the Brazil-Malawi CFIA; Article 24 of the Brazil-Chile CFIA; Article 22 of the Brazil-Columbia CFIA; Article 18 of the Brazil-Mexico CFIA.

[53] See text at n. 44.

decisions followed the first Note of Interpretation on 31 July 2001 regarding the meaning of Article 1105(1) of NAFTA, in particular, the standard of 'fair and equitable treatment' (FET).[54] The Note was issued in between the two phases of *Pope & Talbot*, that is, after the decision on liability but before the decision on damages and quantum, and it determined that FET in Article 1105(1) reflects the minimum standard of treatment under customary international law and requires no treatment beyond what is required by that customary standard.[55]

The *Pope & Talbot* tribunal had decided in the liability phase that Canada's conduct was in breach of Article 1105(1), which it found to guarantee fair and equitable treatment as an independent obligation, 'not subsumed by the obligation to accord treatment required by international law'.[56] In the damages phase, the tribunal criticised the FTC Note of Interpretation, which it perceived as unlawful amendment rather than interpretation.[57] It raised issues regarding the propriety of Canada's participation in the FTC when at the same time it was acting as a respondent in an ongoing dispute.[58] The tribunal further rejected Canada's argument that it was not competent to review whether the FTC Note was indeed an interpretation and not an amendment.[59] It concluded that even considering the Note as binding upon it, its decision would remain the same given the evolution of the international minimum standard of treatment over time.[60]

[54] See C. N. Brower, 'Why the FTC Notes of Interpretation Constitute a Partial Amendment of NAFTA Article 1105', *VaJIL*, 46 (2005–6), 347, 349–53.

[55] The FTC Note reads in relevant part: '1. Article 1105(1) prescribes the customary international law minimum standard of treatment of aliens as the minimum standard of treatments to be afforded to investments of investors of another Party. 2. The concepts of "fair and equitable treatment" and "full protection and security" do not require treatment in addition to or beyond that which is required by the customary international law minimum standard of treatment of aliens.'

[56] *Pope & Talbot* v. *Canada*, UNCITRAL, Award in Respect of Damages of 31 May 2002, paras. 8 and 9.

[57] *Ibid.*, para. 47. The view is shared by C. N. Brower, 'Investor-State Disputes under NAFTA: The Empire Strikes Back', *ColumJTransnL*, 40 (2001–2), 41–88, esp. 56 and n. 71.

[58] *Pope & Talbot*, paras. 11–16.

[59] The circularity of the tribunal's reasoning in *Pope & Talbot* is apparent in para. 24 of the damages award, where it states that 'the Tribunal must therefore consider for itself whether the Commission's action can properly be qualified as an "interpretation"', but then it goes on to admit that this would 'depend on what a proper interpretation of Article 1105 might be'.

[60] *Pope & Talbot*, para. 69.

Subsequent awards of NAFTA Chapter 11 tribunals have treated the FTC Note in varying ways. The tribunal in *Mondev* implicitly accepted that it was bound by the Note by virtue of Article 1131(2) of NAFTA,[61] given also that the NAFTA parties intended to settle by means of the Note the long-standing debate regarding the meaning of Article 1105(1).[62] In the end, however, the tribunal did not accept that the minimum standard of treatment was confined to that formulated by the *Neer* tribunal in 1926 but rather that it was an evolutionary standard which has been influenced by the subsequent conclusion of numerous bilateral and multilateral investment treaties.[63]

The *ADF* tribunal took the view that there was no reason for it to inquire whether the FTC Note of Interpretation constituted interpretation or amendment of Article 1105(1).[64] In any event, as the tribunal stated, '[W]e have the Parties themselves – all the Parties – speaking to the Tribunal. No more authentic and authoritative source of instruction on what the Parties intended to convey in a particular provision of NAFTA is possible. Nothing in NAFTA suggests that a Chapter 11 tribunal may determine for itself whether a document submitted to it as an interpretation by the Parties acting through the FTC is in fact an "amendment" which presumably may be disregarded until ratified by all the Parties under their respective internal law.'[65] As in *Mondev*, however, the *ADF* tribunal found that the customary minimum standard was not frozen in time, that is, at the time of *Neer*.[66]

The *Methanex* tribunal rejected the claimant's arguments that the Note constituted an unlawful amendment of Article 1105(1) of NAFTA, finding it 'entirely legal and binding upon on a Tribunal seized with a Chapter 11 case'.[67] Even if the FTC interpretation constituted a 'far-reaching

[61] *Mondev International LTD* v. *USA*, ICSID Case No. ARB(AF)/99/2, Award of 11 October 2002, paras. 100 and 118.

[62] *Ibid.*, para. 120. [63] *Ibid.*, paras. 114–16, 123, 125. See also *Neer*, *AJIL*, 21 (1927), 555.

[64] *ADF Group, Inc.* V. *USA*, ICSID Case No ARB(AF)/00/1, Award of 9 January 2003, para. 177.

[65] *Ibid.*

[66] *Ibid.*, para. 179. The tribunal in *Loewen Group, Inc. and Raymond L. Loewen* v. *USA*, ICSID Case No. ARB(AF)/98/3, Award of 26 June 2003, para. 128, found that the FTC note had as a result that 'fair and equitable treatment and full protection and security' would have normative content only as long as they were recognised by customary international law.

[67] *Methanex Corporation* v. *USA*, UNCITRAL, Final Award on Jurisdiction and Merits of 3 August 2005, Part IV, Chapter C, para. 20. The tribunal stated further that any NAFTA investor has to be aware both of FTC competence to issue Notes of Interpretation and of the latter's binding character upon a Chapter 11 tribunal (*ibid.*).

substantive change',[68] there would be nothing to support that 'far-reaching changes in a treaty must be accomplished only by formal amendment rather than by some form of agreement between all of the parties'.[69] The tribunal considered the Note also against the background of Article 31(3)(a) of VCLT and drew analogies with domestic legislatures clarifying their intentions when they perceive domestic courts as misconstruing their acts.[70]

Other tribunals have also treated the Note of Interpretation as binding but have adopted the position that the customary minimum standard is essentially evolutive, such as, for example, the tribunal in *Waste Management* v. *Mexico*, which reaffirmed the findings in *Mondev* and *ADF*.[71] In *Glamis Gold*, the tribunal approved the analysis in *Waste Management*.[72] In *Merrill & Ring*, the tribunal went about interpreting Article 1105 by referring to Articles 38 of the ICJ Statute and 31 of VCLT[73] while questioning whether the FTC Note reflected the state of customary international law in light of the fact that the tribunals in *Mondev, ADF*, and *Waste Management* had identified the standard of treatment under Article 1105(1) as an evolutionary one.[74] It then disassociated the standard under Article 1105(1) from the *Neer* standard and identified the existence of another standard of treatment of aliens specifically for 'trade, business and investments', which has developed to be more liberal than the *Neer* standard.[75] Arguably, the range of State conduct that these tribunals have deemed as encompassed by Article 1105(1) goes beyond what the parties had in mind as the 'minimum standard of treatment', that is, conduct much closer to the *Neer* standard.[76]

What arises from the examination of the case law is the following: only the *Pope & Talbot* tribunal openly criticised the FTC Note, but even then it still sought to appear as adhering to it in its findings.[77] Other tribunals treated the Note as binding, even if some of them did

[68] *Ibid.* Note that the tribunal did not believe in the instance that the FTC note constituted such a 'far-reaching substantive change'.

[69] *Ibid.* [70] *Ibid.*, Part II, Chapter H, para. 23, and Part IV, Chapter C, paras. 21 and 22.

[71] *Waste Management, Inc.* v. *United Mexican States*, ICSID Case No. ARB(AF)/00/3, Award of 30 April 2004, paras. 91–93.

[72] *Glamis Gold, Ltd.* v. *USA*, UNCITRAL, Award of 8 June 2009, para. 559.

[73] *Merrill & Ring Forestry L.P.* v. *Canada*, UNCITRAL, Award of 31 March 2010, paras. 184 *et seq.*

[74] *Ibid.*, paras. 190–2, 194. [75] *Ibid.*, paras. 204, 205, 207, 209–13.

[76] See note 68; see also *Glamis Gold*, paras. 601, 612, with further references.

[77] See *Pope & Talbot* and text at note 56.

not go so far as to say so explicitly,[78] whereas some explicitly found that they were in no position to review a Note of Interpretation issued by the competent organ under NAFTA.[79] NAFTA tribunals, however, have sought to moderate the impact of the Note by accepting that the 'customary' standard referred to in the Note (and thus in Article 1105(1)) evolves over time. This may be due to the perception that the Note of Interpretation was issued in order to intervene in pending arbitral proceedings.[80] However, according to some, the Note was in reality an amendment of Article 1105(1) of NAFTA, and the FTC had thus overstepped its competence under the treaty, essentially acting *ultra vires.*[81] These and other relevant objections are further considered in Section D.

(2) *The General International Law of Treaties*

Many investment agreements do not include explicit clauses providing for binding joint interpretation by the States parties. Such joint interpretations then fall to be considered under the general international law of treaties, as reflected in the 1969 VCLT.[82] Taking the term 'joint interpretation' at face value, we are discussing interpretation of a treaty, and thus the relevant rules of the law of treaties are those relating to interpretation. Articles 31 to 33 of the VCLT are widely accepted as reflecting the customary rules of interpretation,[83] so reference will be made to these provisions, in particular, to the general rule of interpretation in Article 31.

Article 31(1) of the VCLT requires that a treaty be interpreted 'in good faith in accordance with the ordinary meaning to be given to the terms of

[78] See e.g. *Mondev; Waste Management; Glamis Gold*; and *Merrill & Ring*.

[79] See e.g. *ADF; Loewen; Methanex; Mobil Investments Canada, Inc. & Murphy Oil Corporation* v. *Canada*, ICSID Case No. ARB(AF)/07/4, Decision on Liability and on Principles of Quantum of 22 May 2012.

[80] At the time of the issuance of the FTC Note, *Pope & Talbot* was ongoing, whereas the Notices of Arbitration for *Mondev, Methanex*, and *ADF* had already been filed.

[81] *Pope & Talbot*, para. 47; T. Weiler, 'NAFTA Article 1105 and the Free Trade Commission: Just Sour Grapes or Something More Serious?' *Int'lBusL*, 29 (2001), 491, 496; Brower, 'Why the FTC Notes of Interpretation Constitute a Partial Amendment of NAFTA Article 1105', 349 *et seq.*

[82] Vienna Convention on the Law of Treaties, 1155 UNTS 331.

[83] *Territorial Dispute (Libyan Arab Jamahiriya* v. *Chad)*, Judgment of 3 February 1994, ICJ Reports 1994, 6, para. 41; *Kasikili/Sedudu Island (Botswana* v. *Namimbia)*, Judgment of 13 December 1999, ICJ Reports 1999, 1045, para. 18; Villiger, *Commentary on the 1969 Vienna Convention on the Law of Treaties*, 439–40.

the treaty *in their context* and in light of its object and purpose'.[84] The provision then defines what is considered as context for the purposes of treaty interpretation (paragraph 2), as well as what shall be taken into account together with the context (paragraph 3). Under paragraph 3, the States parties may guide interpretation either through a subsequent agreement regarding the interpretation or application of its provisions (sub-paragraph a) or through their subsequent practice in the application of the treaty which establishes their agreement regarding its interpretation (sub-paragraph b).

According to Villiger, 'the parties' authentic interpretation of the treaty terms [under Article 31(3)(a) and (b) of the VCLT] is not only particularly reliable, but it is also endowed with binding force.'[85] Indeed, long before adoption of the VCLT, in 1911, the US-Mexico International Boundary Commission in the *Chamizal* case found that joint interpretations are binding not only on the tribunal but indeed also on the parties to the treaty. It found it '*impossible to come to any other conclusion than that the two nations have, by their subsequent treaties and their consistent course of conduct in connection with all cases arising thereunder, put such an authoritative interpretation upon the language of the treaties of 1848 and 1853 as to preclude them from now contending* that the fluvial portion of the boundary created by those treaties is a fixed-line boundary.'[86]

There is apparent tension between the strong statement that authentic interpretation is (authoritative and thus) binding and the somewhat softer language of Article 31(3), which only requires the 'taking into account' of subsequent agreement and subsequent practice.[87] However, it should be noted that all elements of Article 31 are to be thrown in a 'crucible', none of them being hierarchically superior to any other – indeed all of them are equally obligatory.[88] So, to suggest that the

[84] Emphasis added.

[85] Villiger, *Commentary on the 1969 Vienna Convention on the Law of Treaties*, 429.

[86] *The Chamizal Case* (1911), XI *UNRIAA*, 309, 328 (emphasis added).

[87] Cf. J. R. Weeramantry, *Treaty Interpretation in Investment Arbitration* (Oxford University Press, 2012), 40, 80; Wälde, 'Interpreting Investment Treaties', 766, who argues that para. 3 of Article 31 is hierarchically inferior to paras. 1 and 2, with tribunals being free to disregard it under narrow circumstances.

[88] The ILC specifically stated that 'the application of the means of interpretation in article [31] would be a single combined operation . . . But these three elements [Article 31(3)(a), (b) and (c)] are all of an obligatory character and by their very nature could not be considered to be norms of interpretation in any way inferior to those which precede them': *YbILC* (1966) Vol. II, 219–20 (paras. 8 and 9). See also First Report of Special

wording of Article 31(3) somehow moderates the effect of authentic interpretation by the parties is slightly disingenuous at best, especially against the background of the whole of Article 31 in context and of customary international law, which it was meant to reflect.

The difference between the two first sub-paragraphs of Article 31(3) has been articulated by Special Rapporteur Nolte in his first report on subsequent agreements and subsequent practice.[89] The distinction between 'subsequent agreement' under (a) and 'subsequent practice' under (b) of Article 31(3) makes no difference as to their legal effects for interpretation purposes but has the practical consequence that a 'subsequent agreement' would constitute 'an *ipso facto* authentic interpretation', whereas 'subsequent practice' needs to substantiate the common understanding of the parties.[90] The practice of international adjudicatory bodies demonstrates some reluctance to distinguish between the two,[91] while a differentiated 'evidentiary standard' seems to be applicable when determining whether conduct of the parties constitutes either 'subsequent agreement' or 'subsequent practice'.[92] Summing up, a 'subsequent agreement' under Article 31(3)(a) must be an agreement indeed, albeit not necessarily in written form, whereas 'subsequent practice' under Article 31(3)(b) 'encompasses all (other) forms of subsequent conduct by one or more parties . . . which contributes to the manifestation of an agreement'.[93]

Fauchald and Weeramantry observe that the provisions of Article 31(3) have been of very little use in investment disputes,[94] with tribunals

Rapporteur Georg Nolte, 'Subsequent Agreements and Subsequent Practice in Relation to Treaty Interpretation', UN Doc. A/CN.4/660 (19 March 2013), para. 9. See finally Ishikawa, 'Keeping Interpretation in Investment Treaty Arbitration "On Track"', 22.

89 Nolte, 'Subsequent Agreements and Subsequent Practice in Relation to Treaty Interpretation', paras. 65–118.

90 *Ibid.*, para. 70.

91 *Ibid.*, para. 71, referring to the *Territorial Dispute* case, paras. 66ff; *Sovereignty over Pulau Ligitan and Pulau Sipadan (Indonesia* v. *Malaysia)*, Judgment of 17 December 2002, ICJ Reports 2002, 625, para. 61; *Gabčíkovo-Nagymaros Project (Hungary* v. *Slovakia)*, Judgment of 25 September 1997, ICJ Reports 1997, 7, para. 138.

92 Nolte, 'Subsequent Agreements and Subsequent Practice in Relation to Treaty Interpretation', para. 74; as to 'subsequent agreement' and 'subsequent practice' being in an 'evidentiary continuum', see R. Moloo, 'When Actions Speak Louder than Words: The Relevance of Subsequent Party Conduct to Treaty Interpretation' *Berkeley JIL*, 31 (2013), 39, 58.

93 Nolte, 'Subsequent Agreements and Subsequent Practice in Relation to Treaty Interpretation', para. 74.

94 O. K. Fauchald, 'The Legal Reasoning of ICSID Tribunals: An Empirical Analysis', *EJIL*, 19 (2008), 301, 332–3; Weeramantry, *Treaty Interpretation in Investment Arbitration*, 80.

sometimes taking account of the interpretation of the parties solely to confirm conclusions already reached.[95] Indeed, there are not many cases where investment tribunals have resorted to Article 31(3) of the VCLT, and as a general trend, they have disregarded the attempts of the parties *to a treaty* to confer a specific meaning to a treaty provision subsequent to its conclusion.[96] Their reluctance is based primarily on the assumption that this would disturb the balance between the parties *to the dispute*, putting the respondent State in a beneficial position.[97]

The High Court of Singapore, as the court of the seat of the arbitration, reviewed, in the *Laos* v. *Sanum* case, the decision on jurisdiction rendered by an arbitral tribunal.[98] After accepting jurisdiction and confirming justiciability,[99] the court reversed the investment tribunal's ruling.[100] The basis for the reversal was found in letters exchanged between Laos and the People's Republic of China (PRC) after the investment tribunal had already handed down its decision on jurisdiction.[101] The exchange of letters reflected the position of the States parties that the PRC–Laos BIT did not extend to Macau.[102] The court considered the letters as a 'subsequent agreement' of States parties under Article 31(3)(a) of the VCLT[103] and concluded that the BIT did not apply to Macau.[104] The court dismissed due-process concerns as 'parties relying on the provisions of BITs' should be aware of the potential impact of Article 31(3)(a).[105] The letters reflected the 'common understanding' of the parties rather than a drastic retroactive change of the PRC–Laos BIT.[106]

[95] See e.g. *CME Czech Republic B.V.* v. *Czech Republic*, UNCITRAL, Final Award of 14 March 2003, paras. 400, 437; *HICEE B.V.* v. *The Slovak Republic*, UNCITRAL, Partial Award of 23 May 2011, para. 136.

[96] M.-L. Jayme, 'Relying upon Parties' Interpretation in Treaty-Based Investor-Based Dispute Settlement: Filling the Gaps in International Investment Agreements', *Georgetown JIL*, 46 (2014–15), 261, 291.

[97] *Ibid.*, 292; such due-process concerns are dealt with in Section D(4).

[98] *Government of the Lao Peoples' Democratic Republic* v. *Sanum Investments, Ltd.*, SGHC 15 (High Court of Singapore, Judgment of 20 January 2015).

[99] *Ibid.*, paras. 30–6. [100] *Ibid.*, paras. 110–11. [101] *Ibid.*, paras. 39 *et seq.*

[102] *Ibid.*, paras. 39–40. [103] *Ibid.*, paras. 69–70.

[104] Indeed, the court did not base its decision solely on the parties' letters but considered them along with other factors. However, it is evident from the reasoning of the decision (see paras. 50, 70, 88, 98, 105 and 109) that the letters, which did not exist at the time of the original award, were the decisive factor not only for the interpretation of the BIT under Article 31(3)(a) but also for the interpretation of Articles 29 of the VCLT and 15 of the Vienna Convention on the Succession of Treaties, 1946 UNTS 3 (see para. 111: 'With the introduction of the Two Letters and the 2001 report in the present proceedings, the conclusion . . . becomes all the more clear').

[105] *Ibid.*, para. 76. [106] *Ibid.*, para. 77.

In *Gruslin* v. *Malaysia*, the tribunal referred to the '*Notes Verbales*' exchanged between Malaysia and Belgium in order to clarify the meaning of the term 'approved project' under the applicable IIA and in order to determine whether there was a covered investment.[107] The *Gruslin* tribunal concluded that the agreement 'as informed by' the '*Notes Verbales*' did not cover an investment in shares.[108] In *Azpetrol* v. *Azerbaijan*, the tribunal inquired whether subsequent conduct of the parties could be taken into account to determine whether a settlement agreement had been reached, thus precluding jurisdiction.[109] English law being applicable, the tribunal answered this question in the negative.[110] It stated, however, that in any event such recourse would not prove claimant's contention that no settlement agreement had been reached between the two parties.[111]

In *National Grid*, the issue was whether a 'most favoured nation' (MFN) clause applied to the ISDS provision, a matter which was not apparent under Article 3(2) of the Argentina–UK BIT.[112] In order to determine the intention of the parties, the tribunal examined their practice regarding MFN clauses in subsequent BITs as well as their interpretation of such clauses.[113] However, given Argentina's limited specific practice, the tribunal decided that the common intent of the parties was not clearly established.[114] In *Aguas del Tunari*, Bolivia sought to establish the agreement of the parties regarding interpretation of the BIT on the basis of certain statements made by the Netherlands.[115] The tribunal identified Article 31(3)(a) and (b) as applicable in the instance[116] but refused to accept the Dutch statements as constituting subsequent agreement under Article 31(3)(a), disregarding the coincidence of several statements and finding lack of intent that the statements be regarded as an agreement.[117] It examined whether the statements could be considered as 'subsequent

107 *Philippe Gruslin* v. *Malaysia*, ICSID Case No ARB/99/3, Award of 27 November 2000, para. 23.

108 *Ibid.*, para. 25.6.

109 *Azpetrol International Holdings B.V. and Azpetrol Group B.V. and Azpetrol Oil Services Group B.V.* v. *Republic of Azerbaijan*, ICSID Case No ARB/06/15, Award of 8 September 2009, para. 64.

110 *Ibid.*, para. 90. 111 *Ibid.*, para. 92.

112 *National Grid plc* v. *Argentine Republic*, UNCITRAL, Decision on Jurisdiction of 20 June 2006, para. 82.

113 *Ibid.*, para. 85. 114 *Ibid.*

115 *Aguas del Tunari SA* v. *Bolivia*, ICSID Case No. ARB/02/3, Decision on Jurisdiction of 21 October 2005, para. 249.

116 *Ibid.*, para. 250. 117 *Ibid.*, para. 251.

practice' under Article 31(3)(b) but found the evidence adduced to have failed the respective test as well.[118] In *RosInvest* v. *Russia*, the tribunal affirmed the application of Article 31(3)(a) and (b), though only in passing, since it found no reason (and no evidence) to apply it in that case.[119]

D. The Objections

What emerges from our overview of the arbitral practice with respect to joint interpretation is a certain reluctance of investment tribunals to embrace wholeheartedly what the first principles (and indeed the rules) of international law seem to require: the unquestionable vesting with binding force of joint interpretations by the States parties of their own treaties. A number of objections could be gleamed in that jurisprudence more or less clearly, and it is to these express or implied objections that we now turn.

(1) Subjects, Objects and Beneficiaries

One potential objection to the binding force of joint interpretations of IIAs by their States parties is that the States parties to these agreements have endowed individuals coming within the scope of application of the agreements with substantive and(or) procedural rights, which they can no longer take away or affect, including through authentic interpretation (which may be tantamount to amendment). Different positions have been taken in this debate as to whether investors are full subjects enjoying direct rights akin to human rights (despite, among others, the significant 'sociocultural distance' between investment and human rights laws[120]), mere objects along the lines of diplomatic protection, or rather beneficiaries of investment agreements akin to third parties under treaty law.[121]

118 *Ibid.*, para. 262.

119 *RosInvestCo UK, Ltd.* v. *Russian Federation*, Stockholm Chamber of Commerce, SCC No. V079/2005, Award on Jurisdiction of 1 October 2007, paras. 38, 119.

120 See Moshe Hirsch, 'Investment Tribunals and Human Rights Treaties: A Sociological Perspective', in Baetens, *Investment Law within International Law*, 85, 92–100.

121 For an overview of the positions taken, see generally M. Paparinskis, 'Analogies and Other Regimes of International Law', in Z. Douglas, J. Pauwelyn and J. E. Viñuales (eds.), *The Foundations of International Investment Law: Bringing Theory into Practice* (Oxford University Press, 2014), 73, 79–85; and K. Parlett, *The Individual in the International Legal System* (Cambridge University Press, 2011), 105 *et seq.*; see also Z. Douglas, 'The Hybrid Foundations of the International Investment Arbitration',

For our purposes, it is not required to resolve this issue, at least as far as the future application of the joint interpretation reached by the States parties is concerned. Suffice it here to note that from a structural perspective IIAs, be they bilateral or multilateral, are premised upon a bilateralised approach to obligations, very closely connected to the notion of reciprocity. A State grants treaty protection to nationals of another State because, and for as long as, the other State also grants the same level of protection to the first State's nationals.[122] This is further reinforced by the fact that both the law of countermeasures and the defence of necessity are (at least in principle) applicable to IIAs.[123] Furthermore, from a teleological point of view, investment treaties were initially concluded in order to induce foreign direct investment (FDI) flows to States with developmental needs (and quite frankly are still meant to perform the same function).[124] This differs a lot from the very idea at the heart of human rights or other individual-centred regimes (e.g. the law of consular relations), namely, the protection of individuals because of considerations of humanity and due process.

BYbIL, 74 (2003), 151, 162ff; M. Paparinskis, 'Investment Treaty Arbitration and the (New) Law of State Responsibility', *EJIL*, 24 (2013), 617–46; A. Gourgourinis, 'Investors' Rights Qua Human Rights? Revisiting the "Direct"/"Derivative" Rights Debate', in M. Fitzmaurice and P. Merkouris (eds.), *The Interpretation and Application of the European Convention of Human Rights: Legal and Practical Implications* (The Hague, Netherlands: Martinus Nijhoff, 2013), 147–82; F. Gonzáles de Cossio, 'Investment Protection Rights: Substantive or Procedural?', *ICSID Review*, 25 (2010), 107–22; see further *Wintershall Aktiengesellschaft* v. *Argentina*, ICSID Case No. ARB/04/14, Award of November 2008, para. 110; *Archer Daniels Midland Company and Tate & Lyle Ingredients Americas, Inc.* v. *Mexico*, ICSID Case No. ARB(AF)/04/05, Award of 21 November 2007, paras. 161–80; *ADF*, para. 152; *Corn Products International, Inc.* v. *United Mexican States*, ICSID Case No. ARB(AF)/04/1, Decision on Responsibility of 5 January 2008, paras. 167–79; and *Cargill, Inc.* v. *Mexico*, ICSID Case No. ARB(AF)/05/2, Award of 13 August 2009, paras. 403–28.

122 Gourgourinis, 'Investors' Rights Qua Human Rights?', 171 and nn. 110–11; see also e.g. Article 1115 of the NAFTA.

123 Gourgourinis, 'Investors' Rights Qua Human Rights?', 161 *et seq.*; cf. Parlett, *The Individual in the International Legal System*, 110–11, 114; *Impregilo SpA* v. *Argentine Republic*, ICSID Case No. ARB/07/17, Final Award of 21 June 2011, para. 334; *El Paso Energy International Company* v. *Argentine Republic*, ICSID Case No. ARB/03/15, Award of 27 October 2011, paras. 649–65; *Archer Daniels*, para. 179.

124 Valenti, 'Restricting the Scope of International Investment Agreements', 2; Jamie, 'Relying upon Parties' Interpretation', 268–9; J. W. Salacuse and N. P. Sullivan, 'Do BITs Really Work? An Evaluation of Bilateral Investment Treaties and Their Grand Bargain', *HarvILJ*, 46 (2005), 67, 77.

At any rate, what the State(s) first it giveth, the State(s) then it taketh away, at least for the future. This goes not simply for investor 'rights' but even for human rights, which put individuals within a State's jurisdiction (and indeed *all* individuals without discrimination, not just investors) in the strongest possible position that individuals enjoy under current international law. States may not only affect these rights by binding joint interpretation or amendment; they may even unilaterally withdraw from treaties for the protection of human rights, whether the European Convention on Human Rights (ECHR),[125] the Convention against Torture (CAT),[126] the International Convention on the Elimination of All Forms of Racial Discrimination (CERD)[127] or even the Genocide Convention.[128]

Such withdrawal will not, of course, affect the human rights of individuals under customary international law,[129] but it will certainly affect their capacity to bring claims in their own name at the international level against States for the violation of these rights. Crucially, investor 'rights' are clearly not enshrined in customary law – they are granted to investors by States pursuant to treaty arrangements only.[130] So, irrespective of whether investors are to be classed as subjects, objects or beneficiaries of investment treaties, this will in no way affect the position of States as masters of the treaties they have made.

Things become slightly more complicated when considering whether the masters of the treaty may intervene to issue binding interpretations pending a dispute between one of them and an investor under the treaty. However, given that it is the interpretation of the treaty that is at stake in the instance, rather than its modification or termination, this matter is taken up further in Sections D(3) and (4).

[125] Convention on the Protection of Human Rights and Fundamental Freedoms (ECHR), ETC No. 5, Article 58.

[126] Convention against Torture and Other Cruel, Inhuman or Degrading Treatment or Punishment, 1465 UNTS 112 (CAT), Article 31.

[127] International Convention on the Elimination of All Forms of Racial Discrimination, 660 UNTS 212 (CERD), Article 21.

[128] Convention on the Prevention and Punishment of the Crime of Genocide, 78 UNTS 277, Article XIV. On IIA termination see Chapter 9.

[129] Article 43 of the VCLT.

[130] The customary 'minimum standard of treatment' applicable to all aliens prohibits denial of justice. See *Loewen* v. *USA*, para. 129. However, this 'right' is to be realised before the domestic courts of the State, and customary international law does not in its current state provide for a right of foreign investors to have recourse to international arbitration.

(2) *Dependent and Independent Tribunals versus the Agent/Trustee Spectrum*

Another objection could arise on the basis of the understanding of investment tribunals as agents of the States parties or trustees of the legal regime established by the treaty.[131] Many commentators take up this matter,[132] some arguing that the vagueness of the provisions of international investment agreements, combined with their provisions for ISDS, render investment tribunals constituted under them trustees of the treaty regime rather than agents of the States parties. This, indeed, occurs even more so if it is considered that investors are subjects or beneficiaries of investment treaties rather than mere objects.[133]

However, this is yet another battle that does not need to be fought, at least not for the purposes of this chapter. Firstly, these categories are not open-and-closed. At best, they exist on a spectrum.[134] At worst, they are singularly unhelpful in that they put the cart before the horse. Whether the tribunal is meant to function as an agent or trustee will depend on the interpretation of the treaty at hand, and it is over this interpretation that first principles indicate that States parties exercise ultimately authoritative control. Whichever theory one chooses, States parties are the masters of the treaty, and they make the law; they may then delegate through explicit treaty provisions adjudicatory powers to arbitral tribunals to apply that law. However, most treaties do not contain explicit provisions as to whom the power of authoritative interpretation of treaty provisions lies with.[135] Thus, resort is in any event necessary to the general rules of international law, including the rules on treaty interpretation as reflected in the Vienna Convention.

Secondly, for every argument based on categorisation of investment tribunals as agents or trustees, an equal and therefore neutering counter-argument can be made based on some other categorisation. For example, one could juxtapose to the agent/trustee categorisation the

[131] See on this also Chapters 1 and 6.

[132] See e.g. van Aaken, 'Delegating Interpretative Authority in Investment Treaties'; K. Alter, 'Agents or Trustees? International Courts in Their Political Context', *EJIR*, 14 (2008), 33–63; P. B. Stephan, 'Courts, Tribunals and Legal Unification: The Agency Problem' *ChiJIL*, 3 (2002), 333–52.

[133] See van Aaken, 'Delegating Interpretative Authority in Investment Treaties', 11; Alter, 'Agents or Trustees?', 39–40.

[134] See A. Roberts, 'Power and Persuasion in Investment Treaty Interpretation: The Dual Role of States', *AJIL*, 104 (2010), 179, 187; van Aaken, 'Delegating Interpretative Authority in Investment Treaties', 9.

[135] Roberts, 'Power and Persuasion in Investment Treaty Interpretation', 180.

dependent/independent court categorisation.[136] According to the latter, dependent courts are those which take the interests to the parties to the dispute more seriously, which is the case, for example, when their members are directly appointed by the parties to the dispute (as is the case with investment tribunals).[137] Accordingly, investment tribunals would be *structurally* dependent (as their members are party appointed), which would indeed bring them closer to agency and at the same time *substantively* trustees (given the vagueness of the provisions they have been 'entrusted' with interpreting and applying). It is difficult to conceptualise how they could be both at the same time:[138] the usefulness of such categorisations thus breaks down at this point.

(3) *Interpretation and Amendment*

NAFTA tribunals have raised the issue of whether what is put forward as interpretation may in fact be an amendment in violation of the amendment process of the treaty.[139] This potential objection of joint interpretation being tantamount to unlawful amendment must be addressed. Interpretation determines the meaning and scope of a norm.[140] Essentially it is supposed to set out a meaning of the norm that has always been there,[141] whereas amendment alters the norm altogether, adding to or restricting its meaning and scope. Therefore, amendment normally only has prospective effect: it operates *ex nunc*. By contrast, the question of inter-temporal law is

136 See the debate between Posner and Yoo on the one side and Helfer and Slaughter on the other in the *California Law Review*: E. A. Posner and J. C. Yoo, 'Judicial Independence in International Tribunals', *CalLRev*, 93 (2005), 1–75; L. R. Helfer and A.-M. Slaughter, 'Why States Create International Tribunals: A Response to Professors Posner and Yoo', *CalLRev*, 93 (2005), 899–956; E. A. Posner and J. C. Yoo, 'Reply to Helfer and Slaughter', *CalLRev*, 93 (2005), 957–74. See also L. R. Helfer and A.-M. Slaughter, 'Towards a Theory of Effective Supranational Adjudication', *YaleLJ*, 107 (1997–8) 273–391.

137 See van Aaken, 'Delegating Interpretative Authority in Investment Treaties', 11; Posner and Yoo, 'Judicial Independence', 8, 25–7.

138 Notably, the consequences of categorisation seem to be contradictory as well. Posner and Yoo, 'Judicial Independence', 28 *et seq*., 54, 66, indicate that the higher the dependence of the tribunal, the higher is its effectiveness, whereas Roberts, 'Power and Persuasion in Investment Treaty Interpretation', 186–7, and van Aaken, 'Delegating Interpretative Authority in Investment Treaties', 10, credit trusteeship with higher effectiveness.

139 See Section C(1).

140 See F. Dopagne, 'Article 28: Convention of 1969', in O. Corten and P. Klein (eds.), *The Vienna Conventions on the Law of Treaties: A Commentary* (Oxford University Press, 2012), Vol. I, 718, 719.

141 As Hafner, 'Subsequent Agreements and Practice', 113, states that subsequent agreements regarding interpretation 'are not intended to create new obligations for the state'.

'extraneous' to issues of interpretation: the norm is not changed by interpretation, so there is no question as to its prospective or retroactive effect.[142] Determining thus whether it is interpretation or amendment that has taken place when States parties to a treaty purport to jointly interpret it with binding force may be crucial in terms of deciding whether the act produces legal effect 'retroactively' in a manner of speaking, thus affecting also disputes as to interpretation pending before a third-party instance, or whether it may also operate for the future.

Interpretation of a treaty by means of subsequent agreement (and practice) may take place by informal or formal means,[143] as stipulated by Article 31(3)(a) and (b). Particularly, a subsequent agreement under Article 31(3)(a) is not subject to any 'constitutional treaty-making procedure' of the States parties, as it is not intended to create new obligations for the parties.[144] On the contrary, amendments of treaty provisions have to follow the relevant procedure laid down by the treaty in question or by the default rules of Articles 39–41 of the VCLT, reflecting customary law. And, more importantly, an amendment could be made subject to the formal constitutional procedures necessary in each Contracting Party.[145]

The distinction between interpretation and amendment is notoriously difficult to draw in practice, as already stated earlier.[146] According to Special Rapporteur Nolte, there are no formal criteria to distinguish between interpretation and modification or amendment, apart from those that may be potentially provided for in the treaty in question.[147] However, the Kelsenian approach to interpretation explained in Section B helps us to understand the distinction conceptually. Interpretation is the determination of a range of possible meanings, the possible meanings that fall within the interpretative radius of a norm. These meanings are part of the norm as it exists, and the

142 Dopagne, 'Article 28: Convention of 1969', 719.

143 Nolte, 'Subsequent Agreements and Subsequent Practice in Relation to Treaty Interpretation', para. 67.

144 Hafner, 'Subsequent Agreements and Practice', 113.

145 See e.g. Article 2202 of the NAFTA; Hafner, 'Subsequent Agreements and Practice', 116; see further the discussions following the formal amendment of the Singapore-Australia FTA (13 October 2016), available at http://worldtradelaw.typepad.com/ielpblog/2016/10/the-tobacco-carveout-is-spreading.html and http://worldtradelaw.typepad.com/ielpblog/2016/10/does-a-tobacco-carveout-amendment-violate-investment-obligations.html (accessed 21 October 2016).

146 See text at n. 25; Second Report of Special Rapporteur Nolte, 'Subsequent Agreements and Subsequent Practice in Relation to the Interpretation of Treaties', UN Doc. A/CN.4/671 (26 March 2014), paras. 116, 163. According to Nolte (this note), para. 145 and n. 298, in judicial practice it is not even necessary to distinguish between interpretation and amendment in certain cases, as for example in the *Territorial Dispute* case, para. 60.

147 *Ibid.*, para. 163.

selection of one among them as controlling (the outcome of interpretation) is a political act. Amendment would consist in determining that the meaning of a norm is one that would not fit within the range of possible meanings, within the original interpretative radius that is, thereby essentially modifying that interpretative radius, that is, modifying the norm.[148] The examination of both jurisprudence and States practice has led Special Rapporteur Nolte to conclude that both States and international tribunals are inclined to allow States parties wide room for interpretation by means of subsequent agreement.[149] This is further affirmed by the ILC's Draft Conclusion 7(3), which establishes a presumption in favour of interpretation rather than amendment or modification.[150]

Thus, any selection of one among the possible meanings of a norm by States parties constitutes interpretation and not amendment, even if it restricts the range of possible interpretations, the interpretative radius. This joint interpretation is binding both for the parties and for any tribunals called upon to interpret the relevant norm. Moreover, this interpretation controls in a quasi-retroactive manner, therefore being applicable even in pending disputes.[151]

At any rate, the discussion is to some extent circular: even the determination of the range of plausible meanings is incapable of strictly differentiating between interpretation and amendment. Subsequent practice of parties with regard to interpretation may be 'modifying' or 'repealing practice',[152] for example, interpretation *contra legem*, going against the clear wording of the provision. In the context of international organisations, such subsequent practice has been considered as acceptable even though the proper processes for amendment have not been followed: Article 27(3) of the UN Charter serves as a standing reminder to that effect. The point is that flexibility is advised, and indeed wisely adopted by subsequent interpreters, when the masters of the treaty have spoken.

148 Wälde, 'Interpreting Investment Treaties', 765, talks about an 'interpretation [that], however authoritative, *stretches the text so much that it goes beyond the borders* of permissible interpretation' (emphasis added).

149 Nolte, 'Subsequent Agreements and Subsequent Practice in Relation to the Interpretation of Treaties', para. 163.

150 ILC, 'Subsequent Agreements and Subsequent Practice in Relation to the Interpretation of Treaties', text and titles of draft conclusions 6–10 provisionally adopted by the Drafting Committee on 27 and 28 May and on 2 and 3 June 2014, UN Doc. A/CN.4/L.833 (3 June 2014), Draft Conclusion 7(3).

151 *Chamizal*, 328, seems to imply that an agreement which authoritatively (even if indirectly) interprets a previous agreement would be retroactive by virtue of its object alone. Cf. Dopagne, 'Article 28: Convention of 1969', 727.

152 For the term, see J.-M. Sorel and V. Boré Eveno, 'Article 31: Convention of 1969', in Corten and Klein, *The Vienna Conventions on the Law of Treaties*, 804, 826.

(4) *Due Process*

One final objection evident in the reticence of tribunals in accepting joint interpretations canvassed in Section C is that of due-process concerns. When States parties 'intervene' to issue a joint interpretation of a particular provision whose interpretation and application are actually pending before an arbitral tribunal in a dispute between one of them and an investor, it could be argued that the State both party to the treaty and to the dispute is colluding with the other State party to the treaty in order to 'move the goalposts' as it were, to the detriment of the investor.

This objection can be dealt with rather briefly. First of all, it would be up to the State party that is not party to the dispute to protect the investor of its nationality in these circumstances.[153] If it does not, then that must mean something. More importantly, it must be reminded that, as explained in Section D(3), joint interpretation is distinct from amendment, in the sense that it does not 'move the goalposts' beyond the radius within which they could be moved anyway. Furthermore, this objection assumes that there is someone other than the States parties to the treaty (the investor? the tribunal?) who knows better than the masters of the treaty where precisely these goalposts are. But nobody else can presume to know exactly and authoritatively where these goalposts lie, precisely for the reasons explored in Sections B and D(1)–(3): the treaty is the States' treaty, they own it, and there are no 'inherent' rights of the investor that are somehow being infringed. The States parties grant and define these 'rights', and they may continue to define them more precisely as time goes by, not only reacting to, but also pre-empting, decisions of tribunals.[154] The investors, however, make use of an international treaty which grants them 'rights' or benefits: they subject themselves to an international legal regime whose contours they should be aware of and which allows the masters of the treaty to authentically interpret it with binding force, as even tribunals have warned them.[155]

E. Conclusion

The movement of States parties towards the reassertion of control over their investment treaties and, indirectly, investment arbitration demonstrates the

[153] See also V. Prislan, 'Non-Investment Obligations in Investment Treaty Arbitration: Towards a Greater Role for States?', in Baetens, *Investment Law within International Law*, 450, 479–80.

[154] Cf. Crawford, 'A Consensualist Interpretation of Article 31(3)', 31.

[155] See e.g. n. 67; *Sanum* v. *Laos*, para. 76.

undoubted dissatisfaction of States with the way in which their treaties have been interpreted by investment tribunals. Tribunals, for their part, would do well to take heed of such reactions. In terms of cost-benefit analysis much favoured by some of these tribunals, States are only going to continue participating in the system and abiding by the decisions of investment tribunals (or give them competence to decide at all) as long as the 'net profit' of such behaviour is higher than the 'net costs'.[156] States parties remain the masters of their treaties; tribunals may not be their puppets, but they should really not claim to be masters either. *Iznogoud* teaches that attempts to become Caliph in the Caliph's place rarely end in success.[157]

[156] See van Aaken, 'Delegating Interpretative Authority in Investment Treaties', 1; Roberts, 'Power and Persuasion in Investment Treaty Interpretation', 191–8.

[157] No pop (or indeed rock) references have been spared in the making of this chapter.

8

Systemic Integration

An Instrument for Reasserting the State's Control in Investment Arbitration?

RUMIANA YOTOVA*

A. Systemic Integration under General International Law

It is only in the last two decades that the so-called principle of systemic integration became the object of scholarly[1] and judicial debate.[2] This is unusual, given that the principle forms part of the general rule of interpretation set out in the 1969 Vienna Convention on the Law of Treaties (VCLT). Systemic integration is an integral and indeed obligatory part of the general rule on interpretation. The unity of the rule is underlined by the International Law Commission (ILC) Commentary on the provision highlighting that 'the provisions of the article form a single, closely integrated rule'.[3] Notably, the principle is different from paragraphs 1 and 2 of Article 31 in that it requires the taking into account of an element extrinsic both to the text and to the context of the treaty.[4] This is probably the reason why, unlike the other aspects of the

* The author extends special thanks to Andreas Kulick and Martins Paparinskis for their helpful comments on earlier drafts.

1 See e.g. P. Sands 'Treaty, Custom and the Cross-Fertilisation of International Law', *Yale Human Rights and Development Law* Journal 1 (1998), 85; C. McLachlan 'The Principle of Systemic Integration and Article 31(3)(c) of the Vienna Convention', *International and Comparative Law Quarterly*, 54 (2005), 279; 'Report of the Study Group of the International Law Commission on Fragmentation of International Law: Difficulties Arising from the Diversification and Expansion of International Law', *ILC Yearbook*, II(2) (2006).

2 See e.g. *Oil Platforms (Islamic Republic of Iran* v. *Unites States of America)*, Judgment, ICJ Reports 2003, 161; and *Iron Rhine Arbitration* (Belgium/Netherlands), PCA, Award of 24 May 2005.

3 'Report of the ILC on the Work of the Second Part of Its Seventeenth Session', *ILC Yearbook*, II (1966), 169, 220.

4 *Ibid.*

general rule of interpretation, it is not formulated as outcome determinative. According to the ILC Commentary, the wording of Article 31(3)(c) was intended to 'state only the broad principle and not attempt define its results'.[5] This stands in contrast with the formulae used in Article 31(1) and (2), respectively. This is due to the extrinsic elements in paragraph 3 underlying the intention to leave much broader scope for discretion to the interpreter, further reinforced by the generality of the reference to 'any relevant rules of international law', also left open for determination.

The precise meaning and scope of Article 31(3)(c) remain controversial. Scholars disagree on the criteria for assessing 'relevance' in this context. For instance, Linderfalk favours a broad interpretation where relevant are those rules which 'govern the state of affairs, in relation to which the interpreted treaty is examined'.[6] Villiger constructs relevance more narrowly, as a reference to rules which 'concern the subject-matter of the treaty term at issue'.[7] Gardiner takes the middle ground, arguing that relevance refers to rules 'touching on the same subject matter as the treaty provision or provisions being interpreted or which in any way affect that interpretation'.[8] Pauwelyn adopts a functional test where a rule is relevant if it 'sheds light on the meaning of the [treaty] term' under interpretation.[9] This approach is persuasive in linking relevance to the actual term of the treaty under interpretation, which is in line with the wording of the VCLT. The question of relevance is particularly pertinent in investment law, given the specialised subject matter of investment treaties and the frequent attempts of States to 'integrate' in them other special treaties, such as those relating to international human rights and environmental law.

Another area of disagreement relates to determining which rules are 'applicable between the parties'. Whereas a number of scholars seem to agree that 'parties' should be interpreted by reference to Article 2(1)(g) of

[5] Sir Humphrey Waldock, 'Third Report on the Law of Treaties', *ILC Yearbook*, II (1964), 5, 61.

[6] U. Linderfalk, *On the Interpretation of Treaties: The Modern International Law as Expressed in the 1969 Vienna Convention on the Law of Treaties* (Berlin: Springer, 2007), 178.

[7] M. Villiger, *Commentary on the 1969 Vienna Convention on the Law of Treaties* (Leiden, Netherlands: Brill, 2009), 433.

[8] R. Gardiner, *Treaty Interpretation* (Oxford University Press, 2008), 260.

[9] J. Pauwelyn, *Conflict of Norms in Public International Law* (Cambridge University Press, 2003), 263–4.

the VCLT, that is, the parties to the treaty being interpreted,[10] the ILC in its work on fragmentation seemed to prefer an interpretation referring to the parties to the dispute only.[11] Such an approach is difficult to align with the text of the VCLT. Pauwelyn advocates for an interpretation that is even more disjointed from Article 31(3)(c) and its context, where even if a rule is not in force between all parties to the treaty being interpreted or indeed to the dispute at hand, it could still be taken into account if it is 'at least *implicitly* accepted or tolerated by all' parties to the treaty.[12] The first interpretation, relating to the parties of the treaty, is preferable and most in line with the VCLT.

There is a general agreement that the Article 31(3)(c) reference to 'rules of international law' encompasses customary, treaty and conventional rules.[13] This interpretation is fully in line with the open-ended wording of the provision, referring to 'any' rule of international law and is, indeed, supported by practice. What is unclear, however, is whether the formula includes rules which do not form part of general international law but of specialised regimes within it.

The understanding of the function of the principle in Article 31(3)(c) evolved over time, which explains why its formulation as 'systemic integration' is relatively recent. The inception of the principle was informed by the rules of inter-temporal law. More recently, however, it became a key argument, if not a panacea, in the debate concerning the fragmentation of international law.[14] According to Sands, the principle underlines the 'unity of international law',[15] whereas McLachlan goes further in saying that systemic integration 'has the status of a constitutional norm',[16] a 'master key which enables [the interpreter], working at a very practical level, to contribute to the broader task of finding an

[10] Gardiner, *Treat Interpretation*, 263–5; Linderfalk, *On the Interpretation of Treaties*, 177. But see I. Sinclair, *The Vienna Convention on the Law of Treaties*, 2nd edn. (Manchester University Press, 1984), 178.

[11] 'ILC Report on Fragmentation', 238–9, para. 472.

[12] Pauwelyn, *Conflict of Norms*, 260–1.

[13] Villiger, *Commentary on the 1969 Vienna Convention*, 432. See also Linderfalk, On the Interpretation of Treaties, 177; Pauwelyn, *Conflict of Norms*, 254–5; C. McLachlan, 'The Principle of Systemic Integration and Article 31(3)(c) of the Vienna Convention', *ICLQ*, 54 (2005) 279, 290. But see I. Sinclair, *The Vienna Convention*, 119, not including general principles.

[14] See 'ILC Report on Fragmentation', 206–44. See also Sands, 'Treaty, Custom and the Cross-Fertilisation of International Law', 8; and McLachlan, 'The Principle of Systemic Integration', 280–4.

[15] Sands, 'Treaty, Custom and the Cross-Fertilisation of International Law', 8.

[16] McLachlan, 'The Principle of Systemic Integration', 280–1.

appropriate accommodation between conflicting values and interests in international society'.[17]

While Article 31(3)(c) is an important and integral part of the process of treaty interpretation, it is difficult to accord it a meta-status given the considerable discretion it gives to the interpreter both with respect to the weight to be given to the other rules of international law and to their consequences for the outcome of the interpretation. The inherent limitations in the wording of Article 31(3)(c) should be duly observed, namely, that it has as its object the *interpretation* of the *terms* of international treaties, not their modification nor the *application* of other rules of international law, let alone values, that are in conflict with those terms. In practice, States have often tried to use systemic integration in their litigation strategies as a tool with the extraordinary power to trump the express terms of a bilateral investment treaty and transform it into a treaty with an entirely different object. In such cases, systemic integration has proven to be the wrong tool for reasserting the State's control in investment arbitration. Indeed, the most effective way to use systemic integration as a tool for reasserting control is in the process of drafting economic treaties by reference to other rules that the parties consider relevant.

(1) The Vienna Convention on the Law of Treaties and Its Preparatory Works

Precursors of codifying the principle underlying Article 31(3)(c) could be traced back before the VCLT. For instance, the 1935 Harvard Draft Convention on the Law of Treaties in its Article 19 provided that 'the conditions prevailing at the time interpretation is being made are to be considered in connection with the general purpose which the treaty is intended to serve.'[18] According to the Comment, 'the interpreter must consider the effect which his interpretation will produce under current conditions and decide if that effect will be harmonious with the purpose behind the treaty.'[19] This version of the principle is an expression of one of the aspects of inter-temporal law, giving broader discretion to the interpreter compared to the VCLT to consider new developments with reference to the object and purpose of the treaty rather than merely its terms. The object and purpose of the treaty under interpretation, however, are emphatically construed as limitations that cannot be trumped.

[17] *Ibid.*, 318–19. [18] 29 (1935) *AJIL* Supp. 937. [19] *Ibid.*, 970.

Later, in 1956, the Institut de Droit International codified the principle of inter-temporal law, construing it more narrowly by reference to the terms and provisions of the treaty and their interpretation in light of the principles of international law.[20] The preparatory works of Article 31(3)(c) shed light on the meaning and purpose of the provision, as well as on its development. They indicate that the so-called principle of systemic integration is essentially an expression of the principle of inter-temporal law, be it with systemic implications. The rule was included in the ILC draft Convention on the Law of Treaties by the last Special Rapporteur Sir Humphrey Waldock. Draft Article 56 provided that

> 1. A treaty is to be *interpreted* in light of the law in force at the time when the treaty was drawn up.
> 2. Subject to paragraph 1, *the application* of a treaty shall be governed by the rules of international law in force at the time when the treaty is applied.[21]

According to the Commentary, the purpose of the provision was to codify the famous dictum of arbitrator Huber in the *Island of Palmas* arbitration concerning inter-temporal law.[22] Notably, the Rapporteur drew a distinction between the interpretation and the application of treaties, acknowledging that inter-temporal law is 'a rule for the interpretation as much as for the *application* of treaties'.[23] Waldock stressed that 'the *application* of a treaty must, at any given time, take account of the general rules of international law in force at that time', noting that this 'completes and limits the rule' of treaty interpretation in light of the law in force at the time of its conclusion.[24] The Commentary affirmed the ILC understanding that 'the first branch of the inter-temporal law clearly concerns the interpretation of treaties', whereas 'the second can be regarded either as a question of ... the application of the rules of international law to it.'[25]

Following the ILC plenary discussions, the draft provisions concerning inter-temporal law were reduced to one reproducing the general rule of interpretation and omitting the aspect of the rule concerning the application of treaties.[26] The Commentary, however, clarified that this aspect was still implicit in the remaining provisions. Indeed, most ILC members thought that 'the effect of changes in the law upon a treaty is rather

[20] Article 1(1), 'Interpretation des traités, IDI', Session de Grenade 1956.
[21] Waldock, 'Third Report on the Law of Treaties', 5, 9 (emphasis added). [22] *Ibid.*
[23] *Ibid.* (emphasis in original). [24] *Ibid.* (emphasis in original). [25] *Ibid.*, 61.
[26] 'Report of the ILC on the Work of Its Sixteenth Session', 173, 198.

a question of application of the new law to the treaty – a question of modification of the rule laid down in the treaty by a later legal rule rather than one of the interpretation of the terms.'[27] The general rule of interpretation was re-formulated once again in 1966, when it took its current form.[28] The commentary stressed that interpretation depended on the intention of the parties and the principle of good faith.[29]

Based on the preparatory works of Article 31(3)(c), it can be concluded that the underlying principle, now commonly referred to as 'systemic integration', is an expression of the two aspects of inter-temporal law relating both to the interpretation and to the application of treaties by reference to the changes in the system of international law, even if only the former aspect was codified in the end. The latter was implicit in the current provision and governed by the principle of good faith, with due consideration of the intention of the parties. As will be seen in the next section, this dual character of systemic integration is also reflected in case law and has important practical consequences, particularly in investment arbitration.

The ILC revisited Article 31(3)(c) VCLT in its 'Report on Fragmentation [of International Law]'.[30] In this study, the ILC no longer referred to the provision as one of inter-temporal law but rather under the heading 'harmonisation – systemic integration', indicating the shift of emphasis in the understanding of the rule. According to the ILC Study Group, the 'systematic nature of international law has received clearest formal expression in that article'.[31] This is not wrong but surprising in that it completely omits the dynamic temporal aspect which motivated the codification of the rule in the first place. The ILC confirmed the dual character of the principle, noting that 'the *interpretation* and *application* of a treaty takes always place by reference to other rules of international law.'[32]

The report purported to draw another important distinction with respect to systemic integration, observing that the principle manifested into two presumptions:

(a) According to the *positive presumption*, parties are taken 'to refer to general principles of international law for all questions which [the

[27] *Ibid.*, 282–3.

[28] 'Report of the ILC on the Work of the Second Part of Its Seventeenth Session', *ILC Yearbook*, II (1969), 169, 181.

[29] *Ibid.*, 169, 222. [30] 'ILC Report on Fragmentation'. [31] *Ibid.*, 211.

[32] *Ibid.*, 218 (emphasis added).

treaty] does not itself resolve in express terms or in a different way' (*Georges Pinson* case[33]);

(b) According to the negative presumption, in entering into treaty obligations, the parties intend not to act inconsistently with generally recognised principles of international law or with previous treaty obligations towards third States (*Right of Passage over Indian Territory*[34]).[35]

While the negative presumption is a straightforward expression of the principle of systemic integration, the positive one seems to go well beyond the wording of Article 31(3)(c) and indeed the intentions of the drafters. The falling back on rules of general international law for matters not governed by the treaty itself, such as the rules on State responsibility or on treaty interpretation, is hardly a question of interpretation of the treaty but rather one of applying the corpus of general international law for matters not expressly regulated by it. Pauwelyn stresses the difference between the 'interpretation with reference to other law versus *application* of law together with other law', stressing that 'for all issues not explicitly regulated by the treaty, pre-existing norms of international law continue to apply and a "fallback" to, especially general international law is required.'[36]

The ILC itself seemed to be conscious of this distinction when pointing out that '[b]y their very nature, customary law and general principles of law (and general principles of *international law*) exist as *lex generalis* in relation to any particular agreements. They are *fully applicable* and *often applied* alongside particular treaties.'[37] While this statement is unobjectionable, it is hardly regulated by the VCLT, let alone by its rules on the *interpretation* of treaties.

The narrow construction of systemic integration limited to the negative presumption is preferable and in accordance with the wording of the VCLT, which clearly refers to the interpretation of the terms of the treaty by taking into account other relevant rules of international law, rather than to the application of extraneous rules in the absence of any terms to that effect in the treaty. Accordingly, when this study refers to systemic

[33] *Georges Pinson (France)* v. *United Mexican States*, Award of 13 April 1928, UNRIAA, Vol. V, 422.

[34] *Case Concerning the Right of Passage over Indian Territory (Portugal* v. *India)*, Preliminary Objections, ICJ Report of 1957, 142.

[35] *Ibid.*, 234. See also McLachlan, 'The Principle of Systemic Integration', 311.

[36] Pauwelyn, *Conflict of Norms*, 201 (emphasis in the original); see further *ibid.*, 202–5 and 273–4.

[37] 'ILC Report on Fragmentation', 233 (emphasis added).

integration, it will not discuss the application of general international law by way of fallback.

Finally, it should be noted that the border between interpretation and application is a fine and often elusive line. This is not helped by the fact that the two terms are often used interchangeably or together, that is, in the jurisdictional clauses of numerous investment treaties. According to the *Oxford Dictionary*, 'interpretation' is 'the action of explaining the meaning of something',[38] whereas 'application' is 'the action of putting something in operation'.[39] As cautioned by McNair, 'the words "interpret" [and] "interpretation" are often used loosely as if they included "apply" [and] "application"'.[40] The Harvard Draft Convention on the Law of Treaties draws a clear distinction between the two processes too:

> Interpretation is the process of determining the meaning of a text; application is the process of determining the consequences which, according to the text, should follow in a given situation.[41]

The difference between interpretation and application in the context of systemic integration is even more difficult to draw, particularly in the practice of international courts and tribunals. At what point does the interpreter stop extrapolating meaning and start applying other rules of international law? And in the context of investment law, where could the authority to apply other rules of international law to a non-State actor, the investor, come from in the absence of treaty language to this effect? As cautioned by Kammerhofer, 'The techniques of systemic integration cannot produce their intended result if they are understood as interpretation.'[42] One might add that they are often application and, at times, modification.

(2) Systemic Integration before the International Court of Justice: Oil Platforms *Revisited*

The most notable example of systemic integration in the case law of the International Court of Justice (ICJ) is the *Oil Platforms* case.[43] The basis

[38] *Oxford Dictionary* online, available at www.oxforddictionaries.com/definition/english/interpretation (accessed 29 February 2016).

[39] *Ibid.*

[40] A. McNair, *The Law of Treaties*, 2nd edn. (Oxford University Press, 1961), 365.

[41] Harvard Draft Convention on the Law of Treaties, Comment to Article 19, 'Interpretation of Treaties', 938–9.

[42] J. Kammerhofer, 'Systemic Integration, Legal Theory and the ILC', *SSRN* (2009), 9–10.

[43] *Oil Platforms (Islamic Republic of Iran* v. *United States of America)*, 161.

of the ICJ's jurisdiction was the Iran-US Treaty of Amity, Economic Relations and Consular Rights, an economic treaty precursor of modern investment treaties. Iran asked the court to determine whether the US attacks against its oil platforms constituted a breach of the freedom of commerce and navigation. The United States relied on the non-precluded measures (NPM) clause,[44] allowing the adoption of measures 'necessary to protect its essential security interests', to claim that it acted in self-defence. The ICJ interpreted the NPM provision by reference to Article 31(3)(c) of the VCLT so as to include in its consideration the law on the use of force.

The methodology used by the ICJ is instructive. It began its analysis by reference to the limits of the jurisdictional clause of the Treaty of Amity.[45] The Court noted the disagreement between the parties as to the relationship between the law on the use of force and the NPM clause, in particular, the US argument that the Court's jurisdiction does not extend to the determination of the legality of its actions under general international law.[46] The Court dismissed it, constructing the question as 'one of interpretation of the Treaty'.[47]

It interpreted the NPM clause with reference to Article 31(3)(c) of the VCLT, holding that

> The Court cannot accept that Article XX, paragraph 1(d), of the 1955 Treaty was intended to operate wholly independently of the relevant rules of international law on the use of force, so as to be capable of being successfully invoked, even in the limited context of a claim for breach of the Treaty, in relation to an unlawful use of force. The *application* of the relevant rules of international law relating to this question thus forms an integral part of the task of *interpretation* entrusted to the Court by Article XXI, paragraph 2, of the 1955 Treaty.[48]

The first sentence of this paragraph is a classic example of systemic integration in the interpretation of a treaty clause. The second sentence, however, constructs the ICJ's task more broadly – as one of systemic integration in the application of the treaty. The ICJ went beyond interpreting the limits of the NPM clause by reference to legality under the law on use of force and into determining the consequences of the clause by applying extraneous rules of international law. The ICJ justified this by

[44] On NPM, see W. Burke-White and A. von Staden, 'Investment Protection in Extraordinary Times: The Interpretation and Application of Non-Precluded Measures Provisions in Bilateral Investment Treaties' *Virginia Journal of International Law*, 48 (2008), 307.

[45] *Oil Platforms*, 178, para. 31. [46] *Ibid.*, 181, para. 39. [47] *Ibid.*, 181, para. 40.

[48] *Ibid* (emphasis added).

reference to the broad jurisdictional clause of the Treaty of Amity, allowing 'the determination whether action alleged to be justified under that paragraph was or was not an unlawful use of force, by reference to international law applicable to this question'.[49]

After defining its task as one of applying the treaty to the facts of the case, the ICJ went on to apply the criteria of armed attack, necessity and proportionality as conditions for the exercise of the right to self-defence, in great length, to the facts at hand.[50] It anchored its application of the law on the use of force in the NPM clause reference to measures 'necessary' to protect essential security interests. After concluding that US actions in the circumstances did not constitute lawful use of force under international law, the Court drew as a consequence that they 'did not fall within the category of measures contemplated, upon its correct interpretation, by that provision of the Treaty'.[51] The Court was justified in stopping its analysis of the consequences at the level of the NPM clause and not going into the realm of the US State responsibility under general international law, which would have transgressed the limits of its jurisdiction and amounted to applying the law on the use of force in addition to, if not instead of, the treaty.

Some of the separate opinions of the judges draw attention to the controversial aspects of the Court's liberal approach to systemic integration. These judges express discomfort with the Court construing relevance too broadly, as well as going beyond the act of interpretation and engaging in systemic integration when applying the treaty.[52] This is understandable given that systemic integration of this type is not expressly included in the VCLT, but as seen from the preparatory works and subsequent developments, it is arguable that it is part of customary international law that could be reasonably implied in the provision. The criticism that the Court did not engage in enough treaty interpretation is justified, given the limited scope of its jurisdiction and the length at which it discussed and applied the law on the use of force. As to the application of the law on the use of force, the Court did limit its consideration to the effects it had on the application of the treaty. Judge Simma, however, criticised the Court for not going far enough in drawing the consequences under general international law from the US violation of the prohibition of the use of force.[53] With respect to systemic integration, Judge Simma construed relevance broadly, noting

[49] *Ibid.*, 182–3, paras. 41–2. [50] *Ibid.*, 184–99. [51] *Ibid.*, 199, para. 78.

[52] See e.g. Separate Opinion of Judge Higgins, 237, paras. 46–8; Separate Opinion Judge Buergenthal, 279, paras. 22, 29, 282.

[53] Separate Opinion of Judge Simma, 327–9.

> The Court … thus accepts, and rightly so, the principle according to which the provisions of any treaty have to be interpreted and applied in the light of the treaty law applicable between the parties as well as of the rules of general international law 'surrounding' the treaty. If these general rules of international law are of a peremptory nature, as they undeniably are in our case, then the principle of interpretation just mentioned turns into a legally insurmountable limit to permissible treaty interpretation.[54]

Judge Simma's comment could play a role in investment arbitration as an instrument for reasserting the control of the State. It is conceivable to interpret the Court's approach as one of applying the peremptory prohibition against the use of force as a condition or limit to the legality of the US acts.

Other instances where the ICJ engaged in systemic integration include the *Namibia* advisory opinion[55] the *Aegean Sea Continental Shelf*[56] and the *Mutual Assistance in Criminal Matters*[57] cases. In *Questions of Mutual Assistance*, while accepting that the Treaty of Friendship 'does have a certain bearing on the interpretation and application of the Convention on Mutual Assistance in Criminal Matters', the Court stressed that it 'cannot possibly stand in the way of a party to that Convention relying on a clause contained in it which allows for non-performance of a conventional obligation under certain circumstances.'[58] This approach is instructive in showing that the successful invocation of systemic integration is not a guarantee that the State will succeed in its argument based on extraneous rules. There is still a considerable degree of discretion left to the tribunal in deciding upon the relevance and corresponding weight to be given to the extraneous rules, informed by the wording of the treaty being interpreted and by the facts of the case. The intentions of the parties are even more pertinent where the main treaty conferring jurisdiction is a bilateral one, potentially underlined by the intention of the parties to opt out of certain relevant rules of international law in their mutual relations.

In conclusion, the case law of the ICJ supports the proposition that systemic integration is a principle older and broader than what is set out in

[54] *Ibid.*, 330, para. 9.

[55] *Legal Consequences for States of the Continued Presence of South Africa in Namibia (South West Africa) notwithstanding Security Council Resolution 276 (1970)*, ICJ Reports 1971, Advisory Opinion, 16, 31, paras. 52–3.

[56] *Aegean Sea Continental Shelf (Greece* v. *Turkey)*, ICJ Reports 1978, 3, 34, para. 80.

[57] *Certain Questions of Mutual Assistance in Criminal Matters (Djibouti* v. *France)*, ICJ Reports 2008, 177.

[58] *Ibid.*, 219, para. 114.

Article 31(3)(c) of the VCLT as it plays a role not only in the interpretation, but often more crucially, in the dynamic application of treaties – in light of the relevant changes in the law that have occurred after their conclusion. It is in the latter instance where the principle ought to be used with caution to avoid substituting the applicable treaty with other rules of international law. The line between the two acts seems to be defined by the principle of good faith in interpretation with due consideration of the intentions of the parties. Another important lesson is that the criteria of relevance have been construed broadly, not necessarily limited to the subject matter of the treaty or its terms, the most notable example being the *Oil Platforms* case. There seems to be a correlation between the relevance of the extraneous rules and the weight given to them by the interpreter. Notably, in all cases, the consequences of applying systemic integration were strictly limited to those of the interpreted treaty and did not result in findings of violations of the other rules of international law. Where relevant, the principles of the UN Charter and peremptory norms of international law can be construed as an obligatory part of systemic integration, enabling the Court to fulfil its judicial function. Last but not least, the case law of the ICJ indicates that while systemic integration has the potential to be a tool for asserting the control of the State by playing an outcome-determinative role in international dispute settlement, its use and weight are very much dependent on the wording of the main treaty and the degree of relevance of the extraneous rules.

B. Systemic Integration and Investment Treaties

While the broad construction of Article 31(3)(c) with respect to both the interpretation and the application of treaties seems to be increasingly accepted in international law, particularly after its use by the ICJ in the *Oil Platforms* case, the specific character of investment law calls for a more nuanced, if not cautious, approach. States invoke systemic integration as a strategic tool to assert their position and control in international dispute settlement with increasing regularity and some success.[59] The same is not true, however, for investment arbitration, where tribunals have shown caution, if not scepticism, with respect to the attempts of States to invoke systemic integration as an instrument to reassert control.

[59] See e.g. *Iron Rhine Arbitration (Belgium* v. *the Netherlands)*, PCA, Award of 24 May 2005, paras. 58 – 60, 220–23; *OSPAR Arbitration (Ireland* v. *UK)*, PCA, Award of 2 July 2003, paras. 83–6, 101–5. See also *Al Adsani* v. *UK*, ECtHR, Application No. 35763/97, Judgment of 21 November 2001.

This is not because systemic integration is unsuitable as a principle for the interpretation of investment treaties, but rather because there are significant limits to its use. On the one side, this is due to the character of the investor being a non-State actor to whom extraneous rules of international law cannot properly be applied. So, while systemic integration can be used as a tool in interpretation of the investment treaty, there are conceptual objections to *applying* other rules of international law, such as environmental or human rights principles, to impose direct obligations or assess the behaviour of the non-State actor. Investors are not subjects of international law, and accordingly, they do not qualify as 'parties' to which 'other relevant rules of international law' can be applied. As acknowledged by Ruggie, UN Special Representative on the Issue of Human Rights and Transnational Corporations, '[W]ith the possible exception of certain war crimes and crimes against humanity, there are no generally accepted international legal principles that [directly bind corporations].'[60] The second reason is the fact that most investment tribunals derive their authority from specialised bilateral investment treaties (BITs) with narrow economic object and purpose. This imposes limits with respect to both their jurisdiction to use systemic integration in the application of the treaty and also the criteria of relevance and the assessment as to whether or not the parties to the treaty chose to opt out from other relevant rules of international law. This crucial consideration in using systemic integration in the interpretation of investment treaties was highlighted by the Tribunal in *AAPL* v. *Sri Lanka*:

> The construction of the Treaty's comprehensive system governing all aspects related to the extent of the special protection conferred upon the investors in question would permit the evaluation of the Treaty's effective contribution in this respect; i.e. in view of determining with regard to each issue whether the Sri Lanka/UK Treaty intended, merely, to consolidate the pre-existing rules of international law, or, on the contrary, it tended to innovate.[61]

While international law is typically not applicable for assessing the legality of the acts of the investor and does not easily fit through the narrow jurisdictional clauses of some investment treaties, systemic integration can still be a valuable tool for assessing the acts and obligations of

[60] J. Ruggie, 'Interim Report of the Special Representative of the Secretary-General on the Issue of Human Rights and Transnational Corporations and Other Business Enterprises' (2006), para. 60.

[61] *AAPL* v. *Sri Lanka*, ICSID Case No. ARB/87/3, Final Award of 27 June 1990, para. 42.

the host State. For example, systemic integration has been invoked successfully to demonstrate the proper motivation and legitimacy of measures adopted by the host State and challenged by the investor. As observed by Crema, '[T]he most successful vehicle for [investment] tribunals to consider [extraneous rules] and concerns has been the re-affirmation of a domestic sphere of autonomy in which states are free to introduce reasonable new regulations of general public interest, without the need to compensate foreign investors.'[62] State sovereignty and the correlative right to regulate under international law can and should be taken into account[63] by way of systemic integration to accord a degree of deference when interpreting the obligations of States under investment treaties. Their invocation is a suitable tool for reasserting the State's control in investment law and arbitration. A second example of successful invocation of the principle is in the interpretation of what constitutes a protected 'investment' under BITs with reference to its legality not only under the law of the host State but also under general international law.

Systemic integration, being an integral obligatory part of the general rule of treaty interpretation, does not need an explicit legal basis to be applied to investment treaties. However, certain provisions typically found in investment treaties can be of assistance in deciding whether and what rules could be taken into account as being relevant. Certain references to such rules in the BIT could indicate that the parties intended them to complement their agreement rather than to modify them inter se. Examples of such provisions include preambular paragraphs, applicable law clauses, jurisdictional clauses and any other provisions which refer expressly or implicitly to other rules of international law. There is an identifiable trend in the latest generation of BITs to refer to other bodies of international law, providing an express basis for their systemic integration. According to the 2015 United Nations Conference on Trade and Development (UNCTAD) World Investment Report, the majority of investment treaties concluded in 2014 contained clauses

[62] L. Crema, 'Investor Rights and Well-Being: Remarks on the Interpretation of Investment Treaties in Light of Other Rules', in T. Treves, F. Seatzu and S. Trevisanut (eds.), *Foreign Investment, International Law and Common Concerns* (London: Routledge, 2013), 68. See also A. Roberts, 'State-to-State Investment Treaty Arbitration: A Hybrid Theory of Interdependent Rights and Shared Interpretative Authority', *Harvard International Law Journal*, 55 (2014), 1, 21.

[63] See e.g V. Lowe, 'Regulation or Expropriation' *Current Legal Problems*, 55 (2002), 447, 450; and J. Viñuales, 'Sovereignty in Foreign Investment Law', in Z. Douglas, J. Pauwelyn and J. Viñuales (eds.), *The Foundations of International Investment Law: Bringing Theory into Practice* (Oxford University Press, 2014), 317.

referring to the protection of health, safety, the environment and sustainable development.[64] Such types of provisions reaffirm State sovereignty and the wide discretion in regulating matters in the public interest but also, more importantly, the relevance of international rules in these areas in the interpretation of the BIT.

As observed by commentators, the BIT preamble constitutes 'a statement of motives, objectives and circumstances through which a treaty can be seen in its proper perspective'.[65] There are a few typical references to general international law in BIT preambles. These include references to international peace,[66] the respect for internationally recognised workers' rights,[67] the respect for principles of international law,[68] the maintenance of environmental measures of general application,[69] the principle of sustainable development,[70] the principle of non-discrimination[71] and the prohibition against corruption.[72]

References to environmental law are starting to appear in the substantive provisions of the latest generations of BITs and are subject to varying formulations.[73] The Energy Charter Treaty (ECT), for instance, sets out a very detailed provision on its environmental aspects, including the 'pursuit of sustainable development', the 'polluter pays' principle and the 'international agreements concerning the environment' binding on its States Parties.[74] Notably, the new EU investment agreements contain stronger guarantees of the right to regulate public policy objectives, including the protection of the environment.[75] The EU–Vietnam Free Trade Agreement (FTA) is probably the most ambitious and far reaching in integrating environmental and other extraneous considerations in an

[64] 'UNCTAD World Investment Report 2015', available at http://unctad.org/en/PublicationsLibrary/wir2015_en.pdf (accessed 25 September 2016), 112.

[65] R. Dolzer and M. Stevens, *Bilateral Investment Treaties* (The Hague, Netherlands: Martinus Nijhoff, 1995), 20.

[66] See e.g. 1986 USA–Egypt BIT, preambular paragraph 2; 1994 ECT, preambular paragraph 13.

[67] 1992 USA–Bulgaria BIT, preambular paragraph 5; 2012 USA Model BIT, preambular para. 6; 2004 Dominican Republic–Central America–US FTA, preambular para. 14.

[68] 1992 Belgo–Luxembourg Union–Argentina BIT, para. 3.

[69] 2010 Switzerland–Egypt BIT, para. 5; 2012 Japan, Korea and China Investment Agreement, para. 5.

[70] 2004 Canada–China BIT, para. 2. See also 2004 CAFTA-DR, para. 17.

[71] Burundi Model BIT, para. 4.

[72] 2007 Norway Model BIT, para. 11.

[73] See also Chapter 10.

[74] Article 19(1) of the ECT.

[75] See e.g. 2014 Canada-EU Comprehensive Economic and Trade Agreement (CETA), Preamble, paras. 5, 10, Article 8.4(2) and Annex 8-A(3); 2015 EU–Singapore FTA, Preamble, para. 4, Article 9.3(3)(a) and (c), Annex 9-A.

investment treaty so far, as well as in affirming the right of the State to regulate.[76] Such provisions can be used by States to bring in extraneous standards as relevant applicable rules when assessing their measures challenged by the investor, as well as to rely on their right to regulate under customary international law.

The latest US Model BIT sets out progressive and detailed provisions on investment and labour, reaffirming 'the respective obligations as members of the International Labor Organization'.[77] It refers expressly to the freedom of association, the effective recognition of the right to collective bargaining, the elimination of all forms of forced or compulsory labour, the effective abolition of child labour and the prohibition of the worst forms of child labour and the elimination of discrimination in respect of employment.[78] This clause not only provides a clear basis for the systemic integration of international labour law in interpreting the treaty but also contains an express *renvoi* to the law of the ILO as a source of such relevant rules.

Virtually all BITs refer to international law in their applicable law clauses.[79] So does Article 42(1) of the ICSID Convention, applicable in the absence of law chosen by the parties. While these clauses apply to the settlement of investment disputes and could not be used to extend the jurisdiction of the tribunal to international law in general, they do confirm the power of arbitral tribunals to interpret investment treaties with reference to international law by virtue of Article 31(3)(c) of the VCLT, as affirmed by the ICJ in the *Oil Platforms* case. Also in line with this case, the limits of the applicability of systemic integration in investment arbitration are influenced by the jurisdictional clause of the investment treaty. The broader the clause, the more discretion the tribunal has to determine that other rules of international law are relevant to its interpretation.

C. Systemic Integration in Investment Arbitration

The opinions of scholars as to the role of systemic integration in investment arbitration are polarised. On the one side, there are the critics who deny that the principle can play any meaningful role in this context, and

[76] 2015 EU–Vietnam FTA, Article 1(2); 13*bis*(2), Annex Expropriation, para. 3.

[77] Article 13(1) of the 2012 US Model BIT. [78] *Ibid.*, Article 13(3).

[79] 2012 US Model BIT, Article 30(1); 2007 Norway Model BIT, Article 14; Benin Model BIT, Article 9(4); 2002 Austria Model BIT, Article 16(2); 2003 China Model BIT, Article 9(7); ASEAN Comprehensive Investment Agreement, Article 40(1); 1991 Germany–Argentina BIT; 1992 BeLux–Argentina BIT, Articles 12(7) and 10(5); ECT, Article 26(6) et al.

on the other side, there are the optimists who see it as the tool for harmonising investment law with all other areas of international law, including the protection of human rights and the environment.

In the first category, Weeramantry opines that the use of Article 31(3)(c) in investment arbitration has been relatively rare as 'it may be seen to be deploying a rule in a manner that displaces the applicable law.'[80] Desierto cautions in a similar vein that systemic integration inherently licenses overly expansive treaty interpretation by reference to other areas of law.[81] According to Kalderimis, the principle 'must remain, at least in the investment context, an elegant theory which does not, and probably cannot, have a demonstrable effect on practical outcomes' due to the 'risk of muddle'.[82] Paparinskis adopts a more moderate cautionary approach, reasoning that 'an overly enthusiastic integrative argument could result in reintroduction of certain considerations as a matter of interpretation that were excluded as a matter of law-making.'[83]

Among the proponents for a greater role of systemic integration in investment arbitration is Simma, who advocates that extraneous rules, such as human rights, can inform the interpretation of investment treaty clauses concerning expropriation, in particular, 'elements like "public purpose", "non-discrimination" and "just compensation" in lawful regulatory takings'.[84] Crema views the role of systemic integration 'in understanding the legitimacy and reasonableness of a domestic measure implementing human and environmental rights.'[85] Viñuales and Dupuy opine in a similar vein that 'the arbitrators may have to give due consideration to an argument based on the State's obligations' under other areas of international law, such as human rights.[86] This chapter

[80] J. R. Weeramantry, *Treaty Interpretation in Investment Arbitration* (Oxford University Press, 2012), para. 3.149.

[81] D. Desierto, *Necessity and National Emergency Clauses* (The Hague, Netherlands: Martinus Nijhoff, 2012), 230–1, 351.

[82] D. Kalderimis, 'Systemic Integration and International Investment Law: Some Practical Reflections', *SIEL Online Proceedings*, Working Paper No. 2012/46, 2012, 7.

[83] M. Paparinskis, 'Investment Protection Law and Systemic Integration of Treaty and Custom', *SIEL Online Proceedings*, Working Paper No. 2010/21, 2010, 6. See also M. Paparinskis, 'Come Together or Do It My Way: No Systemic Preference', *ASIL Proc.*, 108 (2014), 246.

[84] B. Simma, 'Foreign Investment Arbitration: A Place for Human Rights?', *International and Comparative Law Quarterly*, 60 (2011), 573, 589.

[85] Crema, 'Investor Rights and Well-Being', 70.

[86] P. M. Dupuy and J. Viñuales, 'Human Rights and Investment Disciplines: Integration in Progress', in M. Bungenberg et al. (eds.), *International Investment Law* (Oxford, UK: Hart, 2012).

adopts a moderately optimistic approach to the role of systemic integration as an instrument for reasserting the control of the State in investment arbitration with respect to two categories of cases, which will be discussed in the next section.

(1) Cases Where Systemic Integration Was Successfully Invoked as an Instrument to Reassert the Control of the State

There are three classes of cases where systemic integration has been used as an effective tool of litigation strategy for reasserting the State's control. The first category includes instances where States have relied on the terms of the treaty to invoke the rules of customary international law that define these terms. The use of systemic integration in this category of cases comes very close to applying extraneous rules alongside the investment treaty for matters not expressly regulated by it and could go well beyond the principle incorporated in Article 31(3)(c) of the VCLT. Accordingly, it is doubtful whether they are an example of the use of systemic integration. The second, relatively narrow category of cases involves evaluating the legality of the investment by taking into account general principles of international law. This type of systemic integration has significant consequences as it could disqualify the investment from any protection under the BIT. Understandably, in practice, there are not many investments made in serious violation of international law. The third category of cases involves the use of extraneous rules of international law as relevant rules justifying the measures adopted by the State. This type of systemic integration has the potential to be the most powerful tool for reasserting the State's control in investment arbitration. However, there is significant variation in the case law in this category, both with respect to whether or not other rules of international law could be at all relevant in assessing the acts of the State and also with respect to how much weight they are to be given.

Turning to the first category of cases, *Saluka* v. *Czech Republic* is an example where systemic integration was invoked successfully as an instrument for reasserting the State's control in an investment context by bringing in customary international law. The dispute arose in connection with the reorganisation and privatisation of the Czech banking sector. The host State adopted measures to assist some of its banks, excluding the investor,[87] which was challenged as being in violation of

[87] *Saluka Investments BV* v. *Czech Republic*, UNCITRAL, PCA Case, Partial Award of 17 March 2006, para. 82.

the BIT.[88] The Tribunal interpreted the expropriation clause of the treaty and in particular the term 'deprivation' by relying on systemic integration to apply the customary international law on the State's right to exercise its regulatory powers for the maintenance of public order:

> It is now established in international law that States are not liable to pay compensation to a foreign investor when, in the normal exercise of their regulatory powers, they adopt in a non-discriminatory manner bona fide regulations that are aimed at the general welfare.[89]

The Tribunal applied the so-identified exception in an outcome-determinative way to conclude that the 'CNB's decision is . . . a lawful and permissible regulatory action by the Czech Republic aimed at the general welfare of the State.'[90]

This holding should be understood as an example of applying other rules of international law alongside the treaty by way of fallback for matters not expressly regulated by it. If seen from the prism of systemic integration, however, this approach hardly relates to the *interpretation* of the treaty.

Another case where systemic integration was invoked to import the customary rules on the State's exercise of its police powers, causing non-compensable economic damage, is *Tecmed.*[91] Notably, however, in this case the rules were not weighed as outcome determinative given the wording of Mexico–Spain BIT and the facts:[92]

> After reading Article 5(1) of the Agreement and interpreting its terms according to the ordinary meaning to be given to them (Article 31(1) of the Vienna Convention), we find no principle stating that regulatory administrative actions are per se excluded from the scope of the Agreement, even if they are beneficial to society as a whole – such as environmental protection – particularly if the negative economic impact of such actions on the financial position of the investor is sufficient to neutralize in full the value, or economic or commercial use of its investment without receiving any compensation whatsoever.[93]

This use of systemic integration is more faithful to Article 31(3)(c) and the intentions of the parties to the BIT. Notably, the conclusion reached was opposite to the one in *Saluka* with respect to the applicability of a customary exception for regulatory acts in the absence of treaty

[88] *Ibid.*, para. 164. [89] *Ibid.*, paras. 254 and 255. [90] *Ibid.*, para. 275.

[91] *Técnicas Medioambientales Tecmed, S.A.* v. *United Mexican States*, ICSID Case No. ARB (AF)/00/2, Award of 29 May 2003, para. 119.

[92] *Ibid.*, para. 151. [93] *Ibid.*, para. 121.

language to this effect. However, the main reason for that was the underlying disagreement about the customary rules on regulatory expropriation rather than the understanding of systemic integration.

The second line of case law illustrating the successful invocation of systemic integration as a way to reassert the control of the State relates to the interpretation of the term (protected) 'investment' by implying a condition of legality under international law. This is probably the most outcome-determinative way in which States can use systemic integration to deny protection to investments tainted by a violation of international law. As noted by the Tribunal in *Fraport II*, '[T]here is an increasingly well-established international principle which makes international legal remedies unavailable with respect to illegal investments, at least when such illegality goes to the essence of the investment.'[94]

One example of such use of systemic integration is *Phoenix* v. *Czech Republic*, where the Tribunal held that

> the ICSID Convention's jurisdictional requirements – as well as those of the BIT – cannot be read and interpreted in isolation from public international law, and its general principles. To take an extreme example, nobody would suggest that ICSID protection should be granted to investments made in violation of the most fundamental rules of protection of human rights, like investments made in pursuance of torture or genocide or in support of slavery or trafficking of human organs.[95]

This reasoning was outcome determinative as the Tribunal found that in the instance at hand there was no genuine economic investment but merely a rearrangement of assets for the purposes of bringing an international claim.[96] Notably, the Tribunal saw it as its duty to deny protection of such abusive manipulation.[97] This systemic integration reasoning is convincing and in line with the *Oil Platforms* case, where the ICJ implied that measures contrary to international law could not be intended to fall in the ambit of the bilateral treaty. Furthermore, the fundamental principles of international law are not applied to assess the conduct of the investor but merely to determine whether the investment as a juridical fact qualifies for protection under the treaty. It is difficult to see how a fact in serious violation of international law could benefit from procedural and substantive protection on the international plane or generate rights under an international treaty.

[94] *Fraport AG Frankfurt Airport Services* v. *Republic of the Philippines II*, ICSID Case No. ARB/11/12, Award of 10 December 2014, para. 332.

[95] *Phoenix Action Ltd* v. *Czech Republic*, ICSID Case No. ARB/06/5, Award, 15 April 2009, para. 78.

[96] *Ibid.*, para. 142. [97] *Ibid.*, para. 144.

Other tribunals used systemic integration in their interpretation of what constitutes a protected investment implicitly, without reference to the rule as such but by taking into account other rules of international law, including the prohibition against corruption and fraud, in their interpretation of the treaty terms. Examples include *World Duty Free* v. *Kenya,*[98] *Inceysa* v. *El Salvador*[99] and *Plama* v. *Bulgaria.*[100] For instance, the Tribunal in *Plama* affirmed that 'the protections provided for by the ECT [do not] cover all kinds of investments, including those made contrary to domestic or international law.'[101] Given that investment tribunals derive their authority from BITs, which are an instrument of international law, it is both just and reasonable to imply that their protection should not be extended to acts and juridical facts made in violation of international law.

The third group of cases where States have invoked systemic integration to reassert their control, even if with varying success, is where other rules of international law have been relied upon to demonstrate the motivation, if not the legitimacy, of the measures adopted by the State and challenged by the investor. The approaches of tribunals in this group of cases vary significantly both in deciding what other rules of international law are relevant to their considerations and with respect to what weight, if any, they should have on the outcome of the arbitration.

In *SPP* v. *Egypt*, the respondent relied on its ratification of the United Nations Educational, Scientific and Cultural Organisation (UNESCO) Convention for the Protection of the World Cultural and Natural Heritage as making it 'obligatory on the international plane to cancel the Pyramids Oasis Project' of the investor.[102] The tribunal, however, after acknowledging that the Convention is relevant in the interpretation,[103] opined that 'the UNESCO Convention by itself does not justify the measures taken by the Respondent to cancel the project, nor does it exclude the Claimants' right to compensation.'[104] Nonetheless, the Tribunal admitted that 'as a matter of international law, the Respondent was entitled to cancel

[98] *World Duty Free Company Limited* v. *Republic of Kenya*, ICSID Case No. ARB/00/7, Award of 4 October 2006, para. 148.

[99] *Inceysa Vallisoletana SL* v. *Republic of El Salvador*, ICSID Case No. ARB/03/26, Award of 2 August 2006, para. 249.

[100] *Plama Consortium Limited* v. *Bulgaria*, ICSID Case No. ARB/03/24, Award of 27 August 2008, paras. 138–9, 143–4.

[101] *Ibid.*, paras. 138–9.

[102] *Southern Pacific Properties Limited* v. *Arab Republic of Egypt*, ICSID Case No. ARB/84/3, Award on the Merits of 20 May 1992, para. 150

[103] *Ibid.*, para. 78.

[104] *Ibid.*, para. 154.

a tourist development project situated on its own territory for the purpose of protecting antiquities.'[105] Systemic integration did have a role to play in the application of the investment treaty with respect to reparations, where the Tribunal declined to award *lucrum cessans* and declared any profits non-compensable after 1979 when the UNESCO Convention became binding on Egypt, given that after this date the activities in the area were in violation of international law.[106] This reasoning highlights the discretion that tribunals have in 'taking into account' other rules of international law. It also shows how systemic integration could be used by the tribunal in ways not necessarily intended by the State.

The UNESCO World Heritage Convention was taken into account as relevant and proved outcome determinative in *Glamis Gold* v. *USA*. The broadly understood international *rules* in question were incorporated in US law and relied upon by the Tribunal in finding that the State measures in question were not arbitrary.[107] The Tribunal concluded that there was no manifest lack of reasons for the US legislation and that the State acted in good faith in adopting it.[108]

The respondent State in *Electrabel* v. *Hungary* invoked systemic integration in a similar vein to justify its measures as being adopted on the basis of EU law. The Tribunal had to consider whether EU law formed part of the relevant rules of international law to be taken into account[109] and what weight they ought to be given.[110] It held that EU law was indeed relevant[111] and that it was to be given special weight due to the close relationship between the European Union and the applicable Energy Charter Treaty (ECT). In reaching this conclusion, the Tribunal took into account the historical origin of the ECT and its shared objectives with EU law in combating anti-competitive conduct 'such that the ECT should be interpreted, if possible, in harmony with EU law'.[112] While the Tribunal found that there was no material inconsistency between EU law and the ECT in this case that would necessitate their harmonious interpretation,[113] it did take into account EU law, as requested by Hungary, in evaluating its conduct:

[105] *Ibid.*, para. 158. [106] *Ibid.*, para. 191.
[107] *Glamis Gold, Ltd* v. *USA*, UNCITRAL, Award of 8 June 2009, para. 84.
[108] *Ibid.*, paras. 804–6.
[109] *Electrabel SA* v. *Republic of Hungary*, ICSID Case No. ARB/07/19, Decision on Jurisdiction, Applicable Law and Liability of 30 November 2012, paras. 4.112–16.
[110] *Ibid.*, paras. 4.130–41. [111] *Ibid.*, para. 4.122–6. [112] *Ibid.*, para. 4.130.
[113] *Ibid.*, para. 4.166.

> [T]he acts of the Respondent implementing such a binding decision under EU law have to be taken into account in the evaluation of its conduct under ECT. This means . . . that the ECT does not protect the Claimant, as against the Respondent, from the enforcement by the Respondent of a binding decision of the European Commission under EU law.[114]

This use of systemic integration proved outcome determinative at this stage of the proceedings with respect to rejecting the investor's claims for State liability.[115]

In similar vein, Romania invoked EU law by way of systemic integration in *Micula* v. *Romania*, arguing forcefully that in the event of irreconcilable conflict, EU law should prevail over the BIT.[116] The tribunal dismissed the latter argument by asserting that 'there is no real conflict of treaties.'[117] After noting the lack of reference to EU law in the BIT, as well as its object and purpose set out in the preamble, it concluded that Sweden and Romania did not intend to defeat their obligations under EU law when entering the investment treaty.[118] Accordingly, the Tribunal took into account the relevant rules of EU law in interpreting the fair and equitable treatment clause under the BIT and, in particular, the reasonableness of Romania's revocation of incentives with respect to the investor on the basis that they constituted state aid incompatible with EU competition law.[119] The tribunal rejected the claimant's argument that the State acted unreasonably in revoking the incentives on the basis of the EU law motivation of its conduct.[120] The tribunal, however, did find that Romania violated the legitimate expectations of the investor, even if it did so in pursuit of a rational policy, and thus violated the BIT.[121] The award was confirmed in the course of the annulment proceedings.[122]

This case shows that systemic integration, even when applied by the tribunal, is not a guarantee that the State will succeed in reasserting its control in the arbitration. This is due to the wide discretion given to the decision-makers with respect to the weight to be given to the other relevant rules in the dispute at hand coupled with the fact that the

[114] *Ibid.*, para. 4.169. [115] *Ibid.*, XI, 'Operative Part', paras. 11.4–6.

[116] *Ioan Micula, Viorel Micula, S.C. European Food S.A, S.C. Starmill S.R.L. and S.C. Multipack S.R.L.* v. *Romania*, ICSID Case No. ARB/05/20, Final Award of 11 December 2013, paras. 309–12.

[117] *Ibid.*, paras. 319–20. [118] *Ibid.*, para. 326. [119] *Ibid.*, paras. 786–8.

[120] *Ibid.*, para. 802. [121] *Ibid.*, para. 827.

[122] *Micula* v. *Romania*, ICSID Case No. ARB/05/20, Decision on Annulment of 26 February 2016.

motivation of regulatory measures does not automatically lead to the exculpation of the State.

Canada successfully invoked systemic integration for the purposes of interpreting the term 'in like circumstances' with reference to the Universal Postal Convention and the World Customs Organisation Kyoto Convention.[123] The tribunal upheld Canada's argument to find that the investor UPS and Canada Post were not in like circumstances, and this was outcome determinative. It was held that Canada did not breach its NAFTA Article 1102 obligations as it was justified in differentiating between the investor and its post for the purposes of customs treatment.[124]

It should be noted that this line of case law is not consistent. For instance, in *CDSE* v. *Costa Rica*, the tribunal rejected the argument that international environmental law could be outcome determinative in considering whether the measures at hand constituted expropriation:

> The international source of the obligation to protect the environment makes no difference. Expropriatory environmental measures – no matter how laudable and beneficial to society as a whole – are, in this respect, similar to any other expropriatory measures that a state may take in order to implement its policies: where property is expropriated, even for environmental purposes, whether domestic or international, the state's obligation to pay compensation remains.[125]

Overall, the cases from the third category are inconsistent and their outcomes heavily dependent upon the facts at hand, as well as on the understanding of the Tribunal as to whether or not compensation is owed in cases involving general regulation in the public interest, be it under the treaty or in customary international law. In general, however, tribunals seem open to take into account other relevant rules of international law pertinent to the regulatory measures adopted by the State, and accordingly, systemic integration has a role to play in reasserting the State's control in this way.

(2) Cases Where Systemic Integration Arguments Failed

To give but few examples where systemic integration failed as an instrument to reassert the State's control in investment arbitration, which are

[123] *United Parcel Service of America II* v. *Canada*, UNCITRAL, Award on the Merits of 24 May 2007, para. 117.

[124] *Ibid.*, paras. 119–20.

[125] *Compañía del Dessarrolo de Santa Elena SA* v. *Costa Rica*, ICSID Case No. ARB/96/1, Final Award of 17 February 2008, paras. 71–2.

by no means exhaustive but merely illustrative of how the instrument ought not to be used. The common thread in these cases is that systemic integration was invoked not as an interpretative tool but as a trump card purporting to displace the treaty.

The tribunal in *RosInvest* v. *Russia* rejected the systemic integration arguments of the investor attempting to invoke treaties concluded by the Russian Federation in the interpretation of the applicable investment treaty signed by the Soviet Union. The Tribunal cautioned that

> [i]t cannot conceive of any circumstances in which it would be proper for it to substitute for the treaty actually concluded by the former Soviet Union another treaty which might have been concluded by the Russian Federation had it then been in existence and pursuing different economic policies.[126]

The tribunal reinforced its conclusion by the criteria of 'relevance', noting that none of the invoked agreements had any relation to the interpretation of the provision in question.[127]

Kazakhstan was not successful in using systemic integration as a tool for reasserting control in *KT Asia Investment Group* v. *Kazakhstan*. It tried to invoke the purportedly customary rule of real and effective nationality as applicable instead of the nationality definition in the treaty, under the guise of systemic integration. Customary law here was used not as a fallback tool regulating issues beyond the scope of the treaty but as a tool purporting to modify the express language of the treaty. The tribunal rejected this line of argument, reasoning

> [t]his Tribunal sees no basis for applying a rule of diplomatic protection that would trump the specific regime created by the Treaty. In this respect, the Tribunal agrees with the Claimant that the nationality of a corporation is a legal construct and that in the absence of any obligatory test for the nationality of corporations in international law, it falls to the Contracting States of the relevant investment treaty to define the nationality of a corporation as they see fit.[128]

A line of cases shows Argentina's failure to rely on its obligations under human rights treaties in order to trump the express language of the BIT, based on the former's purported hierarchical superiority under

126 *RosInvest Co UK, Ltd.* v. *Russian Federation*, SCC Case No. V079/2005, Award on Jurisdiction of 1 October 2007, paras. 39 and 42.

127 *Ibid.*, para. 119.

128 *KT Asia Investment Group BV* v. *Republic of Kazakhstan*, ICSID Case No. ARB/09/8, Award of 17 October 2013, paras. 128–9.

the Argentine Constitution.[129] All tribunals rejected this line of argument with different reasoning. Some tribunals accepted systemic integration in principle, including the argument that human rights are one of the sources to be taken into account in resolving the dispute,[130] but found that they were either not in conflict with the treaty and thus not applicable[131] or that they were not determinative under the facts, given the gravity of the treaty violation.[132] Other tribunals dismissed the systemic integration argument all together on the basis of lack of relevance.[133]

It can be concluded that Tribunals are not likely to uphold the State's attempts to use systemic integration as a tool for substituting the language of the treaty with other rules of international law. Such use of systemic integration was not previewed in Article 31(3)(c) of the VCLT as it does not conform with the principle of good faith in the interpretation of treaties, nor does it take into account the intentions of the parties to the BIT. The only type of circumstance where such a tool might succeed would be the invocation of peremptory norms of international law. However, this would not qualify as a question of treaty interpretation by way of systemic integration but rather as application of Articles 53 or 64 of the VCLT to invalidate the treaty.

D. Conclusion

In conclusion, systemic integration can be used as an effective litigation tool by States for reasserting their sovereignty and control in investment arbitration, provided that this is done with due consideration to the inherent limitations of the principle under international law. As seen from the history and preparatory works of Article 31(3)(c), systemic integration can only operate where it is in accordance with the intentions of the parties to the applicable treaty as expressed in its preamble and text. It is not a tool for the modification of treaties by creating exceptions where none exist or by substituting their text with other rules of international law. Ultimately, systemic integration functions in the confines of the processes of interpretation and application of treaties.

[129] See e.g. *SAUR International* v. *Argentine*, ICSID Case No. ARB/04/4, Décision sur la Compétence et sur la Responsabilité of 6 June 2012, para. 328.

[130] *Ibid.*, para. 330. [131] *Ibid.*, para. 331. [132] *Ibid.*, paras. 401–5.

[133] *Siemens AG* v. *Argentine Republic*, ICSID Case No. ARB/02/8, Award of 17 January 2007, para. 79; *CMS Gas Transmission Company* v. *Argentina*, ICSID Case No. ARB/01/8, Award of 12 May 2005, para. 121.

Given that the text of the treaty itself is the key factor in determining the relevance and weight to be given to other rules of international law, the most effective way for States to use systemic integration as a tool for reasserting their control is by factoring it in the drafting of investment treaties. This can be done by referring to other bodies of international law, such as the protection of the environment, international peace and labour rights, in the preambles or texts of BITs. This would be the best way for States to manifest their intention not to modify or displace such other rules in their investment relations.

Investment case law indicates that systemic integration is invoked by States with most success in reasserting their sovereignty to regulate in accordance with their public policy objectives and international obligations. For instance, other rules of international law are relevant in assessing the legality and motivation of measures adopted to implement such rules. However, the case law is inconsistent on the weight to be given to the other rules, which lies largely within the discretion of the arbitral tribunal, also determined by its understanding of the customary rules on the right to regulate. Overall, it seems that the more relevant the other rules of international law, the greater the weight they have in the interpretation. Furthermore, systemic integration has been used in assessing the accordance of investments with other rules of international law. This type of use of the tool is probably the most effective one in investment arbitration as it is outcome determinative given the general recognition that investments made in serious violation of international law cannot be given protection on the international plane.

Moreover, the instances where States failed to use systemic integration in reasserting their control are instructive with respect to the limits of the principle. They indicate that systemic integration is not a rule of hierarchy that could allow extraneous norms to trump the applicable investment treaty. Formulating a systemic integration argument as a trump card virtually guarantees that the State's reassertion of control will fail.

To conclude, systemic integration is a powerful tool that ought to be used with caution in reasserting control in a process governed by specialised economic treaties and involving a non-State actor who is not a party to them. The principle can function effectively as a shield for the State in defending its powers to regulate and to act in accordance with other rules of international law. The invocation of systemic integration as a sword against the investor or the text of the treaty, however, is not normatively justified, nor likely to succeed.

9

Reasserting Control through Withdrawal from Investment Agreements

What Role for the Law of Treaties?

FERNANDO LUSA BORDIN

A. Introduction

When it comes to reasserting control over investment relations, there is no more dramatic measure open to States than seeking to terminate agreements which provide for investment protection and binding third-party dispute settlement. While the many bilateral investment treaties (BITs) concluded in the past few decades may have affected the content and scope of the minimum standard of protection to which foreigners are entitled under general international law,[1] the backbone of the substantive rights enjoyed by investors around the world remains treaty law. Likewise, disputes opposing States and investors can only be brought before international forums if those States give their consent, which they typically do by concluding BITs. Treaty termination may thus come across as an intuitive and effective means to grasp the nettle: by getting rid of the treaties that constrain them, States can recover the room for policy choice that has been taken away by a system of investment protection with which many have become disillusioned.[2]

Treaty termination is, however, a constrained means to reassert control over investment relations, at least in the short term. In *S.S. Wimbledon*, the Permanent Court of International Justice described the 'right of entering into international engagements' as an 'attribute of State

[1] Cf., e.g., the discussion of the Tribunal in *CME Czech Republic B.V.* v. *Czech Republic*, UNCITRAL, Award of 14 March 2003, paras. 498–9.

[2] See generally the contributions in C. Balchin, L. Chung, A. Kaushal and M. Waibel (eds.), *The Backlash against Investment Arbitration* (Alphen aan den Rijn, Netherlands: Kluwer, 2010).

sovereignty',[3] but that judgment made it abundantly clear that once this attribute is exercised, States cannot easily turn back. Indeed, the contemporary law of treaties makes international agreements particularly resilient – or as resilient as the parties wish them to be. To consider to what extent this proposition holds true in relation to investment treaties, this chapter looks into two ways in which States have sought to regain control over their investment relations. The first and most obvious is by attempting to terminate specific BITs by which they are bound. The second is by denouncing the Washington Convention on the Settlement of Investment Disputes between States and Nationals of Other States (the ICSID Convention) with a view to impairing or affecting the application of compromissory clauses in existing BITs.

B. Termination of BITs

(1) *Denunciation and Sunset Clauses*

The termination of BITs is a matter regulated by the general law of treaties, which is authoritatively articulated by the 1969 Vienna Convention on the Law of Treaties (VCLT).[4] The general approach taken by the VCLT is to give ample opportunity for States to agree on rules governing the birth, life and demise of the agreements they conclude as long as by doing so they do not derogate from peremptory norms of general international law.[5] As regards treaty termination, this approach is expressed in Article 54 of the VCLT, which first envisages the possibility of terminating/withdrawing from a treaty 'in conformity with the provisions of [that] treaty' (Article 54(a)) and then adds that termination/withdrawal can always be effected if the 'consent of all the parties' is obtained (Article 54(b)).

In contrast, the VCLT makes it far more difficult for States to seek termination of/denunciation from a treaty unilaterally if that treaty does not establish an individual right to withdraw. The default position on denunciation is that a party can only withdraw if it is established that 'the parties intended to admit the possibility of denunciation or withdrawal' or if 'a right of denunciation or withdrawal may be implied by the nature of the treaty' (Article 56). Failing that, unilateral termination or

[3] *S.S. Wimbledon*, 1923 PCIJ (Ser. A), No. 1, at 25.

[4] Cf. F. Bordin, 'Reflections of Customary International Law: The Authority of Codification Conventions and ILC Draft Articles in International Law', *International & Comparative Law Quarterly*, 63 (2014), 535, 542–3.

[5] Cf. Article 53 of the VCLT.

denunciation can only be sought in the circumstances specified by the VCLT: material breach by the other party (Article 60), supervening impossibility of performance (Article 61) and fundamental change of circumstances (Article 62).

A survey of existing BITs indicates that investment treaties normally fall within the framework laid down by Article 54(a) of the VCLT. Existing BITs tend to include detailed termination provisions that stipulate a period during which they will initially remain in force (typically not less than ten years) and the conditions for their renewal and termination. Those are that unless terminated by the end of the initial period and subject to a twelve-month notice, the treaties are automatically renewed for either an indefinite or a definite period. If the former, they can be terminated at any time by one of the parties, subject to a twelve-month notice. If the latter, they can be terminated only when the subsequent fixed period ends, also subject to a twelve-month notice.[6]

Should a BIT contain no termination clause, the rule in Article 56 of the VCLT comes into play. Given the consistent practice of including termination clauses in BITs, it may be difficult for a party to establish that the 'possibility of denunciation or withdrawal' (Article 56(a)) was intended by the parties absent a clear indication of such intention in the negotiating history of the treaty. Whether BITs entail by their character a right to denunciation (Article 56(b)) is an interesting question. There is little guidance in the practice of States and the case law of international courts as to how to apply Article 56(b), which was not originally formulated by the International Law Commission (ILC) but added subsequently at the Vienna Conference. There is support in legal commentary for the proposition that commercial or trading agreements

[6] Compare e.g. Article 15 of the 2003 China–Germany BIT: 'This Agreement shall remain in force for a period of ten years and shall be extended thereafter for an unlimited period unless denounced … by either Contracting Party twelve months before its expiration … After the expiration of the initial ten years period, either Contracting Party may at any time thereafter terminate this Agreement by giving at least twelve month's written notice … to the other Contracting Party'; Article XIII of the 1998 Belgium–Philippines BIT: 'The Agreement shall remain in force for a period of ten years. Unless notice of termination is given by either Contracting Party at least one year before the expiry of its period of validity, this Agreement shall be tacitly extended each time for a further period of ten years, it being understood that each Contracting Party, reserves the right to terminate the Agreement by notification given at least one year before the date of expiry of the current period of validity'. See also the survey in A. Carska-Sheppard, 'Issues Relevant to the Terminations of Bilateral Investment Treaties', *Journal of International Arbitration*, 26 (2009), 755.

fall under that rule,[7] and BITs arguably belong to this category. Among parties to the Vienna Convention, denunciation under Article 56 will produce effects following a twelve-month notice period. The position under customary international law may be less clear, but at the very least the lapse of a 'reasonable time' would be required.[8]

A feature of existing BITs which further complicates the process of disentanglement from investment obligations is the inclusion of so-called survival or sunset clauses. With some variation, these provide that upon termination, investments made while the BIT was in force will continue to enjoy the protections provided by the treaty (dispute settlement provisions included) for a period of time typically ranging from ten to twenty years.[9] Sunset clauses are meant to guarantee the stability of investment protection and show how elusive the prospects of prompt termination may be for States wishing to reassert control over their investment relations. The point is illustrated by the *Yukos* litigation involving a number of investors and Russia and instituted under the Energy Charter Treaty (ECT). The ECT comprises a twenty-year sunset clause,[10] an unusual feature of which is that it also applies to investments made during the period in which the host State agrees to the provisional application of the Charter.[11] In *Yukos* v. *Russian Federation*, having found that the ECT had applied provisionally to Russia before it notified the depository that it had no intention to proceed with ratification, the Tribunal concluded that 'any investments made in Russia prior to 19 October 2009 will continue to benefit from the Treaty's protections for a period of 20 years, i.e., until 19 October 2029.'[12]

[7] Cf. A. Aust, *Modern Treaty Law and Practice*, 2nd edn. (Cambridge University Press, 2007), 291.

[8] See, with reference to declarations under the optional clause, *Military and Paramilitary Activities in and against Nicaragua (Nicaragua* v. *United States of America)*, ICJ Reports, Jurisdiction and Admissibility, Judgment of 26 November 1984, para. 63.

[9] See the survey in J. Harrison, 'The Life and Death of BITs: Legal Issues Concerning Survival Clauses and the Termination of Investment Treaties', *Journal of World Investment & Trade*, 13 (2012), 928.

[10] Article 47 of the Energy Charter Treaty (1994): 'The provisions of this Treaty shall continue to apply to Investments made in the Area of a Contracting Party by Investors of other Contracting Parties or in the Area of other Contracting Parties by Investors of that Contracting Party as of the date when that Contracting Party's withdrawal from the Treaty takes effect for a period of 20 years from such date.'

[11] Cf. Article 45(3)(b) of the ECT.

[12] *Yukos Universal Limited* v. *Russian Federation*, UNCITRAL, PCA Case No. AA 227, Interim Award on Jurisdiction and Admissibility of 30 November 2009, para. 388. However, note The Hague District Court, Judgment of 20 April 2016, C/09/477160/HA ZA 15-1, quashing the awards of 20 November 2009 and 16 July 2014.

(2) Grounds for Unilateral Termination under General International Law

That BITs are typically agreements comprising detailed termination and survival clauses means that while the opportunity for States to free themselves from their obligations is safeguarded prospectively, there is little room for States to 'reassert control' unilaterally before the agreements run their course. Unless a State is able to secure the consent of the other party to terminate the treaty earlier, the best that it can do is to invoke the grounds for termination envisaged by Articles 60, 61 and 62 of the VCLT. But general international law is unlikely to come to the aid of States seeking to free themselves from obligations under investment treaties. Article 60 (on material breach) does not play much of a role in the termination of BITs because it is the party whose rights were breached that will have the greatest interest in the continuing validity of the treaty. Likewise, Article 61 (on supervening impossibility of performance) only applies in the narrowly defined situation in which an object that is essential for the performance of the obligation in question disappears.[13] Unlike treaties concluded to cater for specific investments, the object of BITs is to create a legal framework for the protection of investments in general. It is difficult to envisage realistic scenarios in which that object – the creation of a legal framework – would 'disappear' rendering performance impossible.

Under general international law, the best option for States to withdraw unilaterally from a BIT is thus to invoke a fundamental change of circumstances pursuant to Article 62 of the VCLT. But the case law of the International Court of Justice (ICJ) illustrates how difficult it can be for a State to make a plea of fundamental change of circumstances. Article 62 imposes two hurdles: (1) to establish that the circumstances in question 'constituted an essential basis of the consent of the parties to be bound by the treaty' and (2) to establish that 'the effect of the change is radically to transform the extent of obligations still to be performed under the treaty.' In *Fisheries Jurisdiction*, the ICJ explained this threshold as requiring an increase in the 'burden of obligations to be executed to

[13] In *Gabcikovo-Nagymaros*, the ICJ took note of the 'narrower concept' that the drafters of VCLT favoured but did not rule on Hungary's contention that 'an economic joint investment which was consistent with environmental protection and which was operated by the two contracting parties jointly' could constitute an 'object' in the sense of Article 61: *Gabcikovo-Nagymaros Project (Hungary/Slovakia)*, Judgment of 25 September 1997, ICJ Reports 1997, paras. 102–3.

the extent of rendering the performance something essentially different from that originally undertaken'.[14] In *Gabcikovo-Nagymaros*, the Court added that a fundamental change of circumstances 'must have been unforeseen' and that 'the stability of treaty relations requires that the plea of fundamental change or circumstances be applied only in exceptional cases.'[15] It should be clear that States cannot make use of Article 62 to 'reassert control' over their investment relations, that is, to implement governmental policies. In this connection, it is noteworthy that in *Gabcikovo-Nagymaros*, the ICJ refused to view changes in the prevailing political situation, the economic viability of the project between Hungary and Slovakia and the state of environmental knowledge as constituting a fundamental change in the sense of Article 62.[16] If that approach is followed in the investment field, the range of political and economic arguments that can be invoked by parties to a BIT to terminate the treaty unilaterally becomes rather limited.[17]

(3) Do the Rights of Investors Constitute an Obstacle to Termination by Mutual Consent?

In short, international law holds States to their promises when it comes to BITs containing detailed termination and sunset clauses. The most promising strategy for a State wishing to reassert control over its investment relations in the short term remains seeking the agreement of the other party either to amend the BIT's terms or to effect an earlier termination. There is, however, a potential caveat here to consider. The fact that BITs are treaties concluded for the benefit of investors gives rise to the question of whether rights acquired by investors are affected if termination does not respect the terms of a specific treaty. If, for example, a clause stipulated that a BIT would be in force for ten years with a survival period of fifteen years following termination, would an investor be entitled to demand additional protection for twenty years if the parties jointly agreed to terminate the treaty (including rights and obligations deriving from the sunset clause) after five years?

[14] *Fisheries Jurisdiction (Federal Republic of Germany* v. *Iceland)*, Merits, Judgment of 25 July 1974, ICJ Reports 1974, para. 43.

[15] *Gabcikovo-Nagymaros Project (Hungary/Slovakia)*, para. 108.

[16] *Ibid.*, para. 104.

[17] There remains, however, the possibility of invoking necessity as a circumstance precluding the wrongfulness of a breach of the BIT, as confirmed by the ICSID Tribunal in *LGE* v. *Argentina*.

Article 54 of the VCLT stands for the proposition that the parties are always at liberty to terminate a treaty by consent, regardless of what the treaty may say.[18] But, as James Harrison has pointed out, the classical approach is open to the criticism that a 'key element' of investment treaties is 'to offer protection to investors from the arbitrary conduct of states', the upshot being that 'mutual termination [should be] subject to some constraint if investors are considered to hold autonomous third party rights under BITs.'[19] Harrison tentatively suggests that the rules on revocation or modification of rights of third States embodied in Article 37 of the VCLT could be extended to investors. Pursuant to Article 37(2), 'When a right has arisen for a third State [under a treaty], the right may not be revoked or modified by the parties [to that treaty] if it is established that the right was intended not to be revocable or subject to modification without the consent of the third State.' If an analogy between investors and third States were admissible so as to extend to individuals the VLCT rules that apply to third States, there would be room for investors to argue that BITs have conferred on them rights that cannot be revoked without their consent.[20] This would constitute an extraordinary limitation on the capacity of States to reassert control over their investment relations by mutual agreement.

There is a lively debate as to the precise character of the rights that investors acquire under BITs, boiling down to the question of whether or not individuals are subjects of 'international investment law' proper.[21] While the position one takes on this debate may make one more or less sympathetic to Harrison's argument, it is doubtful whether that argument obtains as a matter of treaty law as it stands at present. That is so for two reasons. Firstly, the relationship between Article 37 (concerning the application of treaties i.e. their 'lifetime') and Article 54 of the VCLT (concerning the termination of treaties i.e. their 'death') is far from clear. If under Article 36 a third party acquires a right under a treaty, it is sensible to argue that this right must be characterised by 'a measure of

[18] 'Draft Articles on the Law of Treaties with Commentaries', 'Draft Articles on the Law of Treaties with Commentaries', *ILC Yearbook*, 1966, 249, para. 3: 'The Commission considered that, whatever may be the provisions of a treaty regarding its own termination, it is always possible for all the parties to agree together to put an end to the treaty. It also considered that the particular form which such an agreement may take is a matter for the parties themselves to decide in each case.'

[19] J. Harrison, 'The Life and Death of BITs', 928, 943. [20] *Ibid.*, 943–7.

[21] Cf., e.g., K. Parlett, *The Individual in the International Legal System* (Cambridge University Press, 2011), 103–19.

solidity and firmness'[22] while the treaty remains in force. But to read Article 37 as implying a right for a third party to demand that a treaty remain in place when the parties wish otherwise might be going a bit too far, and nothing in the VCLT suggests that this is or should be the case. In short, in the system put in place by the Vienna Convention, the application of Article 37 should be without prejudice to the application of the rule in Article 54.[23]

Secondly, the proposition that Article 37(2) 'represents a general principle which is applicable to all third party right holders'[24] is potentially problematic to the extent that it constitutes a limit to the power of States to create and terminate treaties that goes far beyond the confines of *jus cogens*. In this respect, it should be noted that whether international law imposes restrictions on the power of States to renounce rights that accrue for individuals under treaties and/or custom remains a controversial question. In *Jurisdictional Immunities of the State*, Italy argued that neither Germany nor Italy had the right to renounce the individual right of Italian nationals to compensation for breaches of international humanitarian law and human rights law.[25] Italy attempted to persuade the ICJ that the treaties that had been concluded by the two States with a view towards settling all reparations claims arising from the Second World War did not affect the claims instituted by those nationals before domestic courts. While the Court did not consider this argument in detail (the judgment rather focuses on issues of State immunity), it pointed out that

> [a]gainst the background of a century of practice in which almost every peace treaty or post-war settlement has involved either a decision not to require the payment of reparations or the use of lump sum settlements and set-offs, it is difficult to see that international law contains a rule requiring the payment of full compensation to each and every individual victim as a rule accepted by the international community of States as a whole as one from which no derogation is permitted.[26]

[22] To use the ILC's own words: 'Draft Articles on the Law of Treaties with Commentaries', *ILC Yearbook*, 1966, 249, para. 4.

[23] Rights and obligations vis-à-vis a third party could nevertheless arise for third States under principles of general international law such as good faith, estoppel, etc.

[24] J. Harrison, 'The Life and Death of BITs', 928, 944.

[25] See Italy's Counter-Memorial, paras. 5.15–21, available at www.icj-cij.org/docket/files/143/16648.pdf (accessed 28 February 2016).

[26] *Jurisdictional Immunities of the State (Germany* v. *Italy: Greece Intervening)*, Judgment of 3 February 2012, ICJ Reports 2012, para. 94.

Though one should be careful not to read too much into this passage, implicit in the Court's reasoning is a reluctance to accept that individual rights can survive valid post-war settlements. It may be that an implication of the changes that the emergence of new subjects of international law has brought about to the structure of the international legal system is that a new restriction on the power of States to terminate treaties has to be recognised. It may even be that the rule in Article 54 of the VCLT calls for a reconsideration because there is nothing in international law (classical or contemporary) that would prevent the parties to a treaty from stipulating that termination can only be made by the decision of a third party (e.g. an international organisation or an international tribunal), thus forfeiting the right to terminate a treaty by mutual consent. But these are propositions with wide-reaching implications that have to be considered with caution until they are reflected in developments in the practice of States and decisions of international courts and tribunals. At this stage, accepting Harrison's argument without more makes the notion that States should indeed take steps to reassert control over investment relations all the more appealing.

(4) Recent State Practice on the Unilateral Termination of BITs

While there has not been an extensive practice of terminating BITs as a means of reasserting control over investment relations, a couple of recent examples indicate that this is a path on which certain States – unhappy with restrictions on public policy and the prospects of investor-State arbitration that BITs entail – are ready to embark.

Following a shift in governmental policy, South Africa announced a few years ago a decision by its cabinet to 'refrain from entering into [BITs] in the future, except in cases of compelling and political circumstances'.[27] It terminated BITs concluded with Austria, Belgium and Luxembourg, Germany, the Netherlands, Spain and

[27] See e.g. the press release by the Department of Trade and Industry of South Africa on 26 July 2012, available at www.thedti.gov.za/editmedia.jsp?id=2464 (accessed 28 February 2016). The justification offered for the change in policy is that it 'corresponds in large measure to emerging thinking at the global level. A new generation of investment policies has emerged, with governments pursuing a broader and more intricate development policy agenda within a framework that seeks to maintain a favourable investment climate. New generation investment policies now place inclusive growth and sustainable development at the centre of efforts to attract and benefit from investment.'

Switzerland[28] and is likely to denounce further agreements as their respective terms expire. Interestingly, South Africa does not seem intent on replacing these agreements with new BITs. The current policy is rather to make investment protection a matter for domestic law, for which South Africa has recently enacted a 'Promotion and Protection Investment Bill'.[29] This bill replicates (and occasionally tweaks) standard clauses found in most BITs but does not offer to investors the option of recourse to international investor-State arbitration.

Likewise, Indonesia has announced its intention to terminate dozens of BITs which it has concluded with various States.[30] It has already terminated the 1994 Indonesia–Netherlands BIT and has reportedly denounced investment agreements with France, Slovakia, China, Italy and Bulgaria.[31] In contrast with South Africa, Indonesia's goal does not seem to be replacing BITs with a domestic system of investment protection but rather negotiating better investment agreements in light of contemporary practices and policy concerns.[32]

From the perspective of the law of treaties, the recent practice of South Africa and Indonesia seems to be wholly unproblematic. Both are seeking to terminate their BITs pursuant to the applicable termination clauses, that is, are allowing the agreements to run their course by declining to renew them. There is no indication that either South Africa or Indonesia has called into question the validity and application of the sunset clauses that will continue protecting investments made in the duration of the treaties for the next several years. In short, both South Africa and Indonesia are taking measures to reassert control over their investment relations within the bounds of the international obligations they previously acquired.

28 As recorded e.g. in Investment Policy Hub, a database maintained by the UN Conference on Trade and Development, available at http://investmentpolicyhub.unctad.org/IIA/CountryBits/195 (accessed 28 February 2016).

29 Promotion and Protection Investment Bill, 22 July 2015, available at www.parliament.gov.za/live/commonrepository/Processed/20150729/609997_1.pdf (accessed 28 February 2016).

30 A. Crockett, 'Indonesia's Bilateral Investment Treaties: Between Generations?', *ICSID Review*, 30 (2015), 437.

31 *Ibid.*, 439.

32 See Arif Havas Oegroseno's opinion piece in the *Jakarta Post*, available at www.thejakartapost.com/news/2014/07/07/revamping-bilateral-treaties.html (accessed 28 February 2016).

C. Withdrawal from the ICSID Convention

(1) How Effective a Means to Reassert Control Is ICSID Denunciation?

In the last decade, Bolivia, Ecuador and Venezuela have all shown their discontent with the manner in which investment disputes have been handled under current BITs by withdrawing from the ICSID Convention altogether.[33] Denouncing the ICSID Convention cannot as such restore control over a State's investment relations given that the Convention does not comprise substantive obligations for the protection of investments but rather provides a framework under which disputes arising under BITs can be settled. As a result, withdrawing from the ICISD Convention will often have little more than symbolic value, not least because compromissory clauses in most BITs offer alternatives to ICSID arbitration (e.g. ad hoc arbitrations in accordance with the UNCITRAL Rules or under the auspices of the International Chamber of Commerce) that are left completely unaffected.

That said, withdrawal from the ICSID Convention is hardly without effects. It may create a considerable obstacle for the fulfilment of the obligation to settle disputes agreed in the BITs insofar as it deprives the investor of an alternative that the investor might favour for a number of reasons. These include the possibility to rely on the provisions on interpretation, revision, annulment and recognition of awards found in Chapter IV of the Convention, which may not be available in competing forums. In the case of BITs that only provide for ICISID arbitration (e.g. the Model French BIT[34]), ICSID Convention denunciation will have wide-reaching effects, making performance of the obligation contained in the compromissory clause impossible.

[33] On Latin America's criticism of the ICSID Convention and the reasons that led to withdrawal by the three States, see M. Durney, 'Legal Effects and Implications of the Denunciation of the ICSID Convention on Unilateral Consent Contained in Bilateral Investment Treaties: A Perspective from Latin American Cases', *Max Planck Yearbook of United Nations Law*, 17 (2013), 224, 234–7.

[34] French Model BIT, Article 7: 'Any dispute concerning the investments occurring between one Contracting Party and a national or company of the other Contracting Party shall be settled amicably . . . If this dispute has not been settled within a period of six months . . . it shall be submitted at the request of either party to the arbitration of the International Centre for the Settlement of Investment Disputes (ICSID), created by the Convention for the settlement of disputes in respect of investments occurring between States and nationals of other States signed in Washington on March 18, 1965.' Similar clauses can be found, for example, in the 2005 Belgium–China BIT (Article 8) and in the 1977 Belgium–Egypt BIT (Article IX).

The right to withdraw from the ICISID Convention is provided by Article 71 of the Convention, and some of its effects are regulated by Article 72. The provisions read as follows:

> Article 71. Any Contracting State may denounce this Convention by written notice to the depositary of this Convention. The denunciation shall take effect six months after receipt of such notice.
>
> Article 72. Notice by a Contracting State pursuant to [Article 71] shall not affect the rights or obligations under this Convention of that State or of any of its constituent subdivisions or agencies or of any national of that State arising out of consent to the jurisdiction of the Centre given by one of them before such notice was received by the depositary.

The rule to be distilled from a joint reading of Articles 71 and 72 as regards the effect of withdrawal on consent to arbitration given previously to the notice of denunciation has been the subject of a heated academic debate. The debate focuses on the precise interpretation of the phrase 'consent to the jurisdiction of the Centre given by one of them' in Article 72: what type of previous consent does the Convention protect from the effects of denunciation under Article 71? There are two relatively plausible ways of construing that phrase: (1) as referring to the consent given before the notice of denunciation by *both parties* to the dispute, that is, a State party *and* an investor bearing the nationality of another State party (the 'narrow interpretation') and (2) as referring to consent validly given by *either* of the potential parties by the time when the notice of denunciation is given (the 'broad interpretation'). The controversy is due to the fact that the contemporary and widespread practice of concluding BITs providing for investor-State arbitration had not emerged at the time when the ICISID Convention was drafted.[35] What the drafters had in mind when they formulated Article 72 was the possibility that host States and investors would sign contracts envisaging ICISID arbitration, the idea being that denunciation should not serve as a manoeuvre to circumvent those contracts.[36]

Whether the narrow or the broad interpretation of Article 72 is adopted has considerable impact on the role that ICSID Convention denunciation plays as a means for States to reassert control over their

[35] Cf. C. Schreuer, 'Denunciation of the ICISD Convention and Consent to Arbitration' in C. Balchin, L. Chung, A. Kaushal and M. Waibel (eds.), *The Backlash against Investment Arbitration* (Alphen aan den Rijn, Netherlands: Kluwer, 2010), 353, 357–8.

[36] Cf. C. Schreuer et al., *The ICSID Convention: A Commentary on the Convention on the Settlement of Investment Disputes between States and Nationals of Other States*, 2nd edn. (Cambridge University Press, 2010), 1279–80.

investment relations. If the rights or obligations preserved from denunciation are only those arising from the 'perfected consent' of both parties to the dispute in the sense of Article 25 of the Convention,[37] the notice of denunciation will impose a time bar on the institution of proceedings by investors who have not yet accepted the 'offer to arbitrate' made by the State in the BIT. An interesting feature of Article 72 is that it seems to depart from the default approach of the general law of treaties as regards the effect of denunciation or withdrawal by dispensing with the obligation to give reasonable notice. Though ICSID Convention denunciation only takes effect 'six months' after receipt of the notice, the protection accorded by Article 72 to consent to arbitration previously given extends only up to the date of the notice itself.[38] This means that if the narrow interpretation is adopted, States who have made a pledge to consent to ISCID arbitration through a BIT may take investors by surprise by indirectly withdrawing that pledge with immediate effects. As discussed earlier, that BITs normally include detailed termination and survival clauses means that States may be required to wait for a substantial period of time to reassert control over their investment relations through treaty termination; ICSID Convention denunciation would then provide a 'shortcut' for regaining some control, at least as concerns obligations to submit investment disputes to binding arbitration.

In contrast, if the broad interpretation is adopted and the rights and obligations protected by Article 72 are those arising from consent previously given by one of the parties (whether or not reciprocated by the other), the scope for States to circumvent obligations under BITs by withdrawing from the ICISID Convention is severely restricted. There are two possible solutions if this standpoint is adopted. The more expansive solution is to postulate that as long as there are BITs in force which were concluded previous to the notice of denunciation, investors will be entitled to invoke the compromissory clause before ICSID tribunals. The afterlife of the ICSID Convention for the relevant entities would thus be coextensive with the life and afterlife of the BITs providing for

[37] Article 25(1) of the Convention defines the Centre's jurisdiction to settle investment disputes: 'The jurisdiction of the Centre shall extend to any legal dispute arising directly out of an investment, between a Contracting State (or any constituent subdivision or agency of a Contracting State designated to the Centre by that State) and a national of another Contracting State, which the parties to the dispute consent in writing to submit to the Centre. When the parties have given their consent, no party may withdraw its consent unilaterally.'

[38] As discussed later, the Tribunal in *Venoklim Holding BV* v. *Venezuela* has recently taken a different position on this matter.

ICISID arbitration. The more circumspect solution is that investors would retain the right to accept an offer to arbitrate under a BIT for the six-month period following which denunciation takes effect.

What is then the interpretation of Article 72 to be preferred? Arguably, the mainstream position in legal commentary favours the narrow interpretation – that consent in Article 72 means 'perfected consent' in the sense of Article 25 of the Convention. That is the position taken in Christoph Schreuer's influential *The ICSID Convention: A Commentary.*[39] For Schreuer, the object and purpose of Article 72 are to protect consent to arbitration that is made irrevocable under Article 25 from ICSID Convention denunciation.[40] It is only when both parties consent to ICSID arbitration that they start to enjoy rights and obligations under the Convention, rights and obligations which Article 72 will shield from denunciation.[41] For Schreuer, 'It would run counter to the system of the Convention to provide for the irrevocability of a mere offer of consent to jurisdiction that has not been taken up by the other party.'[42] Commentators disagreeing with Schreuer's position have proposed a grammatical interpretation of Article 72, noting that the consent to which that provision refers is not the mutual consent to which Article 25 refers but rather the 'consent . . . given by one of them', either the State or the investor.[43]

[39] C. Schreuer et al., *The ICSID Convention*, 1279–82.

[40] The argument is further fleshed out in C. Schreuer, 'Denunciation of the ICISD Convention and Consent to Arbitration' in C. Balchin, L. Chung, A. Kaushal and M. Waibel (eds.), *The Backlash against Investment Arbitration* (Alphen aan den Rijn, Netherlands: Kluwer, 2010), 353, 362–4. For a similar position, see J. Fouret, 'Denunciaton of the Washington Convention and Non-Contractual Investment Arbitration', *Journal of International Arbitration*, 25 (2008), 71, 82–6; and A. Tzanakopoulos, 'Denunciation of the ICSID Convention under the General International Law of Treaties' in R. Hofmann and C. Tams (eds.), *International Investment Law and General International Law: From Clinical Isolation to Systemic Integration?* (Baden-Baden, Germany: Nomos 2011), 75, 81–92.

[41] Cf. C. Schreuer, 'Denunciation of the ICISD Convention', 353, 364–7. [42] *Ibid.*, 364.

[43] O. Garibaldi, 'On the Denunciation of the ICSID Convention, Consent to ICSID Jurisdiction and the Limits of the Contract Analogy' in C. Binder, U. Kriebaum, A. Reinisch and S. Wittich (eds.), *International Investment Law for the 21st Century: Essays in Honour of Christoph Schreuer* (Oxford University Press, 2009), 251, 257–8, 272–4. Recent contributions coming to the same conclusion for similar or alternative reasons include F. Sourgens, 'Keep the Faith: Investment Protection Following the Denunciation of International Investment Agreements', *Santa Clara Journal of International Law*, 11 (2013), 335, 390–5; M. Durney, 'Legal Effects and Implications of the Denunciation of the ICSID Convention on Unilateral Consent Contained in Bilateral Investment Treaties: A Perspective from Latin American Cases', *Max Planck Yearbook of United Nations Law*, 17 (2013), 224, 261–72; V. Tejera, 'Unraveling ICSID's Denunciation:

Article 72 would thus be a 'special rule on consent in case of denunciation'.[44]

This had been an academic discussion until proceedings started being instituted against the Latin American States that denounced the ICSID Convention. While a number of such proceedings have been discontinued, an ICSID Tribunal has finally had the chance to pronounce on the matter in *Venoklim Holding BV* v. *Venezuela*.[45] The claimant in that case had instituted proceedings after Venezuela had denounced the Convention but before the six-month period envisaged by Article 71 had lapsed. The respondent then filed its first preliminary objection along the lines of the narrow interpretation of Article 72. Though the Tribunal ultimately found that it lacked jurisdiction to address the merits of the dispute, it rejected this particular preliminary objection. In its opinion, the rule in Article 72 should not be construed as allowing the denunciation of the ICSID Convention to produce immediate effects, that is, to bypass the six-month period envisaged by Article 71.[46] That would be contrary to 'basic principles of legal certainty' because investors cannot anticipate the precise moment at which a host State will file its notice of denunciation, and the purpose of the six-month period in Article 71 is to provide investors with the time to take whatever measures they may be entitled to before denunciation takes effect.[47] For the Tribunal, Articles 71 and 72 fulfil different purposes: the former deals with the prospective effects of denunciation, and the latter makes it clear that denunciation cannot produce effects retrospectively.[48] Most important for present purposes, the Tribunal sided with the broad interpretation of Article 72, finding that 'consent . . . given by one of them' means the unilateral offer to arbitrate made by one of the parties, not 'perfected consent' in the sense of Article 25.[49] It concluded that at the time of the filing of the request to arbitrate, 'Venezuela was still a Contracting Party to the ICSID Convention and, as a result, was bound to respect its obligation to submit to arbitration before this forum.'[50]

Understanding the Interaction between Articles 71 and 72 of the ICSID Convention', *ILSA Journal of International and Comparative Law*, 20 (2014), 423, 431–5.

[44] Cf. M. Durney, 'Legal Effects and Implications of the Denunciation of the ICSID', 224, 271.

[45] *Venoklim Holding B.V.* v *Venezuela*, ICSID Case No. ARB/12/22, Award of 3 April 2015.

[46] *Ibid.*, para. 61. [47] *Ibid.*, para. 63. [48] *Ibid.*, para. 64. [49] *Ibid.*, para. 65.

[50] *Ibid.*, para. 67: 'Lo anterior significa que, cuando la Demandante presentó su Solicitud, Venezuela era todavía un Estado Contratante del Convenio CIADI y, en consecuencia estaba obligada a respetar su obligación de acudir al arbitraje ante ese foro.'

While this recent award has now tipped the balance in favour of the broad interpretation of Article 72, it did not deal with many of the arguments advanced in academic commentary in support of one interpretation or the other. The reasoning of the Tribunal, which heavily relies on an abstract notion of 'legal security', may be criticised as somewhat sketchy. Moreover, the Tribunal did not answer – because it did not need to – the question of whether Article 72 continues protecting rights arising from unilateral consent given previously to the notice of denunciation once the six-month period of Article 71 passes and denunciation takes effect. It will be interesting to see whether the approach taken by the Tribunal will be followed in future decisions.

(2) How Effective a Means to Reassert Control Should ICSID Denunciation Be?

Now that the state of the debate has been discussed, it is important to reflect upon the underlying normative positions that may inform the view that one forms about the interpretation of Articles 71 and 72. Given that so many BITs envisage recourse to ICSID arbitration, should Articles 71 and 72 be construed in a way that makes reasserting control over investment relations easier for States? Should, in other words, one criticise the Tribunal in *Venoklim Holding BV* v. *Venezuela* and side instead with Christoph Schreuer? I shall consider in this section two implications of adopting the narrow interpretation of Article 72.

The first concerns circumvention of treaty obligations. Antonios Tzanakopoulos has persuasively cautioned interpreters of the ICSID Convention against solving the riddle posed by Articles 71 and 72 by reference to an ill-defined conception of what the object and purpose of the Convention may be. It is a mistake to look at the Convention as an agreement whose 'core objective is the accommodation and broadest possible (even if only procedural) protection of foreign private investors'.[51] Rather, Tzanakopoulos suggests that the object and purpose of the ICSID Convention is 'neutral': that of providing 'a *facility* for those states that wish to encourage foreign investment by opting, voluntarily, for the settlement of investment disputes by arbitration in the particular shape and form offered by the Centre'.[52] This is a compelling point. But when one interprets the phrase 'consent ... given by one of them' in Article 72 in light of the 'neutral' object and purpose of the ICSID

[51] Tzanakopoulos, 'Denunciation of the ICSID Convention', 75, 82. [52] *Ibid.*, 83.

Convention, it is also important to consider the system of international investment law that we end up with if it is accepted that States are entitled to denounce the Convention to rid themselves of obligations assumed under the compromissory clauses of BITs.

Even if this is something that the drafters of the Convention did not anticipate, it is a fact that the facility created by the ICSID Convention has been put into motion mostly as a result of the conclusion of BITs. On Schreuer's interpretation, Article 72 is meant to protect 'irrevocable consent', which Article 25 specifies as mutual consent to ICSID arbitration. This stands in contrast with a unilateral offer to agree to ICSID arbitration which a State would be free to revoke at its convenience. But there is a key difference between offers to consent given by States *ex gratia* and *undertakings* to consent under BITs validly concluded by them.[53] Is it sensible to read Article 72, the terms of which are ambiguous, as covering only the mutual consent to arbitrate made irrevocable by Article 25 of the ICSID Convention while disregarding a legal undertaking to consent to arbitrate? Should obligations assumed under a treaty by a State vis-à-vis another State for the benefit of the investor deserve less protection than a contract concluded between the State and the investor? The upshot of endorsing the narrow interpretation of Article 72 is that the treaty which puts into place a facility for the settlement of investment disputes can then be used to create obstacles for the fulfilment of agreements the main point of which is often to provide for dispute settlement.[54]

[53] In this respect, agreements to consent to ICSID arbitration under BITs differ from agreements to arbitrate expressed through domestic legislation. The latter can be unilaterally modified by a State wishing to withdraw from the ICSID Convention without any restrictions imposed by international law. It would thus not be necessarily incoherent to argue that an offer to arbitrate given in a BIT – to the extent that it is irrevocable unilaterally – is protected by Article 72 while an offer to arbitrate given in national legislation – to the extent that it is revocable unilaterally – is not. On consent by national legislation, though coming to the opposite conclusion, see O. Garibaldi, 'On the Denunciation of the ICSID Convention', 251, 267–8.

[54] It should be noted that whether by withdrawing from ICSID a State will violate or otherwise circumvent obligations under a BIT depends on the interpretation of the particular compromissory clause. A breach will clearly arise if the compromissory clause elects ICSID as the only forum for international arbitration (cf. note 35) or if the choice of ICSID arbitration is unequivocally provided for the investor (as is the case e.g. with Article 9(3) of the 2003 Germany–China BIT). If – as it often happens – the compromissory clause offers ICSID as an option for dispute settlement *provided* that both parties to the BIT are also parties to the Convention (e.g. Article 34(3)(a) US Model BIT), it can be argued that the compromissory clause in the BIT is without prejudice to one of the parties deciding subsequently to withdraw from the ICSID Convention. Some BITs, such as the

The oddness of accepting that Article 72 protects mutual consent in contracts but not unilateral consent in BITs becomes more apparent when one considers the course of action that authors espousing the narrow interpretation recommend for investors who wish to benefit from Article 72 protection. For Schreuer, '[I]t is inadvisable for an investor to rely on an ICSID consent clause contained in the host State's domestic law or in a treaty without making a reciprocal declaration of consent' because if the investor 'wait[s] with its acceptance of the offer of consent until it institutes proceedings before the Centre', it will run 'the risk that the offer may be withdrawn before then'.[55] It seems that the solution would be to advise investors to send letters to host States accepting the offer made via the BIT and be quick about it! But given that investors are entitled under international law to rely on the compromissory clause in the BIT for as long as the BIT remains in force, what purpose would that procedural step serve in the system devised by the Convention?[56]

The second implication of adopting the narrow interpretation concerns the legal consequences of ICSID Convention denunciation for a State that remains bound to consent to ICSID arbitration under a BIT. As Tzanakopoulos notes, 'Since [the BIT] is incapable of being implemented because of a unilateral act of the withdrawing state, the latter's international responsibility for breach of the obligation under the treaty will be engaged, exposing it to all possible reactions under general international law, whether of treaties (e.g. termination for material breach) or of State responsibility (countermeasures).'[57] But a question previous to that of the reactions that a State can take under the law of State responsibility (the measures of implementation regulated in Part III of the Articles on State Responsibility (ASR)) is that of the legal consequences which follow from the commission of internationally wrongful acts (the subject of Part II of the ASR). Those are, of course, the obligations of cessation and reparation.

US Model BIT and the 2005 Belgium–Sudan BIT, avoid this problem by prescribing that the investor may have recourse to the ICSID Additional Facility if one of the parties to the BIT happens not to be a party to the ICSID Convention.

55 Cf C. Schreuer, 'Denunciation of the ICISD Convention', 353, 363.

56 If an offer to arbitrate is revocable, that makes sense. It could be even said that the denunciation notice filed by the host State constitutes a valid act of revocation of an offer which the investor failed to accept while it stood. See also note 53.

57 As Tzanakopoulos notes, the remedies available under general international law 'accrue to the other state party to the BIT, and not to any private entity that might have benefited from the promise of ICSID arbitration': Tzanakopoulos, 'Denunciation of the ICSID Convention', 75, 92.

Under the rule articulated in Article 35 of the ASR, a State is under a duty to 'make restitution, that is to re-establish the situation which existed before the wrongful act was committed' as long as that is not 'materially impossible' and 'does not involve a burden out of all proportion to the benefit deriving from restitution instead of compensation'. In the case of a breach of a compromissory clause in a BIT through ICSID Convention denunciation, making restitution means agreeing to submit the dispute to ICSID arbitration (e.g. under the Additional Facility Rules that allow non-parties to the Convention to resort to the services of the Centre). Though there may be room for debate, it would be difficult for a State to establish that consenting to ICSID arbitration is materially impossible or excessively burdensome in the sense of Article 35 of the ASR. It just takes a 'yes' from the host State and the willingness to pay its share of the costs of arbitration to make restitution for the breach of the BIT caused by denunciation of the ICSID Convention.

Restitution is not, however, a remedy that an investor may claim directly, for it is to the State of nationality of the investor that the host State ultimately owes the obligation to consent to ICSID jurisdiction.[58] In practice, this means that the implementation of the host State's responsibility for circumventing a BIT by denouncing the ICSID Convention will ultimately depend on the political will of the State of nationality of the investor. But the point to get from this discussion is that the question of the effects of ICSID Convention denunciation should not be treated as a self-contained issue without regard to the rights and obligations of the parties involved under general international law. If Article 72 can be construed in a way that is conducive to the compliance with dispute settlement obligations in BITs, that interpretation is to be preferred under the principles of 'harmonisation' and 'systemic integration' that the ILC identified in its 2006 'Conclusions of the Work of the Study Group on the Fragmentation of International Law'.[59] As the ILC noted in that study, '[W]hen several norms bear on a single issue they should, to the extent possible, be interpreted so as to give rise to a single set of compatible obligations.'[60]

[58] *Ibid.*

[59] International Law Commission, 'Conclusions of the Work of the Study Group on the Fragmentation of International Law: Difficulties Arising from the Diversification and Expansion of International Law' (2006), paras. 17, 18, 21. On systemic integration, see Chapter 8.

[60] International Law Commission, 'Conclusions of the Work of the Study Group on the Fragmentation of International Law: Difficulties Arising from the Diversification and Expansion of International Law' (2006), Conclusion 4.

Taking into account the international obligations under BITs of the parties to the ICSID Convention in construing Article 72 is indeed a sensible application of the rule of interpretation in Article 31(3)(c) of the VCLT.[61]

In short, the interpretation of Article 72 of the ICSID Convention favoured by Schreuer and others, which would allow States to circumvent obligations to arbitrate under ICSID by denouncing the Convention, remains plausible. If it is correct, ICSID Convention denunciation allows States to reassert some control over how disputes under existing BITs are settled. One may question, however, whether this is a good solution if the international rule of law is a value worth promoting and fulfilling. From a legal perspective, States can only withdraw from obligations under BITs on the terms set by the treaties themselves or on the grounds recognised under general international law. Given the extended protection that termination and survival clauses in existing BITs offer, renegotiating those BITs may be the only option that States have to 'reassert control' while complying with the law. Reading a Convention that protects 'irrevocable' consent to arbitration from the effects of denunciation as providing a shortcut for circumventing – in total or in part – treaty obligations to consent to ICSID arbitration may provide an illusory and normatively problematic means for States to reassert control over their investment relations.

D. Conclusion

The great majority of BITs under which a State party consents to submit disputes with nationals of the other party to ICSID arbitration can only be set aside through the application of detailed termination clauses and enjoy a considerable afterlife by virtue of sunset clauses. On their own terms, they constitute remarkably stable legal regimes.

Denouncing the ICSID Convention is an option open to State parties which can and should be used by those dissatisfied with the current system of investor-State dispute settlement as a first step towards reasserting control. However, the Convention should not be construed as allowing States to circumvent obligations to resort to arbitration provided in existing BITs. While reading the withdrawal provisions of the Convention as protecting contractual arrangements between host States

[61] Pursuant to Article 31(3)(c), which articulates the 'principle of systemic integration', in the interpretation of treaties, '[t]here shall be taken into account, together with the context, any relevant rules of international law applicable in the relations between the parties.'

and investors but not the binding undertakings under BITs is possible, it is a normatively problematic solution. In this light, the recent award of the Tribunal in *Venoklim Holding BV* v. *Venezuela* should be regarded as a positive development.

Ultimately, terminating investment treaties, though essential for reasserting control over investment relations, is a measure constrained by law which is unlikely to provide immediate relief for States disillusioned with investment agreements and investment treaty arbitration. As has been the case with the recent practice of South Africa and Indonesia, it is hoped that States will make use of treaty termination with a view towards negotiating more balanced and fairer agreements, making the system better rather than disowning it with the ensuing conflict and losses.

10

Legitimate Regulatory Interests

Case Law and Developments in IIA Practice

PAUL BARKER

A. Introduction

In response to the global financial crisis, governments around the world took unprecedented measures to avert the collapse of the global economic system.[1] The scale and extent of this State-led intervention in the private sector, using billions of dollars of taxpayers' money, forced a rethink of prevailing economic orthodoxy in a world of freely moving capital.[2] This new reality presents challenges for investor-State dispute settlement, particularly where international investment law is underdeveloped or where the relationship between international law and international community policy is unclear.[3] Take the 2012 Greek government bond exchange, the largest sovereign debt restructuring in history.[4] It was a condition precedent to Greece receiving a €130 billion bail-out from the Eurozone Member States that private holders of Greek debt accept a 53.5 per cent haircut on the value of their bonds.[5] The restructuring followed international best practice, using collective-action clauses to prevent 'holdout' bondholders from refusing to participate in the exchange and suing the State in domestic courts for full repayment under the bond contract.[6] Following this multilateral effort driven by the

[1] See generally B. S. Bernanke, *The Courage to Act: A Memoir of a Crisis and Its Aftermath* (New York: W.W. Norton, 2015).

[2] M. Wolf, *The Shifts and the Shocks* (New York: Penguin, 2014), 27; A. Beattie, 'IMF Drops Opposition to Capital Controls', *Financial Times*, 3 December 2012.

[3] See e.g. M. Waibel, 'Opening Pandora's Box: Sovereign Bonds in International Arbitration', *American Journal of International Law*, 101 (2007), 715.

[4] International Monetary Fund, 'Sovereign Debt Restructuring: Recent Developments and Implications for the Fund's Legal and Policy Framework', 2013, 6.

[5] *Postova* v. *Hellenic Republic*, ICSID Case No. ARB/13/8, Award of 9 April 2015, para. 66.

[6] M. Committeri and F. Spadafora, 'You Never Give Me Your Money? Sovereign Debt Crises, Collective Action Problems, and IMF Lending', IMF Working Papers 20/2013

Eurozone, the European Central Bank and the International Monetary Fund to reduce Greece's debt burden to sustainable levels, holders of restructured bonds commenced investment treaty arbitrations against Greece, arguing that they are entitled to compensation for the haircut under international law.[7]

It is reasonable to expect that such real-world events will have implications for the development of international investment law,[8] particularly as regards host States' 'legitimate regulatory interests', a concept introduced but not defined by the tribunal in *Saluka* v. *Czech Republic.*[9] Indeed, the altered global political economy since 2008 is reflected in the current focus on the right of States parties to international investment agreements (IIAs) to enact regulatory measures for the general welfare without incurring liability to foreign investors.[10] This is now widely described as the State's 'right to regulate'.[11]

Mindful of this recent history, the purpose of this chapter is to survey how Contracting Parties to IIAs are reasserting their right to regulate in investment arbitration proceedings and in the drafting of their IIAs. This trend precedes the global financial crisis. In 2004, Canada and the United States both substantially reformulated their model bilateral investment treaties (BITs) to reflect concerns that some tribunals had interpreted IIAs too much in favour of investor rights at the expense of host States' regulatory sovereignty.[12] Special interest groups have similarly criticised IIAs for having a chilling effect on government regulation. For example, environmental campaigners have argued that trade and investment agreements promote carbon

(2013); M. Sandbu, 'Free Lunch: Flat-Pack Sovereign Debt Restructuring – How to Build Flexibility into Government Financing Instruments', *Financial Times*, 28 July 2015.

7 *Postova and ISTROKAPITAL* v. *Hellenic Republic*, ICSID Case No. ARB/13/8, Award of 9 April 2015 (annulment proceedings pending); *Cyprus Popular Bank Public Co., Ltd.* v. *Hellenic Republic*, ICSID Case No. ARB/14/16.

8 See e.g. 'Trans-Pacific Partnership' (2015), Chapter 9 ('Investment'), Annex 9G ('Public Debt'), available at https://ustr.gov/sites/default/files/TPP-Final-Text-Investment.pdf (accessed 24 February 2016).

9 *Saluka Investments B.V.* v. *Czech Republic*, UNCITRAL, Partial Award of 17 March 2006, para. 306.

10 *Suez et al.* v. *Argentine Republic*, ICSID Case No. ARB/03/17, Separate Opinion of Arbitrator Nikken of 30 July 2010, para. 36.

11 See e.g. 'EU-Canada Comprehensive Economic and Trade Agreement' (CETA), Preamble, available at http://trade.ec.europa.eu/doclib/docs/2014/september/tradoc_152806.pdf (accessed 12 January 2016).

12 UNCTAD, 'Expropriation: A Sequel', UNCTAD Series on Issues in International Investment Agreements II (2012), 71.

use and damaging environmental practices.[13] Furthermore, over the past decade, a crescendo of practitioners and scholars has called for a re-conceptualisation of investor-State arbitration as a 'public order control and accountability mechanism', more akin to judicial review than to international commercial arbitration.[14]

Yet few of these developments or critiques have entered the mainstream political debate until recently. One significant consequence of the global financial crisis, however, has been growing public disquiet over the functioning of the global economic system, including investor-State arbitration. This has translated into heightened public scrutiny of IIA negotiations – which have traditionally been conducted behind closed doors by diplomats and technocrats – and of investor-State arbitration awards. As discussed in greater depth in Chapters 1 and 13, widely reported debates continue across four continents among politicians, civil society advocates and other stakeholders regarding the conclusion of two new regional mega-treaties containing investment protection provisions: the Transatlantic Trade and Investment Partnership (TTIP) and the Trans-Pacific Partnership (TPP).[15] And it is the right of States to regulate in the public interest that is at the heart of these debates.

This is so because most investor-State arbitrations do not concern bright-line cases of direct expropriation and may instead arise out of host States' measures which have 'nothing to do with economic considerations, but intend to protect fundamental public goods, for example, the environment, public health and national security'.[16] Investor-State tribunals have recently considered, *inter alia*, emergency powers exercised during national economic crises,[17] the regulation of public

[13] G. Monbiot, 'All Give and No Take', *The Guardian*, 11 March 2014.

[14] S. Schill, 'The Sixth Path: Reforming Investment Law from Within', *Transnational Dispute Management*, 11 (2014), 11; see also A. Roberts, 'Clash of Paradigms: Actors and Analogies Shaping the Investment Treaty System', *American Journal of International Law*, 107 (2013), 52; *CME Czech Republic B.V.* v. *The Czech Republic*, UNCITRAL, Separate Opinion of Sir Ian Brownlie of 14 March 2003, 74.

[15] See Section B(3).

[16] C. Conyan, 'China-US BIT Negotiations and the Future of Investment Treaty Regime: A Grand Bargain with Multilateral Implications', *Journal of International Economic Law* 457 (2009), 477.

[17] *CMS Gas Transmission Co.* v. *Argentine Republic*, ICSID Case No. ARB/01/8, Award of 12 May 2005; *LG&E Energy Corp, LG&E Capital Corp, LG&E International, Inc.* v. *Argentine Republic*, ICSID Case No. ARB/02/1, Decision on Liability of 3 October 2006; *Sempra Energy International* v. *Argentine Republic*, ICSID Case No. ARB/02/16, Award of 28 September 2007; *Enron Corp and Ponderosa Assets, LP* v. *Argentine Republic*, ICSID Case No. ARB/01/3, Award of 22 May 2007; *BG Group plc* v. *Argentine Republic*,

utilities,[18] the regulation of harmful substances,[19] the protection of cultural property or heritage[20] and non-discrimination and affirmative action policies.[21] Two claimants in particular have caught the public's attention[22]: Phillip Morris, which introduced two claims (now dismissed) against Australia and Uruguay relating to tobacco plain-packaging legislation,[23] and Vattenfall, which commenced an arbitration under the Energy Charter Treaty (ECT) against Germany for the termination of that country's nuclear energy programme following the Fukushima disaster.[24]

A major challenge to any survey of this subject is that most of the more than 3,000 existing IIAs do not typically address with sufficient clarity the relationship between investor protection and the host State's right to pursue legitimate public policy objectives – although, as discussed later, new treaties attempt to do so. This begs the question, what arguments does

UNCITRAL, Final Award of 24 December 2007; *Continental Casualty Co.* v. *Argentine Republic*, ICSID Case No. ARB/03/9, Award of 5 September 2008; *National Grid plc* v. *Argentine Republic*, UNCITRAL, Award of 3 November 2008; *Suez et al.* v. *Argentine Republic*, ICSID Case No. ARB/03/17, Award of 30 July 2010; *Daimler Financial Services AG* v. *Argentine Republic*, ICSID Case No. ARB/05/1, Award of 22 October 2012; *Postova and ISTROKAPITAL* v. *Hellenic Republic*, ICSID Case No. ARB/13/8, Award of 9 April 2015; *Cyprus Popular Bank Public Co., Ltd.* v. *Hellenic Republic*, ICSID Case No. ARB/14/16 (pending).

18 *Biwater Gauff (Tanzania), Ltd.* v. *United Republic of Tanzania*, ICSID Case No. ARB/05/22, Award of 24 July 2004; *Aguas del Tunari SA* v. *Republic of Bolivia*, ICSID Case No. ARB/02/3, Decision on Respondent's Objections to Jurisdiction of 21 October 2005.

19 *Methanex Corp.* v. *US*, NAFTA, Final Award of the Tribunal on Jurisdiction and Merits of 3 August 2005.

20 *Southern Pacific Properties (Middle East), Ltd.* v. *Arab Republic of Egypt*, ICSID Case No. ARB/84/3, Award on the Merits of 20 May 1992; *Glamis Gold, Ltd.* v. *United States of America*, UNCITRAL, Final Award of 8 June 2009.

21 *Piero Foresti, Laura de Carli and others* v. *Republic of South Africa*, ICSID Case No. ARB(AF)/07/1, Award of 4 August 2010.

22 European Commission, 'Fact Sheet: Investment Protection and Investor-to-State Dispute Settlement in EU agreements', Brussels, 2013, 5, available at http://trade.ec.europa.eu/doclib/docs/2013/november/tradoc_151916.pdf (accessed 24 February 2016).

23 *Philip Morris Brands Sàrl, Philip Morris Products S.A. and Abal Hermanos S.A.* v. *Oriental Republic of Uruguay*, ICSID Case No. ARB/10/7, Award of 8 July 2016 (published shortly before this book went to print), in which the tribunal dismissed Philip Morris's claims on the merits, finding that the measures were a reasonable bona fide exercise of police powers for the protection of public health, were not arbitrary, grossly unfair, unjust, discriminatory or disproportionate, and were therefore non-compensable, paras. 307, 420; *Philip Morris Asia Limited (Hong Kong)* v. *Commonwealth of Australia*, UNCTAD, PCA Case No. 2012–12, Award on Jurisdiction and Admissibility of 17 December 2015, in which the tribunal dismissed Philip Morris's claims on jurisdictional grounds.

24 *Vattenfall* v. *Germany*, ICSID Case No. ARB/12/12.

a tribunal find persuasive in distinguishing between a non-compensable regulation, on the one hand, and an indirect expropriation (or 'regulatory taking'), on the other? And when might a measure directed at a legitimate regulatory interest still violate the fair and equitable treatment (FET) standard, for example?

The balancing between the 'public regulatory needs of states and the private interests of investors' is closely related to another contested subject of international investment law: the standard of review.[25] The standard of review applied by tribunals is 'a central means by which to calibrate the balance of power between host states and foreign investors in international investment law'.[26] A deferential standard can allow a tribunal to recognise the State's discretion or margin of appreciation in pursuing a legitimate regulatory interest, but, as demonstrated later, tribunals remain divided over the level of scrutiny that should be accorded policy decisions made by respondent States. A deferential standard of review will not, however, necessarily result in the State avoiding liability for a regulatory measure that harms an investor. For example, the tribunal may nonetheless determine that the alleged regulatory interest is a pretext, or the measure's implementation was arbitrary, discriminatory, disproportionate or otherwise unfair.

It is clear that international investment law recognises the State's right to regulate in the public interest.[27] For instance, in the *Chemtura* NAFTA arbitration, Canada submitted the following:

> Fundamentally, this case is about a government banning the use of a dangerous chemical in order to protect public health ... [W]as the government acting to protect public health in a manner that was non-discriminatory, not excessive, non-arbitrary, and in good faith? If the answer to this question is yes, then the Claimant does not – at international law – have a right to compensation.[28]

Canada relied in part on the oft-cited award in *Saluka* v. *Czech Republic*, where the tribunal held in respect of the expropriation and FET standards, respectively, that

[25] A. Mills, 'Antinomies of Public and Private at the Foundation of International Investment Law and Arbitration', *Journal of International Economic Law*, 14 (2011), 469.

[26] C. Henckels, 'Balancing Investment Protection and the Public Interest: The Role of the Standard of Review and the Importance of Deference in Investor-State Arbitration', *Journal of International Dispute Settlement*, 4 (2013), 197.

[27] *Philip Morris* v. *Uruguay*, Award of 8 July 2016, paras. 292–301.

[28] *Chemtura Corporation* v. *Canada*, NAFTA, Respondent's Rejoinder, paras. 283, 288.

> [i]t is now established in international law that States are not liable to pay compensation to a foreign investor when, in the normal exercise of their regulatory powers, they adopt in a non-discriminatory manner bona fide regulations that are aimed at the general welfare. . . .
>
> The determination of a breach of [the FET standard] by the Czech Republic . . . requires a weighing of the Claimant's legitimate and reasonable expectations on the one hand and the Respondent's *legitimate regulatory interests* on the other.[29]

But, as we shall see, the exercise of the right to regulate is subject to legal limits, both procedural and substantive. Indeed, having found no expropriation, the *Saluka* tribunal went on to hold that the State had nonetheless violated the FET standard of the BIT.[30] Even when considering national crises, some tribunals have taken a more robust approach to the host State's regulatory power. For example, in *Daimler* v. *Argentina*, the tribunal stated that it was

> [m]indful of the Respondent's right to regulate its economy as it sees fit. This right adheres in the sovereign Government of Argentina both in times of economic crisis and otherwise. But the Respondent's general sovereignty is not at issue in these proceedings. What is at issue is the Respondent's obligation to observe its treaty commitments under the German-Argentine BIT. The Claimant has not alleged that Argentina may not exercise its powers to regulate its economy nor that such regulation may never negatively affect the Claimant. Rather, it has alleged that where Argentina elects to exercise its powers in a manner that contravenes one of Argentina's voluntarily assumed international obligations to German investors under the German-Argentine BIT, and where such contravention specifically harms the Claimant's investment, Argentina must compensate the Claimant for the violation.[31]

Ultimately, this issue is about the balance that is struck within the IIA regime between the protection of private investors and the public regulatory imperatives of sovereign States and how tribunals strike this balance when interpreting a treaty's often indeterminate standards of protection and applying them in light of the particular facts of the case.[32]

[29] *Saluka Investments B.V.* v. *Czech Republic*, UNCITRAL, Partial Award of 17 March 2006, paras. 255, 306.

[30] *Ibid.*, para. 511c.

[31] *Daimler Financial Services AG* v. *Argentine Republic*, ICSID Case No. ARB/05/1, Award of 22 October 2012, para. 100. Compare with *Philip Morris* v. *Uruguay*, Award of 8 July 2016, paras. 289–301.

[32] See P. Barker, 'International Investment Arbitration as International Public Law', in I. Laird, B. Sabahi, F. Sourgens and T. Weiler (eds.), *International Law and Investment Treaty Arbitration* (New St, Huntington, NY: Juris, 2015), 235–69.

The upshot of an IIA regime that concerns the interpretation of many broadly drafted treaties and lacks a doctrine of precedent or an appellate court is that some awards are not easy to reconcile with others. Moreover, it is necessary to consider the consequences of new language on legitimate regulatory interests that States are including in their latest IIAs. Over the past decade, new IIAs have sought to clarify that they 'do not purport to promote and protect investment at the expense of other key values such as health, safety, labour protection and the environment'.[33] But how does this trend affect the interpretation of older IIAs that do not contain express provisions on the State's regulatory powers?

Accordingly, this chapter will entail an examination of both State and arbitral tribunal practice. *State practice* will be demonstrated primarily by (1) treaty practice, namely, the language that parties agree to in their IIAs regarding the host State's regulatory authority; and (2) States' advocacy in investor-State arbitration proceedings. *Tribunal practice*, will be demonstrated by select published awards.

This chapter is structured as follows. Section B introduces the concept of legitimate regulatory interests in customary international law and international investment law. It also provides a brief overview of how States have sought or are seeking to protect their legitimate regulatory interests in new IIAs. Section C will use select awards from the past fifteen years to demonstrate host States' reassertion of control over their regulatory sovereignty in investment treaty arbitrations. Section D concludes.

B. Legitimate Regulatory Interests: Context and Development

(1) Relationship between Customary International Law and IIAs

State regulation permeates all aspects of the modern economy.[34] By entering into IIAs, however, States delegate sovereignty to arbitral tribunals to determine when an investor is entitled to compensation for a State-attributed measure affecting its investment. Tribunals cannot strike down State measures, but an award of damages can have a 'chilling effect on future governmental conduct by preventing governments from

[33] UNCTAD, 'Bilateral Investment Treaties 1995–2006: Trends in Investment Rulemaking', UN (2007), 4, available at http://unctad.org/en/docs/iteiia20065_en.pdf (accessed 24 February 2016).

[34] UNCTAD, 'Expropriation: A Sequel', 80.

adopting certain courses of action for fear of future liability.'[35] As practitioner Toby Landau explains:

> [F]or all the passing similarity with the deliberation room in commercial arbitration, this setting [in international investment arbitration] is totally different. [There is a] tribunal in place because of inter-State consent as well as investor consent, but your very existence depends upon two or more states having agreed to you being there. Your mandate unlike commercial arbitration is to review the exercise of discretion by a sovereign by way of its executive, its legislative, even its judiciary. You are tasked in this exercise with applying extremely broadly worded standards. They do not give you much guidance. They are skeletal. They are skeletal because [of] the dynamics . . . of inter-State negotiations . . . and so you are faced with a very concrete problem. You are supposed to rule upon the interest of an individual investor and yet in doing so, you may well impact upon a whole community. If you are going to rule that a carbons emission quota system is contrary to a [IIA], in order to safeguard the interest of a particular coal-fires power plant in a country, then, you may well be impacting upon the whole environment policy of an entire nation. If you are going to rule upon the rights of an investor in the water system of Tanzania, you may well be affecting 350[,]000 water users in Dar Es Salaam. If you are going to question and rule upon South Africa's policy in favour of black economic empowerment, in order to safeguard the interest of the individual mining interest before you the wider impact is obvious. And, you do so with the ability to impose damages unlike many public law municipal systems and those damages may be significant. You have the power to affect the most extraordinary allocation of public funds.[36]

Earlier generations of IIAs are indeed often skeletal and merely include 'provisions for investor rights without addressing in a comprehensive fashion the relationship of these to continuing powers of State regulation'.[37] Although 'it is likely that States parties typically did not intend a severe occlusion of these regulatory powers',[38] tribunals have

[35] A. Roberts, 'The Present: Investment Arbitration as a Governance Tool for Economic International Relations? The Next Battleground: Standards of Review in Investment Treaty Arbitration', in A. J. van den Berg (ed.), *Arbitration: The Next Fifty Years* (ICCA Congress Series 16) (2010), 7.

[36] T. Landau, 'Response to the Report, Rethinking the Substantive Standards of Protection under Investment Treaties', in *Proceedings of the Mauritius International Arbitration Conference* (2010), 368, available at www.lcia.org/media/Download.aspx?MediaId=119 (accessed 24 February 2016).

[37] B. Kingsbury and S. Schill, 'Investor-State Arbitration as Governance: Fair and Equitable Treatment, Proportionality and the Emerging Global Administrative Law', NYU School of Law, Public Law Research Paper No. 09–46 (2009), 23.

[38] *Ibid.*

not typically been given much guidance to determine where the State's discretion ends and the investor's rights begin.[39]

Nevertheless, IIAs are creatures of public international law. It is therefore necessary as a matter of treaty interpretation to consider the place of States' legitimate regulatory interests within that body of law and how IIAs relate to it.[40] Under customary international law, the State's right to regulate in the public interest is well established.[41] The jurisprudential foundation is the 'police powers' doctrine, which

> must be understood as encompassing a State's full regulatory dimension. Modern States go well beyond the fundamental functions of custody, security and protection. They intervene in the economy through regulation in a variety of ways: preventing and prosecuting monopolistic and anticompetitive practices; protecting the rights of consumers; implementing control regimes through licences, concessions, registers, permits and authorizations; protecting the environment and public health; regulating the conduct of corporations; and others.[42]

Although Judge Higgins has questioned the intellectual viability of the distinction between an expropriation, on the one hand, and a non-compensable regulation based on public purpose, on the other,[43] authorities suggest that States may exercise such police powers without incurring liability to alien investors under customary international law.[44] As demonstrated later, influential tribunals have incorporated this principle into international investment law.[45] Indeed, the United Nations Conference on Trade and Development (UNCTAD) concludes that expropriation provisions in IIAs 'may not be read as preventing

[39] See T. Landau, *Mauritius International Arbitration Conference*, 369.

[40] See *Philip Morris* v. *Uruguay*, Award of 8 July 2016, para. 290.

[41] J. Viñuales, 'Sovereignty in Foreign Investment Law', in Z. Douglas, J. Pauwelyn and J. E. Viñuales (eds.), *The Foundations of International Investment Law* (Oxford University Press, 2014), 326.

[42] UNCTAD, 'Expropriation: A Sequel', 79.

[43] R. Higgins, 'The Taking of Property by the State: Recent Developments in International Law', *Recueil des Cours* (1982), 331; *Azurix* v. *Argentine Republic*, ICSID Case No. ARB/01/12, Award of 14 June 2006, para. 310.

[44] 'Restatement (Third) of Foreign Relations of the United States', American Law Institute (1987), Section 712, Comment (g).

[45] *Saluka Investments B.V.* v. *Czech Republic*, UNCITRAL, Partial Award of 17 March 2006, para. 254; *Methanex Corp.* v. *US*, NAFTA, Final Award of the Tribunal on Jurisdiction and Merits of 3 August 2005, Part IV, Chapter D, para. 7. *Chemtura Corporation* v. *Canada*, NAFTA, Award, para. 306; see also *Philip Morris* v. *Uruguay*, Award of 8 July 2016, paras. 289–301.

States from *bona fide* regulation in the public interest'.[46] Accordingly, in respect of the expropriation standard:

> [T]here are also nondiscriminatory regulatory measures, i.e. acts taken by States in the exercise of their right to regulate in the public interest that may lead to effects similar to indirect expropriation but at the same time are not classified as expropriation and do not give rise to the obligation to compensate those affected.[47]

And, in respect of the FET standard:

> [T]he application of FET provisions has brought to light the need to balance investment protection with competing policy objectives of the host State, and in particular, with its right to regulate in the public interest.[48]

As discussed further in Section C, in order to avoid liability under their IIAs, States have argued in numerous cases that the impugned measure is aimed at a legitimate regulatory interest and is therefore non-compensable. This argument has frequently been raised in the related areas of environmental and health protection but also in cases concerning measures related to cultural heritage, human rights and national security, among others. Most IIAs do not, however, expressly state what constitutes a legitimate regulatory interest or a non-compensable regulatory measure. Tribunals must therefore not only decide as a substantive matter whether there is a legitimate regulatory interest to which the measure is genuinely addressed but also from a more procedural or due-process perspective on whether the way in which the measure was implemented conforms to the standards of protection in the IIA.

(2) Saluka *v.* Czech Republic

The award in *Saluka* expressly refers to the State's 'legitimate regulatory interests' and is frequently cited as one of the original investment tribunal decisions recognising non-compensable regulatory measures.[49] *Saluka* concerned the State's refusal to provide financial assistance to a bank, IPB. The tribunal acknowledged that the expropriation clause of the BIT was broadly drafted and did not contain any exception for the exercise of regulatory power. Nevertheless, the tribunal held that it would take

46 UNCTAD, 'Expropriation: A Sequel', 85. 47 *Ibid.*, xi.

48 UNCTAD, 'FET: A Sequel', UNCTAD Series on Issues in International Investment Agreements II (2012), xiii.

49 *Saluka Investments B.V.* v. *Czech Republic*, para. 306.

account of 'any relevant rules of international law applicable in relations between the parties', including the police powers exception.[50]

Accordingly, the tribunal decided that the BIT's expropriation clause imported 'the customary international law notion that a deprivation can be justified if it results from the exercise of regulatory actions aimed at the maintenance of public order'.[51] In the absence of more concrete guidance in the BIT, the tribunal held that it

> inevitably falls to the *adjudicator* to determine whether particular conduct by a state 'crosses the line' that separates valid regulatory activity from expropriation. Faced with the question of *when, how and at what point an otherwise valid regulation becomes, in fact and effect, an unlawful expropriation*, international tribunals must consider the circumstances in which the question arises. The context within which an impugned measure is adopted and applied is critical to the determination of its validity.[52]

The tribunal concluded that the forced administration of IPB was

> a lawful and permissible regulatory action by the Czech Republic aimed at the general welfare of the State, and does not fall within the ambit of any of the exceptions to the permissibility of regulatory action which are recognised by customary international law . . . notwithstanding that the measure had the effect of eviscerating Saluka's investment in IPB.[53]

The tribunal nevertheless went on to find that the Czech Republic's treatment of the investor violated the FET provision of the BIT. In making its assessment, the tribunal said that it would interpret the FET standard so as not to 'undermin[e] [the State's] legitimate right to take measures for the protection of the public interest'.[54] Having quoted with approval the *SD Myers* v. *Canada* award that 'the determination of a breach of the obligation of "fair and equitable treatment" by the host State must be made in the light of *the high measure of deference* that international law generally extends to the right of domestic authorities to regulate matters within their own borders',[55] the tribunal found that the State had, *inter alia*, failed to act in an 'unbiased, even-handed, transparent and consistent way' and discriminated against the claimant without reasonable justification. The tribunal did, however, conclude that there was no FET violation in respect of the State's obligation to provide a predictable and transparent framework for *Saluka*'s investment.[56]

[50] *Ibid.*, paras. 254–5; VCLT, Article 31(3)(c). [51] *Ibid.*, para. 254.
[52] *Ibid.*, para. 264 (emphasis in the original). [53] *Ibid.*, paras. 275–6.
[54] *Ibid.*, para. 309. [55] *Ibid.*, para. 305 (emphasis added). [56] *Ibid.*, para. 500.

(3) IIA Provisions on Legitimate Regulatory Interests

The awards discussed in Section C arise out of an earlier generation of IIAs that did not contain detailed guidance on legitimate regulatory interests. Although some tribunals – including in *Saluka* – have relied on language in the preamble to interpret the treaty's object and purpose in a more balanced way, many tribunals have held that investor protection is the primary aim of the IIA.[57]

In the newer generation of IIAs, States parties have therefore added express language clarifying the scope and balance of the substantive standards, for example, on how to distinguish between indirect expropriation and a non-compensable regulatory measure. Take the 2004 US Model BIT, which expressly considers the relevance of States' legitimate regulatory interests for indirect expropriation claims:

> Except in rare circumstances, non-discriminatory regulatory actions by a Party that are designed and applied to protect legitimate public welfare objectives, such as public health, safety, and the environment, do not constitute indirect expropriations.[58]

Since 2004, both the United States and Canada have included this or similar language in their IIAs, and such language is now included in most provisions on indirect expropriation.[59] Some States parties have included additional distinguishing criteria, including proportionality or breach of the State's written commitments to the investor.[60] Other IIAs include 'general exceptions' or 'non-precluded measures' (NPM) clauses derived from the General Agreement on Tariffs and Trade (GATT), Article XX, such as Article 18 of the Canadian Model BIT, which provides that the host State may take measures to protect human, animal or plant life or health, or the environment, or take prudential action to maintain the financial system.[61] The result of these significant drafting changes is that – unlike the skeletal treaties of old – many IIAs are now quite substantial. The investment chapter of the TPP, for instance, is fifty-two pages long.[62]

[57] *Ibid.*, para. 300.

[58] 2012 US Model Bilateral Investment Treaty (US Model BIT (2012)), Article 4(b), Annex B, available at https://ustr.gov/sites/default/files/BIT%20text%20for%20ACIEP%20Meeting.pdf (accessed 12 January 2016).

[59] UNCTAD, 'Expropriation: A Sequel', 60. [60] *Ibid.* [61] *Ibid.*, 89.

[62] Trans-Pacific Partnership (2015), Chapter 9 (Investment), available at https://ustr.gov/sites/default/files/TPP-Final-Text-Investment.pdf (accessed 24 February 2016).

UNCTAD's 2015 review of IIA trends indicates that most new IIAs include sustainable development-orientated features, including references to the protection of health and safety, labour rights, the environment or sustainable development in the preamble and clauses such as those just sampled stating that States parties should not relax health, safety or environmental standards in order to attract investment.[63] Of the thirteen IIAs concluded in 2014 that UNCTAD surveyed, eleven contain general exceptions, for example, for the protection of human, animal or plant life or health, or the conservation of exhaustible natural resources. In addition to indirect expropriation language, these new treaties also seek to protect legitimate regulatory interests by providing a more detailed description of the FET standard or expressly permitting prudential measures.[64]

Indeed, the protection of legitimate regulatory interests has been central to TTIP and TPP negotiations. Having included an express right to regulate provision in the revised text of the EU-Canada Free Trade Agreement (CETA),[65] the European Commission's policy is that all future EU IIAs will provide a detailed set of provisions giving guidance to tribunals: '[i]n particular, when the state is protecting the public interest in a non-discriminatory way, the right of the state to regulate should prevail over the economic impact of those measures on the investor.'[66] Similarly, the Obama administration has stated its belief that

> TPP will result in higher levels of labor and environmental protections in most TPP countries than they have today . . . We can't change the standards in the more than 3,000 agreements among other countries. Most of those agreements will continue to exist, with or without TPP. But through TPP, we can set a new, higher set of standards, stronger safeguards and better transparency provisions.[67]

The TPP was signed by its twelve Contracting Parties on 5 October 2015, and its text was made public a month later. The TPP's investment chapter generally tracks the approach of the 2012 US Model BIT. It does not therefore contain a GATT Article XX–type exception, instead integrating

63 UNCTAD, IIA Issues Note No. 1, February 2015, 3. 64 *Ibid.*

65 CETA (Revised Text, February 2016), Article 8.9 ('Investment and Regulatory Measures').

66 European Commission, 'Fact Sheet: Investment Protection and Investor-to-State Dispute Settlement in EU Agreements', Brussels, 26 November 2013, 2, 7–8.

67 J. Zients, 'Investor-State Dispute Settlement (ISDS) Questions and Answers', White House Blog, 26 February 2015, available at www.whitehouse.gov/blog/2015/02/26/investor-state-dispute-settlement-isds-questions-and-answers (accessed 24 February 2016).

public welfare considerations into the substantive obligations. There are certain headline provisions that address high-profile stakeholder concerns, such as the denial of benefits to claims 'challenging a tobacco control measure', directed at *Phillip Morris*–type claims.[68] By contrast to an earlier draft text, however, the preamble does not contain language affirming that States have the right to regulate. Nevertheless, the US government asserts that the right to regulate is underscored.[69] Article 9.15 of the Investment Chapter states

> Nothing in [the investment chapter] shall be construed to prevent a Party from adopting, maintaining, or enforcing any measure otherwise consistent with this Chapter that it considers appropriate to ensure that investment activity in its territory is undertaken in a manner sensitive to environmental, health or other regulatory objectives.[70]

Critics question whether the language 'otherwise consistent with this Chapter' negates the protection purported to be given by Article 9.15.[71] Elsewhere in the Chapter there is further evidence of a cautious rebalancing in favour of States' legitimate regulatory interests. For example, Article 9.6(4) does not exclude legitimate expectations from the FET standard but does provide that 'the mere fact that a party takes or fails to take action that may be inconsistent with an investor's expectations does not constitute a breach of this article.' In determining whether treatment is accorded in 'like circumstances' for the purposes of the non-discrimination standard, the tribunal is directed to consider 'the totality of the circumstances, including whether the relevant treatment distinguishes between investors or investments on the basis of legitimate public welfare objectives'.[72] Interestingly, the investment chapter prefaces forty-four provisions with the language 'for greater certainty' or the 'avoidance of doubt'.

Crucially, the TPP retains the prevailing ad hoc arbitration mechanism for investor-State dispute settlement and, like the 2004 and 2012 US Model BITs, merely notes that the Parties retain the option to

[68] TPP, Chapter 9 (Investment), Article 29.5.

[69] United States Trade Representative, 'The Trans-Pacific Partnership: Upgrading and Improving Investor-State Dispute Settlement', available at https://ustr.gov/sites/default/files/TPP-Upgrading-and-Improving-Investor-State-Dispute-Settlement-Fact-Sheet.pdf (accessed 24 February 2016).

[70] TPP, Chapter 9, Article 9.15.

[71] L. Johnson and L. Sachs, 'The TPP's Investment Chapter: Entrenching, Rather Than Reforming, a Flawed System', CCSI Policy Paper (2015), 2.

[72] TPP, Article 9.4, 'Drafting Note'.

incorporate an appellate mechanism 'developed in the future under other institutional arrangements'.[73] By contrast, at the time of this writing, the European Union is demanding that in the TTIP a standing Tribunal of First Instance and Appeal Tribunal, with publicly appointed judges, replace the current model of investor-State arbitration and the practice of Party-appointed arbitrators. In December 2015, the European Union and Vietnam concluded a free trade agreement (FTA) that includes such an investment court system, and in February 2016, the European Commission announced that Canada had agreed to incorporate the court system into a revised version of CETA.[74] The EU's TTIP negotiating position expressly ties the proposed new dispute settlement mechanism to State control over legitimate regulatory interests:

> The EU text proposal on investment protection for TTIP has a simple objective: to effectively safeguard the EU and its Member States' right to regulate, while providing effective protection to European companies against unfair treatment, discrimination or other basic obligations. This will be ensured through a new fully transparent system for resolving investment disputes, with publicly appointed judges, the highest ethical standards and the possibility to have errors corrected through an appeal instance.[75]

A radical alternative future for IIAs is set out in India's recently published draft model BIT, which is intended to serve as the basis for the re-negotiation of that State's eighty-six existing BITs. The Indian government is responding to 'public outcry' over seventeen arbitration notices submitted since 2012 relating to retrospective changes to tax legislation that have left companies such as Vodaphone with billion-dollar tax bills.[76] Article 12 of the draft stipulates that investors and their investments must comply with host State laws and regulations, including employee protection, environmental law, human rights, consumer

[73] TPP, Article 9.22.11.

[74] European Commission, 'EU-Vietnam Free Trade Agreement Now Available Online', Brussels (2016), available at http://trade.ec.europa.eu/doclib/press/index.cfm?id=1449; European Commission, 'CETA: EU and Canada Agree on New Approach on Investment in Trade Agreement', Brussels (2016), available at http://europa.eu/rapid/press-release_IP-16-399_en.htm.

[75] European Commission, 'Fact Sheet: Why the New EU Proposal for an Investment Court System in TTIP Is Beneficial to Both States and Investors', Brussels (2015), available at http://europa.eu/rapid/press-release_MEMO-15-6060_en.htm (accessed 24 February 2016).

[76] J. Singh, 'Guest Post: India and Bilateral Investment Treaties – Are They Worth It?', *Financial Times*, 21 January 2015.

protection and corporate governance standards. Moreover, an investor must 'demonstrate compliance' with Article 12 in any notice of dispute submitted under the investor-State dispute settlement clause.[77] It is too early to tell how successful India will be in negotiating such a forceful reassertion of host State regulatory power, particularly when this goes beyond what has been agreed by States parties in the TPP, CETA and other major new IIAs.

C. Awards

Having provided an overview of the basis in international investment law for non-compensable regulatory measures, this section now surveys how tribunals have addressed States' assertion of a legitimate regulatory interest in the context of indirect expropriation and FET claims.

(1) Sole Effects

Several earlier tribunals applied a 'sole effects' test according to which the State's intent behind a measure is irrelevant to the question of whether an indirect expropriation has occurred. The fact that a measure causing the investor loss was in furtherance of a legitimate regulatory interest would therefore have no bearing on the determination of liability.

In *Santa Elena*, the government enacted a decree directly expropriating the claimant's property for the purpose of protecting flora and fauna of scientific, recreational, educational and tourism value, including sea turtle breeding beaches. The claimant alleged that it had received inadequate compensation. In contrast to the approach subsequently adopted in *Saluka* and *Methanex* (discussed later), the tribunal in *Santa Elena* was unconcerned with the purpose of the expropriation, holding that

> [w]hile an expropriation or taking for environmental reasons may be classified as a taking for a public purpose, and thus may be legitimate, the fact that the Property was taken for this reason does not affect either the nature of the measure or the compensation to be paid for the taking. That is, the purpose of protecting the environment for which the Property was taken does not alter the legal character of the taking for which adequate compensation must be paid. The international source of the obligation to protect the environment makes no difference.

[77] Draft Model Text for the Indian Bilateral Investment Treaty (2015), Article 14.3(iii), available at https://mygov.in/sites/default/files/master_image/Model%20Text%20for%20the%20Indian%20Bilateral%20Investment%20Treaty.pdf (accessed 24 February 2016).

> Expropriatory environmental measures – no matter how laudable and beneficial to society as a whole – are, in this respect, similar to any other expropriatory measures that a state may take in order to implement its policies: where property is expropriated, even for environmental purposes, whether domestic or international, the state's obligation to pay compensation remains.[78]

Similarly, *Metalclad* concerned Mexico's ecological decree declaring the site of the claimant's landfill waste operation to be a protected area for cactus plants.[79] The North American Free Trade Agreement (NAFTA) tribunal said that it did not need to consider the 'motivation or intent' of the adoption of the decree by preventing continued operation of the landfill and found that the decree had indirectly expropriated the claimant's investment.[80]

(2) Purpose

The award in *SD Myers*, rendered the same year as *Santa Elena* and *Metalclad*, did not adopt the sole effects doctrine. Rather, the tribunal held that regulatory measures tantamount to expropriation do not give rise to a claim for compensation if taken for a public purpose. The state's assertion of legitimate regulatory interests is therefore central to the question of liability. However, in *SD Myers*, the impugned export ban on a pesticide called PCB was found to have breached the FET and national treatment standards in the NAFTA. The tribunal concluded that there was 'no legitimate environmental reason for introducing the ban', which was 'intended primarily to protect the Canadian PCB disposal industry from US competition'.[81] 'Insofar as there was an indirect environmental objective – to keep the Canadian industry strong in order to assure a continued disposal capability – it could have been achieved by other measures.'[82] This notwithstanding the tribunal's statement, frequently cited in subsequent awards, that it would accord due deference to the state's regulatory decisions.[83]

78 *Compañía del Desarrollo de Santa Elena. S.A.* v. *Republic of Costa Rica* ('*Santa Elena*'), ICSID Case No. ARB/96/1, Award, 17 February 2000, paras. 71–2.

79 *Metalclad Corporation* v. *Mexico*, ICSID Case No. ARB(AF)/97/1, Award, 30 August 2000, para. 59.

80 *Ibid.*, para. 111. The tribunal also held that Mexico violated the FET standard of the NAFTA. *Ibid.*, para. 101.

81 *SD Myers, Inc.* v. *Canada*, paras. 194–5.

82 *Ibid.*, para. 195.

83 *Ibid.*, para. 263.

In 2004, the United States and Canada introduced new model BITs explicitly rejecting the sole effects doctrine.[84] The subsequent award in *Methanex* confirmed the departure from the sole effects doctrine and marks a new line of cases in which tribunals have rejected indirect expropriation claims where the purpose of the impugned measure was to protect a legitimate regulatory interest. In *Methanex*, the NAFTA tribunal found that a measure banning the fuel additive MTBE on environmental and health grounds was legitimate and therefore not expropriatory. The tribunal agreed with the United States that the ban was objectively justified by scientific evidence.[85] Nor did the claimant have a legitimate expectation that the government would not introduce such a prohibition in the highly regulated industry.[86] The tribunal stated:

> In the tribunal's view, Methanex is correct that an intentionally discriminatory regulation against a foreign investor fulfils a key requirement for establishing expropriation. But as a matter of general international law, a non-discriminatory regulation for a public purpose, which is enacted in accordance with due process and, which affects, inter alios, a foreign investor or investment is not deemed expropriatory and compensable unless specific commitments had been given by the regulating government to the then putative foreign investor contemplating investment that the government would refrain from such regulation.[87]

(3) *Standard of Review*

Closely tied with the concept of legitimate regulatory interests is the standard of review, which has been employed by tribunals in order to 'strike an appropriate balance between national autonomy and the need for compliance with international obligations'.[88] The standard of review reflects the degree of deference that tribunals accord respondent States' decisions, including out of recognition of States' regulatory sovereignty and the proximity of State authorities to their populations – essentially, the view that governments are best placed to decide what is in the public interest – as well as the State decision-makers' relevant competence and expertise.[89] Drawing on German constitutional law, European Union law, the European Convention on Human Rights (ECHR) jurisprudence or World Trade Organisation (WTO) law, several tribunals have adopted a deferential standard of review that allows

[84] UNCTAD, 'Expropriation: A Sequel', 71. [85] *Methanex Corporation* v. *US*, para. 20.
[86] *Ibid.*, paras. 9–10. [87] *Ibid.*, para. 7.
[88] Henckels, 'Balancing Investment Protection and the Public Interest', 197. [89] *Ibid.*

for greater regulatory flexibility – such as proportionality balancing or a 'margin of appreciation' – as opposed to strict scrutiny, although the awards betray a lack of consistency and doctrinal clarity.[90]

A notable award in this regard is *Tecmed* v. *Mexico*, in which an investment tribunal first articulated the concept of the proportionality of the disputed measure to the public interest in order to determine whether a regulatory measure amounted to a compensable indirect expropriation. In that case, the State decided not to renew the claimant's waste landfill site permit. The tribunal found that the measure was not solely motivated by environmental or public health concerns. Rather, the State was responding to political imperatives, namely, community pressure to relocate the landfill.[91] The tribunal held that the measure's impact on the investor was not proportionate to the aim sought to be realised because there was no 'present or imminent risk to the ecological balance or to people's health'.[92] The measure therefore amounted to an indirect expropriation.

Adopting the proportionality analysis in *Tecmed*, tribunals have held that a measure which severely affects an investor will amount to a compensable expropriation unless the measure is justified by a substantial public interest[93] and that 'proportionality has to exist between the public purpose fostered by the regulation and the interference with the investors' property rights.'[94]

A deferential standard of review does not mean that the State will avoid liability. For example, in *Lemire* v. *Ukraine*, the claimant alleged that he was denied frequencies by the government for his radio broadcasting

90 W. Burke White and A. von Staden, 'Private Litigation in a Public Law Sphere: The Standard of Review in Investor-State Arbitrations', *Yale Journal of International Law*, 35 (2010), 310; Henckels, 'Balancing Investment Protection and the Public Interest', 197; see e.g. *Occidental Petroleum Corporation and Occidental Exploration and Production Company* v. *Republic of Ecuador*, ICSID Case No. ARB/06/11, Award of 5 October 2012, paras. 402–9; *Bernhard von Pezold and Others* v. *Republic of Zimbabwe*, ICSID Case No. ARB/10/15, Award of 28 July 2015, para. 460. *Philip Morris* v. *Uruguay*, Award of 8 July 2016, paras. 398–9.

91 *Técnicas Medioambientales Tecmed S.A.* v. *Mexico ('Tecmed')*, ICSID Case No. ARB(AF)/00/02, Award of 29 May 2003, para. 144.

92 *Ibid.*, paras. 122, 149.

93 *Deutsche Bank AG* v. *Democratic Socialist Republic of Sri Lanka*, ICSID Case No. ARB/09/2, Award of 31 October 2012, para. 522; *Azurix* v. *Argentine Republic*, ICSID Case No. ARB/01/12, Award of 14 June 2006, para. 311; *LG&E Energy Corp, LG&E Capital Corp, LG&E International, Inc.*, v. *Argentine Republic*, ICSID Case No. ARB/02/1, Decision on Liability of 3 October 2006, para. 189.

94 *El Paso Energy International Company* v. *Argentine Republic*, ICSID Case No. ARB/03/15, Award of 31 October 2011, para. 243.

business. Quoting the *SD Myers* v. *Canada* award, the ICSID tribunal held that

> [a]s a sovereign State, Ukraine has the inherent right to regulate its affairs and adopt laws in order to protect the common good of its people, as defined by its Parliament and Government. The prerogative extends to promulgating regulations which define the State's own cultural policy. The promotion of domestic music may validly reflect a State policy to preserve and strengthen cultural inheritance and national identity. The '*high measure of deference that international law generally extends to the right of domestic authorities to regulate matters within their own borders*' is reinforced in cases when the purpose of the legislation affects deeply felt cultural or linguistic traits of the community.[95]

Nevertheless, the tribunal went on to conclude that the FET provision had been violated because the radio-frequency tender process was irregular, arbitrary and discriminatory. The case therefore illustrates that a measure directed at a legitimate regulatory interest must still comply with procedural or due-process standards of investor protection.

The *Glamis* case, in which the United States maintained its undefeated investor-State arbitration record, concerned what the tribunal called the 'thorny issue'[96] of a regulatory taking arising out of measures taken to address the environmental and cultural consequences of open-pit gold mining on Native American sacred land.[97] *Glamis* alleged that the measures were arbitrary, discriminatory and not genuinely addressed to protect environmental and cultural interests from the claimant's mining activities.

The United States briefed extensively on the distinction between a compensable and non-compensable measure, arguing that a non-discriminatory regulation aimed at the general welfare would not ordinarily be deemed an expropriation.[98] In addition to *Saluka*, the United States also cited its 2004 Model BIT, which provides

> [e]xcept in rare circumstances, non-discriminatory regulatory actions by a Party that are designed and applied to protect legitimate public welfare objectives, such as public health, safety and the environment, do not constitute indirect expropriations.

On the contrary, the United States argued, *Glamis* had 'failed to demonstrate that its claim presents the "rare circumstances" where a regulatory

[95] *Joseph C. Lemire* v. *Ukraine*, ICSID Case No. ARB/06/18, Decision on Jurisdiction and Liability, 21 January 2010, para. 505 (emphasis in the original).

[96] *Glamis Gold, Ltd.* v. *United States of America*, para. 356. [97] *Ibid.*, para. 674.

[98] *Glamis Gold, Ltd.* v. *United States of America*, UNCITRAL, US Counter-Memorial, 197.

expropriation claim might succeed'.[99] Rather, the measure under scrutiny was a bona fide non-discriminatory regulation of general application, enacted for the public welfare, and thus did not constitute an expropriation.[100]

The tribunal interpreted the US Model BIT's 'indirect expropriation' provision to mean that it should determine whether a measure constitutes a non-compensable regulation or a compensable expropriation 'by examining, *inter alia*, (1) the extent to which the measures interfered with reasonable and investment-backed expectations of a stable regulatory framework, and (2) the purpose and character of the governmental actions taken.'[101] Ultimately, the tribunal did not need to take this analysis further because Glamis's property rights retained significant value and therefore could not amount to an expropriation.

The concept of deference was integral to US arguments on the FET standard. As well as citing European jurisprudence according States a 'margin of appreciation',[102] the United States argued that the relevant government decision-maker conducting itself in a regular and transparent manner was entitled to 'great deference' in making regulatory or legislative decisions that affect foreign investments.[103] In support, the United States cited to the *SD Myers* Chapter 11 tribunal:

> When interpreting and applying the 'minimum standard' a Chapter Eleven tribunal does not have an open-ended mandate to second-guess government decision-making. Governments have to make many potential controversial choices. In doing so, they may appear to have made mistakes, to have misjudged the facts, proceeded on the basis of a misguided economic or sociological theory, placed too much emphasis on some social values over others and adopted solutions that are ultimately ineffective or counterproductive. The ordinary remedy, if there were one, for errors in modern governments is through internal political and legal processes, including elections.[104]

The United States further argued that every State is free under international law to 'change its regulatory policy' as long as the measure is rationally related to a legitimate governmental purpose.[105]

[99] *Ibid.*, 199. [100] *Ibid.*

[101] *Glamis Gold, Ltd.* v. *United States of America*, UNCITRAL, Final Award of 8 June 2009, 356.

[102] *Glamis Gold, Ltd.* v. *United States of America*, UNCITRAL, US Rejoinder, 189.

[103] *Ibid.*, 188. [104] *Glamis Gold, Ltd.* v. *United States of America*, n. 956.

[105] *Ibid.*, paras. 591–3.

Whereas Glamis had been 'one of the most active public participants in the [decision-making] process at every level of state and federal government', Glamis, the United States argued, was effectively requesting that the tribunal

> second-guess California's democratically established means of addressing the public interest in protecting the environment and irreplaceable, sacred Native American resources from the threat posed by open-pit cyanide heap leach mining, and the federal government's interpretation of its own regulations – a request this Tribunal lacks authority to grant.[106]

Indeed, although it did not expressly say as much, the tribunal adopted a deferential standard of review in recognition of the State's relative competence and expertise, stating that the sole inquiry was whether there was a 'manifest lack of reasons' for the measure.[107] Noting the US argument that mining is a highly regulated activity and therefore that 'any reasonable investor would have anticipated the possibility of regulatory changes',[108] the tribunal held that the claimant's legitimate expectations can only be based on a 'quasi-contract'.[109] The tribunal appears to have been persuaded that the measure was directed at legitimate regulatory interests, concluding that

> the bill addresses some, if not all, of the harms caused to Native American sacred sites by open-pit mining. The Tribunal agrees with Respondent's assertion that governments must compromise between the interests of competing parties and, if they were bound to please every constituent and address every harm with each piece of legislation, they would be bound and useless.[110]

(4) Legitimate Expectations and Regulation

In the *Saluka* award, the tribunal expressly weighed the State's legitimate regulatory interests against the investor's legitimate expectations in assessing liability under the FET standard.[111] Moreover, *Saluka* and several other awards have held that investors cannot expect a host State's regulatory framework to remain unchanged.

The *Parkerings* ICSID case concerned the privatisation of municipal parking enforcement powers, including the termination of a contract to

[106] *Glamis Gold, Ltd.* v. *United States of America*, UNCITRAL, US Counter-Memorial, 217.
[107] *Glamis Gold, Ltd.* v. *United States of America*, UNCITRAL, Final Award of 8 June 2009, para. 805.
[108] *Ibid.*, paras. 715, 729. [109] *Ibid.*, para. 766. [110] *Ibid.*, para. 804.
[111] *Saluka Investments B.V.* v. *Czech Republic*, paras. 306, 499–500.

build a car park because of its impact on heritage buildings. The tribunal held that there was no indirect expropriation. In finding no FET violation either, the tribunal rejected the claimant's broad conceptualisation of legitimate expectations, holding that although a State could not act 'unfairly, unreasonably or inequitably in the exercise of its legislative power',

> [i]t is each State's undeniable right and privilege to exercise its sovereign legislative power. A State has the right to enact, modify or cancel a law at its own discretion. Save for the existence of an agreement, in the form of a stabilisation clause or otherwise, there is nothing objectionable about the amendment brought to the regulatory framework existing at the time an investor made its investment. As a matter of fact, any businessman or investor knows that laws will evolve over time.[112]

Chemtura concerned a pesticide ban. The NAFTA tribunal held that the measure was non-discriminatory and 'motivated by the increasing awareness of the dangers presented by lindane for human health and the environment'.[113] The tribunal also noted that Canada was acting on its international environmental obligations.[114] The ban was therefore 'a valid exercise of the Respondent's police powers' and did not constitute an expropriation.[115]

As for the investor's legitimate expectations, Canada submitted:

> In the absence of specific assurances or guarantees that the legal framework will not change such as through a stabilization clause, it is unreasonable for an investor to expect that the legal and regulatory environment will remain static, particularly in an environment that is highly regulated and constantly influenced by the advances of science.[116]

In rejecting the FET claim, the tribunal agreed that Canada had amply demonstrated serious scientific concerns over the pesticide.[117] Moreover, the claimant was well aware that it operated in a highly regulated industry.[118] In finding that due process had been followed, the tribunal placed weight on the fact that a board of review established under statute had decided on the measure on the basis of scientific evidence. The tribunal therefore accorded due deference; it was not the place of the tribunal to

[112] *Parkerings-Compagniet AS* v. *Lithuania*, ICSID Case No. ARB/05/08, Award of 11 September 2007, para. 332.

[113] *Chemtura Corporation* v. *Canada*, NAFTA, Award of 2 August 2010, para. 266.

[114] *Ibid.*, para. 138. [115] *Ibid.*, para. 266.

[116] *Chemtura Corporation* v. *Canada*, NAFTA, Canada Rejoinder, para. 200.

[117] *Chemtura Corporation* v. *Canada*, NAFTA, Award of 2 August 2010, para. 135.

[118] *Ibid.*, paras. 138, 145, 149.

'second-guess the correctness of the science-based decision-making of highly specialised national regulatory agencies'.[119]

Compare, however, *Chemtura* with the recent award against Canada in *Bilcon*, where a majority of the tribunal found that Canada had violated the minimum standard (FET) and national provision provisions of the NAFTA.[120] The case concerned the rejection by a joint federal-provincial environmental review panel (the JRP) of the claimants' application to develop a mining and marine terminal project in Canada. The JRP recommended that the project not proceed, including on the basis that the project could not operate consistently with 'core community values'.

Such JRPs are generally made up of scientists and environmental experts and not necessarily lawyers used to employing technical legal language.[121] The JRP's mandate was to 'identify, evaluate and report on the potential environmental effects of the Project on the physical, biological and human environments'.[122]

In the award, the tribunal stated that it was not conducting its own environmental assessment, in substitution for that of the JRP.[123] In determining whether a FET violation had occurred, the tribunal agreed that the NAFTA Article 1105 standard is high, as set out in *Waste Management*:

> The minimum standard of treatment of fair and equitable treatment is infringed by conduct attributable to the State and harmful to the claimant if the conduct is arbitrary, grossly unfair, unjust or idiosyncratic, is discriminatory and exposes the claimant to sectional or racial prejudice, or involves a lack of due process leading to an outcome which offends judicial propriety – as might be the case with a manifest failure of natural justice in judicial proceedings or a complete lack of transparency and candour in an administrative process.[124]

A majority of the tribunal concluded that the JRP violated Canadian law when it relied on the concept of 'community core values', which was not a term used in the environmental guidelines for the JRP, to

119 *Ibid.*, para. 134.

120 *William Ralph Clayton, William Richard Clayton, Douglas Clayton, Daniel Clayton and Bilcon of Delaware, Inc.* v. *Government of Canada*, NAFTA, PCA Case No. 2009–04, Award on Jurisdiction and Liability of 17 March 2015.

121 *Bilcon* v. *Canada*, Dissenting Opinion of Professor Donald McRae, 17 March 2015, para. 46.

122 *Ibid.*, para. 15.

123 *Bilcon* v. *Canada*, Award, para. 602.

124 *Waste Management, Inc.* v. *United Mexican States*, ICSID Case No. ARB(AF)/00/3, Award of 30 April 2004, paras. 98, 99, cited in *Bilcon* v. *Canada*, Award, para. 442.

recommend rejection of the project.[125] On this basis, the majority held that the conduct of the JRP was arbitrary for the purposes of NAFTA Article 1105 because it departed from the methodology required by Canadian law and created a new legal standard – 'community core value' – that was not notified in advance to the claimant and constituted an 'unprecedented and unexpected approach' to the review.[126] In short, the claimants were not afforded a fair opportunity to have their proposal considered in accordance with applicable laws, frustrating the claimants' legitimate expectations that the project would obtain environmental permission if the project satisfied the JRP requirements prescribed by domestic law.[127]

The majority stated that there was no issue under NAFTA with Canada adopting high environmental standards; the tribunal was concerned that the review process prescribed by Canadian law was not in fact carried out.[128] By contrast, the dissenting arbitrator concluded that whether Canadian law had been complied with was arguable, and 'the Tribunal did not have the benefit of a determination by a Canadian federal court on the matter.'[129] The dissent also dismisses the idea that the claimants had 'legitimate expectations' that Canadian law would be applied properly because any investor would have this expectation.[130] The dissent further cautions that treating such a potential violation of domestic law as itself a violation of NAFTA Article 1105 allows an investor to seek damages for what is a breach of Canadian law, even though Canadian law does not afford damages for such a breach.[131] The dissent concludes that the award constitutes a 'significant intrusion into domestic jurisdiction and will create a chill on the operation of environment review panels.'[132]

(5) *Non-Precluded Measures*

Notoriously, tribunals hearing claims arising out of measures taken during the Argentine financial crisis have taken irreconcilable views in interpreting Article XI of the US–Argentina BIT, which provides:

> This treaty shall not preclude the application by either Party of measures necessary for the maintenance of public order, the fulfilment of its obligations

[125] *Bilcon* v. *Canada*, Award, paras. 451–2. [126] *Ibid.*, paras. 591, 594, 601.
[127] *Ibid.*, paras. 603, 447. [128] *Ibid.*, paras. 595, 597, 598, 600.
[129] *Bilcon* v. *Canada*, Dissenting Opinion, para. 34. [130] *Ibid.*, para. 33.
[131] *Ibid.*, para. 43. [132] *Ibid.*, para. 48.

> with respect to the maintenance or restoration of international peace and security, or the protection of its own essential security interests.[133]

Whereas the tribunals in *CMS, Enron* and *Sempra* read Article XI as reflecting the customary international law defence of necessity and concluded that Argentina failed to meet that high threshold,[134] the tribunal in *Continental* held that the conditions of Article XI were satisfied and Argentina's measures were therefore not precluded by its BIT obligations (save for one minor FET breach).[135]

The *Continental* tribunal appears to have been influenced by, and quoted at length from, Argentina's memorials on the severity of the economic situation at the time the measures were implemented.[136] Contrary to the strict standard of review applied in *CMS, Enron* and *Sempra*, the *Continental* tribunal accorded Argentina a 'significant margin of appreciation', stating that 'a time of grave crisis is not the time for nice judgments, particularly when examined by others with the disadvantage of hindsight.'[137] The tribunal was not, however, so deferential as to accept Argentina's argument that Article XI was 'self-judging'.[138] In determining whether Argentina's measures were 'necessary', the tribunal applied a proportionality balancing test derived from GATT/WTO jurisprudence rather the strict 'only means' customary international law concept of necessity.[139]

Other than a broad acceptance that economic crises can threaten 'essential security interests' or 'maintenance of public order', however, the Argentina cases (and subsequent annulment committee proceedings) demonstrate the continued uncertainty surrounding the interpretation and effect of NPM provisions. Indeed, the United States has amended its model BIT accordingly to clarify that the provision is self-judging.[140]

[133] Treaty between the United States of America and the Argentine Republic Concerning the Reciprocal Encouragement and Protection of Investment (1991), Article XI, available at http://www.state.gov/documents/organization/43475.pdf (accessed 24 February 2016).

[134] *CMS* v. *Argentine Republic*, ICSID Case No. ARB/01/8, Award of 12 May 2005; *Enron Corporation Ponderosa Assets, L.P.* v. *Argentine Republic*, ICSID Case No. ARB/01/3, Award of 22 May 2007; *Sempra Energy International* v. *Argentine Republic*, ICSID Case No. ARB/02/16, Award of 28 September 2007.

[135] *Continental Casualty Company* v. *Argentine Republic*, ISCID Case No. ARB/03/09, Award of 5 September 2008, para. 164; see also *LG&E Energy Corp., LG&E Capital Corp. and LG&E International, Inc.* v. *Argentine Republic*, 201–16.

[136] *Continental Casualty Company* v. *Argentine Republic*, ISCID Case No. ARB/03/09, Award of 5 September 2008, para. 53.

[137] *Ibid.*, para. 181. [138] *Ibid.*, para. 187. [139] *Ibid.*, para. 192.

[140] US Model BIT (2012), Article 18.

D. Conclusion

Having overviewed general developments in treaty practice and several notable awards concerning host States' legitimate regulatory interests, it is possible to draw five broad conclusions:

1. The concept of legitimate regulatory interests is widely recognised in international investment law. The archetypal examples given in IIAs are public health and the environment. Tribunals have had regard to the existence of scientific evidence and a transparent and lawful decision-making process, including 'public hearings, testimony and peer-review', in assessing whether there is a legitimate regulatory interest at stake.[141]
2. The right of States parties to regulate in the public interest has been affirmed in select IIAs and in awards.[142] Moreover, a number of tribunals have held that the nature, purpose and character of a measure are relevant to distinguishing an indirect expropriation from a non-compensable regulation. However, the distinction, when applied, remains imprecise and turns on the facts of each case.[143] There also remains uncertainty about precisely how the balance is struck between the investor's legitimate expectations and the State's right to regulate.[144] Several tribunals considering regulatory measures have required 'specific assurances' or representations be made to investors, who have been subjected to a due-diligence obligation and presumed to understand that the regulatory framework can change over time, particularly in highly regulated industries.[145]
3. The right to regulate without incurring liability to foreign investors is circumscribed by both custom and treaty. As Canada submitted in *Chemtura*, the police powers doctrine operates within certain limits 'so that it is not abused by governments who might enact police measures as a pretext to an expropriation'.[146] In distinguishing a lawful regulation from a compensable measure, tribunals have considered whether the measure is arbitrary, grossly unfair, unjust,

[141] *Methanex*, Part III, Chap. A, para. 102.
[142] *Philip Morris* v. *Uruguay*, Award of 8 July 2016, paras. 292–301.
[143] *Saluka Investments B.V.* v. *Czech Republic*, 2006, para. 264; UNCTAD, 'Expropriation: A Sequel', 72–3.
[144] The risk also remains that more expansive FET standards could be incorporated via an MFN clause; see also *Bayindir* v. *Pakistan*, ICSID Case No. ARB/03/29, Award, 27 August 2009.
[145] *Philip Morris* v. *Uruguay*, Award of 8 July 2016, paras. 422–427.
[146] *Chemtura Corporation* v. *Canada*, NAFTA, Award of 2 August 2010, para. 594.

excessive or discriminatory; follows due process; was adopted in good faith or is proportionate to the public interest.[147] It has been further suggested that IIAs may not permit host States to place a high individual burden on foreign investors in pursuit of regulatory objectives for the benefit of a national community of which the investor is not a member without the payment of compensation.[148]

4. In the absence of more detailed guidance in the language of the IIA, a number of tribunals have adopted a deferential standard of review, including for reasons that States have 'direct knowledge of their society and its needs',[149] and therefore, tribunals may be reluctant to second-guess the legitimacy of public policy objectives or the means by which such objectives are achieved.[150] However, the doctrinal basis for according deference remains unclear, and tribunals have applied it inconsistently. Moreover, the award in *Bilcon* v. *Canada* demonstrates how potentially far-reaching investor-State tribunals' jurisdiction can be, even where the tribunal is not substituting its judgment for that of the domestic decision-maker.[151]
5. Under greater public scrutiny than ever before, States parties are drafting their IIAs to reassert control over their regulatory space, for example, by enhancing guidance on indirect expropriation, clarifying the FET standard or including general exceptions for legitimate regulatory interests. The *Glamis* award illustrates how tribunals have had regard to subsequent developments in IIA practice, such as the guidance on non-compensable regulatory measures introduced in the 2004 US Model BIT, as an aid for interpreting

[147] *El Paso Energy International Company* v. *Argentine Republic*, ICSID Case No. ARB/03/15, Award of 31 October 2011, para. 241 ('If general regulations are unreasonable, i.e. arbitrary, discriminatory, disproportionate or otherwise unfair, they can . . . be considered as amounting to indirect expropriation if they result in a neutralisation of the foreign investor's property rights.'). *Philip Morris* v. *Uruguay*, Award of 8 July 2016, para. 420.

[148] *Renta 4 S.V.S.A, Ahorro Corporación Emergentes F.I., Ahorro Corporación Eurofondo F.I., Rovime Inversiones SICAV S.A., Quasar de Valors SICAV S.A., Orgor de Valores SICAV S.A., GBI 9000 SICAV S.A.* v. *The Russian Federation*, SCC No. 24/2007, Award of 20 July 2012, para. 23; *Deutsche Bank AG* v. *Democratic Socialist Republic of Sri Lanka*, ICSID Case No. ARB/09/2, Award of 31 October 2012, para. 522.

[149] *Continental Casualty Company* v. *Argentine Republic*, ISCID Case No. ARB/03/09, Award of 5 September 2008, para. 270.

[150] *Joseph C. Lemire* v. *Ukraine*, ICSID Case No. ARB/06/18, Decision on Jurisdiction and Liability, 21 January 2010, para. 505; *Continental Casualty Company* v. *Argentine Republic*, ISCID Case No. ARB/03/09, Award of 5 September 2008, paras. 198–9, 233. *Philip Morris* v. *Uruguay*, Award of 8 July 2016, para. 399.

[151] *Bilcon* v. *Canada*, paras. 591–601.

earlier treaties.[152] The European Union favours replacing investor-State arbitration with a standing court and appellate mechanism, which it believes will bring greater consistency and transparency to international investment law and will safeguard States' right to regulate.

[152] *Philip Morris* v. *Uruguay*, Award of 8 July 2016, para. 300.

11

State Controls over Available Remedies in Investor-State Arbitration

DIANE A. DESIERTO

> The emergence of other actors in the international system means that the observer has to take these changes into account and may consider that in certain domains (e.g. economic relations) other actors may often function more effectively than states. But the state is still, and in the foreseeable future will remain (notwithstanding the relative decline of its strength), the main and the most powerful actor ... [States] still provide the chief institution through which societies will try to respond to change.[1]

> Traditionally, arbitration has been used for disputes in which the issues are legal and the desire to improve relations makes the idea of a binding settlement handed down by a third party attractive ... [A] further advantage of arbitration is that the parties define the question or questions they want the tribunal to answer and can also specify the basis of its decision.[2]

A. Introduction: State Power in Investor-State Arbitration

The shifting balance of power between States and foreign investors has always been a central theme in the ongoing debate over the content and force of international investment law.[3] In the decolonisation era, it was critical to newly independent States and former colonies regaining their independence to emphasise the 'full permanent sovereignty of every State over its natural resources and all economic activities',[4] alongside

[1] R. Müllerson, *International Law, Rights, and Politics* (London: Routledge, 1994), 10.

[2] John Merrills, 'The Place of International Litigation in International Law', in N. Klein (ed.), *Litigating International Law Disputes: Weighing the Options* (Cambridge University Press, 2014), 3, 4.

[3] See K. J. Vandevelde, 'A Brief History of International Investment Agreements', *U.C. Davis J. Int'l & Policy*, 12 (2005), 157; K. Miles, *The Origins of International Investment Law: Empire, Environment, and the Safeguarding of Capital* (Cambridge University Press, 2013), 19–99.

[4] United Nations General Assembly, Declaration on the Establishment of a New International Economic Order, A/RES/S-6/3201, 1 May 1974, para. 4(e).

their power of 'regulation and supervision of the activities of transnational corporations, by taking measures in the interest of the national economies of the countries where such transnational corporations operate on the basis of the full sovereignty of those countries'.[5] In contemporary debates involving investor-State dispute settlement procedures for new behemoth economic agreements such as the recently concluded Trans-Pacific Partnership (TPP) and the proposed Trans-Atlantic Trade and Investment Partnership (TTIP),[6] there has been a growing narrative expressing discontent that States are somehow becoming powerless, taken advantage of or otherwise short-changed by the predatory acts of foreign investors able to seek direct recourse against States to challenge their regulatory actions through investor-State arbitration.[7] Notwithstanding the deeply contested nature of these narratives about the balance of power between States and foreign investors, however, the fundamental dilemma about addressing both State and investor moral hazards remains much the same as Lord Shawcross described in 1961:

> The economic, social, and political problem is how to promote this flow of private capital to those countries where it can do the most good. And it is here that one at once sees the importance of adherence to acceptable rules of International Law. For the fact that whilst there is still a very great deal of private capital available for investment abroad, the flow is largely to advanced countries ... rather than to those where the need for economic progress is greatest. Nor is the reason far to seek. Private investors invest to make profit, not for reasons of benevolence. They are prepared to take the often very considerable commercial risks which are inherent in the establishment of new enterprises. But if they make profits they not unnaturally expect that, subject to normal taxation, they will be entitled to keep them. If they acquire property they expect to be entitled to keep it. It is the feeling of insecurity in these respects, caused by bitter experience

[5] *Ibid.*, para. 4(g).

[6] See, among others, L. Mistelis, 'ISDS in TTP and TTIP Negotiations: Lessons for the EU, 2015', available at http://efilablog.org/2015/11/10/isds-in-tpp-and-ttip-negotiations-lessons-for-the-eu/ (accessed 25 September 2016); J. Meltzer, 'Investment', in S. Lester, B. Mercurio and L. Bartels (eds.), *Bilateral and Regional Trade Agreements: Commentary and Analysis*, 2nd edn. (Cambridge University Press, 2015), 245, 296.

[7] This is best illustrated by the public exchange of letters on investor-State dispute settlement between law professors, scholars, policy experts, advocates and lobbyists. See 2015 Alliance for Justice letter, available at www.afj.org/wp-content/uploads/2015/03/ISDS-Letter-3.11.pdf (accessed 25 September 2016); and 2015 open letter about investor-State dispute settlement signed by professors and scholars of international law, arbitration and dispute settlement, available at www.mcgill.ca/fortier-chair/isds-open-letter (accessed 25 September 2016).

> in the past, which is perhaps the main deterrent to the flow of private capital to the developing countries. What then does Public International Law do, or can it do, to regulate these relationships and provide the order and security that we are accustomed to find for them under civilised municipal systems?[8]

States created the investor-State arbitration system, and it can hardly be said that they have been passive recipients of this system. It is not coincidental that the modern International Centre for Settlement of Investment Disputes (ICSID) investor-State arbitration system was designed under the acknowledged premise that a vast power disparity exists between States and foreign investors.[9] Precisely because States have a demonstrated history of having deployed coercive force against foreign investors' property interests in the past, and even, on occasion, also having violated the personal rights of foreign investor nationals,[10] States decided to take the route of negotiating investment treaties in order to govern and regulate the consequences of any unlawful and injurious host State acts against the investor nationals of home States.[11] Even in investor-State arbitral disputes, where States may admittedly have less time and resources to prepare their defences to investment claims,[12] it cannot be denied that States still have a greater inherent

[8] Q. C. Shawcross, 'The Problems of Foreign Investment in International Law', *Recueil des Cours*, 102 (1961) (Leiden, Netherlands: Martinus Nijhoff), 342.

[9] See A. R. Parra, *The History of ICSID* (Oxford University Press, 2012), 11–26 (on the origins of the decision to provide for an arbitral body as the dispute settlement mechanism in the ICSID Convention); J. E. Alvarez, 'The Public International Law Regime Governing Foreign Investment', *Recueil des Cours*, 344 (2011), 295–308.

[10] See, among others, J. A. Ortiz, 'The Illegal Expropriation of Property in Cuba: A Historical and Legal Analysis of the Takings and a Survey of Restitution Schemes for a Post-Socialist Cuba', *Loyola of Los Angeles International and Comparative Law Review*, 22 (2000), 321; K. J. Vandevelde, *Bilateral Investment Treaties: History, Policy, and Interpretation* (Oxford University Press, 2010), nn. 152–4 ('throughout the 1960s and 1970s, host states unilaterally repudiated concession agreements with foreign investors').

[11] J. W. Salacuse, *The Law of Investment Treaties*, 2nd edn. (Oxford University Press, 2015), 87–124.

[12] See J. K. Sharpe, 'Representing a Respondent State in Investment Arbitration', in C. Giorgetti (ed.), *Litigating International Investment Disputes: A Practitioner's Guide* (Leiden, Netherlands: Martinus Nijhoff, 2014), 41, 43: 'Many States thus lack standard operating procedures for responding to claims . . . While the best-prepared claimant may be ready on day one, a State may still be struggling to figure out what is happening, let alone how to respond . . . those responsible for handling the defence of the State often are unaware of the underlying facts and sometimes even of the existence of the dispute until after the claim is filed . . . the records of the original transaction or investment may be difficult to find, turnover in personnel is significant and institutional memory is not what it is in the case of the typical private claimant.'

capability and domestic authority to control access to governmental documents, project documentation, witnesses and other related evidence necessary to prove the investor's claim.[13] State power is at the forefront of defining the international rules governing investment and the web of international institutions that enforces the rules States agree should govern foreign investment – including extending the benefit of direct arbitral recourse against States to non-State actors such as foreign investors.[14] By defining international investment law's substantive and procedural rules, States markedly retain the full authority to weed out frivolous claims at the outset and long before disputes materialise:

> There are procedural rules that prevent abuses of ISDS claims. First, the disputing parties must first attempt to settle any claim through consultation or negotiation. Note that in BITs [bilateral investment treaties] and FTAs [free trade agreements], a claim may be generally made only after six months have elapsed since the events giving rise to a claim. This means that at least a six month period for consultation and/or negotiation is guaranteed. Second, the disputing investor must deliver written notice of intention to submit a claim to arbitration at least ninety days before the claim is submitted. This prior notification will give the defending state some degree of predictability and time to prepare for the defence. Third, there exists a certain period of statute of limitation. In NAFTA [North American Free Trade Agreement], an investor may not bring an ISDS claim if more than three years have elapsed from the date of the alleged breach or damage. Therefore, investors may not take action on a long-standing grudge against a host state by acting 'from the closet', so to speak. Claims are required to be brought with 'good faith' and very importantly, a transparency that allows the claim to be considered on its formal merits. Fourth, an investment company that is registered in the host state, by itself, may not make an ISDS claim. Fifth, once ISDS proceedings have started, they must proceed to the exclusion of any other remedies, again, upping the ante for participants to only bring claims for which they authentically want an actual adjudication. No 'forum shopping' between domestic courts and arbitration proceedings is permitted to the complaining investor.[15]

[13] See N. D. O'Malley, *Rules of Evidence in International Arbitration: An Annotated Guide* (London: Taylor & Francis, 2013), 47: '[I]n an investor-State dispute, the investor typically will not have access to internal government documents necessary to establish its claim.'

[14] See K. Nadakavukaren Schefer, 'State Powers and Investor-State Dispute Settlement', in S. Lani and R. Polanco Lazo (eds.), *The Role of the State in Investor-State Arbitration* (Leiden, Netherlands: Martinus Nijhoff, 2014), 15–22.

[15] W.-M. Choi, 'The Present and Future of the Investor-State Dispute Settlement Paradigm', *Journal of International Economic Law*, 10 (2007), 725, 738–9.

This chapter contextualises the fundamental dilemma of eliciting accountability from morally hazardous State as well as investor conduct, more from the lens of State power and how this is deployed in the modern investor-State arbitration system. Rather than focus macroscopically on geopolitical, empirical or ideologically laden narratives,[16] many of which depict States as somehow impotent or largely powerless against the bias in favour of foreign investors in investor-State arbitration[17] (narratives that are themselves also contested by other scholars[18]), this chapter instead examines how States retain and assert control over available remedies in investor-State arbitration.[19] Using examples from recent investor-State jurisprudence, I show how some States are not choosing to automatically abandon the investor-State arbitration system but rather appear to opt for more strategically engaging this system to ensure that they exercise more control over the transparency, even-handedness and reasonableness of investor-State arbitration as an international dispute resolution

[16] On the full spectrum of issues involved in determining the fairness or unfairness of investor-State arbitration, see J. E. Kalicki and A. Joubin-Bret (eds.), *Reshaping the Investor-State Dispute Settlement System* (Leiden, Netherlands: Martinus Nijhoff, 2015).

[17] See, among others, G. Van Harten, 'Arbitrator Behaviour in Asymmetrical Adjudication: An Empirical Study of Investment Treaty Arbitration', *Osgoode Hall Law Journal*, 50 (2012), 211–68; M. Sornarajah, 'Power and Justice in Foreign Investment Arbitration', *Journal of International Arbitration*, 14 (1997), 103–40; P. Eberhardt and C. Olivet, 'Profiting from Injustice: How Law Firms, Arbitrators, and Financiers Are Fuelling an Investment Arbitration Boom', Corporate Europe Observatory and the Transnational Institute, November 2012, available at http://corporateeurope.org/sites/default/files/publications/profiting-from-injustice.pdf (accessed 25 September 2016).

[18] See, among others, S. D. Franck, 'Development and Outcomes of Investment Treaty Arbitration', *Harvard International Law Journal*, 50 (2009), 435–89; L. E. Trakman and K. Sharma, 'Jumping Back and Forth between Domestic Courts and ISDS: Mixed Signals from the Asia-Pacific Region', in S. Hindelang and M. Krajewski (eds.), *Shifting Paradigms in International Investment Law: More Balanced, Less Isolated, Increasingly Diversified* (Oxford University Press, 2016), 316, 337; S. W. Schwebel, 'In Defence of Bilateral Investment Treaties', ICCA Keynote Address, 6 April 2014, available at http://sccinstitute.com/media/49810/iccamiamispeechfinalrendering.pdf (accessed 25 September 2016).

[19] This is not a proposal to 're-Statify' or inject new State-driven mechanisms into investor-State arbitration as it is to explore, within the parameters of actual investor-State jurisprudence, how some States have acted successfully to use and control available remedies within the system. See C. N. Brower and S. Blanchard, 'From "Dealing in Virtue" to "Profiting from Injustice": The Case against "Re-Statification" of Investment Dispute Settlement', *Harvard International Law Journal Online*, 55 (2014), 45–59; C. N. Brower and S. Blanchard, 'What's in a Meme? The Truth about Investor-State Arbitration: Why It Need Not, and Must Not, Be Repossessed by States', *Columbia Journal of Transnational Law*, 52 (2014), 689–777.

mechanism.[20] I demonstrate this emerging trend of State control over available remedies in four areas: (1) challenges to third-party funding arrangements of investors, (2) challenges to arbitrator qualifications and conflicts of interest, (3) expanding fact-finding to include information from non-disputing parties and (4) challenging the bases and suitability of compensation as the mode of reparations for alleged breaches of investment treaty obligations. This brief review of more recent jurisprudential practices might illuminate on how some States reject their seeming 'powerlessness'[21] in international dispute settlement – and in particular, in investor-State arbitration.[22]

B. Challenges to Third-Party Funding Arrangements of Investors

States raise serious concerns about the lack of transparency over investors' use of third-party funding arrangements[23] and how these could affect the particular accountability and control mechanisms built into investor-State arbitration.[24] The main concerns over the lack of transparency of these funding arrangements[25] involve (1) the uncertainty over the nature of the third-party funders' influence on the claimant's

[20] See A. Joubin-Bret and J. E. Kalicki, 'Introduction to TDM Special Issue on Reform of Investor-State Dispute Settlement: In Search of a Roadmap', *Transnational Dispute Management* (2014).

[21] There has been some empirical data put forward that poorer WTO members tend to participate less in the WTO's dispute settlement proceedings. See M. Klamberg, *Power and Law in International Society: International Relations as a Sociology of International Law* (London: Routledge, 2015), 65; M. Sornarajah, *The International Law on Foreign Investment*, 3rd edn. (Cambridge University Press, 2010), 225: '[I]nvestment treaties have nearly always provided for the interests of multinational corporations without taking into account the possible harm that may be caused by such corporations and the plight of the developing state that stands powerless in the face of this problem.'

[22] Note that the argument has been made that States retain a continuing power to influence the interpretation of investment treaties over time, notwithstanding interpretations contained in investor-State arbitral awards. See A. Roberts, 'Power and Persuasion in Investment Treaty Interpretation: The Dual Role of States', *American Journal of International Law*, 104 (2010), 179. See also Chapter 7.

[23] On third-party funding in international commercial arbitration generally, see D. Yeoh, 'Third-Party Funding in International Arbitration: A Slippery Slope or Levelling the Playing Field?', *Journal of International Arbitration*, 33 (2016), 115–22.

[24] See J. von Goeler, *Third-Party Funding in International Arbitration and Its Impact on Procedure* (Alphen aan den Rijn, Netherlands: Kluwer Law International, 2016), 9–120.

[25] For a brief survey of investor-State jurisprudence that addresses aspects or consequences of third-party funding in investment arbitration, see J.-C. Honlet, 'Recent Decisions on Third-Party Funding in Investment Arbitration', *ICSID Review*, 30 (2015), 699–712.

decision-making in the arbitration, including any possibility of settlement with the respondent State,[26] (2) the extraordinarily limited nature of the consent given by a State to be sued directly by investors, which does not contemplate the moral hazards that could be created by having third-party funders sustain otherwise impecunious or frivolous claims,[27] (3) the difficulty of investigating arbitrator conflicts of interest, when there is an undisclosed 'party' working in tandem with the claimant such as a third-party funder[28] and (4) the difficulty for the respondent State in establishing the factual basis of any application it would make for security for costs and the counterpart difficulty for an arbitral tribunal to ensure the enforceability of any future order for costs that a tribunal might award against the impecunious claimant whose third-party funder could well disappear at any time.[29] While States have repeatedly sought disclosure of third-party funding arrangements from tribunals,[30] it was not until the 12 June 2015 Procedural Order No. 3 in *Muhammet Çap &*

[26] C. B. Lamm and E. R. Hallbeck, 'Third-Party Funding in Investor-State Arbitration and Overview', in B. M. Cremades Roman and A. Dimolitsa (eds.), *Third-Party Funding in International Arbitration* (Paris: ICC Dossier, International Chamber of Commerce, 2013), 101–21. See also I. Torterola, 'Third Party Funding in International Investment Arbitration', UNCTAD Investment Policy Hub, 8 April 2013, available at http://investmentpolicyhub.unctad.org/Blog/Index/21 (accessed 25 September 2016); P. Pinsolle, 'Comment on Third-Party Funding and Nationality Issues in Investment Arbitration', in K. P. Sauvant (ed.), *Yearbook on International Investment Law and Policy 2010–2011* (Oxford University Press, 2012), 639–48 (stating that third-party funding arrangements do not affect nationality of claims unless the investment treaty provides for this effect).

[27] See Organisation for Economic Cooperation and Development (OECD), *Investor-State Dispute Settlement Public Consultation 16 May–9 July 2012* (OECD, 2012), 36–41, available at www.oecd.org/investment/internationalinvestmentagreements/50291642.pdf (accessed 25 September 2016).

[28] See A. Bjorklund, 'Constraints on Power and Authority in International Investment Arbitration', in A. W. Rovine (ed.), *Contemporary Issues in International Arbitration and Mediation: The Fordham Papers 2013* (Leiden, Netherlands: Martinus Nijhoff, 2014), 15, 22. See also Chapter 15.

[29] See 'Draft Report of the ICCA-QMUL Task Force on International Arbitration Subcommittee on Security for Costs and Costs', 1 November 2015, available at www.arbitration-icca.org/media/6/09700416080661/tpf_taskforce_security_for_costs_and_costs_draft_report_november_2015.pdf (accessed 25 September 2016).

[30] See, among others, *KT Asia Investment Group* v. *Kazakhstan*, ICSID Case No. ARB/09/8, Award of 17 October 2013, para. 50; *Teinver SA and others* v. *Argentine Republic*, ICSID Case No. ARB/09/1, Decision on Jurisdiction of 21 December 2012, paras. 254–9; *Giovanni Alemanni and others* v. *Argentine Republic*, ICSID Case No. ARB/07/8, Decision on Jurisdiction and Admissibility of 17 November 2014, para. 278; *RosInvest Co. UK, Ltd.* v. *Russian Federation*, SCC Case No. V079/2005, Final Award of 12 September 2010, paras. 5, 322–3, 381–3; *Quasar de Valors and others* v. *Russian Federation*, SCC Case No. 24/2007, Award of 20 July 2012, para. 33.

Sehil Inşaat Endustri ve Ticaret, Ltd. Sti. v. *Turkmenistan*[31] that a State succeeded in obtaining a fully reasoned[32] order from an arbitral tribunal that compels disclosure of third-party funding arrangements in investment arbitration. In that order, the *Ticaret* arbitral tribunal asserted 'inherent powers to make orders of the nature requested where necessary to preserve the rights of the parties and the integrity of the process.'[33] As Turkmenistan proved in this case, disclosure of third-party funding arrangements is crucial to truly safeguard arbitrator conflicts of interest with the third-party funder,[34] as well as to provide adequate information for the State to be able to apply for security for costs and ensure that the same could be enforced against the investor-claimant's real financier.[35]

[31] *Muhammet Çap & Sehil Inşaat Endustri ve Ticaret, Ltd. Sti.* v. *Turkmenistan*, ICSID Case No. ARB/12/6, Procedural Order No. 3 of 12 June 2015, [hereafter *Ticaret* Procedural Order No. 3], para. 13.

[32] A report indicates that the arbitral tribunal in *EuroGas* v. *Slovakia* issued an oral order to parties compelling disclosure of third-party funders, which has not yet been set down or indicated in any explicit written order in this case. See Procedural Order Nos. 1 to 4 in *EuroGas Inc. and Belmont Resources* v. *Slovak Republic*, ICSID Case No. ARB/14/14, available at www.italaw.com/cases/3210 (accessed 225 September 2016); J. Hepburn, 'ICSID Tribunal Orders Identification of Third-Party Funder, But Denies State's Request for Security for Costs and Claimants' Request for Provisional Measures', *Investment Arbitration Reporter*, 3 August 2015, available at www.iareporter.com/articles/icsid-tribunal-orders-identification-of-third-party-funder-but-denies-states-request-for-security-for-costs-and-claimants-request-for-provisional-measures/ (accessed 225 September 2016).

[33] *Ticaret* Procedural Order No. 3, para. 6.

[34] See 'International Bar Association (IBA) Guidelines on Conflicts of Interest in International Arbitration', 23 October 2014, 13, General Standard 6(b): 'If one of the parties is a legal entity, any legal or physical person having a controlling influence on the legal entity, or a direct economic interest in, or a duty to indemnify a party for, the award to be rendered in the arbitration, may be considered to bear the identity of such party'; and 14–15: 'Third-party funders and insurers in relation to the dispute may have a direct economic interest in the award, and as such may be deemed to be the equivalent of the party. For these purposes, the terms "third-party funder" and "insurer" refer to any person or entity that is contributing funds, or other material support, to the prosecution or defence of the case and that has a direct economic interest in, or a duty to indemnify a party for, the award to be rendered in the arbitration.'

[35] See L. Reed, J. Paulsson and N. Blackaby, *Guide to ICSID Arbitration*, 2nd edn. (Alphen aan den Rijn, Netherlands: Kluwer Law International, 2011), 156: 'ICSID tribunal decisions on the allocation of costs between the parties depend on the arbitrators' perception of the reasonableness with which the parties pursued their claims and defences, the parties' general cooperativeness in achieving cost-effective results, and the novelty of the legal issues presented. Tribunals are especially likely to award costs to the prevailing party in the face of misconduct, fraudulent activity or abuse of process by the losing party.'

C. Challenges to Arbitrator Qualifications and Conflicts of Interest

ICSID arbitrators are expected to be 'persons of high moral character and recognised competence in the fields of law, commerce, industry or finance, who may be relied upon to exercise independent judgment. Competence in the field of law shall be of particular importance in the case of persons on the Panel of Arbitrators.'[36] Additionally, in designating persons to serve as arbitrators in ICSID panels, the chairman of the ICSID Administrative Council is mandated to 'pay due regard to the importance of assuring representation on the Panels of the principal legal systems of the world and of the main forms of economic activity.'[37]

Notwithstanding these stringent standards for appointment as an international arbitrator in investor-State disputes, many criticisms have been levelled against the alleged bias and/or incompetence of arbitrators to resolve investor-State disputes.[38] Other more theoretical works investigate the conceptual underlying critique against the seeming injustice of States (and their regulatory prerogatives) being left to the judgment of unelected international arbitrators.[39] What is implicit (and still contested) from the critique is the impression that States have no feasible or meaningful controls whatsoever over the appointment, selection and

[36] 1965 Convention on the Settlement of Disputes between States and Nationals of Other States (ICSID Convention), 575 UNTS 159, Article 14(1); on arbitrator challenges as a means of reassertion of control, see also Chapter 15.

[37] ICSID Convention, Article 14(2).

[38] For a sampling of the literature examining the spectrum of these criticisms, see, among others, M. Lalonde, 'Quo Vadis Disqualification?', in M. N. Kinnear et al. (eds.), *Building International Investment Law: The First 50 Years of ICSID* (Alphen aad den Rijn, Netherlands: Kluwer Law International, 2015), 641–54; M. N. Kinnear, 'Challenge of Arbitrators at ICSID: An Overview', *Proceedings of the Annual Meeting of the American Society of International Law*, 108 (2014), 412–16; J. D. Fry and J. I. Stampalija, 'Forged Independence and Impartiality: Conflicts of Interest of International Arbitrators in Investment Disputes', *Arbitration International*, 30 (2014), 189–264; S. D. Franck, 'Conflating Politics and Development? Examining Investment Treaty Arbitration Outcomes', *Virginia Journal of International Law*, 55 (2014), 23, 60; G. Van Harten, 'Arbitrator Behaviour in Asymmetrical Adjudication: An Empirical Study of Investment Treaty Arbitration', *Osgoode Hall Law Journal*, 50 (2012), 211, 233–4; S. Puig, 'Social Capital in the Arbitration Market', *European Journal of International Law*, 25 (2014), 387–424.

[39] See, among others, L. E. Trakman, 'The ICSID Under Siege', *Cornell International Law Journal*, 45 (2012), 603; J. Resnik, 'Diffusing Disputes: The Public in the Private of Arbitration, the Private in the Courts, and the Erasure of Rights', *Yale Law Journal*, 124 (2015), 2680–3203.

institutional oversight of international arbitrators in investor-State disputes.[40]

As the records show, however, 'despite a low success rate',[41] States increasingly challenge arbitrators based on conflicts of interest and other grounds for disqualification.[42] In recent years, States' challenges against arbitrators have been sustained in a few instances where it was shown that (1) a proposed arbitrator and his or her law firm were also representing the same claimants in other pending investment treaty-based proceedings against the respondent State,[43] (2) a proposed arbitrator gave a published media interview where he gave comments about the actions of the respondent State in relation to the pending ICSID proceedings brought against it by investors,[44] (3) an arbitrator had been repeatedly appointed by the claimant's law firm in eight ICSID cases over a six-year period, which the proposed arbitrator did not disclose, coupled with the arbitrator's conduct (dissent to the tribunal's decision on jurisdiction and decision on liability, conduct during pre-hearing telephone conferences and explanations for such conduct)[45] and (4) a proposed arbitrator is

[40] See S. W. Schill, *The Multilateralisation of International Investment Law* (Cambridge University Press, 2009), 252–3.

[41] Preface, xxxvi, in K. P. Sauvant (ed.), *Yearbook on International Investment Law and Policy 2011–2012* (Oxford University Press, 2013).

[42] See D. D. Caron and L. M. Caplan (eds.), *The UNCITRAL Arbitration Rules: A Commentary*, 2nd edn. (Oxford University Press, 2013), 178–93 (providing an overview of challenges made to arbitrators in UNCITRAL-governed investment disputes); M. N. Kinnear and F. Nitschke, 'Disqualification of Arbitrators under the ICSID Convention and Rules', in C. Giorgetti (ed.), *Challenges and Recusals of Judges and Arbitrators in International Courts and Tribunals* (Leiden, Netherlands: Martinus Nijhoff, 2015), chap. 2.

[43] *ICS Inspection and Control Services, Ltd.* v. *Argentine Republic*, UNCITRAL, Decision on Challenge to Arbitrator (Mr Stanimir Alexandrov) of 17 December 2009, para. 22.

[44] *Perenco Ecuador Limited* v. *Ecuador and Empresa Estatal Petroleos del Ecuador*, ICSID Case No. ARB/08/6, Decision on Challenge to Arbitrator (Hon. Charles N. Brower) of 8 December 2009, para. 27 and *dispositif* in Part V: 'NOW THEREFORE, I, Christiaan M.J. Kröner, Secretary-General of the Permanent Court of Arbitration, having considered the comments submitted by the Parties and by Judge Brower, and having established to my satisfaction my competence to decide this challenge applying the IBA Guidelines in accordance with the October 2008 Agreement between the Parties, HEREBY SUSTAIN the challenge against the Hon. Charles N. Brower as arbitrator in the above-referenced matter for the reason that, from the point of view of a reasonable third person having knowledge of the relevant facts, the comments made by Judge Brower in an interview published in the August 2009 edition of *The Metropolitan Corporate Counsel* constitute circumstances that give rise to justifiable doubts as to Judge Brower's impartiality or independence.'

[45] *Burlington Resources Incorporated* v. *Ecuador*, ICSID Case No. ARB/08/5, Decision on the proposal for disqualification of Professor Francisco Orrego Vicuña of 13 December 2013, paras. 70, 81.

a partner in a global law firm, where a country branch of the same global law firm is also representing the claimant in other proceedings against the respondent State, even if the proposed arbitrator has no involvement or participation in the latter proceedings.[46] While these are undoubtedly select incidents thus far of successful challenges out of a much more substantial pool of ongoing State challenges against arbitrators in other cases, they nonetheless evidence a modest trend of States being able to successfully raise objections, based on justifiable doubts, against the actual or perceived impartiality and/or independence of arbitrators in investor-State arbitration.[47]

Much work remains to be done by States, however, to ensure the a priori enlargement and diversification of the pool of international arbitrators for investor-State disputes, especially for those administered by ICSID. Chiara Giorgetti rightly argues that the case for diversity in investor-State arbitration is one based on advancing greater deliberative quality of judgments, as well as enhancing the legitimacy of the investor-State tribunal to all its stakeholders.[48] As a practical matter, States can, to a certain extent (and only because parties are not mandated to nominate arbitrators from the ICSID Panel of Arbitrators), affect the quality and composition of future investor-State tribunals by purposely diversifying their nominees to the ICSID Panel of Arbitrators and other lists of arbitrators in other international arbitration institutions that may be called upon to administer investor-State disputes.[49]

D. Expanding Arbitral Fact-Finding to Include Information from Non-Disputing Parties

The December 2014 United Nations Convention on Transparency in Treaty-Based Investor-State Arbitration (Mauritius Convention on Transparency), which makes it obligatory for States to apply the United Nations Commission on International Trade Law (UNCITRAL) Rules

[46] *Blue Bank International and Trust (Barbados) Limited* v. *Venezuela*, ICSID Case No. ARB/12/20, Decision on the Parties' Proposals to Disqualify a Majority of the Tribunal of 12 November 2013, para. 71 (sustaining the disqualification of Mr Jose Maria Alonso, Partner, at Baker MacKenzie).

[47] See B. S. Vasani and S. A. Palmer, 'Challenge and Disqualification of Arbitrators at ICSID: A New Dawn?', *ICSID Review*, 30 (2015), 194–216.

[48] C. Giorgetti, 'Who Decides Who Decides in International Investment Arbitration?', *University of Pennsylvania Journal of International Law*, 35 (2014), 431, 474–84.

[49] See Eric de Brabandere, *Investment Treaty Arbitration as Public International Law: Procedural Aspects and Implications* (Cambridge University Press, 2014), 73–88.

on Transparency to any investor-State arbitration,[50] demonstrates how some States have resorted to a treaty mechanism in order to broaden the scope of information sources in investor-State arbitration.[51] As of September 2016, however, the Mauritius Convention has not yet entered into force, with only one State (Mauritius) ratifying this Convention so far out of the required three, and there being only seventeen States signatory thus far to this treaty.[52] In contrast to these treaty-driven efforts, transparency gains have been achieved incrementally in the investor-State arbitration system,[53] largely from the initiative of international arbitration institutions such as ICSID and those of States Parties to the ICSID Convention. From his examination of investor-State arbitration jurisprudence, Lucas Bastin identifies eight emerging trends: '(1) amici curiae are seeking to participate more regularly; (2) amici curiae are no longer only non-governmental organisations; (3) amici curiae are participating outside the ICSID and NAFTA context; (4) within the NAFTA context, the scope of the requests made by amici curiae, and the procedure used to decide those requests, are now well settled; (5) outside the NAFTA context, the requests made by amici curiae have been consistently ambitious; (6) amici curiae participation favours States; (7) the system has become more permissive of amici curiae; and (8) despite increasing tolerance for amici curiae, the system is still a long way from granting them full participation rights.'[54]

ICSID tribunals have articulated different reasons and conditions for participation, in the few instances when they admitted non-disputing party-written submissions. In *Suez* v. *Argentine Republic*,[55] the tribunal

[50] United Nations Convention on Transparency in Treaty-Based Investor-State Arbitration, Article 2(1), available at www.uncitral.org/pdf/english/texts/arbitration/transparency-convention/Transparency-Convention-e.pdf (accessed 25 September 2016).

[51] UNCITRAL Rules on Transparency in Treaty-Based Investor-State Arbitration, available at www.uncitral.org/pdf/english/texts/arbitration/rules-on-transparency/Rules-on-Transparency-E.pdf Article 5 (accessed 25 September 2016).

[52] See Status of the UN Convention on Transparency in Treaty-Based Arbitration, available at https://treaties.un.org/pages/ViewDetails.aspx?src=IND&mtdsg_no=XXII-3&chapter=22&lang=en (accessed 25 September 2016).

[53] See ICSID Arbitration Rule 37(2); C. Knahr, 'The New Rules on Participation of Non-Disputing Parties at ICSID Arbitration: Blessing or curse?', in C. Brown and K. Miles (eds.), *Evolution in Investment Treaty Law and Arbitration* (Cambridge University Press, 2011), 319–38.

[54] L. Bastin, Amici Curiae in Investor-State Arbitration: Eight Recent Trends, *Arbitration International*, 30 (2014), 125–44.

[55] *Aguas Provinciales de Santa Fe S.A., Suez, Sociedad General de Aguas de Barcelona S.A. and InterAguas Servicios Integrales del Agua S.A.* v. *Argentine Republic*, ICSID Case No.

concluded that pursuant to its residual power to resolve procedural questions under Article 44 of the ICSID Convention, the tribunal could set three basic criteria for the acceptance of *amicus curiae* submissions, without at the same time granting access to documents in the arbitration to the proposed amicus: 'a) the appropriateness of the subject matter of the case; b) the suitability of a given nonparty to act as amicus curiae in that case, and c) the procedure by which the amicus submission is made and considered.'[56] The arbitral tribunal in *Biwater Gauff (Tanzania), Ltd.* v. *United Republic of Tanzania* rejected a broad *amicus curiae* designation for non-disputing party submissions under ICSID Arbitration Rule 37(2) and instead granted the request of five public interest non-governmental organisations (NGOs) to make written submissions based on their 'reasonable potential to assist the Arbitral Tribunal by bringing a perspective, particular knowledge or insight that is different from that of the disputing parties [where such] submissions would address matters within the scope of the dispute [and] each of the Petitioners has a sufficient interest in this proceeding'.[57] In contrast, the tribunal in *Piero Foresti and others* v. *Republic of South Africa* opened access to documents in the proceedings under narrow terms, stressing that non-disputing party (NDP) participation 'is intended to enable NDPs to give useful information and accompanying submissions to the Tribunal, but is not intended to be a mechanism for enabling NDPs to obtain information from the Parties ... NDPs must be allowed access to those papers submitted to the Tribunal by the Parties that are necessary to enable the NDPs to focus their submissions upon the issues arising in the case and to see what positions the Parties have taken on those issues. NDPs must also be given adequate opportunity to prepare and deliver their submissions in sufficient time before the hearing for the Parties to be able to respond

ARB/03/17, Order in Response to a Petition for Participation as Amicus Curiae of 17 March 2006.

[56] *Ibid.*, para. 11. Note that the tribunal took the same position with respect to other petitioners. *See Aguas Provinciales de Santa Fe S.A., Suez, Sociedad General de Aguas de Barcelona S.A. and InterAguas Servicios Integrales del Agua S.A.* v. *Argentine Republic*, ICSID Case No. ARB/03/19, Order in Response to a Petition for Participation as Amicus Curiae of 19 May 2005, para. 17; *Aguas Provinciales de Santa Fe S.A., Suez, Sociedad General de Aguas de Barcelona S.A. and InterAguas Servicios Integrales del Agua S.A.* v. *Argentine Republic*, ICSID Case No. ARB/03/19, Order in Response to a Petition for Participation as Amicus Curiae of 12 February 2007, para. 12.

[57] *Biwater Gauff (Tanzania), Ltd.* v. *United Republic of Tanzania*, ICSID Case No. ARB/05/22, Procedural Order No. 5, para. 50.

to those submissions.'[58] The tribunal in *Pac Rim Cayman LLC* v. *Republic of El Salvador* granted requests to file written submissions as non-disputing parties or *amicus curiae*, without stating reasons, but clarifying instead that the written submissions would be limited only to the jurisdictional issues with a view towards assisting the tribunal, and without risking the disruption of the proceedings or otherwise unduly burdening or unfairly prejudicing any of the parties to the dispute.[59]

More recently, in procedural orders issued in 2015 in the *Philip Morris* v. *Uruguay* case, however, the tribunal accepted applications to submit *amicus curiae* briefs from international or intergovernmental public organisations such as the World Health Organisation (WHO) and its Secretariat on the Framework Convention on Tobacco Control (FCTC),[60] as well as by the Pan-American Health Organization (PAHO),[61] on the identical reasoning that these institutions stood to contribute important particular knowledge and expertise regarding the matters in the dispute and that the public interest involved in the case further warranted supporting greater transparency of the proceedings.[62] In both applications, the *Philip Morris* tribunal gave particular significance to observations previously made by the tribunal in the *Methanex* v. *United States* case:

> [T]here is an undoubtedly public interest in this arbitration. The substantive issues extend far beyond those raised by the usual transnational arbitration between commercial parties. This is not merely because one of the Disputing Parties is a State: there are of course disputes involving States which are of no greater interest in this arbitration than a dispute between private persons. The public interest in this arbitration arises from its subject-matter, as powerfully suggested in the Petitions. There is also a broader process argument, as suggested by the Respondents and Canada: the . . . arbitral process could benefit from being perceived as more open or transparent; or conversely be harmed if seen as unduly secretive. In this regard, the Tribunal's willingness to receive amicus submissions might

[58] *Piero Foresti and others* v. *Republic of South Africa*, ICSID Case No. ARB(AF)/07/1, Letter to the Disputing Parties of 5 October 2009, paras. 1 and 2.

[59] *Pac Rim Cayman LLC* v. *Republic of El Salvador*, ICSID Case No. ARB/09/12, Procedural Order No. 8 of 23 March 2011, paras. (ii) to (iv).

[60] *Philip Morris Brand Sàrl (Switzerland), Philip Morris Products S.A. (Switzerland), and Abal Hermanos S.A. (Uruguay)* v. *Oriental Republic of Uruguay*, ICSID Case No. ARB/10/7, Procedural Order No. 3 of 17 February 2015 [hereafter WHO and FCTC Amicus Order].

[61] *Philip Morris Brand Sàrl (Switzerland), Philip Morris Products S.A. (Switzerland), and Abal Hermanos S.A. (Uruguay)* v. *Oriental Republic of Uruguay*, ICSID Case No. ARB/10/7, Procedural Order No. 4, 24 March 2015 [hereafter 'PAHO Amicus Order'].

[62] WHO and FCTC Amicus Order, para. 28; PAHO Amicus Order, para. 30.

support the process in general and this arbitration in particular, whereas a blanket refusal could do positive harm.[63]

These procedural orders in the *Philip Morris* case are highly significant for States seeking to affect arbitral discretion over their fact-finding procedures. They imply that non-disputing-party States – as members of international or inter-governmental scientific and other technical organisations – could indeed also seek to expand the information sources available to investor-State arbitral tribunals tasked with determining complex public policy and regulatory questions.[64] By purposely expanding the information provided to investor-State arbitral tribunals through these technical submissions and reports of inter-governmental bodies on public policy and regulatory matters affecting investment operations in host States, States can themselves widen the lens of investment arbitral decision-making beyond its often-critiqued purely 'commercial'[65] confines.

E. Challenging the Bases and Suitability of Compensation as a Mode of Reparations in Investor-State Arbitration

It should also be pointed out that States have also been quite vigilant in challenging the bases and suitability of compensation as a mode of reparation in investor-State arbitration.[66] *Biwater Gauff* v. *Tanzania* is a crystal example of a case where a respondent State was declared to have breached investment treaty obligations but ultimately was not made to

[63] *Methanex Corporation* v. *United States of America*, UNCITRAL, Decision of the Tribunal on Petitions from Third Persons to Intervene as Amici Curiae under the North American Free Trade Agreement and the UNCITRAL Arbitration Rules of 15 January 2001.

[64] Bruno Simma and I previously made this observation about inter-governmental participation in investor-State arbitration in relation to the UN Committee on Economic, Social and Cultural Rights. See B. Simma and Diane A. Desierto, 'Bridging the Public Interest Divide: Committee Assistance for Investor-Host State Compliance with the ICESCR', in D. Hanschel, S. Graf Kielmansegg, U. Kischel, C. Koenig and R. A. Lorz (eds.), *Mensch und Recht: Festschrift für Eibe Riedel* (Berlin: Duncker & Humblot, 2013), 49, 53.

[65] See N. Hachez and J. Wouters, 'International Investment Dispute Settlement in the Twenty-First Century: Does the Preservation of the Public Interest Require an Alternative to the Arbitral Model?', in F. Baetens (ed.), *Investment Law within International Law: Integrationist Perspectives* (Cambridge University Press, 2013), 417, 424.

[66] Note that the European Commission reported that 'studies point to the fact that where the Tribunals have found in favour of the investor (which is in 25% of all ISDS cases according to UNCTAD), investors are on average granted only a small part of their original claim'; see European Commission, *Investor-State Dispute Settlement (ISDS): Some Facts and Figures*, 12 March 2015, 8, available at http://trade.ec.europa.eu/doclib/docs/2015/january/tradoc_153046.pdf (accessed 25 September 2016).

pay any amount of compensation because, as successfully pointed out by the respondent State, the investor itself failed to substantiate and provide sufficient evidence of any of its monetary or financial claims against Tanzania.[67] Timely and correct challenges to the evidentiary support submitted to substantiate investor claims for compensation is one way for States to assert control over available remedies in investor-State arbitration.

More importantly, however, State control over available remedies in investor-State arbitration could also be extended to thoroughly scrutinise investor claims for compensation on the basis of alleged State breaches of non-expropriation provisions in investment treaties.[68] While many investment treaties' clauses on expropriation generally include a requirement to pay compensation,[69] other investment treaty standards (e.g. guarantees of non-discriminatory treatment such as most favoured nation (MFN) treatment, national treatment and fair and equitable treatment (FET)) are often silent on the issue of compensation.[70] Compensation for breach of non-expropriation investment treaty provisions has been heatedly contested ever since the very first bilateral investment treaty award rendered by an arbitral tribunal, *Asian Agricultural Products, Ltd.* v. *Sri Lanka.* In this case, the dissenting arbitrator nominated by Sri Lanka strongly protested the finding of the tribunal majority that Sri Lanka's breach of the UK-Sri Lanka BIT's 'war clause' (e.g. granting national treatment or MFN treatment to investors for losses suffered owing to war or other armed conflict, revolution, state of national emergency, revolt, resurrection or riot in the territory of the host State) – which was altogether silent on the issue of

[67] *Biwater Gauff (Tanzania), Ltd.* v. *Tanzania*, ICSID Case No. ARB/05/22, Award and Concurring and Dissenting Opinion of 24 July 2008, paras. 797–807.

[68] See Diane A. Desierto, 'ICESCR Minimum Core Obligations and Investment: Recasting the Non-Expropriation Compensation Model during Financial Crises', *George Washington International Law Review*, 44 (2012), 473–520.

[69] See United Nations Conference on Trade and Development (UNCTAD), *Expropriation: A Sequel, UNCTAD Series on International Investment Agreements II* (New York: United Nations, 2012), 40–50, 111–15.

[70] See United Nations Conference on Trade and Development (UNCTAD), *Fair and Equitable Treatment: A Sequel* (UNCTAD Series on International Investment Agreements II) (New York: United Nations, 2012), 88–9: 'Investment treaties typically set out an explicit standard of compensation for expropriation cases only – most frequently, IIAs require prompt, adequate and effective compensation equal to fair market value of the expropriated investment. When non-expropriatory treaty violations are found, damages have been awarded in accordance with the rules of international law that require "full compensation". In a number of cases concerning FET breaches, this resulted in an award of the fair market value of the investment calculated by reference to future cash flows.'

compensation or remedies for the breach of this clause – should result in an award of compensation despite Sri Lanka not having granted any such compensation to either its nationals or third-State nationals for losses arising under the same emergency situation that gave rise to Asian Agricultural Products, Ltd.'s losses.[71]

Where investors assert a claim for compensation arising from the host State's breach of a non-expropriation investment treaty provision, tribunals thus far often gloss over the threshold question of the suitability of compensation to redress the non-expropriation breach.[72] The suitability of compensation as the mode of reparation arises vividly when *causation* (between the alleged infringing host State acts and the asserted damage to foreign investors) appears to be inadequately established or discussed in an arbitral award.[73] Two cases against the Czech Republic lodged by different foreign investors – over essentially the same governmental actions and inactions – well illustrate this phenomenon. In *Lauder* v. *Czech Republic*,[74] the arbitral tribunal found that the acts of the Czech Media Council in reversing its initial position that a direct investment in a Czech company was permitted to operate a media license (instead requiring the foreign investor to create a local joint-venture company) amounted to a 'discriminatory and arbitrary measure'[75] in breach of the bilateral investment treaty between the United States and the Czech Republic. Despite the finding of breach, however, the arbitral tribunal held that such a breach 'was too remote to qualify as a relevant cause for the harm caused. A finding on damages due to the Claimant by the Respondent would therefore not be appropriate.'[76] In contrast, the

[71] *Asian Agricultural Products Limited* v. *Sri Lanka*, Final Award on Merits and Damages, ICSID Case No. ARB/87/3 of 21 June 1990, Dissenting Opinion of Arbitrator Asante, paras. 38–42 and 53.

[72] Although note the position taken by some scholars that 'the absence of explicit standards of compensation for non-expropriatory breaches of international investment law does not preclude the use of standards applicable in case of expropriation.' P.-Y. Tschanz and J. E. Viñuales, 'Compensation for Non-Expropriatory Breaches of International Investment Law: The Contribution of the Argentine Awards', *Journal of International Arbitration*, 26 (2009), 735.

[73] See *Biwater Gauff* v. *Tanzania*, ICSID Case No. ARB/05/22, Award and Concurring and Dissenting Opinion of 18 July 2008, para. 807 (finding that declaratory relief could be appropriate rather than damages when causation is not proven): 'Given that none of the Republic's violations of the BIT caused the loss and damage for which BGT now claims compensation, it follows that each of BGT's claims for damages must be dismissed, and that the only appropriate remedies for the Republic's conduct can be declaratory in nature.'

[74] *Ronald Lauder* v. *Czech Republic*, UNCITRAL, Final Award of 3 September 2001.

[75] *Ibid.*, para. 222. [76] *Ibid.*, para. 235.

tribunal majority in *CME Czech Republic* v. *Czech Republic*[77] did not elaborate the issue of causation in awarding compensation to the claimant for the same actions of the Czech Media Council. The *CME* majority in the tribunal reached a factual conclusion on causation in one paragraph (where nine previous paragraphs simply restated the Articles of State Responsibility principles on damages), where, without further factual discussion, it held that the 'Media Council, when coercing CNTS in 1996 to amend its MOA [Memorandum of Agreement] and to implement the Service Agreement *must have understood the foreseeable consequences of its actions*, depriving CME of the legal safety net for its investment in the Czech Republic.'[78] The *CME* tribunal majority ultimately awarded US$270 million in damages for the same actions of the Czech Media Council that the *Lauder* tribunal did not find to have caused compensable harm.[79]

One can well observe how much the *CME* v. *Czech Republic* arbitral award contrasts starkly with the significance that the International Court of Justice (ICJ) attaches to properly establishing causation for claims of compensation for material and non-material injuries. In its Judgment on Compensation in *Case Concerning Ahmadou Sadio Diallo (Guinea* v. *Congo)*,[80] the ICJ found that non-material injuries caused by the Democratic Republic of Congo to businessman Mr Diallo for his arrest and detention were compensable but noted qualifications based on equity:

> 24. Quantification of compensation for non-material injury *necessarily rests on equitable considerations.* As the umpire noted in the *Lusitania* cases, non-material injuries 'are very real, and the mere fact that they are difficult to measure or estimate by money standards makes them none the less real and affords no reason why the injured person should not be compensated therefore as compensatory damages' (*RIAA*, Vol. VII, p. 40). When considering compensation for material or non-material injury caused by violations of the Covenant or the African Charter, respectively, the Human Rights Committee and the African Commission on Human and Peoples' Rights recommended 'adequate compensation' without specifying

[77] *CME Czech Republic* v. *Czech Republic*, UNCITRAL, Partial Award and Separate Opinion of 13 September 2001.

[78] *Ibid.*, para. 585.

[79] *CME Czech Republic* v. *Czech Republic*, UNCITRAL, Final Award and Separate Opinion of 14 March 2003, Part IX.

[80] *Case Concerning Ahmadou Sadio Diallo (Guinea* v. *Congo)*, Judgment on Compensation of 19 June 2012, ICJ Reports 2012, 324.

> the sum to be paid (see, for example, *A.* v. *Australia*, HRC, 3 April 1997, communication No. 560/1993, United Nations Doc. CCPR/C/59/D/560/1993, para. 11; *Kenneth Good* v. *Republic of Botswana*, ACHPR, 26 May 2010, communication No. 313/05; *28th Activity Report*, Ann. IV, p. 110, para. 244). Arbitral tribunals and regional human rights courts have been more specific, given the power to assess compensation granted by their respective constitutive instruments. Equitable considerations have guided their quantification of compensation for non-material harm. . . .
>
> 25. With regard to the non-material injury suffered by Mr. Diallo, the circumstances outlined in paragraphs 21 to 23 lead the Court to consider that the amount of US$85,000 would provide appropriate compensation. The sum is expressed in the currency to which both Parties referred in their written pleadings on compensation.[81]

The ICJ further relied on equitable considerations in assessing compensation due for material injury caused to Mr Diallo by the DRC's actions against his businesses or properties, while requiring specific evidence for each asserted claim of compensation:

> 33. Despite the shortcomings in the evidence related to the property listed on the inventory, the Court recalls that Mr. Diallo lived and worked in the territory of the DRC for over thirty years, during which time he surely accumulated personal property. Even assuming that the DRC is correct in its contention that Guinean officials and Mr. Diallo's relatives were in a position to dispose of that personal property after Mr. Diallo's expulsion, the Court considers that, at a minimum, Mr. Diallo would have had to transport his personal property to Guinea or to arrange for its disposition in the DRC. *Thus, the Court is satisfied that the DRC's unlawful conduct caused some material injury to Mr. Diallo with respect to personal property that had been in the apartment in which he lived, although it would not be reasonable to accept the very large sum claimed by Guinea for this head of damage. In such a situation, the Court considers it appropriate to award an amount of compensation based on equitable considerations (see paragraph 36 below). . . .*
>
> 36. The Court therefore awards no compensation in respect of the high-value items and bank account assets described in paragraphs 34 and 35 above. However, in view of the Court's conclusions above (see paragraph 33) regarding the personal property of Mr. Diallo and on the basis of equitable considerations, the Court awards the sum of US$10,000 under this head of damage.[82]

[81] *Ibid.*, paras. 24–5 (emphasis added).

[82] *Ibid.*, paras. 33–6 (emphasis added).

Apart from issues on the suitability of compensation as a mode of reparations for non-expropriation breaches, States can also make sure that they scrutinise the appropriateness of valuation measures used by tribunals. While fair market value often appears to be the valuation measure of choice used for breaches of non-expropriation investment treaty standards such as the FET standard,[83] it should be stressed that this measure is not necessarily controlling in all cases. For example, in *PSEG Global Incorporated and Konya Ilgin Elektrik Üretim ve Ticaret Limited Širketi* v. *Turkey*,[84] while the arbitral tribunal found that Turkey breached the FET standard by its 'failure to conduct negotiations in a proper way and other forms of interference … [t]he appropriate remedies thus do not relate to a compensation for the market value of those assets but to a different objective'.[85] The *PSEG* tribunal declared that 'fair market value shall not be retained as the measure for compensation in this case',[86] and neither would it apply 'the lost profits heading of claim as the measure of compensation because it cannot be justified from a legal or economic point of view in the circumstances of the case'.[87] Instead, the tribunal ordered Turkey to pay compensation in the amount of US$9 million, representing the cost of PSEG's proven investment expenditures, plus interest from the date of injury.[88] Similarly, the tribunal in *Lemire* v. *Ukraine* differentiated the choice of valuation measure and awarded almost US$9 million in damages, finding that 'in situations where the breach of the FET standard does not lead to total loss of the investment, the purpose of the compensation must be to place the investor in the same pecuniary position in which it would have been if respondent had not violated the BIT.'[89] The *Lemire* tribunal stressed that 'the actual calculation of damages cannot be made in the abstract, it must be case specific: it requires the definition of a financial methodology for the

[83] See, among others, *Enron Creditors Recovery Corporation and Ponderosa Assets L.P.* v. *Argentine Republic*, ICSID Case No. ARB/01/3, Award of 22 May 2007, para. 363; *Sempra Energy International* v. *Argentine Republic*, ICSID Case No. ARB/02/16, Award of 28 September 2007, para. 403; *CMS Gas Transmission Company* v. *Argentine Republic*, ICSID Case No. ARB/01/8, Award of 12 May 2005, paras. 409–10; *SD Myers* v. *Government of Canada*, UNCITRAL, Second Partial Award of 21 October 2002, para. 311; *MTD Equity Sdn Bhd and MTD Chile SA* v. *Chile*, ICSID Case No. ARB/01/7, Award of 25 May 2004, para. 253.

[84] *PSEG Global Incorporated and Konya Ilgin Elektrik Üretim ve Ticaret Limited Širketi* v. *Turkey*, ICSID Case No. ARB/02/5, Award and Annex of 19 January 2007.

[85] *Ibid.*, para. 308. [86] *Ibid.*, para. 309. [87] *Ibid.*, para. 315. [88] *Ibid.*, para. 353.

[89] *Joseph Charles Lemire* v. *Ukraine*, ICSID Case No. ARB/06/18, Award of 28 March 2011, para. 149.

determination of a sum of money which, delivered to the investor, produces the equivalent economic value which, in all probability, the investor would enjoy, "but for" the State's breach.'[90] The tribunal pragmatically articulated the difficulties and intricacies of an armchair reconstruction of these pre-breach and post-breach values:

> 248. While the existence of damage is certain, calculating the precise amount of the compensation is fraught with much more difficulty, inherent in the very nature of the 'but for' hypothesis. *Valuation is not an exact science. The Tribunal has no crystal ball and cannot claim to know what would have happened under a hypothesis of no breach; the best any tribunal can do is to make an informed and conscientious evaluation, taking into account all the relevant circumstances of the case*, not unlike that made by anyone who assesses the value of a business on the basis of its likely future earnings.
>
> 249. The issues surrounding the measure of compensation for breaches of the FET standard are – as the Tribunal in LG & E said – 'particularly thorny'. To estimate the damages, the Tribunal will inevitably have to accept certain assumptions. These assumptions can and must be checked, applying tests of reasonableness. But in the end, there is no denying that the calculation of damages in a case like this, inevitably requires a certain amount of conjecture as to how things would have evolved 'but for' the actual behaviour of the parties. This difficulty in calculation cannot, however, deprive an investor, who has suffered injury, from his fundamental right to see his losses redressed.[91]

Neither the *PSEG* nor the *Lemire* tribunals questioned the suitability of compensation as the mode of reparation for the asserted breaches of non-expropriation investment treaty provisions, although both tribunals ultimately whittled down the investors' compensation claims considerably by rejecting the automatic applicability of the fair-market-value standard.

Finally, while compensation appears to be the dominant mode of reparation favoured by tribunals for host State breaches of non-expropriation investment treaty provisions, there are a few who do recognise that other modes of reparation may also be more appropriate than compensation. The tribunal in *Al-Baloul* v. *Tajikistan*, for example, found that Article 26 of the Energy Charter Treaty (ECT) did not rule out the possibility for the tribunal to order specific performance (e.g. such as the issuance of licenses sought by the claimant),[92] even if the claimant

[90] *Ibid.*, para. 152. [91] *Ibid.*, paras. 243–4 and 246–9 (emphasis added).

[92] *Al-Baloul* v. *Tajikistan*, SCC Case No. 064/2008, Final Award of 8 June 2010, paras. 47–63.

was thereafter not able to present evidence to substantiate its right to this form of relief. Notwithstanding this possibility, the *Al-Baloul* tribunal ultimately adjudicated the claims for compensation, using valuation methods prescribed by other tribunals, intuiting that since the ECT did not provide guidance on the standard of compensation for non-expropriation breaches,

> it need not decide which of the various standards and methodologies applied in other cases by other tribunals might be suitable in this case. The Claimant has chosen its own methodology. The Claimant has submitted a valuation based on the difference in the value of the licenses in the [hypothetical scenario in 2001, had there been no breach and Tajikistan issued the licenses; and the hypothetical scenario in 2009]. The Tribunal notes that a value-based approach has been applied by a number of investment tribunals for treaty breaches other than expropriation.[93]

Restitution can also be a preferable mode of reparations as opposed to compensation. In *Arif* v. *Moldova*, the arbitral tribunal sided with the respondent State and explicitly acknowledged that 'restitution is more consistent with the objectives of bilateral investment treaties, as it preserves both the investment and the relationship between the investor and the host State.'[94] The *Arif* tribunal sequentially approached the modes of reparation possible – restitution and compensation – and held the latter in abeyance until parties could demonstrate that restitution was impossible:

> 571. The Tribunal considers restitution to be the preferable remedy, but as in the present case Respondent has not been able to confirm that restitution is possible, and the Tribunal cannot supervise any restitutionary remedy, the best course is to order restitution and compensation as alternatives, with the remedy of compensation suspended for a period of ninety days. This provides Respondent with the opportunity, in light of the findings of this award, to formulate and propose to Claimant the exact mechanism of restitution. If restitution is not possible, or the terms of restitution proposed by Respondent are not satisfactory to Claimant then the damages awarded will satisfy the violation of Claimant's right to fair and equitable treatment. This solution provides a final opportunity to preserve the investment, while also preserving Claimant's right to damages if a satisfactory restitutionary solution cannot be found.[95]

[93] *Ibid.*, paras. 67–8.
[94] *Arif* v. *Moldova*, ICSID Case No. ARB/11/23, Award of 8 April 2013, para. 570.
[95] *Ibid.*, paras. 569–72 (emphasis added).

A tribunal's power to order restitution may exist both as a matter of its inherent authority to order pecuniary and non-pecuniary remedies under the ICSID Convention and as when such a mode of reparation is not precluded under a BIT.[96] While restitution is 'rarely ordered'[97] by tribunals, it remains a primary mode of reparation that should not be easily discarded or assumed to be impracticable.

In sum, States could challenge – and as seen from the emerging jurisprudence discussed earlier, several already have challenged – the bases and suitability of compensation as a mode of reparation for alleged host State breaches of investment treaties in investor-State arbitrations. They can readily challenge the sufficiency of the evidentiary support presented as the basis for compensation claims. They need not cede threshold legal issues on the validity and appropriateness of compensation as the mode of reparation for breaches of non-expropriation provisions of investment treaties – particularly in situations where the claimant has not established the material impossibility of restitution for these kinds of treaty breaches. Assuming that compensation is found to be the appropriate mechanism, States can scrutinise the causation and proportionality elements of the compensation sought by the investor to redress non-expropriation treaty breaches, put forward equitable considerations to tribunals and contest fair-market-valuation methodologies and assumptions made by the claimant.

F. Conclusion

It is difficult to imagine today that States – the architects of modern international investment law and the ongoing reform of the investor-State dispute resolution system – would ever be characterised as utterly powerless or deemed wholly defenceless against foreign investors. The multimillion- and multibillion-dollar onerous scale of compensation awards alone that have been issued in favour of investors against respondent States in investor-State arbitrations – and how these awards stand in marked contrast to other economic claims against sovereign States made at the ICJ and other international tribunals – facially establishes a systemic disproportionality that currently exists in international dispute settlement mechanisms to resolve claims against States for international economic

[96] *Micula and others* v. *Romania*, ICSID Case No. ARB/05/20, Decision on Jurisdiction and Admissibility of 24 September 2008, paras. 166–8.

[97] *Ibid.*, para. 166.

damage.[98] But one also cannot lose sight of the fact that there are internal currents in investor-State arbitration that demonstrate States pushing back to reassert control over available remedies. This chapter merely lays out the most promising recent jurisprudential trends demonstrating the reassertion of State control in circumscribing the role of interested parties and third-party funders, policing the ranks of qualified and impartial international arbitrators, expanding information sources for tribunals and challenging the bases and suitability of compensation as a mode of reparation for breach of non-expropriation provisions of investment treaties. States cannot thus be said to have truly lost control over available remedies in investor-State arbitration, even if only a few States to date have been effective at rapidly evolving new creative policy, treaty, and dispute settlement strategies to continuously defend their interests and resources from unjustified, unlawful, exaggerated, impecunious or spurious investment claims.

98 See Diane A. Desierto, 'Postmodern Reparations in International Law' (manuscript on file with author).

PART IV

Reassertion of Control

Policy and Trends

12

States' Reassertion of Control over International Investment Law

(Re)Defining 'Fair and Equitable Treatment' and 'Indirect Expropriation'

ERIC DE BRABANDERE

'Fair and equitable treatment' (FET) without doubt is the most invoked standard in investment treaty arbitration, and its importance as a standard of investment protection cannot be underestimated. The prohibition of indirect expropriation commonly found in international investment treaties is less frequently successful as a stand-alone claim in investment disputes,[1] but it constitutes nevertheless one of the most invoked provisions in investment disputes. Both investment protection provisions share many common principles, such as their standardly vague formulation or definition in the vast majority of international investment agreements. They also share the reputation of being generally considered as detrimental impediments to the States' right to regulate and to take measures in the public interest. This is precisely why both FET and the prohibition of indirect expropriation have attracted much criticism over recent years.[2]

This chapter investigates how States, through definitions of the FET standard and the prohibition of indirect expropriation, have sought to assert or reassert control over investment law. Indeed, there are clear differences in the formulation of the FET standard and the prohibition of indirect expropriation. 'Western hemisphere' bilateral investment treaties (BITs) used in Western European States tend to include FET as a stand-alone standard of treatment, whereas North American investment treaties, as exemplified, *inter alia*, in the North American Free Trade

[1] See A. K. Hoffmann, 'Indirect Expropriation', in A. Reinisch (ed.), *Standards of Investment Protection* (Oxford University Press, 2008), 167.

[2] See J. Bonnitcha, *Substantive Protection under Investment Treaties: A Legal and Economic Analysis* (Cambridge University Press, 2014), 21 *et seq.*

Agreement (NAFTA)[3] and the US Model BIT 2012[4], tend to equate FET with the customary norm on the minimum standard of treatment. Similarly, distinctions in the formulation of what constitutes a prohibited indirect expropriation are widespread, and here again, the contrast between the practice of North American treaties and those based on the 'western hemisphere' BITs show that the former tend to more precisely define what constitutes a prohibited indirect expropriation and which regulatory measures cannot amount to an expropriation, while the latter more generally contain a generic definition of the term. These differences highlight one important issue: States generally have full discretion in how to formulate these provisions in their treaties. And while 'tradition' has in the past influenced the choice of one model or formulation over the other, increasingly policy-related arguments now define the precise formulation of FET and the prohibition of indirect expropriation, provided, of course, that all States parties to the treaty agree on the terminology.

In this chapter I will focus on the recent treaty practice of States in showing how States have – to use a more neutral term – reacted to the application and interpretation of FET and indirect expropriation by arbitral tribunals in the abundant case law that exists in that respect. I will first give an overview of the FET standard of treatment and the prohibition of indirect expropriation in order to better grasp the recent treaty practice of States to redefine such terms. I will next analyse the causes and concerns surrounding the FET standard of treatment and the prohibition of indirect expropriation, which have led to certain reactions by States, which will be discussed in the third part of this chapter. These reactions will be grouped into, firstly, procedural reactions and, secondly, reactions on substance through the redefinition of the FET standard of treatment and the prohibition of indirect expropriation.

A. The FET Standard of Treatment and the Prohibition of Indirect Expropriation: An Overview

(1) Fair and Equitable Treatment

FET generally is referred to as a non-contingent, absolute standard of treatment as opposed to contingent, relative standards, such as national

[3] North American Free Trade Agreement (NAFTA), 17 December 1992, in force 1 January 1994 (1993) 32 ILM 289, 605.

[4] US Model Bilateral Investment Treaty (2012), available at www.ustr.gov/sites/default/files/BIT%20text%20for%20ACIEP%20Meeting.pdf (accessed 25 February 2016).

treatment (NT) or most favoured nation (MFN) treatment.[5] The latter category of standards of treatment imposes on the host State the obligation to act in a certain way by reference to how *other* investors or investments are treated, for example, national investors or investments in case of NT or investors or investments from third States in case of MFN treatment. The objective of such standards is that States may not discriminate between investors and investments; whether or not the State has exercised due diligence in this respect is irrelevant. Standards such as FET, however, ask the State to act in a certain way as required under international law (either custom or treaty law), irrespective of how other investors or investments are treated.

The obligation to treat foreign investors fairly and equitably is stipulated in the vast majority of BITs and in some regional or sectoral multilateral investment agreements, such as the NAFTA or the Energy Charter Treaty (ECT).[6] According to Dolzer and Schreuer, '[T]he purpose of the [fair and equitable treatment] clause as used in [investment treaty] practice is to fill gaps that may be left by the more specific standards, in order to obtain the level of investor protection intended by the treaties.'[7] Another explanation, offered by McLachlan, Shore and Weiniger, is that the clause 'affords a basis by which international law judges the adequacy of treatment meted out to a foreign investor by the judicial and administrative agencies of the host State. It reflects treatment which all civilized nations should accord to their citizens as well as to aliens.'[8]

In a passage which has been repeatedly quoted by subsequent tribunals,[9] the tribunal in *Tecmed* v. *Mexico* said that the FET standard 'requires the Contracting Parties to provide to international investments treatment that does not affect the basic expectations that were taken into

[5] See C. McLachlan, L. Shore and M. Weiniger, *International Investment Arbitration: Substantive Principles* (Oxford University Press, 2008), 207, para. 7.19; N. Angelet, 'Fair and Equitable Treatment', in R. Wolfrum (ed.), *Max Planck Encyclopedia of Public International Law* (Oxford University Press, 2012), online edition, para. 3.

[6] R. Kläger, 'Fair and Equitable Treatment: A Look at the Theoretical Underpinnings of Legitimacy and Fairness', *Journal of World Investment & Trade*, 11 (2010), 436.

[7] R. Dolzer and C. Schreuer, *Principles of International Investment Law* (Oxford University Press, 2008), 122.

[8] McLachlan, Shore and Weiniger, *International Investment Arbitration: Substantive Principles*, para. 7.17.

[9] See e.g. *Sempra Energy International* v. *The Argentine Republic*, ICSID Case No. ARB/02/16, Award of 28 September 2007, para. 298.

account by the foreign investor to make the investment.'[10] More recently, the tribunal in *Bayindir* v. *Pakistan* stated that

> the different factors which emerge from decisions of investment tribunals as forming part of the [fair and equitable treatment] standard . . . comprise the obligation to act transparently and grant due process, to refrain from taking arbitrary or discriminatory measures, from exercising coercion or from frustrating the investor's reasonable expectations with respect to the legal framework affecting the investment.[11]

The FET standard clearly is a flexible and rather vague concept. One should keep in mind, however, that the framing and labelling of the different sub-elements continue to vary considerably and continue to be influenced heavily by arbitral jurisprudence. However, based on the abovementioned cases and scholarship, it is generally accepted that the following obligations form part of fair and equitable treatment: observance of the investor's legitimate expectations, non-discrimination, proportionality, due process, transparency, freedom from coercion and harassment, stability, predictability and a general duty of due diligence.[12] The two most important components of FET in practice are the requirement of a certain form of legal stability and protection of the legitimate expectation of foreign investors.[13] Yet, one can notice, in the practice of arbitral tribunals, a tendency to a more cautious approach to FET through recognition of the States' right to regulate and thus for States to maintain sufficient regulatory space.[14] This has been reflected, moreover, in certain treaties, as I will explain later.

[10] *Tecnicas Medioambientales Tecmed SA* v. *United Mexican States*, ICSID Case No. ARB (AF)/00/2, Award of 29 May 2003, para. 154.

[11] *Bayindir Insaat Turizm Ticaret Ve Sanayi AS* v. *Islamic Republic of Pakistan*, ICSID Case No. ARB/03/29, Award of 27 August 2009, para. 178.

[12] A. Newcombe and L. Paradell, *Law and Practice of Investment Treaties: Standards of Treatment* (Alphen aan den Rijn, Netherlands: Kluwer Law International, 2009), 277–9; I. Tudor, *The Fair and Equitable Treatment Standard in the International law of Foreign Investment* (Oxford University Press, 2008), 157, 186; R. Kläger, 'Fair and Equitable Treatment: A Look at the Theoretical Underpinnings of Legitimacy and Fairness', *Journal of World Investment & Trade*, 11 (2010), 436. See also for an overview of the contents of the standard in function of arbitral practice K. Yannaca-Small, 'Fair and Equitable Treatment Standard: Recent Developments', in A. Reinisch (ed.), *Standards of Investment Protection* (Oxford University Press, 2008), 118 *et seq.*

[13] See for a discussion K. Yannaca-Small, 'Fair and Equitable Treatment Standard: Recent Developments', in A. Reinisch (ed.), *Standards of Investment Protection* (Oxford University Press, 2008), 118.

[14] See for a discussion also U. Kriebaum, 'FET and Expropriation in the (Invisible) EU Model BIT', *Journal of World Investment & Trade*, 15 (2014), 471.

Moreover, in any case, FET requires at least treatment in accordance with the international minimum standard (IMS) as understood in general international law.[15] Indeed, IMS and FET share many features. Their exact relation and the question of whether FET exists as a self-contained standard[16] or is merely a re-badged version of the IMS[17] still are subject to much debate. More recently, tribunals have considered the FET to be the 'new' customary minimum standard of treatment.[18] Commentators indeed have suggested that the evolving nature of the IMS appears well established today and seems to have evolved to the point where the current arbitral jurisprudence has refused to discern any practical difference between the interpretation of FET in line with the evolved minimum standard and the application of FET as a self-contained norm.[19]

In practical terms, there are roughly four models of FET clauses, exception made of the possibility, of course, of not including any FET provision, such as in the Australia–Singapore Free Trade Agreement (FTA) of 2003.[20] Firstly, FET can be a stand-alone (unqualified) clause, in that FET is included without any specific reference to another treaty standard or to its content – the 'European model'.[21] Such clauses, because of their stand-alone and unqualified character, usually are interpreted very broadly by tribunals.[22] Secondly, FET can be coupled to the phrase

[15] Newcombe and Paradell, *Law and Practice of Investment Treaties*, 277.

[16] See for a discussion C. Schreuer, 'Full Protection and Security', *Journal of International Dispute Settlement*, 1 (2010), 1–17.

[17] Kläger, 'Fair and Equitable Treatment', 436–8.

[18] *William Ralph Clayton, William Richard Clayton, Douglas Clayton, Daniel Clayton and Bilcon of Delaware, Inc.* v. *Government of Canada*, UNCITRAL, PCA Case No. 2009–04, Award on Jurisdiction and Liability of 17 March 2015, paras. 433 *et seq*. See also *Merrill & Ring Forestry L.P.* v. *Government of Canada*, UNCITRAL, ICSID Administered Case, Award of 31 March 2010, paras. 210 *et seq*.

[19] Kläger, 'Fair and Equitable Treatment', 439.

[20] All investment treaties referred to here are available on the website of UNCTAD: http://investmentpolicyhub.unctad.org/IIA (accessed 25 February 2016).

[21] See e.g. Article 3 of the Belgium–Luxembourg Economic Union–Tajikistan BIT (2009): 'All investments made by investors of one Contracting Party shall enjoy a fair and equitable treatment in the territory of the other Contracting Party.' See for a discussion also U. Kriebaum, 'FET and Expropriation in the (Invisible) EU Model BIT', *Journal of World Investment & Trade*, 15 (2014), 454.

[22] See for a discussion M. C. Porterfield, 'A Distinction without a Difference? The Interpretation of Fair and Equitable Treatment under Customary International Law by Investment Tribunals', *Investment Treaty News Quarterly*, 22 March 2013, available at www.iisd.org/itn/2013/03/22/a-distinction-without-a-difference-the-interpretation-of-fair-and-equitable-treatment-under-customary-international-law-by-investment-tribunals/0 (accessed 25 February 2016).

'in accordance with international law'.[23] Such clauses are aimed at ensuring that the interpreter uses principles of international law, including international customary law and general principles, to identify the scope and content of the standard.[24] Thirdly, FET can be equated to the IMS, as is the case, for instance, in the 2012 US Model BIT.[25] And fourthly, FET can be used in combination with some specific substantive content, such as the prohibition of a denial of justice or non-discrimination.[26]

(2) Indirect Expropriation

The regulation of direct expropriation under international law has existed for a long time. Indeed, most international investment treaties, while having some variation as to the exact formulation, have crystallised the traditional customary norm on expropriation which requires taking for a public purpose, in a non-discriminatory manner, with respect of due process of law and the payment of a compensation.[27]

While outright direct expropriations no longer occur very often in practice – at least, they do not often lead to a dispute based on the alleged breach of an international investment treaty – indirect expropriations have over recent years been the subject of several disputes between foreign investors and host States. An indirect expropriation, however, is characterised by a measure that has an effect equivalent to a direct expropriation in that there is, because of a measure, a substantial or total deprivation of an investment.[28] The effect is measured by a variety of

[23] See e.g. Article 3(2) of the Croatia–Oman BIT (2004): 'Investments or returns of investors of either Contracting Party in the territory of the other Contracting Party shall be accorded fair and equitable treatment in accordance with international law and provisions of this Agreement.'

[24] UNCTAD, *Fair and Equitable Treatment* (UNCTAD Series on Issues in International Investment Agreements II) (New York: United Nations, 2012), 22.

[25] See Article 5 of the US Model BIT (2012).

[26] See e.g. Article 11 ASEAN Comprehensive Investment Agreement:

1. Each Member State shall accord to covered investments of investors of any other Member State, fair and equitable treatment and full protection and security.
2. For greater certainty:
   (a) fair and equitable treatment requires each Member State not to deny justice in any legal or administrative proceedings in accordance with the principle of due process.

[27] UNCTAD, *Expropriation* (UNCTAD Series on Issues in International Investment Agreements II) (New York: United Nations, 2012), 27.

[28] See for a discussion S. López Escarcena, *Indirect Expropriation in International Law* (Cheltenham, UK: Edward Elgar, 2014), 200 *et seq.*

factors, such as the economic impact of the measure on the investment or the degree of interference of the measure with the use of or control over the investment.[29] An indirect expropriation differs from a direct expropriation in that there is no deliberate intent to formally transfer title over the property of the foreign investor or to seize the property.[30]

Most investment treaties signed today include, often coupled to a provision or paragraph on direct expropriation, a prohibition of indirect expropriations as well. Here there are roughly two models. The 'European' model has traditionally included a generic prohibition of indirect expropriation, without any specific definition or requirements. Article 4(2) of the 2008 German Model BIT, for example, provides that 'investments by investors of either Contracting State may not directly or indirectly be expropriated, nationalised or subjected to any other measure the effects of which would be tantamount to expropriation or nationalisation in the territory of the other Contracting State except for the public benefit and against compensation.' More specific requirements only are added in relation to the compensation requirement.[31] Similar provisions can be found in the Indian Model BIT[32] and the French Model BIT.[33]

The second – 'North-American' – model contains more detailed provisions, which had been introduced in the 2004 US Model BIT and the 2004 Canadian Model Foreign Investment Promotion and Protection

[29] See for an analysis UNCTAD, *Expropriation*, 63. [30] *Ibid.*, 7.

[31] German Model BIT (2008), Article 4(2): 'Such compensation must be equivalent to the value of the expropriated investment immediately before the date on which the actual or threatened expropriation, nationalization or other measure became publicly known. The compensation must be paid without delay and shall carry the usual bank interest until the time of payment; it must be effectively realizable and freely transferable. Provision must have been made in an appropriate manner at or prior to the time of expropriation, nationalization or other measure for the determination and payment of such compensation. The legality of any such expropriation, nationalization or other measure and the amount of compensation must be subject to review by due process of law', available at www.italaw.com/investment-treaties (accessed 25 February 2016).

[32] Indian Model BIT (2015), Article 5(1): 'Neither Party may nationalize or expropriate an Investment (hereinafter 'expropriate'), or take Measures having an effect equivalent to expropriation, except for reasons of public purpose, in accordance with the procedure established by Law, and on payment of adequate compensation', available at www.italaw.com/investment-treaties (accessed 25 February 2016).

[33] French Model BIT (2006), Article 5(2): 'Neither Contracting Party shall take any measures of expropriation or nationalization or any other measures having the effect of dispossession, direct or indirect, of nationals or companies of the other Contracting Party of their investments on its territory and in its maritime area, except in the public interest and provided that these measures are neither discriminatory nor contrary to a specific commitment', available at www.italaw.com/investment-treaties (accessed 25 February 2016).

Agreement (FIPA). The 2012 US Model BIT contains even more detailed provisions. Prior to the introduction of this 'model', the United States generally followed the European approach explained in the preceding paragraph.[34]

The basic provisions in the US and Canadian Model BITs are generally formulated and do not deviate much from the 'European model'. Yet the US and Canadian Model BITs comprise specific annexes which contain details and limitations as to which measures may constitute indirect expropriations, such as Annex B.13(1) of the 2004 Canadian Model BIT or paragraph 4 of Annex B to the 2012 US Model BIT.

B. Causes and Concerns Surrounding FET and Indirect Expropriation

The contemporary meaning of the FET standard rests very much on interpretations by the arbitral tribunals tasked with settling disputes between foreign investors and host States. This, in essence, is the result of the often general and vague formulations of the FET standard, which leaves much room for expansive interpretations by tribunals of what constitutes an 'unfair and un-equitable' treatment. Likewise, in relation to indirect expropriations, and although the test to be applied in that context is much different from the one applied in relation to FET, the appraisal of the effect of a State measure on the property of the foreign investor, and notably whether such a measure has an effect equivalent to direct expropriation, also leaves much discretion to arbitral tribunals.

It is beyond doubt that the main trigger for what this book terms Contracting Parties' 'reassertion of control' over investment law, and notably in relation to the contents of the FET standard and indirect expropriation, has been the arbitral jurisprudence over recent decades.[35]

In relation to the FET standard specifically, two issues have triggered specific reactions. Firstly, the minimalist[36] and open-ended formulations of FET in investment treaties have resulted in an interpretation of that standard which includes a vast variety of sub-categories or elements, which clearly has been considered by certain States as going beyond their original intention. The inclusion, notably, of the requirement of

[34] See e.g. Argentina-US Bilateral Investment Treaty (1991), Article 4, available at http://tcc.export.gov/Trade_Agreements/All_Trade_Agreements/exp_000897.asp (accessed 25 February 2016).

[35] See also Chapter 1.

[36] UNCTAD, *Fair and Equitable Treatment*, 11.

a stable legal framework[37] and the extensive reliance on the legitimate expectations of the foreign investor,[38] has been the subject of much criticism in recent years.[39]

The second issue, which is very much the consequence of the first, is the expansive interpretation of FET provisions which has resulted from tribunals' purely semantic approaches to defining what constitutes 'unfair and un-equitable' treatment. The vagueness of the standard[40] and the lack of precise guidance on how to interpret the standard – apart from the treaties' preambles – in practice will result in tribunals considering on a case-by-case basis whether they consider the treatment accorded to the foreign investor to be 'unfair' or 'un-equitable'.[41] Such a semantic approach and the resulting expansive interpretation of what constitutes 'fair and equitable treatment', while not necessarily contrary to the rules on treaty interpretation, have nevertheless resulted in a clear tendency to restrict the scope of the FET provision and clearly define the standard 'without leaving unwelcome discretion to arbitrators'.[42]

As far as indirect expropriation is concerned, the main issue has been the fact that certain regulatory measures of States have been deemed to constitute an indirect expropriation despite the fact that the measure was considered to have been taken to protect legitimate public interests of the State. While certain arbitral awards have ruled that 'a non-discriminatory regulation for a public purpose, which is enacted in accordance with due

37 See e.g. *Occidental Exploration and Prod. Co.* v. *Republic of Ecuador*, UNCITRAL, LCIA Case No. UN3467, Final Award of 1 July 2004, para. 18: 'The stability of the legal and business framework is thus an essential element of fair and equitable treatment'. See also *CMS Gas Transmission Company* v. *The Republic of Argentina*, ICSID Case No. ARB/01/8, Award of 12 May 2005, para. 274.

38 See e.g. *Saluka Investments B.V.* v. *Czech Republic*, UNCITRAL, Partial Award of 17 March 2006, paras. 301 *et seq.*

39 On the 'stability' element, see M. Hirsch, 'Between Fair and Equitable Treatment and Stabilization Clause: Stable Legal Environment and Regulatory Change in International Investment Law', *Journal of World Investment & Trade*, 12 (2001), 783–806. On the 'legitimate expectations' element, see notably *Suez, Sociedad General de Aguas de Barcelona S.A.* v. *Argentine Republic*, ICSID Case No. ARB/03/19, Separate Opinion of Arbitrator Pedro Nikken of 30 July 2010, para. 19.

40 See generally for a criticism on the vagueness of the FET standard and the resulting lack of legitimacy M. C. Porterfield, 'An International Common Law of Investors Rights', *University of Pennsylvania Journal of International Law*, 27 (2014), 99 *et seq.*

41 See for a discussion UNCTAD, *Fair and Equitable Treatment*, 10 *et seq.*

42 European Commission, 'Concept Paper: Investment in TTIP and Beyond – The Path for Reform Enhancing the Right to Regulate and Moving from Current Ad Hoc Arbitration towards an Investment Court', 12 May 2015, 2, available at http://trade.ec.europa.eu/doclib/docs/2015/may/tradoc_153408.PDF (accessed 25 February 2016).

process, and, which affects, *inter alios*, a foreign investor or investment is not deemed expropriatory and compensable unless specific commitments had been given,'[43] others have nonetheless considered that 'expropriatory environmental measures – no matter how laudable and beneficial to society as a whole – are, in this respect, similar to any other expropriatory measures that a state may take in order to implement its policies: where property is expropriated, even for environmental purposes, whether domestic or international, the state's obligation to pay compensation remains.'[44] And it is precisely to avoid the potential for regulatory non-discriminatory measures taken for a public purpose to constitute indirect expropriations that States have redefined the formulation of the prohibition of indirect expropriation. As the European Commission has noted in its Concept Paper on the negotiations of the investment chapter of the Transatlantic Trade and Investment Partnership (TTIP) with the United States, 'detailed language has been agreed upon to clarify what constitutes indirect expropriation, particularly excluding claims against legitimate public policy measures.'[45] This evidences a clear fear that 'legitimate public policy measures' may be considered an indirect expropriation. Yet I should reiterate here that the prohibition of indirect expropriation has not very often been successful as a stand-alone claim in investment disputes,[46] at least compared to FET. Fears and concerns in this respect are thus frequently more hypothetical and future oriented than based on persistent findings of indirect expropriations in arbitral practice.

More generally, of course, a general impression underlying the criticism of both FET and indirect expropriation is that the State's right to regulate has been unduly restricted in the sense that legitimate regulatory acts of States have been considered to be in breach of the FET standard or of a provision prohibiting indirect expropriations.

[43] *Methanex Corporation* v. *United States of America*, UNCITRAL, Final Award of the Tribunal on Jurisdiction and Merits of 3 August 2005, para. 7 (Part IV, Chapter D). See also *S.D. Myers, Inc.* v. *Government of Canada*, UNCITRAL, Partial Award of 13 November 2000, para. 281.

[44] *Compañía del Desarrollo de Santa Elena, S.A.* v. *Republic of Costa Rica*, ICSID Case No. ARB/96/1, Final Award of 17 February 2000, para. 72.

[45] European Commission, 'Concept Paper: Investment in TTIP and Beyond', 2, available at http://trade.ec.europa.eu/doclib/docs/2015/may/tradoc_153408.pdf (accessed 25 February 2016).

[46] A. K. Hoffmann, 'Indirect Expropriation', in A. Reinisch (ed.), *Standards of Investment Protection* (Oxford University Press, 2008), 167; U. Kriebaum, 'FET and Expropriation in the (Invisible) EU Model BIT', *Journal of World Investment & Trade*, 15 (2014), 458–9.

C. A New Generation of FET and Indirect Expropriation Clauses? States' (Re)asserting Control through Substantive Re-Formulations

In order to (attempt to) reduce the concerns expressed in the preceding section, there are various strategies States have adopted and can adopt for both their future and existing FET and indirect expropriation provisions. These strategies can be viewed from two perspectives. Firstly, procedurally, States can react and redefine (directly or indirectly) through the termination, amendment and interpretation of existing treaties.[47] These options are explored, with regard to FET, indirect expropriation and beyond, in the contributions by Antonios Tzanakopoulos and Eleni Methymaki (Chapter 7) and Fernando Lusa Bordin (Chapter 9) and therefore will not be further discussed here. Secondly, from a substantive perspective, States can redefine and re-formulate the specific contents and formulations of FET and the prohibition of indirect expropriation. In this context, three specific possibilities will be examined. It needs to be noted that the three options discussed here can, of course, take place in the event of an amendment or an interpretative statement in relation to existing treaties as well. Since I will focus here on the *substantive* rather than the *procedural* options open to States, there is, as explained, an inevitable overlap between these two categories. I have grouped, for the purposes of this chapter, three specific ways in which States have, in their recent treaty practice, attempted to redefine or re-formulate provisions on FET and indirect expropriation, which are, of course, very much in line with the causes and concerns in relation to those provisions which I identified earlier. However, before engaging in a discussion of the treaty practice of States in this respect, I should add that there is in fact a fourth option which consists of simply not excluding any FET or indirect expropriation clause in a treaty. While practice still is scarce, notably in relation to indirect expropriation, there have been a couple of recently concluded investment treaties which have simply not included the FET among the substantive protection clauses.[48] India's most recent Model BIT, for instance, does not include any FET clause.[49] Brazil also has signed

[47] See generally L. Johnson and M. Razbaeva, 'State Control over Interpretation of Investment Treaties', Vale Columbia Centre on Sustainable International Investment, April 2014, available at http://ccsi.columbia.edu/files/2014/04/State_control_over_treaty_interpretation_FINAL-April-5_2014.pdf (accessed 25 February 2016).

[48] For an overview and discussion, see UNCTAD, *Fair and Equitable Treatment*, 18–19.

[49] Indian Model BIT (2015), available at https://mygov.in/sites/default/files/master_image/Model%20Text%20for%20the%20Indian%20Bilateral%20Investment%20Treaty.pdf (accessed 25 February 2016).

new Cooperation and Facilitation Investment Agreements (CFIAs) aimed at providing an alternate approach to both investment promotion and investment protection, since neither of the CFIAs signed so far (with Angola and Mozambique) contain an FET provision.[50] Moreover, Contracting Parties may also introduce a 'right to regulate' in their international investment agreements (IIAs). The implications of such a 'right to regulate' for matters of reassertion of control are discussed in detail by Paul Barker in Chapter 10 and hence will not be further explored here.

(1) *Curtailing the Semantic Approach to FET*

As noted in previous sections, one of the specific concerns of States relates to the overbroad discretion arbitral tribunals have in determining what constitutes a 'fair and equitable treatment', something which has been termed a 'semantic approach' to FET.[51]

While this concern is very much linked to the next section on the scope of the provision, there have been certain specific reactions of States which consist of linking the content of FET to international law or to an international customary norm not only to give a specific or narrower content to the provision but also to move away from a semantic and hence expansive interpretation of that provision. As mentioned earlier in relation to the different forms of FET clauses one usually finds in BITs, linking the content of the FET standard to international law aims at preventing a semantic approach by arbitral tribunals in defining that content by requiring a review of the various international law sources to that effect.[52] While this practice, in fact, may not necessarily be evidence of States reasserting control over investment law, since it has been visible in treaties in the 1990s already,[53] it may well be evidence of States' attempt to simply 'assert' control over international law from the start. A step further is to link FET to the IMS found in customary international law, which often combines the previous approach – general link of FET to international law – with the further clarification that FET under international law requires nothing more than the IMS in order to further

[50] J. C. Hamilton and M. Grando, 'Brazil and the Future of Investment Protections', 8 May 2015, available at www.latinarbitrationlaw.com/brazil-and-the-future-of-investment-protections/ (accessed 25 February 2016).

[51] UNCTAD, *Fair and Equitable Treatment*, 22. [52] *Ibid.*, 22 *et seq.*

[53] See e.g. Albania–France BIT (1994), available at http://investmentpolicyhub.unctad.org/IIA/country/72/treaty/16; and the Bahrain–US BIT (1999), available at www.state.gov/documents/organization/43479.pdf (both accessed 25 February 2016).

narrow the scope of the obligation. This latter provision firstly sets a ceiling to what constitutes FET, secondly indirectly gives content to FET, and thirdly, and most important for our purposes here, removes the possibility of applying a semantic methodology to identify the content of the standard. In other words, by linking FET to the international minimum standards, arbitral tribunals tasked with assessing the content of that standard no longer are able to determine what constitutes 'fair and equitable treatment' by using semantic approaches, since the content of what constitutes fair and equitable treatment is to be found in the customary norms in that respect. But this leaves open the question of the precise content of the customary norm and the usual problems accompanying the formation and identification of custom.

It is in this context that the aforementioned NAFTA Free Trade Commission's Interpretative Note on the FET standard contained in Chapter 11 of the NAFTA needs to be viewed. NAFTA's response to the FET standard's interpretation is highlighted because NAFTA's preferred interpretation of the FET standard has found its way into a number of other model and actual BITs, notably the 2012 US Model BIT, as well as the 2004 Canadian Model BIT.[54] The Japan–Mexico FTA also mirrors the US approach to FET almost entirely.[55]

Article 1105(1) of the NAFTA, which entered into force on 1 January 1994, stipulates that 'each Party shall accord to investments of investors of another Party treatment in accordance with international law, including fair and equitable treatment and full protection and security.' Arbitral tribunals which have dealt with this provision in the early stages of NAFTA investment disputes gave different interpretations of the NAFTA's FET provision. In order to clarify the interpretation of Article 1105(1), the NAFTA Free Trade Commission (FTC) issued a binding interpretation on 31 July 2001, which provides

> 1. Article 1105(1) prescribes the customary international law minimum standard of treatment of aliens as the minimum standard of treatment to be afforded to investments of investors of another Party.
> 2. The concepts of 'fair and equitable treatment' and 'full protection and security' do not require treatment in addition to or beyond that which

[54] See Article 5 of the US Model BIT (2012) and Article 5 of the Canadian Model BIT (2004), available at www.italaw.com/documents/Canadian2004-FIPA-model-en.pdf (accessed 25 February 2016).

[55] Agreement between Japan and the United Mexican States for the Strengthening of the Economic Partnership, Article 60, available at www.mofa.go.jp/region/latin/mexico/agreement/agreement.pdf (accessed 25 February 2016).

is required by the customary international law minimum standard of treatment of aliens.

3. A determination that there has been a breach of another provision of the NAFTA, or of a separate international agreement, does not establish that there has been a breach of Article 1105(1).[56]

The objective of the note was to clarify further the content of the FET standard, yet one cannot overlook the fact that the direct *renvoi* to 'the customary international law minimum standard of treatment of aliens' operates first and foremost as a means to avoid the semantic approach. This language has been taken over in various other treaties involving non-NAFTA States.[57]

Such clauses, however, are in view of recent arbitral jurisprudence no longer really effective in achieving both the limitation of the content of FET and the attempts to limit the discretion tribunals otherwise would have in interpreting the standard. As explained earlier, indeed, certain tribunals have considered the FET to be the 'new' customary minimum standard of treatment[58], and in so doing, they have thus simply bypassed the narrowing down of FET attempted by States which had adopted such a formulation.[59] It remains, however, that tribunals are required, in interpreting such a provision, to rely on the customary law content of the standard instead of following the semantic approach. This discussion, however, may have triggered the more recent tendency to simply enunciate in the treaty what the Parties' understanding of the content of FET is.

(2) Giving Specific Content to FET

As explained earlier, traditionally, FET clauses had been framed in rather vague terms, and the few words used to formulate the standard were

[56] Available at www.international.gc.ca/trade-agreements-accords-commerciaux/topics-domaines/disp-diff/NAFTA-Interpr.aspx?lang=eng (accessed 25 February 2016).

[57] UNCTAD, *Fair and Equitable Treatment*, 25 *et seq.*

[58] *William Ralph Clayton, William Richard Clayton, Douglas Clayton, Daniel Clayton and Bilcon of Delaware Inc.* v. *Government of Canada*, UNCITRAL, PCA Case No. 2009–04, Award on Jurisdiction and Liability of 17 March 2015, paras. 433ff. See also *Merrill & Ring Forestry L.P.* v. *Government of Canada*, UNCITRAL, ICSID Administered Case, Award of 31 March 2010, paras. 210ff.

[59] See for a discussion M. C. Porterfield, 'A Distinction without a Difference?', available at www.iisd.org/itn/2013/03/22/a-distinction-without-a-difference-the-interpretation-of-fair-and-equitable-treatment-under-customary-international-law-by-investment-tribunals/ (accessed 25 February 2016).

inversely proportional to the practical relevance of these clauses in investment disputes between foreign investors and host States. Yet, because of the unsettled and multi-threaded aspect of the FET standard, there is an increasing tendency by states to narrow the ambit of FET.[60] The most recent treaties have shown a clear tendency by States to move away from open-ended formulations of FET and indirect expropriation clauses via formulations by which the specific content of what constitutes fair and equitable treatment is explicitly included. At the same time, one should keep in mind that many newly signed treaties still very much stick to the 'old' formulations. European States, for instance, still use the generic FET (and indirect expropriation clauses) discussed earlier in their BITs.[61]

There are many examples of this recent trend, and I will therefore limit myself to the most recent ones. Besides the 'indirect content'–based formulations of FET in which the content of the standard is indirectly formulated by a general reference to international law or the IMS, the recent negotiations between the European Union and its trading partners have exhibited an interesting new form of FET clauses in which the precise content of what constitutes FET is listed in the treaty itself. But this practice in fact is the continuation of the treaty language of the 2012 US Model BIT, which consists of listing certain elements of the FET standard in a non-exhaustive way:

> '[F]air and equitable treatment' includes the obligation not to deny justice in criminal, civil, or administrative adjudicatory proceedings in accordance with the principle of due process embodied in the principal legal systems of the world.[62]

As is widely known, the recent negotiations of investment treaties by the European Union with Canada and the United States most notably have sparked a vigorous debate not only on the entire investment law system as it currently stands but also in relation to such provisions as FET and indirect expropriation.[63] Article 8.10 of the final text of the Comprehensive Economic and Trade Agreement (CETA) between

[60] Kläger, 'Fair and Equitable Treatment', 436.

[61] See U. Kriebaum, 'FET and Expropriation in the (Invisible) EU Model BIT', *Journal of World Investment & Trade*, 15 (2014), 454.

[62] Article 5(2)(a) of the US Model BIT (2012).

[63] European Commission, 'Concept Paper: Investment in TTIP and Beyond', available at http://trade.ec.europa.eu/doclib/docs/2015/may/tradoc_153408.pdf (accessed 25 February 2016). See also 'Special Issue: The Anatomy of the (Invisible) EU Model BIT', *Journal of World Investment & Trade*, 15(3–4) (2014). See also Chapter 1.

Canada and the European Union[64] of February 2016 enumerates the types of measures which can constitute a breach of FET:

> Each Party shall accord in its territory to covered investments of the other Party and to investors with respect to their covered investments fair and equitable treatment and full protection and security in accordance with paragraphs 2 to 6.
>
> A Party breaches the obligation of fair and equitable treatment referenced in paragraph 1 where a measure or series of measures constitutes:
>
> (a) Denial of justice in criminal, civil or administrative proceedings;
> (b) fundamental breach of due process, including a fundamental breach of transparency, in judicial and administrative proceedings;
> (c) manifest arbitrariness;
> (d) targeted discrimination on manifestly wrongful grounds, such as gender, race or religious belief;
> (e) abusive treatment of investors, such as coercion, duress and harassment; or
> (f) a breach of any further elements of the fair and equitable treatment obligation adopted by the Parties in accordance with paragraph 3 of this Article.[65]

The preceding seems to be intended to constitute an exhaustive list as it states that contracting parties shall accord 'fair and equitable treatment in accordance with paragraphs 2 to 6', which list all the possible breaches. Yet, the text is not explicit on this point.

The list contains many elements which are usually considered part of FET (see Section A(1)), yet a notable absence from the list is the 'stability' element, which, as noted, has been considered problematic. The recent draft of the TTIP between the United States and the European Union goes further and explicitly includes, in the general provision on the right to regulate, the rule that 'the provisions of this section shall not be interpreted as a commitment from a Party that it will not change the legal and regulatory framework, including in a manner that may negatively affect the operation of covered investments or the investor's expectations of profits.'[66]

64 Final CETA Text (29 February 2016), available at http://trade.ec.europa.eu/doclib/docs/2016/february/tradoc_154329.pdf (accessed 25 September 2016).

65 Article 8.10(1) and (2), final CETA Text (29 February 2016), available at http://trade.ec.europa.eu/doclib/docs/2016/february/tradoc_154329.pdf (accessed 25 September 2016).

66 Article 2(2), Transatlantic Trade and Investment Partnership (TTIP) EU Draft (12 November 2015), available at http://trade.ec.europa.eu/doclib/docs/2015/november/tradoc_153955.pdf (accessed 25 February 2016).

Another notable absence is the 'legitimate expectation' element, also a highly criticised FET component. Nevertheless, Article 8.10(4) of the CETA provides that:

> when applying the above fair and equitable treatment obligation, a tribunal may take into account whether a Party made a specific representation to an investor to induce a covered investment, that created a legitimate expectation, and upon which the investor relied in deciding to make or maintain the covered investment, but that the Party subsequently frustrated.

The 'legitimate expectations' component of FET is thus abandoned as a 'core' element of FET and relegated to a mere potential or subsidiary issue the arbitral tribunal may take into account in assessing whether FET as defined in the preceding paragraphs has been breached.

The list is not carved in stone, however. The draft provision further provides that 'the Parties shall regularly, or upon request of a Party, review the content of the obligation to provide fair and equitable treatment. The Committee on Services and Investment may develop recommendations in this regard and submit them to the Trade Committee for decision.'[67] The need to revise the content of the obligation further shows the intention of both the European Union and Canada perhaps to consider the list as an exhaustive list of breaches that define the content of FET.

The clause clearly is a reaction to what the European Commission has termed 'abuses'.[68] In this respect, several scholars had already advocated for the need to address the content of the FET obligation in investment protection instruments[69] and have noted that such an approach might contribute to, but cannot guarantee, greater predictability and consistence in arbitral practice.[70] However, others have noted that such

[67] Article 8.10(3), final CETA Text (29 February 2016), available at http://trade.ec.europa.eu/doclib/docs/2016/february/tradoc_154329.pdf (accessed 25 September 2016).

[68] European Commission, 'Concept Paper: Investment in TTIP and Beyond', 2, available at http://trade.ec.europa.eu/doclib/docs/2015/may/tradoc_153408.pdf (accessed 25 February 2016).

[69] P. Dumberry, 'Drafting the Fair and Equitable Treatment Clause in the TPP and RCEP: Lessons Learned from the NAFTA Article 1105 Experience' *Transnational Dispute Management*, 1 (2015); W. Zhang, 'Will Greater Specificity with respect to the Fair and Equitable Treatment Obligation Lead to Greater Predictability in Investment Treaty Cases?, *Transnational Dispute Management*, 1 (2015); E. Boomer, 'Rethinking Rights and Responsibilities in Investor-State Dispute Settlement: Some Model International Investment Agreement Provisions', *Transnational Dispute Management*, 1 (2015).

[70] W. Zhang, 'Will Greater Specificity with respect to the Fair and Equitable Treatment Obligation Lead to Greater Predictability in Investment Treaty Cases?', *Transnational Dispute Management*, 1 (2015).

a provision 'creates new uncertainties, rather than reducing them' and 'shift[s] the focus away from traditional European BITs approaches to certain topics which have not led to major discussions in the arbitral case law'.[71] The 'new uncertainties' resulting from such a provision are, of course, difficult to anticipate, yet it is evident that every provision, even narrowly and exhaustively formulated, will require interpretation and application by the tribunal charged with a dispute in that respect. At the same time, the 'shift' away from traditional European BITs is a clear and conscious political and policy decision of the European Commission which has been made after careful consideration. And – whether one agrees with this or not – it is clear and unambiguous evidence of the intent of the European Union and Canada to restrict the content of FET and thereby disavow certain arbitral jurisprudence which has given – according to the Commission – unbridled content to the provision. The most recent version of the FET provision in the TTIP contains a similar – yet not completely identical – provision.[72] A similar provision was included also in the final draft of the TPP accepted in November of 2015.[73]

(3) Harnessing Indirect Expropriation

Similarly to the recent attempts to further define and narrow down the FET standard, certain recent investment treaties show a strong inclination towards redefining what constitutes an 'indirect expropriation'. While traditionally the prohibition of indirect expropriation was framed in relatively general terms without really defining what an 'indirect expropriation' really is, recent (draft) investment treaties attempt to more clearly define (1) what constitutes an indirect expropriation and (2) which regulatory measures taken by a State cannot amount to an indirect expropriation.

As noted earlier, the United States and Canadian Model BITs for more than a decade have already included a specific annex, worded in similar terms, which contains details and limitations as to which measures may constitute indirect expropriations. The formulations adopted

[71] U. Kriebaum, 'FET and Expropriation in the (Invisible) EU Model BIT', *Journal of World Investment & Trade*, 15 (2014), 482.

[72] Article 3, TTIP.

[73] Article 9, *io* Annex 9A, Trans Pacific Partnership (TPP) (November 2015), available at https://ustr.gov/trade-agreements/free-trade-agreements/trans-pacific-partnership/tpp-full-text (accessed 25 February 2016).

by the US and Canadian Model BITs are more restrictive than the open-ended formulations one usually finds in treaties modelled on the European practice which consists simply of allowing direct and indirect expropriations only if the customary requirements on the legality of such takings are met. The re-definitions found in the most recent US and Canadian model treaties clearly were inspired by the US doctrine of takings under domestic law.[74] The objective of such an annex precisely shows the two points mentioned in the preceding paragraphs, namely, a more clear definition of what constitutes an indirect expropriation and which regulatory measures taken by a State cannot amount to an indirect expropriation.

Annex B.13(1) of the 2004 Canadian Model BIT, for example, in order to define more clearly what constitutes an indirect expropriation, includes, besides a clear definition of what constitutes an 'indirect expropriation'[75] and the need for a 'case-by-case, fact-based inquiry',[76] the factors that need to be taken into account by an arbitral tribunal, namely

> i) the economic impact of the measure or series of measures, although the sole fact that a measure or series of measures of a Party has an adverse effect on the economic value of an investment does not establish that an indirect expropriation has occurred;
> ii) the extent to which the measure or series of measures interfere with distinct, reasonable investment-backed expectations; and
> iii) the character of the measure or series of measures.[77]

Some other treaties have included, among the factors, also the duration of the measure or series of measures[78] or have added to the 'character of the

[74] See Kriebaum, 'FET and Expropriation', 462–3.

[75] 'Indirect expropriation results from a measure or series of measures of a Party that have an effect equivalent to direct expropriation without formal transfer of title or outright seizure.' Annex B.13(1)(a), Canadian Model BIT (2004). See also Article 5(2), Indian Model BIT (2015), available at https://mygov.in/sites/default/files/master_image/Model%20Text%20for%20the%20Indian%20Bilateral%20Investment%20Treaty.pdf (accessed 25 February 2016).

[76] Annex B.13(1)(b), Canadian Model BIT (2004). Cf. However, the more elaborate definition contained in the November 2015 Draft TTIP: '[I]ndirect expropriation occurs where a measure or series of measures by a Party has an effect equivalent to direct expropriation, in that it substantially deprives the investor of the fundamental attributes of property in its investment, including the right to use, enjoy and dispose of its investment, without formal transfer of title or outright seizure' (Annex I(1)(b), TTIP).

[77] Annex B.13(1)(b), Canadian Model BIT (2004).

[78] Article 6(8), Norwegian Model BIT (2015), available at www.italaw.com/investment-treaties (accessed 25 February 2016).

measure or series of measures' an additional phrase 'notably their object, context and intent'.[79]

Recent treaty practice has revealed a far more widespread use of the North American model in order to restrict the scope of the prohibition of indirect expropriation and a tendency to go even further by providing additional clarification as to what is meant by some of these requirements. For example, the TPP provides in a footnote to the phrase 'the extent to which the government action interferes with distinct, reasonable investment-backed expectations', that

> for greater certainty, whether an investor's investment-backed expectations are reasonable depends, to the extent relevant, on factors such as whether the government provided the investor with binding written assurances and the nature and extent of governmental regulation or the potential for government regulation in the relevant sector.[80]

Some treaties, such as CETA, have further characterised what is understood by 'the character of the measure or series of measures' by adding the term 'notably their object, context and intent'.[81] Other treaties have followed this example yet have omitted the term 'intent',[82] which may be problematic in view of the fact that indirect expropriations are precisely characterised by the lack of an intent to expropriate.[83]

Other recent treaties have further narrowed the types of measures that could constitute an indirect expropriation or added requirements. An example is the 2008 China–New Zealand Free Trade Agreement, which contains, beside the general prohibition of indirect expropriations in Article 145, a specific and narrower definition of what constitutes an indirect expropriation in Annex 13:

> 1. Expropriation may be either direct or indirect:
>   a) direct expropriation occurs when a state takes an investor's property outright, including by nationalisation, compulsion of law or seizure;
>   b) indirect expropriation occurs when a state takes an investor's property in a manner equivalent to direct expropriation, in that it deprives the investor in substance of the use of the investor's property, although the means used fall short of those specified in subparagraph (a) above.
> 2. In order to constitute indirect expropriation, the state's deprivation of the investor's property must be:

[79] *Ibid.* [80] Annex 9B(3)(a)(ii) of the TPP. [81] Annex 8A(2)(d) of the CETA.
[82] Annex I(2)(c) of the TTIP.
[83] See for a discussion also Kriebaum, 'FET and Expropriation', 466.

a) either severe or for an indefinite period; and
b) disproportionate to the public purpose.

3. A deprivation of property shall be particularly likely to constitute indirect expropriation where it is either:
   a) discriminatory in its effect, either as against the particular investor or against a class of which the investor forms part; or
   b) in breach of the state's prior binding written commitment to the investor, whether by contract, licence, or other legal document.
4. Except in rare circumstances to which paragraph 4 applies, such measures taken in the exercise of a state's regulatory powers as may be reasonably justified in the protection of the public welfare, including public health, safety and the environment, shall not constitute an indirect expropriation.[84]

Despite the similarity of certain sections with US or Canadian models, this provision is much narrower. Indeed, this treaty requires that the 'state's deprivation of the investor's property must be (a) either severe or for an indefinite period; and (b) disproportionate to the public purpose'.

The 2007 Columbian Model BIT[85] has similar wording in the substantive provision on expropriation, with some more restrictive phrasing. The provision excludes, for example, the term 'amongst other factors' in the list of indicators of an indirect expropriation, thus effectively limiting the factors indicating an indirect expropriation to the economic impact of the measure and the interference of the measure 'on the reasonable and distinguishable expectations concerning the investment'.[86]

In the recent 2015 Norwegian Model BIT, one similarly finds a more detailed provision on the prohibition of indirect expropriation partly inspired by the US and Canadian models. Paragraph 8 of Article 6 contains the general rule that an indirect expropriation is the result of a measure which 'substantially deprives the investor of the fundamental attributes of property in its investment, including the right to use, enjoy and dispose of its investment, without formal transfer of title or outright seizure'. This definition is a more specific and detailed definition of an indirect expropriation in that it specifically mentions the requirement of a 'substantial deprivation of the fundamental attributes of property'.[87]

[84] Annex 13 of the China–New Zealand Free Trade Agreement (2008), available at www.chinafta.govt.nz/1-The-agreement/2-Text-of-the-agreement/index.php (accessed 25 February 2016).

[85] Columbian Model BIT (2007), available at www.italaw.com/investment-treaties (accessed 25 February 2016).

[86] *Ibid.*, Article 6(2)(b).

[87] Cf. US Model BIT (2012), which makes no mention of this.

The same paragraph then further elaborates on the factors to be used in the determination of the occurrence of an indirect expropriation.[88]

The second aim of redefining indirect expropriation is to make clear which regulatory measures taken by a State cannot amount to an indirect expropriation. This is done through the inclusion of a phrase, such as in lit. (c) of Annex B.13(1) of the 2004 Canadian Model BIT, which explains that

> Except in rare circumstances, such as when a measure or series of measures are so severe in the light of their purpose that they cannot be reasonably viewed as having been adopted and applied in good faith, non-discriminatory measures of a Party that are designed and applied to protect legitimate public welfare objectives, such as health, safety and the environment, do not constitute indirect expropriation.

Similar provisions can be found in the recent November 2015 EU draft of the TTIP[89] or the November 2015 text of the TPP.[90] The 2007 Columbian Model BIT[91] excludes measures adopted 'for public purposes or social interests' from potentially constituting an indirect expropriation 'except in rare circumstances',[92] which are terms not found in the US or Canadian models. Article 6 of the 2015 Norwegian Model BIT also contains a paragraph noting that the rules on direct expropriation – which apply *mutatis mutandis* to indirect expropriations[93] – 'shall not, however, in any way impair the right of a Party to enforce such laws as it deems necessary to control the use of property in accordance with the general interest or to secure the payment of taxes or other contributions or penalties'. Such a provision closely mirrors the objective of general provisions which attempt to generally safeguard 'the right to regulate'.[94]

D. Conclusion

Both the FET standard and the prohibition of indirect expropriation are very common provisions in international investment treaties. While use of the FET provision has been much more successful in substantiating investment claims than the prohibition of indirect expropriation,

[88] Article 6(8) of the Norwegian Model BIT (2015).
[89] Annex I (3) of the EU TTIP draft.
[90] Annex 9B(3)(b) of the TPP. See also Annex 13(4) of the China–New Zealand Free Trade Agreement (2008).
[91] Columbian Model BIT (2007). [92] *Ibid.*, Article 6(2)(c).
[93] Article 6(8) of the Norwegian Model BIT (2015).
[94] On the right to regulate, see also Chapter 10.

they have both triggered much attention and criticism in recent years. Notably, their indeterminate and open-ended formulations have required arbitral tribunals to give substance and content to the notions with little guidance. This has triggered a reaction by States which has had as a main objective to limit the scope of the provisions and to avoid the discretion arbitral tribunals previously had in delineating the precise content of the FET standard and the prohibition of indirect expropriation. These two provisions have also been targeted specifically because of their – effective or perceived – detrimental impact on States' right to regulate.

This chapter has investigated how States, through re-formulations of the FET standard and the prohibition of indirect expropriation in their recent treaty practice, have sought to assert or reassert control over investment law. This (re)assertion of control has analysed three specific ways in which States have, in their recent treaty practice, attempted to redefine or re-formulate provisions on FET and indirect expropriation, in view of the causes and concern in relation to those provisions which I identified.

Firstly, States have attempted to curtail the semantic or subjective approach to FET by linking the standard to international law or customary international law, more specifically, in order to objectivise the methodology of arbitral tribunals in defining that content. This method of (re)asserting control, however, is not a novelty and has existed for many years. It has, moreover, in the practice of arbitral tribunals, not shown to be effective in achieving more objectivity in the methodology tribunals' use in defining the exact content of FET.

Secondly, certain States have moved away from open-ended formulations of FET clauses by formulating FET clauses in which the precise content of what constitutes FET is listed in the treaty itself. The very recently proposed text for the TTIP clearly (exhaustively) lists the elements of FET and builds on current trends in BITs to enumerate the conduct that constitutes a breach of FET, and notably the 2012 US Model BIT, which had already included a non-exhaustive list of what may fall under the FET.

Thirdly, in relation to indirect expropriation, recent (draft) investment treaties have adopted narrower and more detailed formulations of the prohibition in order to, firstly, more clearly define what constitutes an indirect expropriation and, secondly, exclude certain regulatory measures taken by a State from the ambit of the indirect expropriation provision.

Whether or not States have, in so doing, in fact, reasserted control or simply asserted control is a question I have deliberately not answered. Yet it is beyond doubt that these recent trends and tendencies constitute strong reactions to certain arbitral jurisprudence. It is difficult to agree or disagree with such developments, since the formulation of international investment agreements is entirely left to the discretion of the States parties to the treaty and the policy choices made by States. These developments do show, however, that while 'tradition' has in the past influenced the choice of one model or formulation over the other, States increasingly rely on policy arguments to choose the precise formulation of FET and the prohibition of indirect expropriation. It is notable, for instance, that the European Union's recent practice in this respect has clearly and unambiguously moved away from traditional European BITs based on a clear, admitted and conscious policy.

13

How the European Commission and the EU Member States Are Reasserting Their Control over Their Investment Treaties and ISDS Rules

NIKOS LAVRANOS

A. Setting the Scene

Over the past fifty years, States have signed and ratified more than 3,300 investment treaties – either in the form of bilateral investment treaties (BITs) or free trade agreements (FTAs) with an investment protection chapter. With the exception of the very early BITs (e.g. the Germany–Pakistan BIT of 1959 and the Netherlands–Cameroon BIT of 1966) and the famous US–Australia FTA (which entered into force in 2005), most of the more than 3,300 existing investment treaties contain some form of dispute settlement rules, usually including investor-State dispute settlement (ISDS).

By signing and ratifying investment treaties, States have consciously consented to the possibility that investors could bring a claim against them. Apparently, there was and is consensus that concluding investment treaties is beneficial for both Contracting Parties. In fact, States continue to negotiate, sign and ratify investment treaties.[1] Indeed, recent studies show that after ratification of a BIT, foreign direct investment (FDI) flows increase on average by about 30 per cent.[2]

However, as the United Nations Conference on Trade and Development (UNCTAD) and the European Commission repeatedly

[1] According to the United Nations Conference on Trade and Development (UNCTAD), as of September 2016, the total number of IIAs stands at 3,316 worldwide; see UNCTAD Investment Policy Hub website: http://investmentpolicyhub.unctad.org/IIA/IiasByCountry (accessed 25 September 2016).

[2] A. Lejour and M. Salfi, 'The Regional Impact of Bilateral Investment Treaties on Foreign Direct Investments', CPB Discussion Paper 298 (The Hague, 2015), available at www.cpb.nl/publicatie/de-regionale-effecten-van-bilaterale-investeringsverdragen-op-directe-buitenlandse-investeringen (accessed 25 September 2016).

have noted, it cannot be denied that an increasing uneasiness is felt within States, governments, parliaments and certain non-governmental organisations (NGOs) about ISDS and investment treaties. The public debate, though based largely on misperceptions and misrepresentations,[3] has triggered a drive to reform the current ISDS system.[4] In this context, it is important to note that this drive to reform is not limited to Europe but is also taking place in some of the BRICS (Brazil, Russia, India, China and South Africa) countries. For example, Brazil has concluded BITs on the basis of a new model text which does not include ISDS.[5] India has recently published its new Model BIT, which departs significantly from the current ISDS system.[6] Also, South Africa has moved away from 'old school' BITs by terminating many of them with EU Member States and replacing them with a new domestic investment law.[7]

More recently, within the context of the Transatlantic Trade and Investment Partnership (TTIP) negotiation, the European Commission has proposed the creation of an Investment Court System (ICS) that would create a semi-permanent two-tier court system, which would constitute a significant departure from the existing ISDS system.[8] Indeed, the FTA between Canada and the European Union (Comprehensive Economic and Trade Agreement (CETA)) already contains the ICS proposal.

[3] See for an extensive analysis of the misperceptions EFILA, 'EFILA's Response to the Criticism against ISDS' (May 2015), available at http://efila.org/wp-content/uploads/2015/05/EFILA_in_response_to_the-criticism_of_ISDS_final_draft.pdf (accessed 25 September 2016).

[4] See e.g. UNCTAD, 'Reform of ISDS: In Search of a Roadmap', *UNCTAD IIA Issue Note 2* (June 2013), available at http://unctad.org/en/PublicationsLibrary/webdiaepcb2013d4_en.pdf (accessed 25 September 2016).

[5] See further F. Morosini and M. Ratton Sanchez Badin, 'The Brazilian Agreement on Cooperation and Facilitation of Investments (ACFI): A New Formula for International Investment Agreements?' (IISD, 4 August 2015), available at www.iisd.org/itn/2015/08/04/the-brazilian-agreement-on-cooperation-and-facilitation-of-investments-acfi-a-new-formula-for-international-investment-agreements/ (accessed 25 September 2016); J. de Paiva Muniz and L. Peretti, 'Brazil Signs New Bilateral Investment Treaties with Mozambique and Angola: New Approach to BITs or "Toothless Lions"?', *Global Arbitration News*, 7 April 2015, available at http://globalarbitrationnews.com/20150407-brazil-signs-new-bilateral-investment-treaties/ (accessed 25 September 2016).

[6] 'India Model BIT Text', published in December 2015, available at http://finmin.nic.in/the_ministry/dept_eco_affairs/investment_division/ModelBIT_Annex.pdf (accessed 25 September 2016).

[7] See www.southafrica.info/business/investing/regulations/protection-bill-051113.htm#.VbsUVDYVhPY (accessed 25 September 2016).

[8] Text of 12 November 2015 containing the proposal of the European Commission for an ICS, available at http://trade.ec.europa.eu/doclib/docs/2015/november/tradoc_153955.pdf (accessed 25 September 2016).

These 'reforms' are implemented at different levels and by various means. This chapter focuses on how the European Commission and the Member States are reasserting their control in the new EU investment treaties. In addition, the analysis also looks at the efforts of the European Commission to reassert control over existing BITs of the Member States. It also tries to forecast how the Court of Justice of the European Union (CJEU) would react to these reforms.

B. From One-Off Treaty Making to Continuous Treaty Modification and Dispute Intervention

In the good old days, investment treaties were negotiated, signed, ratified, published in the official gazette and forgotten about. Once in a while, an investor would contact his or her home state and complain about the acts or omissions of a host State. If the home State considered those complaints to be reasonable and serious enough, it would first informally and, if necessary, formally contact the host State asking to resolve the issue. If the host State failed to address the issue, the investor would occasionally bring a claim against the host State, and if the investor won, the host State would normally duly pay the award.[9] All this worked by and large pretty well and operated without much attention from politicians, parliaments, the public and the media. In short, the 'old school' BITs of the EU Member States were rather 'static' and only required a one-off treaty-making effort. In other words, after ratification, the BITs were forgotten about and would only be occasionally used by an investor as a final resort after all other methods of solving the dispute had failed.

In more recent times, the situation has dramatically changed from the perspective of the investor. Starting with the Federal Trade Commission (FTC) Note of Interpretation of the North American Free Trade Agreement (NAFTA) Contracting Parties issued in 2001[10], States have shown increasing appetite for 'correcting' in their eyes 'wrong' interpretations of investment treaty provisions by ad hoc international arbitral tribunals. Since then, more recent (model) BIT texts, such as the US BIT

[9] Although it must be admitted that some states such as Argentina, Bolivia and Venezuela have been rejecting the investment arbitration system and have either not paid awards or even stepped out of the ICSID and terminated their BITs. More recently, EU Member States such as the Slovak Republic and Romania also have used all possible means to avoid paying awards.

[10] NAFTA FTC Note of Interpretation (31 July 2001), available at www.sice.oas.org/tpd/nafta/Commission/CH11understanding_e.asp.

Model Text of 2012[11] and the recently concluded CETA text[12] include several tools which explicitly provide Contracting Parties with the ability to continuously monitor treaties, modify and interpret them as well as intervene in on-going disputes. This 'pro-active' toolbox as contained in CETA is one of the most significant changes adopted by the European Union compared to the static BITs of the EU Member States.

The reasons for including the 'pro-active' toolbox are numerous. Clearly, the rising number of ISDS cases and the fact that, according to a report of *Notre Europe*, ninety-eight States worldwide have now been respondents in ISDS disputes are cause for concern for States.[13] Also, many States have the perception that arbitral tribunals decide cases without taking the views and intentions of the 'Masters of the BITs' sufficiently into account. Moreover, the high amounts of some awards, going sometimes into several hundred millions or even billions of US dollars, has sparked complaints by members of parliaments, NGOs and the public at large. Finally, some awards are considered 'wrong' or unacceptable because States perceive them as having encroached upon their prerogatives as democratically elected legislators.

In short, there are sufficient reasons or at least perceptions for States to get more involved in ISDS and investment treaties by monitoring and managing them on a continuous basis rather than treating them as one-off affairs. Since Article 207 of the Treaty on the Functioning of the European Union (TFEU) has given the European Union exclusive competence regarding FDI – or rather, as the European Commission argues, regarding all investment-related issues, including ISDS – the European Union has become a forerunner in including a 'pro-active' toolbox in all its on-going investment treaty negotiations.

In the following sections, several elements of the 'pro-active' toolbox as proposed by the European Commission and now contained in CETA will be discussed in more detail.[14] Although the analysis is limited to CETA

[11] 'US 2012 Model BIT Text', available at www.state.gov/documents/organization/188371.pdf (accessed 25 September 2016).

[12] 'CETA Text', published on 5 July 2016, COM(2016) 443 final, available at http://eur-lex.europa.eu/legal-content/EN/TXT/?qid=1467909007204&uri=COM:2016:443:FIN#document2 (accessed 26 September 2016).

[13] E. Fabry and G. Garbasso, 'ISDS in the TTIP: The Devil Is in the Detail', Policy Paper 122, 16 January 2015, available at www.institutdelors.eu/media/ttipisds-fabrygarbasso-nejdi-jan15.pdf?pdf=ok (accessed 25 September 2016).

[14] This analysis complements in particular the contributions of Friedrich Rosenfeld, Freya Baetens and Eleni Methymaki and Antonios Tzanakopoulos in Chapters 4, 5 and 7.

provisions, the conclusions are in analogy also applicable to all other EU investment treaties which are currently being negotiated.

(1) *Joint Binding Interpretations*

As far as the European Union and its Member States are concerned, CETA is the first investment treaty which contains the explicit option of adopting interpretations concerning CETA provisions, which are binding on the tribunal and can be issued with retroactive effect.[15] Moreover, and as will be discussed later, Article 8.44(3) of the CETA allows the CETA Parties to adopt any further elements of the 'fair and equitable treatment' (FET) obligation.[16]

Accordingly, these provisions contain two specific 'pro-active' tools, which give the CETA Parties the possibility to re-interpret the CETA provisions. While Article 8.31(3) of the CETA provides a *general* tool for adopting binding interpretations for any CETA provision concerning 'investment', Article 8.44(3)(d) of the CETA is a *specific* tool for re-interpreting the FET standard by allowing for the addition of any elements to the FET standard.

These two tools contain a number of 'innovative' features. While it is not unusual that Contracting Parties decide that their interpretations shall be binding, the 'innovative' feature in this provision refers to the fact that the Contracting Parties can determine the specific date for the entry into force of that interpretation. Since there is no explicit exclusion of the possibility to fix a date in the past, the CETA Parties are in a position to adopt binding interpretations retroactively. The possibility of a retroactive application of the interpretation has also been confirmed by representatives of the European Commission. As a consequence thereof, a retroactively applicable binding interpretation can directly interfere in on-going CETA arbitral proceedings by determining the outcome of the case.

[15] Article 8.31(3) of the CETA states: '3. Where serious concerns arise as regards matters of interpretation that may affect investment, the Committee on Services and Investment may, pursuant to Article 8.44.3(a), recommend to the CETA Joint Committee the adoption of interpretations of this Agreement. An interpretation adopted by the CETA Joint Committee shall be binding on the Tribunal established under this Section. The CETA Joint Committee may decide that an interpretation shall have binding effect from a specific date.'

[16] Article 8.44(3)(d) of the CETA states: 'recommend to the CETA Joint Committee the adoption of any further elements of the fair and equitable treatment obligation pursuant to Article 8.10.3.'

It is interesting to note that during the CETA negotiations the European Commission rejected the proposal by the Netherlands to at least adopt the terminology used in the failed draft Norwegian Model BIT Text of 2007.[17] Article 23(4)(ii) of the draft Norwegian Model BIT Text explicitly stated that

> the Joint Committee may: . . .
>
> ii. interpret this Agreement, bearing in mind that this competence shall not be used to undermine the amendment provisions of Article [Amendments]. The Joint Committee *should refrain from adopting interpretations of provisions already submitted to a Tribunal in a dispute between a Party and an Investor of the other Party.*[18]

This kind of language strikes a more appropriate balance between protecting the legitimate rights of the investor who is involved in arbitral proceedings against one of the Contracting Parties of the investment treaty and the right of the Contracting Parties to adopt binding interpretations. In contrast, the fact that Article 8.31(3) of the CETA enables the CETA Parties to retroactively intervene in on-going cases by modifying the interpretation of CETA provisions permits them to interfere in on-going disputes in a manner that is clearly an unacceptable violation of rule of law principles, which belong to the European constitutional law tradition and which are binding on the EU institutions and EU Member States.[19]

(2) Closed List of FET Breaches

The second innovative tool concerns the new way of limiting the scope of the FET standard *ab initio* by listing all the breaches that may be considered breaches of the FET standard. The first part of the first sentence of Article 8.10 of the CETA is comparable to what is normally found in EU Member States' BITs. However, Article 8.10(2) of the CETA

[17] 'Draft Norwegian Model BIT Text', 2007, available at www.italaw.com/sites/default/files/archive/ita1031.pdf (accessed 25 September 2016).

[18] Emphasis added.

[19] See the new 'Rule of Law Framework of the EU', Commission Communication COM(2014)158 final/2, 19 March 2014, available at http://ec.europa.eu/justice/effective-justice/files/com_2014_158_en.pdf (accessed 25 September 2016). See further N. Lavranos, 'The Rule of Law as the Common Foundation of EU Law and International Investment Law', EFILA blog, 1 September 2015, available at http://efilablog.org/2015/09/01/the-rule-of-law-as-the-common-foundation-of-eu-law-and-international-investment-law/ (accessed 25 September2016).

contains the 'innovative' element by prescribing in a closed list the types of breaches which would constitute breaches of the FET standard.[20]

Article 8.10(3) of the CETA provides a 'pro-active' tool of constant monitoring of the FET standard coupled with the possibility of modifying the list of breaches that also allows for a further limitation of the FET standard. Article 8.10(4) gives further directions to the tribunal in particular regarding legitimate expectations, which may be considered a sort of 'limited umbrella clause' which has been left out of CETA, while Article 8.10(5) and (6) contain 'clarifications' on the concept of full protection and security and the relationship with other breaches of CETA or other international agreements.

Consequently, any acts or omissions not listed in Article 8.10(2) of the CETA cannot be considered by the tribunal as breaches of the FET standard in the CETA. While the elements listed in Article 8.10(2) of the CETA may be considered to be a restatement of the case law on FET and as such would not be a huge innovation, the innovative element lies in the fact that it is a closed list, which prevents the tribunal from developing the FET standard any further. Indeed, the European Commission and many anti-ISDS critics have argued that this list brings much-needed clarity and specificity of the traditional unqualified, open-text FET standard, which they consider far too broad and vague. However, if one carefully analyses the terminology used in the FET list, it appears that the items in the list are similarly vague. For example, when is a breach 'fundamental', 'manifest' or 'targeted'? Conversely, are breaches which do not meet these thresholds in conformity with the CETA? It is important to underline that none of these terms are defined in the CETA, which means that they will have to be defined and applied on a case-by-case basis by the tribunal and will potentially be 'corrected' by the CETA Parties. Accordingly, in my view, the use of such vague terminology provides an excellent opportunity for lawyers to initiate more rather than fewer disputes in order to test the limits of the FET

[20] Article 8.10(2) states: 'A Party breaches the obligation of fair and equitable treatment referenced in paragraph 1 if a measure or series of measures constitutes: (a) denial of justice in criminal, civil or administrative proceedings; (b) fundamental breach of due process, including a fundamental breach of transparency, in judicial and administrative proceedings; (c) manifest arbitrariness; (d) targeted discrimination on manifestly wrongful grounds, such as gender, race or religious belief; (e) abusive treatment of investors, such as coercion, duress and harassment; or (f) a breach of any further elements of the fair and equitable treatment obligation adopted by the Parties in accordance with paragraph 3 of this Article.'

list. In short, it is an illusion to think that these 'clarifications' will prevent any disputes.[21]

Be that as it may, the closed FET list in the CETA is a significant limitation of the powers of the tribunal. More generally, the closed FET list is a major departure from the traditional unqualified, open-text FET standard which is contained in most Member States' BITs. The CETA Parties thus can further restrict the FET standard, for instance, by adding that the level of protection does not have to go beyond the minimum standard of customary international law or that the FET standard does not apply to disputes involving indirect expropriation and the protection of public policy. In this way the CETA Parties are able to further define and thus limit the scope of application of the FET-standard, which is one the key protection standards invoked in most if not all investment arbitration cases. In fact, the CETA Parties can immediately take action to 'correct' an award that has been issued which they do not consider to adequately protect the policy space of the CETA Parties. Obviously, from the perspective of an investor, this introduces an element of unpredictability, which makes it very unattractive for initiating proceedings against a CETA Party.

(3) Joint Committees

In addition to these more ad hoc type of tools, another innovative 'pro-active' tool is the creation of several joint committees, which are tasked with constantly reviewing the application and implementation of the CETA provisions and make proposals for solving any issues. While joint committees have been a regular feature in FTAs, in particular, in light of the vast areas covered by FTAs, such committees are unknown to traditional Member States' BITs. Besides resolving any problems, joint committees also have the task of thinking ahead and proposing new innovative elements. For example, Article 8.44(1)(b) entrusts the joint committee to consider possible improvements in the investment chapter in the light of experience and developments in other international forums and under the Parties' other agreements. More specifically, Article 8.29 of the CETA states that the Parties shall pursue with other trading partners the establishment of a multilateral investment tribunal and appellate

[21] See for a detailed analysis N. Lavranos, 'The Lack of an FET-Standard in CETA', presentation at the McGill CETA Conference, 1 November 2014, available at www.mcgill.ca/fortier-chair/events/ceta-conference-2014 (accessed 25 September 2016).

mechanism for the resolution of investment disputes. Upon establishment of such a body, the joint committee shall adopt a decision providing that investment disputes under CETA will be decided by this multilateral investment tribunal. Again, this is another feature of continuous treaty management, which is in contrast with the traditional one-off approach of the EU Member States' BITs.

Moreover, joint committees are also tasked to act as a preliminary filter in certain specific sectors, which the CETA Parties consider politically very sensitive, such as financial services and taxes. For example, Article 13.18 of Chapter 13 on financial services establishes a Financial Services Committee. Article 13.21 of the same chapter modifies the general ISDS rules for disputes relating to financial services. Accordingly, the respondent party in a financial services dispute may refer the dispute to the Financial Services Committee in order to determine whether or not a defence of the respondent based on a prudential carve out or an exception is valid. If the Financial Services Committee – or the CETA Joint Committee as the higher political body – makes a joint determination that the defence of the respondent has been valid, the claim is dismissed and cannot be pursued anymore under the ISDS rules of the CETA.

A similar filter mechanism exists also for ISDS claims related to tax measures (Article 28.7(7) in the chapter on exceptions). Accordingly, in that sector, investors must firstly present their claim to the joint committee, which consists of governmental experts of the CETA Parties who determine whether (1) a measure is a taxation measure, (2) the measure, if it is found to be a taxation measure, breaches an obligation under the CETA investment protection chapter and (3) there is an inconsistency between the obligations in CETA that are alleged to have been breached and those of a tax convention. If the CETA Parties agree that the measure is not a taxation measure or that it does not breach any obligations, the claim cannot be pursued further. The introduction of these filter mechanisms is a reaction to the perception by some States and NGOs that many investment claims are 'frivolous' and should be kicked out before full proceedings can commence.

Obviously, the introduction of States Parties' experts in determining as a kind of first-tier judge whether or not a claim may be pursued re-politicises the arbitral proceedings and thus undermines one of the virtues of ISDS, which is to de-politicise the dispute by bringing it before an independent international ad hoc tribunal.[22] It is very likely that the

[22] See I. Shihata, 'Towards a Greater Depoliticization of Investment Disputes: The Roles of ICSID and MIGA', *ICSID Review*, 1 (1986), 1–25.

joint committees will be inclined to kick out as many cases as possible, thus reducing the general risk of being exposed to arbitral proceedings. Consequently, in these cases the CETA Parties are replacing the tribunal by taking over the decision on the admissibility of a claim in certain sensitive sectors – without any possibility of the claimant to challenge or appeal that decision. Clearly, this is another important tool for the CETA Parties to exercise control over ISDS claims from the moment they are initiated. The result is that the actual possibility of investors using ISDS in cases relating to financial services or taxes is *de facto* removed.

(4) *Interfering in Disputes as Non-Disputing State Party*

After arbitral proceedings have been initiated, Article 8.38 of the CETA further enlarges the possibilities of the other CETA Parties which are not respondents by explicitly enabling them to intervene in the proceedings as 'non-disputing Party'. Indeed, this provision not only allows the non-disputing Parties to participate in the proceedings but also to request copies of all relevant documents pertaining to the disputes. Again, this tool has been copied from NAFTA, which also allows the NAFTA Parties to interfere in all NAFTA cases as non-disputing parties, which happens on a regular basis.[23]

Obviously, if all CETA Parties agree on a certain position which should be followed by the tribunal, the common and co-ordinated intervention by all CETA Parties in a dispute can have a very powerful impact on the tribunal. Indeed, it is difficult to imagine that the tribunal faced with such a co-ordinated intervention would adopt a totally divergent view. But more generally, this tool allows non-disputing Parties to make their views on certain points of law publicly known and thus shape the interpretation

[23] Article 1128 of the NAFTA allows non-disputing Parties to send submissions to the arbitral tribunal. See e.g. the various submissions by the United States, Canada and Mexico in several cases. Regarding the *Methanex* case, see http://investorstatelawguide.com/documents/documents/UN-0015–41%20-%20Methanex%20v.%20US%20-%20Canada%201128%20Subm%203.pdf; www.uncitral.org/res/transparency-registry/registry/data/can/s_d__myers_inc_html/myers-31.pdf; www.iisd.org/pdf/methanexsubMX.pdf; and www.state.gov/documents/organization/3946.pdf (all accessed 25 September 2016). Regarding the *Mesa Power* case, see www.international.gc.ca/trade-agreements-accords-commerciaux/assets/pdfs/disp-diff/mesa-usa-1128-submission.pdf (accessed 25 September 2016). Concerning the *Bilcon* case, see L. Johnson, 'As Decision in *Mesa* v. *Canada* looms, investor and all three NAFTA parties weigh in on significance of *Bilcon*', *IAReporter*, 10 August 2015, available at www.iareporter.com/articles/as-decision-in-mesa-v-canada-looms-investor-and-all-three-nafta-parties-weigh-in-on-significance-of-bilcon/ (accessed 25 September 2016).

of the law in future cases. This possibility is also an important tool for addressing any concerns of States' own citizens by showing that they are united against a certain interpretation argued by claimants. While this may enhance transparency, it can also politicise the proceedings, which, in turn, can have a significant intimidating effect on the tribunal and the claimant.

(5) Determining the Correct Respondent

Another interesting innovation concerns the determination of the correct respondent as regards claims against the European Union and its Member States. According to Article 8.21 of the CETA, a Canadian investor who intends to initiate proceedings against the European Union and/or a Member State must first send a notice to the European Union requesting a determination of the correct respondent. Within fifty days, the European Union will inform the investor of the determination of the correct respondent. If the European Union fails to make this determination within fifty days, the respondent will be determined on the basis of whether the disputed measure is attributable to the European Union or the Member State. This is further regulated in the so-called Financial Liability Regulation 912/2014.[24] More importantly, Article 8.21(7) of the CETA explicitly states that the tribunal is bound by the determination made by the European Union and its Member States pursuant to this provision. From the perspective of a Canadian investor who intends to initiate an ISDS case, the choice of the respondent is of utmost importance and has significant consequences.[25]

For example, in the case of the CETA, if an EU Member State (with the exception of Poland) is the respondent, the investor can select the ICSID Arbitration Rules,[26] whereas if the European Union is the respondent, neither the ICSID Arbitration Rules nor the ICSID Additional Facility would be available because the European Union is not Party to the ICSID

[24] Regulation (EU) No. 912/2014 of 23 July 2014, establishing a framework for managing financial responsibility linked to investor-to-State dispute settlement tribunals established by international agreements to which the European Union is party, OJ 2014 L 257/121, 28 August 2014.

[25] A similar system has been proposed by the European Commission for the TTIP.

[26] Canada ratified the ICSID Convention only in November 2013; see www.international.gc.ca/media/comm/news-communiques/2013/11/01a.aspx?lang=eng (accessed 25 September 2016).

Convention and not a State.[27] However, the non-availability of the ICSID Convention has substantial disadvantages for the investor, particularly regarding the recognition and enforcement of awards. If the ICSID Arbitration Rules are not available, the investor must select the United Nations Commission on International Trade Law (UNCITRAL) Arbitration Rules. The disadvantage of these arbitration rules is that the respondent can turn to national courts to prevent the recognition and enforcement of such awards. Moreover, in the case of national courts situated within the European Union, the option of preliminary ruling requests by national courts to the CJEU is available. All this significantly increases the duration and costs of the proceedings – not only for the investor but also for the taxpayer of the respondent.[28]

Finally, it is very problematic that the tribunal is bound by the determination of the European Union and its Member States, in particular, if it appears during the proceedings that the wrong respondent has been determined. There are no provisions which enable the tribunal to correct such a situation. The consequences of a wrong respondent can be fatal for the case: the case may be declared inadmissible or the award becomes unenforceable. This risk is fully borne by the investor turned claimant.

(6) The European Commission's Proposal for an Investment Court System (ICS)

After the European Commission had published a 'concept paper' in May 2015[29] suggesting new proposals to transform the current ISDS system into a court-like system, it followed up with a more detailed draft investment chapter for the TTIP in September 2015,[30] which was

[27] F. Pascual Vives, 'Shaping the EU Investment Regime: Choice of Forum and Applicable Law in International Investment Agreements', *Cuadernos de Derecho Transnacional*, 6 (2014), 269–93, 273, available at http://e-revistas.uc3m.es/index.php/CDT/article/download/1918/911 (accessed 25 September 2016).

[28] The *Eureko/Achmea* v. *Slovakia* and *Micula* v. *Romania* disputes illustrate the many options that lead to delays and obstructions against the recognition and enforcement of awards within the European Union.

[29] See EU Commission, 'Concept Paper: Investment in TTIP and Beyond–The Path for Reform', available at http://trade.ec.europa.eu/doclib/html/153408.htm (accessed 25 September 2016).

[30] See EU Commission, 'Draft Proposal for an Investment Court System', 16 September 2015, available at http://trade.ec.europa.eu/doclib/docs/2015/september/tradoc_153807.pdf (accessed 25 September 2016).

finally adopted on 12 November 2015[31] and presented to the United States as part of the TTIP negotiations.[32]

In parallel, the European Commission also presented its ICS proposal to Canada, indicating that without the inclusion of the ICS proposal, a ratification of the CETA by the European Parliament and EU Member States would be highly unlikely. Canada, being keen to ratify the CETA as quickly as possible, agreed to amend the already finalised 2014 CETA text to incorporate the ICS proposal.

The ICS proposal constitutes a significant departure from the current ISDS system by proposing a new semi-permanent two-tier court system. As will be explained later in more detail, it is a hybrid *sui generis* body which incorporates elements from the WTO Appellate Body and the CJEU while at the same time maintaining some standard arbitration features.

Article 8.27 of the CETA establishes the tribunal, which consists of fifteen members appointed jointly by the European Union and Canada, with five EU nationals, five Canadian nationals and five nationals of third countries. The members would be appointed for a five-year term, renewable once. However, the terms of seven of the fifteen members appointed immediately after the entry into force of the CETA would be six years. The cases would be heard by chambers of three members, always comprised of one EU, one Canadian and one third-party tribunal member (with the third-party member as chair). Besides, the disputing Parties could agree on a sole arbitrator (to be appointed out of the five nationals of third countries). The tribunal would resolve disputes under the rules chosen by the investor, that is, ICSID Rules (if available), ICSID Additional Facility Rules (if available) or the UNCITRAL Rules.

Article 8.28 of the CETA establishes the Appellate Tribunal (AT). The CETA does not specify the number of AT members nor the length of their appointments, but defers that decision to the CETA Joint Committee. However, the ICS proposal for TTIP mentions six members who would be appointed for a six-year term, with two EU and two US nationals and a further two nationals of third countries. The appeals would be heard by chambers of three members. The ICS proposal for TTIP specifies timelines

[31] See the EU Commission's proposed TTIP investment chapter containing the proposal for an investment court system (ICS), 12 November 2015, available at http://trade.ec.europa.eu/doclib/docs/2015/november/tradoc_153955.pdf (accessed 25 September 2016).

[32] See for an in-depth analysis 'EFILA Task Force Paper on the ICS Proposal', published 5 February 2016, available at http://efila.org/wp-content/uploads/2016/02/EFILA_TASK_FORCE_on_ICS_proposal_1-2-2016.pdf (accessed 25 September 2016).

for the duration of the proceedings, which are not mentioned in the CETA but are deferred for decision of the CETA Joint Committee. Accordingly, there would be strict time limits for the Parties to appeal an award (ninety days from issuance) and for the appeal proceedings themselves (usually not to exceed 180 days from notification of appeal to decision but subject to a longstop of 270 days).

The grounds of appeal are extensive by comprising not only those contained in Article 52 of the ICSID Convention but in addition cases where the tribunal has made 'errors in the application or interpretation of applicable law' or 'manifest errors in the appreciation of the facts, including the appreciation of relevant domestic law'.[33] Accordingly, the appellate review also covers points of facts, which goes beyond the usual limited scope of points of law.

Regarding the qualifications of the judges, it is interesting to note that CETA does distinguish between members of the tribunal and the AT. For both bodies, Article 8.27(4) states that members must possess the qualifications required in their respective countries for appointment to judicial office or be jurists of recognised competence. More specifically, the members shall have demonstrated expertise in public international law, and it is 'desirable' that they have expertise, in particular, in international investment law, in international trade law and the resolution of disputes arising under international investment or international trade agreements.

As far as the fees of the members are concerned, this decision is deferred to the CETA Joint Committee. However, Article 8.27(14) provides that unless the CETA Joint Committee adopts a decision, the amount of the fees and expenses of the members of the tribunal shall be in line with the ICSID Convention. In contrast to that, the ICS proposal for TTIP indicates retainer fess of (€2,000 and €7,000, respectively, per month). In this context, it is important to emphasise that initially the members will not be appointed on a permanent basis, but remain free to engage in other non-conflicting occupations.

Moreover, even though Article 8.30 of the CETA provides that the members shall be independent and not affiliated with any government, a footnote states that the 'fact that a person receives remuneration from a government does not in itself make that person ineligible.'[34] This clarifies that governmental officials may become member of the tribunal, while the same provision states that members shall not take instructions from any organisation or government with regard to matters of

[33] Article 8.28(2)(a) and (b) of the CETA. [34] Footnote 12 to Article 8.30.

dispute. Moreover, the members shall comply with the International Bar Association Guidelines on Conflicts of Interest in International Arbitration or any supplemental rules adopted. In addition, upon appointment, the members shall refrain from acting as counsel or as Party-appointed expert or witness in any pending or new investment dispute under this or any other international agreement.

In the context of dealing with conflicts of interest, CETA contains an interesting improvement compared to the ICS proposal for TTIP. Whereas the ICS proposal for TTIP assigns the presidents of the tribunal and the AT to decide upon any conflict-of-interest challenges, Article 8.30(2) of the CETA assigns that task to the president of the ICJ. In other words, a person who is not associated in any way with the tribunal or AT. This should ensure swift and impartial decisions.

Furthermore, it should be noted that Article 8.27(16) of the CETA explicitly provides that the ICSID Secretariat shall act as the Secretariat for the tribunal and provide it with appropriate support.

Despite the obvious efforts to move the ICS away from arbitration, the CETA text prescribes that the decisions of the ICS are to be treated similar to ICSID and New York Convention awards as the case may be, which proves how close the ICS actually remains within the current arbitration system – at least as far as the recognition and enforcement of awards are concerned.[35]

In sum, the main features of the ICS proposal underline the clear shift towards more control of the Contracting Parties while eliminating any influence of the claimant. The States alone appoint the members of the ICS; they determine all the rules of procedure and are able to 'correct' any decisions which they consider to be 'wrong'. Obviously, there is a high risk that States will create a pro-State-biased body, which will not gain the trust of investors.

(7) The A Priori Exclusion of Any Direct Effect of the CETA

A final tool to exert control over investment disputes, which the CETA Parties have included in the CETA text, is the explicit a priori exclusion of any direct effect of CETA provisions. Article 30.16 of the CETA states:

> Nothing in this Agreement shall be construed as conferring rights or imposing obligations on persons other than those created between the

[35] Article 8.41(5) and (6) of the CETA.

> Parties under public international law, nor as permitting this Agreement to be directly invoked in the domestic legal systems of the Parties.
>
> A Party shall not provide for a right of action under its domestic law against the other Party on the ground that a measure of the other Party is inconsistent with this Agreement.

Accordingly, no private party is able to rely on CETA provisions such as, for example, the national treatment (NT), most favoured nation (MFN) or FET clauses before their domestic courts. The exclusion of any direct effect of international trade agreements is, of course, nothing new. For example, in its decisions to sign recent bilateral FTAs, such as the one with South Korea and Columbia and Peru, the Council added provisions specifying that

> the Agreement shall not be construed as conferring rights or imposing obligations which can be directly invoked before Union or Member State courts and tribunals.[36]

Moreover, the CJEU also has been very cautious in accepting a direct effect of provisions of international trade agreements, such as regarding the WTO agreements (General Agreement on Tariffs and Trade (GATT), General Agreement on Trade in Services (GATS) and the Agreement on Trade-Related Aspects of Intellectual Property Rights (TRIPS)).[37] A similar reluctance of the CJEU can also be detected regarding international environmental agreements.[38]

The consequence of excluding any direct effect of the CETA *a priori* is that even if an investor would give preference to bringing a claim against a CETA Party before a domestic court instead of the tribunal established under CETA, the CETA Parties have effectively excluded this option. This is a clear denial of justice and access to domestic courts. Moreover, the CETA Parties can be sure that none of the domestic courts (including the CJEU) gets the opportunity to interpret and apply the CETA provisions in a way which may not have been foreseen or intended by the CETA Parties. But this also prevents domestic courts from reviewing any measures of the CETA

[36] See Council Decision 2011/265/EU of 16 September 2010 on the signing, on behalf of the European Union, and provisional application of the free trade agreement between the European Union and its Member States, of the one part, and the Republic of Korea, of the other part, OJ 2011 No. L 127/1, 14 May 2011; Council Decision 012/735/EU of 31 May 2012 on the signing, on behalf of the Union, and provisional application of the trade agreement between the European Union and its Member States, of the one part, and Columbia and Peru, of the other part, OJ 2012 No. L 354/1, 21 December 2012.

[37] See M. Bronckers, 'Schizophrenia in the EU about International Law', Leiden Law blog, 21 January 2015, available at http://leidenlawblog.nl/articles/schizophrenia-in-the-eu-about-international-law (accessed 25 September 2016).

[38] *Ibid.*

Parties in light of the CETA provisions and thus prevents them from striking down any inconsistent measures. Instead, that task is left to the tribunal and AT, although Article 8.31 (2) explicitly excludes any binding effect on the domestic courts or the authorities of the CETA Parties. This is a rather schizophrenic outcome in light of the current criticisms against arbitral tribunals and the obvious intention to limit their powers. But ultimately it would be the CETA Parties themselves who decide whether or not a measure is inconsistent. In other words, the same entities which adopted any disputed measure are the ones which decide about their inconsistency. Obviously, the Contracting Parties are not impartial.

However, there are also voices, such as Daniel Thym, who are glad that any direct effect of the CETA is excluded since

> the absence of direct effect in domestic proceedings shows that the legal implications of CETA and TTIP would be less dramatic than some commentators in the public debate suggest. Courts in Europe would not hold the power to annul domestic or supranational legislation, which violates the agreements – a power that also the dispute settlement bodies would be denied explicitly, together with the option for the state parties to force their reading of the agreements upon the arbiters by means of an authoritative interpretation. This would orientate the dispute settlement rules in CETA and TTIP towards inter-state bargaining, pretty much like in the WTO context.[39]

In my view, this statement illustrates very little trust in any court – be it domestic, European or international – which raises the very fundamental question, why should we trust domestic courts and the CJEU when they apply and interpret EU law or any kind of law? But Thym's statement correctly identifies the ultimate goal of the CETA Parties, which is to keep all forms of dispute resolution within an inter-State bargaining setting while excluding any independent and impartial court or tribunal. This is the real intention behind these 'reforms', which goes against the very same rule-of-law principles, which the European Union and its Member States are so proud of.

C. Forecasting the CJEU's Approach towards BITs and ISDS

Whereas previous sections dealt with the future EU investment policy, in particular, the 'innovations' introduced in the new EU investment

[39] D. Thym, 'The Missing Link: Direct Effect, CETA/TTIP and Investor-State Dispute Settlement', *EU Law Analysis*, 7 January 2015, available at http://eulawanalysis.blogspot.nl/2015/01/the-missing-link-direct-effect-cetattip.html (accessed 25 September 2016).

treaties such as in the CETA (and most likely in the TTIP), the situation regarding the more than 1,500 existing Member States' BITs must not be forgotten. Also regarding those BITs, the European Commission has been stepping up its efforts to increase its control over these BITs and disputes brought under them. In this context, it is important to recall that the efforts of the European Commission are not necessarily supported by the Member States but rather are directed against them.[40] The main reason for this is the continuous struggle of the European Commission to impose a total exclusive EU competence over all investment law and ISDS aspects, whereas most Member States are of the view that the European Union's competence is strictly limited to FDI issues.[41] That issue will soon be resolved by the CJEU, since the European Commission requested on Advisory Opinion concerning the question of whether the EU–Singapore FTA falls within the exclusive competence of the European Union or is a 'mixed' agreement that needs to be signed and ratified by the Member States as well.[42]

Since the European Commission has now successfully managed to get the CJEU involved as the final and authoritative judge to determine the future place of BITs, ISDS and arbitral tribunals within the European Union's legal order, this section analyses the recent CJEU case law that will be relevant to its approach towards these issues. Two related issues will have to be decided by the CJEU: firstly, what is the extent of the exclusive common and commercial policy (CCP) competence of the European Union, and secondly, whether and, if so, to what extent

[40] In the original draft proposal for the grandfathering regulation, the European Commission had proposed that the Member States must terminate all their 1,500 extra-EU BITs within seven years. See for a detailed description N. Lavranos, 'In Defence of Member States' BITs Gold Standard: The Regulation 1219/2912 Establishing a Transitional Regime for Existing Extra-EU BITs – A Member State's Perspective', *Transnational Dispute Management*, 2 (2013), 1–14. More recently, the European Commission initiated infringement procedures against five Member States because it considers their intra-EU BITs to be in violation of European Union law; see 'Commission Asks Member States to Terminate Their Intra-EU BITs', press release, 18 June 2015, available at http://europa.eu/rapid/press-release_IP-15-5198_en.htm (accessed 25 September 2016).

[41] See e.g. a presentation by the European Commission in which it explicitly states that the FDI competence is full and includes investment protection, available at trade.ec.europa.eu/doclib/html/150853.htm (accessed 25 September 2016). See generally A. Reinisch, 'The EU on the Investment Path: Quo Vadis Europe? The Future of EU BITs and Other Investment Agreements', available at http://law.scu.edu/wp-content/uploads/investment/Reinisch-EU-Investment-Law-Quo-Vadis-26-01-2013.pdf (accessed 25 September 2016).

[42] See the request for an opinion submitted by the European Commission pursuant to Article 218(11) of the TFEU, (Opinion 2/15), (2015/C 363/22), OJ 2015 No. C363/18, 3 November 2015.

international arbitral tribunals may operate within the European Union's legal system. Regarding the first issue, it can be expected that the CJEU will define the exclusive CCP competence as broadly as possible and most likely will grant full exclusive CPP competence for all investment issues to the European Union.[43] Concerning the second issue, the CJEU has not yet specifically decided the relationship between itself and international arbitral tribunals. However, over the years, the CJEU has developed a line of jurisprudence concerning its relationship with various international courts and tribunals which have been established in other fields of international law.[44]

To cut a long story short, the attitude of the CJEU towards accepting other international courts and tribunals that could potentially interpret and apply EU law, which includes international treaties concluded by the European Union and/or its Member States, has been rather negative.[45] This applies to the European Free Trade Association (EFTA) Court,[46] the WTO Appellate Body,[47] dispute settlement under Article 287 of the United Nations Convention on the Law of the Sea (UNCLOS) Arbitral Tribunal[48] and the envisaged Patent Court.[49]

For example, in its *Opinion 1/09* regarding the Patent Court, the CJEU underlined that the 'tasks attributed to the national courts and to the Court of Justice respectively are indispensable to the preservation of the

[43] This position has also been argued for by e.g. A. Dimopoulos, *EU Foreign Investment Law* (Oxford University Press, 2011).

[44] See for an extensive analysis N. Lavranos, 'Is An International Investor-State Arbitration System Possible under the Auspices of the ECJ?', in N. Jansen Calamita, D. Earnest and M. Burgstaller (eds.), *The Future of ICSID and the Place of Investment Treaties in International Law* (London: BIICL, 2013), 129–48, also available at http://papers.ssrn.com/sol3/papers.cfm?abstract_id=1973491 (accessed 25 September 2016).

[45] See extensively N. Lavranos, *Jurisdictional Competition: Selected Cases in International and European Law* (Groningen: Europa Law Publishing, 2009).

[46] It should be recalled that in its Opinion 1/91, *EEA Agreement* [1991], ECR I-6079, the CJEU rejected the first EEA Treaty creating the EFTA Court. Subsequently, in its Opinion 2/91, *EEA Agreement II* [1992], ECR I-2821, the CJEU accepted the EFTA Court after its powers to interpret EU law were restricted.

[47] As is well known, the CJEU has always consistently refused to be bound by final, definite WTO Appellate Body Reports, see e.g. Case C-21/14 P, *Commission* v. *Rusal Armenal ZAO*, Judgment of 16 July 2015, available at http://curia.europa.eu/juris/document/document.jsf?text=BIRET&docid=165927&pageIndex=0&doclang=EN&mode=req&dir=&occ=first&part=1&cid=1188965#ctx1 (accessed 25 September 2016), paras. 38 *et seq.* See generally F. Snyder, 'The Gatekeepers: The European Courts and WTO Law', *Common Market Law Review*, 40 (2003), 313–67.

[48] Case C-459/03, *Commission* v. *Ireland (Mox plant)* [2006], ECR-I 4635.

[49] Opinion 1/09, *Patent Court* [2011], ECR I-1137.

very nature of the law established by the Treaties'.[50] Thus, the CJEU concluded that

> [C]onsequently, the envisaged agreement, by conferring on an international court which is *outside* the institutional and judicial framework of the European Union an exclusive jurisdiction to hear a significant number of actions brought by individuals in the field of the Community patent and to interpret and apply European Union law in that field, would deprive courts of Member States of their powers in relation to the interpretation and application of European Union law and the Court of its powers to reply, by preliminary ruling, to questions referred by those courts and, consequently, would *alter the essential character of the powers which the Treaties confer on the institutions of the European Union and on the Member States and which are indispensable to the preservation of the very nature of European Union law.*[51]

More recently, in *Opinion 2/13*,[52] the CJEU followed the same line of reasoning regarding its relationship with the European Court of Human Rights (ECtHR). In essence, the CJEU recalled that an international agreement that establishes bodies which can bind the EU institutions, including the CJEU itself, can only be accepted if there 'is no adverse effect on the autonomy of the EU legal order'.[53] However since the ECtHR would be in a position to interpret and apply EU law in a manner that would also be binding on the CJEU,[54] the CJEU found that this is 'liable adversely to affect the specific characteristics of EU law and its autonomy'.[55]

Thus, the CJEU concluded that the European Union may not accede to the ECHR – at least not on the basis of the envisaged agreement. The conclusions of the CJEU are remarkable to say the least. First, the CJEU ignores the explicit will of the 'Masters of the Treaties' who clearly prescribed in Article 6 of the Treaty of the European Union (TEU) that the Union shall accede to the ECHR. Second, the CJEU itself has been applying the ECHR for decades,[56] while at the same time the ECtHR indicated that it will not review EU law measures because they are presumed to be compatible with the ECHR unless it is shown that the

[50] *Ibid.*, para. 85. [51] *Ibid.*, para. 89 (emphasis added).

[52] See Opinion 2/13, *Accession of the EU to the ECHR*, 18 December 2014, available at http://curia.europa.eu/juris/document/document.jsf?text=&docid=160882&pageIndex=0&doclang=EN&mode=lst&dir=&occ=first&part=1&cid=512776 (accessed 25 September 2016).

[53] *Ibid.*, paras. 183–4. [54] *Ibid.*, para. 185. [55] *Ibid.*

[56] See e.g. Joined Cases C-402/05 P and C-415/05 P, *Kadi and Al Barakaat* v. *Council and Commission* [2008], ECR I-6351, para. 284, with reference to its long-standing jurisprudence.

standard of human rights protection is 'manifestly deficient'.[57] Thus, there seems to be no danger or risk that the ECtHR would undermine the CJEU's exclusive jurisdiction to interpret and apply EU law *in fine*. But apparently the CJEU saw reasons to make it very clear that the ECtHR will not be allowed under any circumstances to potentially trespass on its jurisdiction regarding EU law.

If one applies this approach to international arbitral tribunals established under an investment agreement to which the European Union and/or a Member State is a Party, it can be safely concluded that such arbitral tribunals would be considered unacceptable for the CJEU. Although it has not yet been tested, it is generally assumed that international arbitral tribunals do not meet the criteria of a 'national court' of a Member State, which would enable international arbitral tribunals to request preliminary rulings from the CJEU.[58] So far the CJEU has ruled that arbitral tribunals established under the law of the Member States do not qualify as a 'national court'[59] and that there is no reason why that would be any different for international arbitral tribunals. Hence, international arbitral tribunals would fall 'outside' the EU judicial system and thus would have to be considered incompatible with the European Union's legal order. This is so because such arbitral tribunals could always potentially interpret EU law provisions in a manner binding for EU institutions and Member States without allowing the CJEU to correct such interpretations. This would not only apply to international arbitral

[57] See ECtHR, *Bosphorus* v. *Ireland*, Judgment of 30 June 2005, App. No. 45036/98, paras. 155 *et seq.*

[58] In contrast, P. Paschalidis, 'Arbitral Tribunals and Preliminary References to the EU Court of Justice', *Arbitration International*, 1 (2016), 1–23, argues that international arbitral tribunals may well qualify as domestic courts of a Member State and thus be empowered to submit preliminary references to the CJEU.

[59] See Case C-125/04, *Denuit & Cordenier* v. *Transorient* [2005], ECR I-923: 'In order to determine whether a body making a reference is a court or tribunal of a Member State for the purposes of Article 234 EC, the Court takes account of a number of factors, such as whether the body is established by law, whether it is permanent, whether its jurisdiction is compulsory, whether its procedure is *inter partes*, whether it applies rules of law and whether it is independent (see, in particular, Case C-54/96, *Dorsch Consult* [1997], ECR I-4961, para. 23, and the case-law there cited, and Case C-516/99, *Schmid* [2002], ECR I-4573, para. 34). Under the Court's case-law, an arbitration tribunal is not a 'court or tribunal of a Member State' within the meaning of Article 234 EC where the parties are under no obligation, in law or in fact, to refer their disputes to arbitration and the public authorities of the Member State concerned are not involved in the decision to opt for arbitration nor required to intervene of their own accord in the proceedings before the arbitrator (Case 102/81, *'Nordsee' Deutsche Hochseefischerei* [1982], ECR 1095, paras. 10–12 and Case C-126/97, *Eco Swiss* [1999], ECR I-3055, para. 34).'

tribunals established under intra-EU and extra-EU BITs but similarly also to the ICS established under the CETA and proposed for the TTIP or a permanent multilateral investment court. This is particularly the case for the ICS under the CETA because the tribunal may consider domestic law as fact and because one of the grounds for appeal concerns the manifestly wrong appreciation of facts. Accordingly, the AT is in a position to review EU law, even though the CETA text states that any findings are not binding on the courts and authorities of the CETA Parties.[60]

Consequently, in my opinion, it must be concluded that on the CJEU's reasoning in *Opinion 2/13*, there is no room within the European Union's legal order for any permanent international investment court or arbitral tribunal operating 'outside' the preliminary ruling system. Obviously, such a conclusion would make the proposed ICS unacceptable to the CJEU, which puts the whole proposal of the European Commission into question. One solution, of course, would be to change the TEU and TFEU and make it explicitly possible that such international courts and arbitral tribunals can request preliminary rulings from the CJEU.

D. Outlook

One thing is clear: Contracting Parties to investment treaties are not staying at the sidelines anymore but are applying a whole range of tools to (re)gain control over their investment treaties, ISDS rules and investment disputes. More specifically, Contracting Parties have moved away from the traditional one-off treaty making towards continuous treaty monitoring, treaty modification by interpretation and active dispute intervention. The consequences of this new approach are significant and hitting two different targets: (1) arbitral tribunals and (2) investors turned claimants who intend to initiate ISDS proceedings.

Regarding arbitral tribunals, the CETA Parties have created numerous possibilities to impose binding interpretations and decisions on the tribunal and the AT. In sensitive areas such as financial services and

[60] Article 8.31(2) of the CETA states: 'The Tribunal shall not have jurisdiction to determine the legality of a measure, alleged to constitute a breach of this Agreement, under the domestic law of the disputing Party. For greater certainty, in determining the consistency of a measure with this Agreement, the Tribunal may consider, as appropriate, the domestic law of the disputing Party as a matter of fact. In doing so, the Tribunal shall follow the prevailing interpretation given to the domestic law by the courts or authorities of that Party and any meaning given to domestic law by the Tribunal shall not be binding upon the courts or the authorities of that Party.'

taxes, the CETA Parties are in fact replacing the tribunal at the jurisdictional phase by acting as filters deciding whether or not a claim is frivolous or may proceed. The CETA Parties also interfere into the process by exclusively selecting the members of the tribunal and AT, thereby removing any influence of the claimant in the proceedings. The CETA Parties are also able to add further obligations in terms of codes of conduct, transparency and so on. Consequently, in the long run and if the ICS proposal is adopted by more States, arbitral tribunals could be totally replaced by the envisaged ICS, which would incidentally prevent practicing lawyers – who are perceived by many anti-ISDS critics as being biased – from acting as arbitrators.

Regarding investors, it is very obvious that more obstacles are created to prevent the initiation and pursuit of ISDS claims. This is a clear attempt to discourage ISDS claims – preferably from the very beginning. In addition, the substantive protection standards are also further lowered.[61] As a result, investors are deprived of a useful and effective dispute settlement tool.

All in all, one gets the impression that many States would prefer to eradicate the whole system of investment treaties and ISDS. There seems to be little trust anymore in the usefulness of international arbitration. But if this is indeed the case, the question arises, why are States – as 'Masters of the BITs' – not simply eradicating the current ISDS system? Could it be that most States continue to consider BITs beneficial for their investors and for attracting FDI? One notable example is the United Kingdom, which recently came out with a strong support for ISDS in the TTIP, which is an exceptional voice against the anti-ISDS trend in many Member States.[62] But perhaps Brazil is setting the new trend with its recently concluded new type of BIT, which does not include ISDS but instead an ombudsman and State-State dispute settlement (SSDS) procedures and is the example that may well be followed by other States.[63] Time will tell.

As far as the European Union and its Member States are concerned, incremental but continuous 'improvements' and 'innovations' will be included in the new EU investment treaties, and the European

[61] Cf. also Chapter 12.

[62] See the UK government's response to the House of Commons Business, Innovation and Skills Committee's Eleventh Report of Session 2014–15: TTIP (July 2015), available at www.gov.uk/government/uploads/system/uploads/attachment_data/file/448208/Cm_9103_TTIP_Government_response_to_Business_Innovation_and_Skills_Committee_report_PRINT.pdf (accessed 25 September 2016).

[63] See note 5.

Commission will continue to play an even more active role in this development. The CETA already contains an extensive 'pro-active' toolbox which enables CETA Parties to exert significantly more control over the investment provisions and ISDS proceedings compared to the traditional Member States' BITs. Indeed, if CETA enters into force and creates the semi-permanent two-tier court system, this could be the start of a new era in the settlement of investment treaty disputes between investors and States.

As has been argued in this contribution, the ICS proposal contains even more elements which will further increase the control of States parties while at the same time reducing the interpretative room of the tribunal and AT and restricting access of investors to the ICS. In this context, the trend towards a permanent, institutionalised investment court is clearly visible, whereas at the same time it seems highly unlikely that the CJEU would accept such a (semi)permanent investment court as part of the EU legal order.

While such solutions look attractive at first sight – at least for States – there are negative aspects which must also be taken into account in the equation of whether or not such efforts to 'reform' actually help to address some of the more legitimate concerns.[64] One thing that is certain is that the current developments illustrate that the need for and advantages of investment protection and arbitration, in particular, for the stimulation of FDI, creation of jobs and promotion of the rule of law, are lost out of sight in this 'reform process'.

[64] See C. Tietje, 'Ein internationales Handels- und Investitionsgericht für CETA (und TTIP)?', *TELC Policy Paper on Transnational Economic Law*, 42 (March 2015), available at http://telc.jura.uni-halle.de/sites/default/files/PolicyPaper/PolicyPaper_No42.pdf (accessed 25 September 2016).

14

Arbitrator Selection

Towards Greater State Control

MICHAEL WAIBEL*

A. Introduction

Two defining characteristics of international arbitration are the absence of a standing tribunal and the selection of the adjudicators by the disputing parties.[1] Investment arbitral tribunals are constituted for particular cases with decision-makers appointed for one particular dispute only by the disputing parties directly or in accordance with their agreement. The lifetime of such tribunals comes to an end when they issue their final awards. By contrast, national courts or international tribunals, such as the International Court of Justice (ICJ), have a permanent existence, and their decision-makers are typically appointed for long, fixed terms or for life.[2]

The principle of party autonomy has traditionally played a central role in arbitrator selection.[3] 'Party autonomy' means that the composition of

* Thanks to Jonathan Bonnitcha, Gabriel Bottini, Dirk Pulkowski, Andreas Kulick, Lauge Poulsen, Yanhui Wu and all the participants of the Tübingen workshop in June 2015 for discussions and Christine Barthelemy for research assistance.

1 However, ad hoc judges appointed by State Parties without representation on the bench of a standing tribunal remain an important feature of international dispute settlement e.g. before the ICJ and ITLOS; see generally I. R. Suh, 'Voting Behavior of National Judges in International Courts', *American Journal of International Law*, 63 (1969), 224–36; and Y. Shany, 'Squaring the Circle – Independence and Impartiality of Party-Appointed Adjudicators in International Legal Proceedings', *Loyola International & Comparative Law Review*, 30 (2008), 473–90.

2 See generally R. Mackenzie, *Selecting International Judges: Principle, Process, and Politics* (Oxford University Press, 2010).

3 On the value of party autonomy, see J. D. H. Karton, *The Culture of International Arbitration and the Evolution of Contract Law* (Oxford University Press, 2013), chap. 4; P. Fouchard, E. Gaillard, B. Goldman and J. Savage, *Fouchard, Gaillard, Goldman on International Commercial Arbitration* (Alphen aan den Rijn, Netherlands: Kluwer Law International, 1999), 1.

investment tribunals depends on the will of the disputing parties.[4] Disputing parties have traditionally attached considerable weight to their input into the selection of arbitral tribunals. It gives them an important degree of influence to ensure that the arbitral tribunal includes qualified members and that the tribunal will fully and diligently consider their arguments.

The long-standing principle is that it is up to the disputing parties to select the arbitrators for appointment to arbitral tribunals – severally for party-appointed arbitrators and jointly for presiding arbitrators. As a result, investment disputes are not decided by adjudicators assigned to those disputes according to some formula or even randomly, as is commonly the case with judges on domestic courts. Rather, the parties select the make-up of their investment tribunals.[5]

To the disputing parties, their influence in choosing the arbitrators is one of arbitration's main attractions vis-à-vis national courts and other forms of dispute resolution. Party input into arbitrator selection remains a condition for the litigants to regard the tribunal as legitimate and as a viable alternative to domestic courts.[6] In part, the appeal of arbitration relative to national courts depends on the arbitrators selected to decide these disputes reflecting the preferences of both parties.[7] By opting for arbitration, the disputing parties minimise the risk of their dispute being decided by judges who may lack specialised expertise for their dispute or who may be perceived as biased decision-makers because they are embedded in a national legal system, particularly the host country's legal system.

4 Article 37(2)(a) of the ICSID Convention; cf. also Article V(1)(d) of the New York Convention (providing for an exception to the Convention's general obligation to recognise arbitral awards in cases where the arbitral tribunal was not constituted in accordance with the Parties' agreement).

5 The EU's proposal for an 'investment court system' which the EU-Canada Free Trade Agreement (CETA) and the EU-Vietnam Free Trade Agreement (EVFTA) adopt, however, breaks with this approach and align the selection processes of other standing international courts and tribunals, see Chapter 8, Chapter II, Section 3, Sub-sections 4 and 5 of the EU-Vietnam Free Trade Agreement as of January 2016, available at http://trade.ec.europa.eu/doclib/press/index.cfm?id=1437 (accessed 16 March 2016); Chapter 8, Section F of the CETA as of 29 February 2016, available at http://trade.ec.europa.eu/doclib/docs/2016/february/tradoc_154329.pdf (accessed 16 March 2016); EU Commission, 'Concept Paper: Investment in TTIP and Beyond–The Path for Reform', 11–12, available at http://trade.ec.europa.eu/doclib/docs/2015/may/tradoc_153408.PDF (accessed 16 March 2016). See also Section F.

6 T. Wälde, J. Werner and A. H. Ali (eds.), *A Liber Amicorum: Thomas Wälde: Law beyond Conventional Thought* (Manhasset, NY: CMP Publishing, 2009), 187.

7 G. de Clippel, K. Eliaz and B. Knight, 'On the Selection of Arbitrators', *American Economic Review*, 104 (2014), 3434–58, 3435.

At the same time, however, the central role of the disputing parties in selecting arbitrators has fuelled a debate on the legitimacy of arbitrators deciding investment disputes.[8] To some critics, the 'little formal control over the overall group of professionals who serve on ICSID [International Centre for Settlement of Investment Disputes] tribunals' by states amounts to a 'smear on the legitimacy of the [investment treaty] system'.[9] Arbitrator selection, particularly by the disputing parties, may feed the perception that investment treaty arbitration – despite the prominence of the public interest in at least some cases – is at heart a purely private system of dispute resolution, designed to benefit only the disputing parties.

The main problems associated with the existing rules of arbitrator selection are that the disputing parties may appoint arbitrators with conflicts of interest to these ephemeral tribunals; the patterns of arbitrator appointments may lead to systematic biases in arbitration outcomes; and arbitrators may be drawn from a small network that scarcely represents the contemporary world economy (e.g. the under-representation of female arbitrators or of arbitrators from developing countries). As this chapter explores, States have sought to reassert control over investment arbitration through limitations on the traditional party autonomy in selecting arbitrators. In the case of a permanent investment tribunal (e.g. the EU-Canada Comprehensive Economic and Trade Agreement (CETA)), such party autonomy disappears altogether.

This chapter focuses on the formal and informal rules for nominating arbitrators, how the parties and arbitral institutions choose arbitrators in practice, the patterns of arbitral appointment that these rules produce and possible avenues for reform. The chief question is how parties and arbitral institutions select arbitrators to serve on arbitral tribunals rather than the separate question of when there are grounds for *challenging* arbitrators.[10] This chapter focuses on ICSID arbitration, as all investment

[8] E.g. J. Paulsson, 'Moral Hazard in International Dispute Resolution', *ICSID Review – Foreign Investment Law Journal*, 25 (2010), 339–55, 354; C. Giorgetti, 'Who Decides Who Decides in International Investment Arbitration?', *University of Pennsylvania Journal of International Law*, 35 (2014), 431–86; S. Hindelang and S. Wernicke (eds.), *Essentials of a Modern Investment Protection Regime – Objectives and Recommendations for Action* (Karnack-Haus Reflections, 2015), 14.

[9] I. M. Penusliski, 'A Dispute Systems Design Diagnosis of ICSID', in M. Waibel, A. Kaushal, K.-H. L. Chung and C. Balchin (eds.), *The Backlash against Investment Arbitration: Perceptions and Reality* (Alphen aan den Rijn, Netherlands: Kluwer Law International, 2010), 507–36, 533.

[10] See Chapter 15.

disputes and the identity of arbitrators appointed to each tribunal under the ICSID Convention are in the public domain. Conversely, no comprehensive data are available for the United Nations Commission on International Trade Law (UNCITRAL) and other sets of arbitral rules. Only a subset of such arbitrations is in the public domain, and the identity of the arbitrators is not known for all cases.

B. The Formal Rules for Nominating Arbitrators in Investment Arbitration

Parties frequently agree to arbitrate pursuant to institutional rules, incorporated by reference into their investment treaty/agreement to arbitrate. The States party to investment treaties can (and usually do) agree to a particular appointing authority simply by agreeing to arbitrate under a set of institutional arbitration rules. As I examine in this section, each set of arbitration rules has rules for appointing arbitrators. One important factor for States entering into investment treaties for deciding which arbitration rules to refer to is the role of arbitral institutions in constituting the tribunal and removing or replacing arbitrators.

It is rare for investment treaties themselves to set out procedures for the appointment of arbitrators. Traditionally, investment treaties have simply referred to the International Centre for Settlement of Investment Disputes (ICSID) Convention, UNCITRAL Rules or another set of procedural rules when it comes to the rules for appointing arbitrators. As a result, the default rules for the appointment of arbitrators set out in these arbitration rules apply (even though it is perfectly possible for the States parties to investment treaties to vary them). For example, Article 27 of the US Model BIT 2012, entitled, 'Selection of Arbitrators', does not modify the ICSID default rules on appointing arbitrators in any significant respect.[11] Increasingly, however, as part of a wider trend of States reasserting control over investment dispute settlement examined in this book, investment treaties provide greater specificity and depart in important respects from the default rules set out in the ICSID Convention and the UNCITRAL Rules 2010.[12]

The UNCITRAL Rules, the International Chamber of Commerce (ICC) Rules, the Permanent Court of Arbitration (PCA) Rules, the American

[11] It provides for a three-member tribunal as the default option; for the ICSID Secretary-General to appoint within seventy-five days from the date of request for arbitration for arbitrators not yet appointed.

[12] See Section F.

Arbitration Association (AAA) Rules, and the ICSID Rules on arbitrator selection are representative of arbitral rules more generally.[13] As a rule, the disputing parties may agree directly on a sole arbitrator; in the case of three-person tribunals, each disputing party nominates one party-appointed arbitrator. Under some of these rules (e.g. 2010 UNCITRAL Rules), the two party-appointed arbitrators jointly select the president of the arbitral tribunal, while other rules (e.g. 2012 ICC Rules) contain a default rule whereby an arbitral institution (rather than the party-appointed arbitrators) selects the presiding arbitrator. If the parties or the party-appointed arbitrators fail to agree, the appointing authority appoints the president.

A central theme of these rules is party autonomy, in terms of deciding on both the number and the identity of the arbitrators. Notwithstanding, they also provide for a 'backup' method of institutional appointments to ensure that the disputing parties cannot frustrate the arbitration (e.g. by failing to appoint their arbitrator).This section describes methods of nominating arbitrators found in the various international arbitral rules, starting with the most established and most-often-used rules: ICSID and UNCITRAL, followed by the ICC and London Court of International Arbitration (LCIA) Rules.

With respect to party appointments, the disputing parties are subject to few constraints as to who to choose as their arbitrator; most important is the prohibition against arbitrators who lack impartiality and/or independence. Requirements of impartiality and independence matter for both the selection of arbitrators, challenges to arbitrators and the enforcement of arbitral awards.[14] Such limitations curtail party autonomy in the interest of the integrity of the arbitration. More significant restrictions, for example that the disputing parties must select the arbitrators from a roster of arbitrators, are traditionally rare.[15]

[13] Articles 7–10 of the 2010 UNCITRAL Rules, Articles 11–13 of the 2012 ICC Rules, Articles 8–13 of the 2012 PCA Arbitration Rules and Rules 11–16 of the AAA Commercial Arbitration Rules.

[14] However, an arbitrator's lack of independence and impartiality is insufficient grounds for the annulment of ICSID awards. Pursuant to Article 52 of the ICSID Convention, corruption of the arbitrator is required – a dormant provision thus far in ICSID arbitration: C. H. Schreuer, L. Malintoppi, A. Reinisch and A. Sinclair, *The ICSID Convention: A Commentary* (Cambridge University Press, 2009), Article 52, paras. 271–7 (corruption requires improper 'compensation'; predisposition by a Party-appointed arbitrator is insufficient); Article 12(2) of the UNCITRAL Model Law ('justifiable doubts regarding [the arbitrator's] impartiality or independence'); Article 12 of the 2010 UNCITRAL Rules; Article 57 of the ICSID Convention (manifest lack of the qualities listed in Article 14, notably lack of independence).

[15] But see the CETA as of September 2014 as a recent exception discussed in Section F.

This chapter focuses on arbitrator selection. What is the difference between 'selection' and 'appointment'? Appointment is the formal delegation of decision-making authority by an arbitral institution in accordance with the applicable rule. By contrast, 'selection' focuses on who the parties/institution chooses to sit as arbitrator and what characteristics these arbitrators have.

(1) ICSID

Articles 36–40 of the ICSID Convention, as well as Rules 1–4 of the ICSID Arbitration Rules, set out the rules governing the nomination and appointment of arbitrators. Parties must establish the tribunal (by an agreed mechanism or according to the default procedure) within ninety days from the notice of request for arbitration (Article 38 of the ICSID Convention), unless they agree on another timescale. This timescale applies regardless of the method by which parties choose to nominate the arbitrator(s).[16]

Article 37 of the ICSID Convention provides that the tribunal shall consist of a single arbitrator or an uneven number of arbitrators (Article 37(2)(a)) – typically three arbitrators.[17] The disputing parties nominate by agreement – either before or after the commencement of proceedings – or in accordance with the default rule (Article 37(2)(b)). Article 37(2)(b) provides:

> Where the parties do not agree upon the number of arbitrators and the method of their appointment, the Tribunal shall consist of three arbitrators, one arbitrator appointed by each party and the third, who shall be the president of the Tribunal, appointed by agreement of the parties.

The default appointment procedure under Article 37(2)(b) is sequential and unfolds in three stages (Rule 3 of the ICSID Arbitration Rules). Firstly, party A appoints one arbitrator and proposes a president of the tribunal. Second, party B appoints its own arbitrator and either approves party A's proposal for president or proposes an alternative president. Third, if party B rejects party A's proposal for President and proposes an alternative president instead, party A either agrees with party B's choice or refuses to concur.

[16] E.g. if the disputing parties cannot agree on the appointment of a president of the arbitral tribunal or if no member the tribunal is appointed within ninety days for any reason.

[17] Sole arbitrators are the exception. Only twelve of the more than 450 ICSID tribunals constituted to date consisted of a sole arbitrator.

The disputing parties can choose to nominate an arbitrator from ICSID's panel of arbitrators. The panel of arbitrators is composed of almost 500 individuals.[18] Each Contracting Party to the ICSID Convention may designate up to four individuals to the panel (Article 13(1)), while the chairman of the ICSID Administrative Council may nominate up to ten individuals to the panel (Article 13(2)).

Crucially, however, the disputing parties can also look beyond the panel of arbitrators. They can choose any individual who meets the required minimum qualifications in Article 14 of the Convention (Article 40(2) of the ICSID Convention). In practice, parties often appoint arbitrators from outside the panel of arbitrators. By contrast, ICSID chairman appointments must be from the panel of arbitrators (Article 40(1)).[19] According to Sergio Puig's data, nearly 55 per cent of ICSID appointments were unilateral, 12 per cent by agreement of the disputing parties and 16.5 per cent by the ICSID.[20]

All arbitrators, whether chosen from the panel or otherwise, must comply with the requirements set out in Article 14 of the ICSID Convention:

> Persons designated to serve on panel shall be persons of high moral character and recognized competence in the fields of law, commerce, industry or finance, who may be relied upon to exercise independent judgment.

All arbitrators must be neutral and impartial and must exercise independent judgment. Their actual and perceived neutrality is essential for confidence in the system. To further this objective, no arbitrator can be a national of a State party to the dispute (Rule 3 of the ICSID Arbitration Rules).

(2) UNCITRAL

The UNCITRAL procedure (Articles 7–10 of the UNCITRAL Arbitration Rules 2010) resembles that of the ICSID in important respects: the disputing parties decide on the number of arbitrators who will sit on the tribunal (be it either one or three) and their identity (Articles 7–9). The default number of arbitrators is also three (Article 7(1)). Under Article 6(7), the disputing parties are encouraged to take into account all considerations relevant to

[18] See the ICSID website: https://icsid.worldbank.org/apps/ICSIDWEB/icsiddocs/Pages/Panels-of-Arbitrators-and-Conciliators.aspx (accessed 16 March 2016).

[19] Yet the ICSID often seeks the Parties' agreement to appoint someone who is not on the panel of arbitrators. I am grateful to Gabriel Bottini for this point.

[20] S. Puig, 'Social Capital in the Arbitration Market', *European Journal of International Law*, 25 (2014), 387, 406.

appointing independent and impartial arbitrators, including selecting arbitrators with a nationality other than those of the disputing parties.

There are also some significant differences between ICSID and UNCITRAL tribunals. Firstly, for tribunals composed of three arbitrators, the two party-appointed arbitrators select the presiding arbitrator by agreement rather than by the two disputing parties, as under the ICSID Convention (Article 9(1)). Secondly, the backup mechanism for nominating arbitrators also differs. If the two arbitrators fail to agree on the presiding arbitrator, then an 'appointing authority' will appoint the president by way of a list procedure (Article 8(2)(a)–(d) and Article 9(3)). If the parties have not chosen an appointing authority, the Secretary-General of the Permanent Court of Arbitration (PCA) designates the appointing authority (Article 6(2)). The Secretary-General's role is not to appoint an arbitrator but instead merely to designate an authority that will then make such appointment.

The UNCITRAL list procedure works as follows: the appointing authority makes a list containing at least three names and sends it to both parties (Article 8(2)(a)). Each party then simultaneously vetoes some (or none or all) of the names on that list, ranks the remaining names and then returns the list to the appointing authority (Article 8(2)(b)). The appointing authority then picks the name on the returned lists with the highest rank (Article 8(2)(c)). If the list procedure fails, the appointing authority will exercise its discretion and appoint the remaining arbitrator (Article 8(2)(d) and Article 9(3)).

If the Secretary-General of the Permanent Court of Arbitration acts as appointing authority, then the procedures set out in the PCA Rules 2012 apply. Articles 6–10 of the PCA Rules mirror almost exactly Articles 6–10 of the UNCITRAL Rules.

(3) ICC

As under the ICSID and UNCITRAL Rules, the disputing parties to an ICC arbitration can choose whether they wish to appoint one or three arbitrators (Article 12 of the ICC Rules 2012). Yet, importantly, all party nominations are still subject to confirmation by the ICC Court (Article 13).[21] If the disputing parties agree to appoint one arbitrator but fail to

[21] Article 7(4) of the ICC Rules. W. W. Park, 'Arbitrator Integrity', in Waibel et al. (eds.), *The Backlash against Investment Arbitration*, 189–251, 202 (the ICC Court exercises veto power over clearly unqualified Party nominees).

agree on that individual, the ICC Court appoints (Article 12(3)). Likewise, if the parties agree to appoint three arbitrators, then each party is allowed to nominate one candidate, and the Court appoints the third arbitrator. If the parties fail to make the three nominations within a previously agreed period of time (usually thirty days), the ICC Court appoints all three members of the tribunal (Article 12(8)) based on the proposal by a national committee or group (Article 13(3)). The backup power to appoint is thus centralised in the ICC Court.

(4) LCIA

Under the London Court of International Arbitration (LCIA) Rules, parties to an arbitration may agree on the identity of their arbitrator (Article 7.1) or on the method of nominating an arbitrator (Articles 7.2–7.3). In all cases, however, the LCIA Court *appoints* all members of a tribunal (Articles 5.6 and 7.1), taking into account any joint nomination or prior agreement, if applicable (Article 5.7). However, in the absence of prior agreement, the rules vest the power of both nomination and appointment to the LCIA Court (Article 7.3). The default number of arbitrators is one, rather than three, unless the parties otherwise agree or the Court finds it necessary to appoint a three-person tribunal (Article 5.8). While the Court must take into account the method and criteria the parties prefer, ultimately authority rests with the Court in appointing the tribunal based on the nature, subject matter and size of the arbitration (Article 5.9). As with the other arbitral rules, the LCIA Rules recognise the importance of impartiality and independence (Articles 5.3–5.4). For example, arbitrators are discouraged from holding the same nationality as one of the parties, where the disputing parties are of different nationalities (Article 6.1).

C. Informal Rules for Selecting Arbitrators

Institutions such as the PCA and ICSID use various tools to help the disputing parties select their arbitrators – without these informal mechanisms being reflected in the arbitration rules themselves. These mechanisms are particularly important for institutional arbitral appointments or appointments by the agreement of the parties – typically concerning the presidents of arbitral tribunals. The arbitral institutions resort to these rules with the (implicit) agreement of the parties.

Arbitral institutions commonly use list procedures in cases in which both disputing parties participate in the selection of arbitrators. Rather than the arbitral institution selecting the presiding arbitrator as a *deus ex machina* without any party input, the arbitral institution draws up a list of three or more names. Such input by the disputing parties with respect to non-party-appointed arbitrators gives parties the sense that this is 'their' tribunal rather than one imposed on them by an arbitral institution. In this way, arbitral institutions routinely consult the parties on their preferred choices for the presiding arbitrator and at times for the tribunal as a whole.[22]

One important dimension according to which we can class informal methods of arbitrator selection is whether they operate simultaneously or sequentially. With simultaneous methods, the disputing parties make their selection at the same time; with sequential methods, their selections are staggered over time. We can distinguish the following selection methods: (1) 'veto-rank' (VR), (2) 'shortlisting' (SL), (3) 'alternate strikes' and (4) 'voting by alternating offers and vetoes' (VAOV).[23]

With veto-rank, the two disputing parties simultaneously receive a list of n potential arbitrators. Each party independently vetoes $(n - 1)/2$ names; each party ranks the remaining $(n + 1)/2$ names. The selected arbitrator is the individual with the minimal sum rank. As we have seen in Section B(2), Article 8(2) of the UNCITRAL Rules follows this model, and this method of selecting arbitrators from a list seems to be commonly used by arbitral institutions, including the ICSID.[24] This procedure involves a formula and an element of judgment on the part of the appointing authority. For instance, if arbitrator X is party 1's first choice and party 2's fifth choice and arbitrator Y is the second choice for both disputing parties, the appointing authority can appoint arbitrator Y.

With shortlisting, one randomly chosen disputing party chooses an odd number of arbitrators, and the other disputing party picks an arbitrator from that shortlist. This procedure encourages the first mover to come up with at least some arbitrators who are likely acceptable compromises to the other party.

With alternate strikes, a sequential mechanism, each disputing party alternatively removes one name from the list of potential arbitrators (an

[22] Cf. M. Kinnear, 'Appointment to Arbitral Tribunals at ICSID', American Bar Association, Section of International Law, *International Arbitration Committee Newsletter*, 1(1) (2013), 35. According to the ICSID Secretary-General, at the appointment stage, the 'practice of ICSID is to support the disputing parties in reaching consensus whenever possible during this process', instead of imposing a tribunal upon them.

[23] De Clippel et al., 'On the Selection of Arbitrators'.

[24] I am grateful to Dirk Pulkowski and Gabriel Bottini for sharing their practical experiences with regard to arbitrator selection with me.

uneven number). The final remaining individual is the arbitrator. A second sequential mechanism is voting by alternating offers and vetoes[25] – a method not currently used in arbitral practice.[26] Under this procedure, the disputing parties take turns in proposing arbitrators. If the arbitrator proposed by one party is rejected by the other party, that arbitrator is removed from the list, and the rejecting party then proposes a name from the remaining list. The procedure continues until a proposal is accepted or only one individual remains on the list of possible arbitrators.

Arbitral institutions frequently use veto rank. Both disputing parties can use strikes to cancel out certain names on the list. However, it is rare for both parties' strikes, in combination, to cancel out all names on the list.[27] Usually one to three arbitrators remain (depending on the length of the list). The disputing parties have an incentive to behave reasonably because if the list procedure fails, then the appointing authority often proceeds to make a direct appointment (in which case the disputing parties have no direct input in the selection of the arbitrator).

Conversely, SL, AS and VAOV do not appear to be used in arbitrator selection at the moment. Notwithstanding, the disputing parties/co-arbitrators may informally use a mechanism similar to VAOV when selecting presiding arbitrators through direct consultations between themselves. The crucial part of the VAOV mechanism is that the list is finite, creating incentives for both disputing parties to act reasonably so as to avoid being stuck with an arbitrator they disfavour.

For example, with the disputing parties' agreement, the PCA uses a modified list procedure to avoid having the list procedure fail.[28] Under this approach, the disputing parties agree in advance to rank arbitrators acceptable to them. Furthermore, they commit not to strike out more than 50 per cent – 1 arbitrators on the list. In this way, the list procedure is guaranteed to succeed, and the appointing authority needs to make a direct appointment from outside the list.

The next section turns to the question of why arbitrator selection is an important feature of investor-State arbitration – both for arbitration outcomes and for the legitimacy of investor-State arbitration.

[25] N. Anbarci, 'Noncooperative Foundations of the Area Monotonic Solution', *Quarterly Journal of Economics*, 108 (1993), 245–58.

[26] De Clippel et al., 'On the Selection of Arbitrators'.

[27] Nevertheless, a disputing Party may not participate in arbitrator selection at all and never return the list put forward by the arbitral institution.

[28] For further details on this procedure, see B. W. Daly, E. Goriatcheva and H. A. Meighen, *A Guide to the PCA Arbitration Rules* (Oxford University Press, 2014), para. 4.22.

D. Why Arbitrator Selection Matters for Outcomes and Legitimacy

Who the parties select as arbitrators is important for how the investment treaty tribunals operate and for the investment treaty regime's legitimacy.[29] The nomination procedure matters because these procedures may encourage the appointment of conflicted arbitrators or arbitrators biased towards host States or investors. Moreover, because arbitral awards are final, the selection of arbitrators is especially important. The parties to investment arbitration cases and especially their counsel spend considerable time and effort to scrutinise the backgrounds of arbitrators, their relationship with the parties, published works and prior appointments before nominating them for arbitral appointments. The time spent by the disputing parties on choosing the right arbitrators suggests that the personality and background of the arbitrator matter for arbitration outcomes. Otherwise, the behaviour of the parties in selecting the right arbitrators for their investment disputes would be irrational.

The nomination of arbitrators matters to the investment arbitration system because it is the *arbitrators* (their expertise, conduct and performance during arbitrations) who give the system part of its institutional legitimacy.[30] The procedural rules found in the ICSID Convention and UNCITRAL Arbitration Rules do not have, on their own, institutional legitimacy, as does trade regimes (namely, the WTO).[31]

The disputing parties seek to appoint individuals they expect to have some favourable predisposition towards their case without rising to the level of challengeable conflict of interest. For instance, parties may favour arbitrators who share a similar cultural or legal background.[32] Conversely,

[29] J. Pauwelyn, 'The Rule of Law without the Rule of Lawyers? Why Investment Arbitrators are from Mars, Trade Adjudicators from Venus', *American Journal of International Law*, 109 (2015), 761–805; see also I. Venzke, 'Investor-State Dispute Settlement in TTIP from the Perspective of a Public Law Theory of International Adjudication', *Journal of World Investment & Trade*, 17 (2016), 374–400.

[30] S. W. Schill, 'Developing a Framework for the Legitimacy of International Arbitration', in A. J. Van den Berg (ed.), *Legitimacy: Myths, Realities, Challenges* (Alphen aan den Rijn, Netherlands: Kluwer Law International, 2015), 789.

[31] Pauwelyn, 'The Rule of Law without the Rule of Lawyers?', 38–40.

[32] D. Bishop and L. Reed, 'Practical Guidelines for Interviewing, Selecting and Challenging Party-Appointed Arbitrators in International Commercial Arbitration', *Arbitration International*, 14 (1998), 395, 401 (factors might include 'religion, economic ideology and social environment, all of which may condition an arbitrator's way of thinking'); N. Blackaby, C. Partasides, M. Hunter and A. L. Redfern, *Redfern and Hunter on International Arbitration*, 5th edn. (Oxford University Press, 2009), para. 4.52.

the disputing parties may also agree on certain desirable characteristics of arbitrators: lawyers vs. non-lawyers, experienced arbitrators, efficient arbitrators, arbitrators with the requisite language competencies and arbitrators who offer good value for money.

The arbitration rules we examined in Section C allow each disputing party to appoint one arbitrator. Such party-appointed arbitrators may represent the interests of the appointing party on arbitral tribunals. The risk is that such arbitrators assume the role of advocates for their appointing party. In extreme cases, party-appointed arbitrators may seek to engineer results favourable to their appointing party. According to one critique, the persistence of party-appointed arbitrators casts doubt on the legitimacy and perceived neutrality of arbitration as an institution for resolving investment disputes impartially.[33]

More generally, arbitrators appointed only for single investment disputes may be tempted to further their own economic interests. A growing number of investment disputes could mean future appointments for the same arbitrators.[34] Furthermore, at least some arbitrators wear multiple hats: they may render decisions (wearing their arbitrator hat) that could benefit them and their clients (wearing their counsel or expert hat) in pending and future arbitrations. According to one view, investment arbitrators form a type of lucrative, self-serving industry with ties to corporations and prominent roles in academia.[35] Only by granting the adjudicators of investment disputes long-term tenure can we ensure that they decide investment disputes not based on their own private interests and are truly independent of the disputing parties.[36]

Some commentators also take the view that the lack of representativeness of investment arbitrators, a trend described in more detail in Section E, could create bias in arbitration outcomes. The lack of diversity among arbitrators is said to contribute to the regime's legitimacy deficit. Critics

[33] E.g. Paulsson, 'The Rule of Law without the Rule of Lawyers?'. But cf. C. H. Brower and C. B. Rosenberg, 'The Death of the Two-Headed Nightingale: Why the Paulsson–van den Berg Presumption that Party-Appointed Arbitrators Are Untrustworthy Is Wrongheaded', *Arbitration International*, 23 (2013), 7.

[34] G. Van Harten, *Investment Treaty Arbitration and Public Law* (Oxford University Press, 2007), chap. 7.

[35] P. Eberhardt and C. Olivet, *Profiting from Injustice: How Law Firms, Arbitrators and Financiers Are Fuelling an Investment Arbitration Boom* (2012).

[36] Van Harten, *Investment Treaty Arbitration and Public Law*; M. Sornarajah, 'The Neo-Liberal Agenda in Investment Arbitration', in W. Shan, P. Simons and D. Singh (eds.), *Redefining Sovereignty in International Economic Law* (Oxford, UK: Hart, 2008), 218.

argue that the homogeneity of arbitrators not only risks creating bias in arbitration outcomes but also undermines one of the fundamental goals of the investment treaty regime, namely, to furnish a neutral forum for the settlement of investment disputes. Increasing diversity is therefore a priority for investment treaty tribunals.[37]

The empirical literature on the relationship between arbitrator background and arbitration outcomes is split. Some studies concluded that there is no verifiable effect of the arbitrator background on arbitral outcome. For example, using both Organisation for Economic Co-operation and Development (OECD) and World Bank standards of 'development status', Susan Franck concluded that there was no statistically significant causal effect of ICSID arbitrator origin on arbitration outcomes.[38] Daphne Kapeliuk found no causal effect of more 'experienced' investor-appointed arbitrators on outcomes.[39] She also rejected the hypotheses that arbitrators are biased towards the party that appointed them, that 'elite' arbitrators do not behave strategically or that they display biases.[40]

A second group of studies affirms a causal relationship between arbitrators and arbitration outcomes. For example, Van Harten tested the effect of arbitrator origin on the substantive outcome of arbitrations by examining trends in legal interpretation. He found that arbitrators favour claimant investors from developed countries.[41] That said, Van Harten argues that the mere *appearance* of bias too undermines the legitimacy of the investment treaty regime. Arbitration not only needs to be fair in fact, but its users also need to regard it as fair.[42]

The next section examines what patterns of appointment the formal rules and informal mechanisms for the selection of ICSID arbitrators have produced.

[37] S. D. Franck, J. Freda, K. Lavin, T. Lehmann and A. Van Aaken, 'The Diversity Challenge: Exploring the Invisible College of International Arbitration', *Columbia Journal of Transnational Law*, 53 (2015), 429–506.

[38] S. D. Franck, 'Development and Outcomes of Investment Treaty Arbitration', *Harvard International Law Journal*, 50 (2009), 435–89.

[39] D. Kapeliuk, 'Collegial Games Analyzing the Effect of Panel Composition on Outcome in Investment Arbitration', *Review of Litigation*, 31 (2012), 267.

[40] D. Kapeliuk, 'The Repeat Appointment Factor: Exploring Decision Patterns of Elite Investment Arbitrators', *Cornell Law Review*, 96 (2010), 47.

[41] G. Van Harten, 'Arbitrator Behaviour in Asymmetrical Adjudication: An Empirical Study of Investment Treaty Arbitration', *Osgoode Hall Law Journal*, 50 (2012), 211–68.

[42] G. Van Harten, 'Perceived Bias in Investment Treaty Arbitration', in Waibel et al. (eds.), *The Backlash against Investment Arbitration*, 433–53.

E. Patterns of ICSID Arbitral Appointments

The homogeneity and skewed distribution of arbitral appointments to ICSID tribunals is striking when compared to World Trade Organisation (WTO) dispute settlement. We might expect that ICSID arbitrators and WTO panellists have similar backgrounds. However, there is considerable variation across the two regimes.[43] Pauwelyn has identified six key characteristics across which investment arbitrators and WTO panellists differ: (1) nationality, (2) professional background, (3) legal expertise, (4) diversity, (5) status and (6) ideology.[44]

Investment arbitrators tend to be high-performing lawyers with the nationality of OECD States. Moreover, on average, they are white, male and highly polarised in their economic and political ideologies (attaching considerable importance to a high degree of investor protection or to extensive room for host States to regulate).[45] To contrast, WTO panellists are more diverse in nationality, originating more frequently from developing countries (52 per cent); they also come disproportionately from government service positions (80 per cent) or have at least some government experience as diplomats or negotiators (88 per cent).[46] Some WTO panellists are not lawyers, whereas virtually all investment arbitrators are. Further, the re-appointment rate for WTO panellists is lower than for investment arbitrators, so no 'elite club' exists among the former group.[47] Finally, WTO panellists are less ideologically polarised than investment arbitrators: the former cannot be easily separated into 'pro-trade' or 'protectionist' ideologies like investment arbitrators – each of which host States or investors repeatedly appoint. Partly this is a function that in the WTO, all appointments of panellists are institutional ones, whereas in investment arbitration, as we have seen, party appointments have traditionally played a prominent role.

This is not to say that there is no overlap at all between investment arbitrators and WTO panellists: some individuals have been appointed to

[43] J. A. Fontura Costa, 'Comparing WTO Panelists and ICSID Arbitrators: The Creation of International Legal Fields', *Oñati Socio-Legal Series*, 1 (2011); P. C. Mavroidis, 'Selecting the WTO Judges' in J. A. Huerta-Goldman, A. Romanetti and F. X. Stirnimann (eds.), *WTO Litigation, Investment Arbitration, and Commercial Arbitration* (Alphen aan den Rijn, Netherlands: Kluwer Law International 2013), 103–14.

[44] Pauwelyn, 'The Rule of Law without the Rule of Lawyers?'.

[45] Puig, 'Social Capital in the Arbitration Market'; M. Waibel and Y. Wu, 'Are Arbitrators Political', Working Paper 2015, available at www.unisg.ch/~/media/internet/content/dateien/unisg/schools/seps/political%20science/pwdresearchseminarwaibelare%20arbitrators%20political20150506.pdf (accessed 16 March 2016).

[46] Pauwelyn, 'The Rule of Law without the Rule of Lawyers?'. [47] *Ibid.*

both investment treaty tribunals and WTO panels. However, the degree of cross-pollination is low and has not changed over time: only 3 per cent of WTO panellists also served as investment (specifically, ICSID) arbitrators.[48] The overlap is higher within the WTO Appellate Body (AB): 40 per cent of the twenty-five AB Members who have served since 1995 have also served on investment tribunals, but typically only after their appointment as an AB Member ended (e.g. Georges Abi-Saab).

The skewed distribution of appointments to ICISD tribunals is underscored by empirical work on arbitrators. Sergio Puig's social network analysis suggests that a core group of twenty-five arbitrators enjoys disproportionate influence on the development of the investment treaty regime.[49] In his account, to understand which individuals shape the investment treaty regime in crucial respects, it suffices to look at twenty-five 'power-brokers' who are at the core of the investment treaty regime. Members of this elite group of twenty-five are, on average, connected to 11.75 other arbitrators in the network.

The core's cultural and legal homogeneity is striking: there are fourteen Europeans, four Latin Americans, three Canadians, one New Zealander and only one US arbitrator. Similarly, among the top ten countries of origin of ICSID arbitrators overall, five are Euro-Atlantic states (United States, France, United Kingdom, Canada and Switzerland) and five Latin American. By contrast, investors, host States and arbitral institutions have rarely appointed African and Asian arbitrators to ICSID tribunals despite significant inward and outward flows of foreign investment to and from Asia in particular (and associated investment disputes).

Table 14.1 provides summary statistics on appointment patterns to ICSID tribunals and shows that appointments are skewed in important respects. Column 1 provides data on presidents on ICSID tribunals – appointed either by agreement of the disputing parties or by ICSID; column 2 on arbitrators appointed by investors and column 3 on arbitrators appointed by host States.

As Table 14.1 shows, women are particularly underrepresented among ICSID arbitrators.[50] That said, Brigitte Stern has accumulated the highest

[48] *Ibid.* [49] Puig, 'Social Capital in the Arbitration Market'.

[50] N. Grossman, 'Sex on the Bench: Do Women Judges Matter to the Legitimacy of International Courts?', *Chicago Journal of International Law*, 12 (2012), 647–85; R. Mackenzie and P. Sands, 'International Courts and Tribunals and the Independence of the International Judge', *Harvard International Law Journal*, 44 (2003), 271–85, 278; G. Van Harten, 'The (lack of) women arbitrators in investment treaty arbitration', *Columbia FDI Perspectives* (2012), 59.

Table 14.1 *Characteristics of ICSID Arbitrators*

	President	I-Arbitrator	HC-Arbitrator
Male	94%	96%	87%
Developing status	22%	21%	40%
Specialist in public international law (PIL)	42%	32%	48%
Full-time academic	37%	25%	37%
Private practice	65%	81%	62%
Legal origin (common)	38%	51%	34%

Source: Waibel and Wu, based on 460 ICSID arbitrators.

number of appointments of *any* ICSID arbitrator. But, overall, the share of female arbitrators is around 5 per cent. Women account for 20 per cent of all ICSID arbitral appointments largely on account of the multiple appointments of both Brigitte Stern and Gabrielle Kaufmann-Kohler.[51] Apart from these two female arbitrators with multiple appointments, women are at the periphery of the arbitration network.

Table 14.1 also shows that host countries are more likely to appoint arbitrators with the nationality of a developing country; those who are specialists in public international law and those who are full-time academics. Conversely, investors are much more likely to select an arbitrator who is in full-time private practice. More than half of all arbitrators selected by investors belong to the common law legal family, whereas that percentage is one-third for host countries. Anthea Roberts has highlighted how paradigms interact in the investment treaty regime.[52] She conceptualises how different epistemic communities, based on their main expertise (public international law specialists versus commercial arbitrators versus public lawyers) and main occupation (academics versus full-time private practitioners versus government lawyers) influence how the investment treaty system operates. Against this background, it is problematic for the regime's legitimacy that arbitrators are predominantly drawn from a small pool that shares similar characteristics, such as the nationality of an OECD country.

51 Puig, 'Social Capital in the Arbitration Market', 205.

52 A. Roberts, 'Clash of Paradigms: Actors and Analogies Shaping the Investment Treaty System', *American Journal of International Law*, 107 (2013), 45–94.

The barriers to entry for those aspiring to sit as arbitrators in investment treaty arbitration have traditionally been high. As we have seen, the investment treaty network is a highly unequal one. Investment arbitrators do not seem to be created equally. The rise of superstar arbitrators has created a divide between one-time and repeat players with multiple appointments – the latter group constituting the group of 'elite' arbitrators.[53] Puig finds that 10 per cent of repeat arbitrators account for 50 per cent of all appointments. The flip side is that more than 50 per cent of all ICSID arbitrators are 'single shooters' – only ever appointed to a single ICSID tribunal.[54]

This skewed distribution reflects that both institutional and especially party appointers favour arbitrators with a track record of appointments. Despite investing considerable time and money in selecting the 'right' arbitrator, party appointers operate under incomplete information and may not be able to forecast how a freshman arbitrator would behave once appointed. Risk aversion and path dependency may play an important role in skewing the appointment process towards 'insiders'. Disputing parties choose experienced arbitrators because other parties chose them previously. Through this self-reinforcing dynamic, the influence of a small group of superstar arbitrators grew as the regime expanded and gained in salience.

These skewed patterns of appointment to ICSID tribunals have already led to a significant degree of treaty change with respect to the mechanisms for appointing arbitrators, and more far-reaching proposals such as the establishment of a permanent investment tribunal are currently on the table. The overall aim of these reform efforts is to give States greater control and influence over arbitrator selection – arguably the biggest price of all for States seeking to wrest back control over the investment treaty system.[55] Some of the most important recent treaty changes and reform proposals concerning the selection of arbitrators are discussed in Section F.

F. Avenues for Reform and Treaty Change

This section considers the European Commission's proposal for a new approach to dispute settlement in the Trans-Atlantic Trade and

[53] Kapeliuk, 'The Repeat Appointment Factor'.

[54] Puig, 'Social Capital in the Arbitration Market'.

[55] S. W. Schill, *Reforming Investor-State Dispute Settlement (ISDS): Conceptual Framework and Options for the Way Forward, Think Piece for E15 Task Force on Investment Policy* (Geneva: International Centre for Trade and Sustainable Development (ICTSD) and World Economic Forum, 2015).

Investment Partnership (TTIP). It also examines several new mechanisms for arbitrator selection in recent trade and investment agreements, such as the Canada-EU Free Trade Agreement (CETA) and the EU-Vietnam Free Trade Agreement (EVFTA), that adopt this proposal.

Investor-State dispute settlement in the TTIP has been a source of much debate since the European Union and the United States commenced negotiations for this mega-regional agreement in 2013.[56] In light of the criticisms of the current system of appointing arbitrators for each investment dispute, especially the centrality of party appointments, proposals for reform have proliferated. While the suggestions have been many (including the establishment of an appellate court to enhance the system's legitimacy or even abandoning the entire system altogether[57]), the reform of most relevance to the current discussion is a standing investment tribunal modelled after the WTO dispute settlement system.[58] Indications are that the United States is unwilling to contemplate investor-State dispute settlement on the model proposed by the European Union.[59]

So far, the European Union has been the champion of such reform and, jointly with Canada in the form of the CETA, took an important step towards that goal in early 2016. According to EU Trade Commissioner Cecilia Malström, traditional investor-State arbitration with exclusive control by the disputing parties over the selection of arbitrators is 'not fit for purpose in the 21st century'.[60] Following consultations on investor-State dispute settlement by the European Commission in 2014 (with many responses hostile to investor-State dispute settlement), the

[56] S. Hindelang, *Study on Investor-State Dispute Settlement (ISDS) and Alternatives of Dispute Resolution in International Investment Law* (2014); European Parliament, 'Negotiations for the Transatlantic Trade and Investment Partnership (TTIP)', 2015; European Union Committee, *The Transatlantic Trade and Investment Partnership* (London: House of Lords 2014); Schill, *Reforming Investor-State Dispute Settlement*; J. Kleinheisterkamp and L. Poulsen, *Investment Protection in TTIP: Three Feasible Proposals* (Global Economic Governance Programme, Policy Brief, December 2014).

[57] C. Tams, 'An Appealing Option? The Debate about an ICSID Appelate Structure', *Beiträge zum Transnationalen Wirtschaftsrecht*, 57 (2006).

[58] European Commission, 'Investment in TTIP and Beyond – The Path for Reform: Enhancing the Right to Regulate and Moving from Current Ad Hoc Arbitration towards an Investment Court', 11: 'The objective would be to multilateralise the court either as a self-standing international body or by embedding it into an existing multilateral organisation.'

[59] S. W. Schill, 'Editorial: US versus EU Leadership in Global Investment Governance', *Journal of World Investment & Trade*, 17 (2016), 1–6.

[60] S. Donnan, 'EU Calls for Global Investment Court', *Financial Times*, 5 May 2015.

Commission aims to create a permanent court in lieu of arbitrators selected by the disputing parties on an ad hoc basis.

The European Commission's proposal foresees a 'two-tiered' structure or 'Investment Court System'.[61] Firstly, the European Union proposes a Tribunal of First Instance, which would be comprised of fifteen judges (selected jointly by the European Union and the United States) drawn from EU, US and third-country nationals. The States parties would vet judges on the first instance 'roster' to ensure that they have the appropriate qualifications for adjudicating international investment disputes. Importantly, in a departure from the traditional approach, the disputing parties would not be able to choose the composition of their arbitral tribunals from the roster of arbitrators. Rather, the tribunal members would be randomly selected from that roster – and include one member from the European Union, the United States and a third party for each dispute.[62]

Secondly, the proposal also incorporates an 'Appeals Tribunal' of six members – two from each nationality (United States, European Union and third state). The Appeals Tribunal would be modelled after the WTO's Appellate Body: the members of the Appeals Tribunal would be specialists in public international law and investment law.

Among the possible advantages of a move to a permanent investment court, in lieu of ad hoc arbitral tribunals for investment disputes, are the following: it could assist in achieving greater coherence in arbitral outcomes by establishing precedents issued by a single, standing tribunal,[63] and it could alleviate legitimacy concerns related to arbitrator independence and the reality or perception of arbitrator bias.[64] The effects of the creation of such an institution on the investment treaty regime will depend crucially on design features of the investment court system,

[61] European Commission, 'Commission Proposes New Investment Court System for TTIP and other EU Trade and Investment Negotiations', press release of 16 September 2015 (the binding code of conduct for arbitrators was a first in investor-State arbitration).

[62] DG for Trade's 'Reading Guide to the Draft Text on Investment Protection and Investment Court System in the TTIP', 16 September 2015.

[63] Though coherence may not be a desirable objective for all stakeholders in the investment treaty regime, particularly if it is coherence with respect to a set of substantive rules that do not favour that stakeholder's interests. For instance, a coherent interpretation of fair and equitable treatment that grants investors a very high level of protection is not in the interest of states with significant investment inflows.

[64] Schill, Reforming Investor-State Dispute Settlement (ISDS), 8. *See also* K. P. Sauvant, *The Evolving International Investment Law and Policy Regime: Ways Forward* (Geneva: International Centre for Trade and Sustainable Development (ICTSD) and World Economic Forum, 2016), 29.

such as who appoints tribunal members, for what period are they appointed, is re-appointment possible and which concurrent or previous professional activities are incompatible with appointment to the tribunal. Notwithstanding, the establishment of a permanent investment tribunal is not a panacea for States seeking to reclaim control over 'run-away' investment tribunals. Conceivably, it could even lead to a further loss of control by States as a result of the higher degree of delegation of decision-making authority to such a permanent tribunal as compared to ad hoc arbitral tribunals.[65]

The September 2014 version of the CETA was among the first investment treaties to include rules on arbitrator selection that significantly varied from the usual arbitration rules.[66] It adopted a roster approach. Failing agreement by the disputing parties on the composition of the arbitral tribunal, the parties could request that the chair of the CETA Joint Committee draw the arbitrators from the 'List of Arbitrators' by lottery (Article 29.7(3)). The Joint Committee at its first meeting would have drawn up the List of Arbitrators (Article 29.8(1)). This list was designed to include at least fifteen arbitrators nominated by Canada and the European Union. The list was to be divided into three sub-lists of at least five individuals: one sub-list for European nationals, one for Canadian nationals and one for nationals of neither party (from which the presidents of the arbitral tribunals will be chosen). As Dupuy and Maupin highlight, the 'real proof of the CETA innovations will be in the pudding of the CETA states' joint roster designations, [whether] the designated arbitrators are persons of high repute – known for their legal acumen, open-mindedness, and sense of duty to justice, rather than for their particular investor or state sympathies'.[67]

[65] See also Chapter 15.

[66] 'Consolidated CETA Text', published on 26 September 2014. NAFTA's roster of presiding arbitrators (Article 1124(4) of the NAFTA) is a precursor (however, it has not become operational because the NAFTA states did not fill the roster); see G. Van Harten, 'Comments on the European Commission's Approach to Investor-State Arbitration in TTIP and CETA', *Osgoode Legal Studies Research Paper Series Paper* (2014), 30, 46. The NAFTA Parties undertook to maintain a roster of forty-five potential presiding arbitrators by consensus. Unusually, in addition to the requirements for ICSID arbitrators under the ICSID Convention, these individuals need to be also 'experienced in international law and investment matters'.

[67] P.-M. Dupuy and J. A. Maupin, 'Of Wit, Wisdom and Balance: Reflections on the Tokyo Resolution of the Institut de Droit International', in D. D. Caron, S. W. Schill, A. Cohen Smutny and E. Triantafilou (eds.), *Practising Virtue: Inside International Arbitration* (Oxford University Press, 2015), 717.

The revised version of the CETA of February 2016 goes much further than the September 2014 version. It does away with arbitral appointments altogether.[68] Instead, in keeping with the European Union's proposal for a standing international investment court in relation to the TTIP, it establishes a standing investment tribunal composed of fifteen judges (Article 8.27 of the CETA). They serve five-year terms, renewable once. Three members of this tribunal will hear each investment dispute, made up of one Canadian national, one EU national and one national of a third country. The revised text also foresees the establishment of an appellate mechanism (Article 8.28 of the CETA). The European Union regards the CETA as a bilateral stepping stone towards a multilateral investment court.[69]

CETA, the European Union–Singapore Free Trade Agreement (EUSFTA) and the European Union–Vietnam Free Trade Agreement EUVFTA also formally incorporate a 'Code of Conduct for Arbitrators and Mediators'.[70] The codes explicitly set out requirements for experience and independence, as well as disclosure of all interests on matters likely to affect the arbitrator's independence (Annex 29B(3)). Article 8.30 of the CETA provides that members of the tribunals cannot participate in deciding disputes involving a 'direct or indirect conflict of interest'. Crucially, upon appointment, they shall refrain from 'acting as counsel or as party-appointed expert or witness in any pending or new investment dispute under this or any other international agreement'.[71]

G. Conclusion

Arbitrator selection under the current default rules in leading arbitration rules privileges arbitrator appointments aligned with the preferences of

[68] Comprehensive Economic and Trade Agreement (CETA) between Canada and the European Union and Its Member States, February 2016 (not yet ratified); cf. also 'EU-Vietnam FTA Agreed Text' (not yet ratified), January 2016, available at http://trade.ec.europa.eu/doclib/press/index.cfm?id=1437 (accessed 16 March 2016).

[69] European Commission, 'CETA: EU and Canada Agree on New Approach on Investment in Trade Agreement', press release, 29 February 2016.

[70] Annex 29B (CETA); Annex 15B (EUSFTA) and Annex II (EVFTA); European Commission, 'Investment Provisions in the EU-Canada Free Trade Agreement (CETA)', press release, 3 December 2013.

[71] A French proposal (aimed primarily at the TTIP) goes even further. It prescribes a cooling-off period of five years such that tribunal members cannot work as a private attorney for a period of five years prior to appointment and five years after stepping down from the tribunal; M. Fekl, *Vers un nouveau moyen de régler les différends entre États et investisseurs* (2015).

the disputing parties. More recently, the investment regime – triggered by legitimacy concerns – has moved beyond the interests of the disputing parties to take account of broader systemic concerns. This partial shift away from party autonomy, or its possible abandonment altogether in investment treaty arbitration, is one way in which the pendulum is likely to swing towards an accrued role for States in this regime. Indeed, as this chapter has shown, this shift is already underway. Treaty parties have begun to seek a more vocal role in arbitrator selection.

As States seek to re-balance the investment treaty regime and maintain more control over central features of this regime such as arbitrator appointments, we are likely to see the default rules for the appointment of arbitrators evolve towards mandatory rules that are not at the disposition of disputing parties (such as a requirement for all arbitrators to be drawn from a roster) or even more pronounced shifts such as the creation of permanent investment tribunals for particular treaties as an interim step towards a multilateral investment court. To the extent that ad hoc appointments of arbitrators by the disputing parties survive in investment treaty arbitration, States might increasingly insist that they choose the individuals eligible for such appointments. The main mechanism is for States to restrict the disputing parties to appointments from a roster of arbitrators.

The changing rules for arbitrator appointments may affect the relative attractiveness of investment treaty arbitration/dispute settlement before a permanent investment tribunal vis-à-vis dispute settlement before national courts. They could also affect the make-up of investment tribunals in significant ways. Future investment tribunals may well come to resemble WTO panels, with more diverse panels and more adjudicators with experience in government.[72]

As this chapter has shown, appointment mechanisms that account for the parties' preferences as to the decision-makers may well leave both disputing parties better off than mechanisms that appoint arbitrators on a rotating basis or purely based on institutional appointments. As a result, party input into the selection process – an emanation of the traditional principle of party autonomy – is valuable to the disputing parties. To that extent, the shifts on appointing arbitrators currently under way could dent the attractiveness of investor-State arbitration to investors.

[72] Pauwelyn, 'The Rule of Law without the Rule of Lawyers?'.

15

Arbitrator (Issue) Challenge

What's the Real Issue?

STEPHAN WILSKE AND MELANIE ECKARDT

Just another room, just another town, same old crazy people hanging around.[1]

A. How Arbitrator Challenges Contribute to Current Criticism of Investment Dispute Settlement

International investment law truly has experienced an enormous boost in the twenty-first century. Likewise, its investor-State dispute settlement mechanism has been frequently used during this time by economic players advised by global law firms.[2] Surprisingly, this area of law has been treated with indifference by the public until recently. This has changed drastically. After being a 'sleeping beauty' for decades – well known to its admirers but unnoticed by its opponents – international investment law and investor-State dispute settlement (ISDS) stepped into the centre of public attention mainly in connection with the Transatlantic Trade and Investment Partnership (TTIP), an envisaged comprehensive free trade agreement (FTA) between the United States and the European Union.[3] Negotiations of FTAs such as TTIP, but also the EU-Canada Comprehensive Economic and Trade Agreement (CETA) and the Trans-Pacific Partnership

[1] Nils Lofgren, 'Shine Silently', A&M, 1979.

[2] C. Harris, 'Arbitrator Challenges in International Investment Arbitration', *Transnational Dispute Management*, 5(4) (2008), 1; see also R. Michaels, 'Roles and Role Perceptions of International Arbitrators', in W. Mattli and T. Dietz (eds.), *International Arbitration & Global Governance* (Oxford University Press, 2014), 47 (calling international commercial arbitration a 'success story in many regards').

[3] 'Erfolg für TTIP-Gegner', *Handelsblatt*, 23 April 2015; 'Aufstand gegen die Wirtschaft', *Handelsblatt*, 10 April 2015; and – somewhat esoteric – 'TTIP Protestors to "Exorcise" King & Spalding's London Office', *The Lawyer*, 30 April 2015.

Agreement (TPP)[4], have initiated a heated public and academic debate on the legitimacy and the *raison d'être* of this system with its ISDS mechanism.[5] The degree of criticism has varied from concerns regarding its democratic legitimacy and its necessity to accusations of it being a money-making machine for a small circle of financial beneficiaries and of it being a shadow justice (*Schattenjustiz*), a 'cartel' or even the 'mafia'.[6]

In such circumstances, the growing number of (partly successful) bias challenges has contributed to recent criticism by exacerbating mistrust in private investment dispute settlement.[7] Trust in the independence and impartiality of decision makers, however, is a major prerequisite for the continuing viability of investment arbitration. Recent proposals for disqualification under the ICSID Convention were based on grounds of so-called issue conflict or issue challenges. In such an issue challenge, an arbitrator appears inappropriately predisposed to the subject matter in dispute or to one of the parties and thereby raises doubts as to his or her ability to approach the dispute with an open mind.[8] The phenomenon of issue challenges has acutely heated up the discussion on the lack of transparency in ISDS and has aggravated the current legitimacy crisis of international

[4] The text of the Trans-Pacific Partnership was released by New Zealand on 5 November 2015. Despite all public criticism, it includes a comprehensive investor-State dispute settlement mechanism.

[5] For recent criticism regarding the TPP in particular voiced by American presidential candidate Hillary Clinton, see 'Hillary Clinton Opposes Obama's Trans-Pacific Trade Deal', *New York Times*, 23 October 2015.

[6] 'Es wird ein Sonderklagerecht für die Wirtschaft eingeführt', *Handelsblatt*, 10 April 2015, 54. 'Geheimgerichte', *Frankfurter Allgemeine Zeitung*, 23 October 2014; R. A. Lorz, 'The Transnational Trade and Investment Partnership and Investment-Dispute Settlement: Observations on a Paradox', Columbia FDI Perspectives No. 132, 13 October 2014; for a summary of the most detailed and varied criticism, see S. Wilske and M. Raible, 'The Arbitrator as Guardian of International Public Policy? Should Arbitrators Go Beyond Solving Legal Issues?' in C. Rogers and R. Alford (eds.), *The Future of Investment Arbitration* (Oxford University Press, 2009), 249, 253 *et seq.*

[7] A. Ross, 'Time to Rename "Issue Conflicts"?', *Global Arbitration Review News*, 24 April 2015; J. Paulsson, 'Metaphors, Maxims, and Other Mischief: The Freshfields Arbitration Lecture', *Arbitration International*, 30(4) (2014), 615; D. Thomson, 'Stern Faces New Challenge over Repeat Appointments', *Global Arbitration Review News*, 31 March 2015.

[8] International Council for Commercial Arbitration of the American Society of International Law (ICCA), 'Discussion Draft', 10 March 2015, para. 2. Following the release of this 'Discussion Draft', the ICCA Task Force held a special panel during the ASIL Annual Meeting on 9 April 2015 to present a summary of the outcomes and to instigate discussion; see R. Teitelbaum, 'ICCA Review', *ICCA Newsletter*, August 2015, 4; e.g. an arbitrator (Brigitte Stern) currently faces a new challenge due to her previous six appointments for Venezuela: Thomson, 'Stern Faces New Challenge over Repeat Appointments'.

investment law. Against this background, the topic of arbitrator issue challenge merits a closer analysis.

B. Institutional Background to Arbitrator (Issue) Challenge

(1) Appointment of Arbitrators: Qualities to Look for in an Arbitrator

Since 'the quality of the arbitral tribunal ... makes or breaks the arbitration',[9] the appointment of the 'right' arbitrator is critical for a successful arbitration or – to use the words of William 'Rusty' Park – '[j]ust as in real estate the three key elements are 'location, location, location', so in arbitration the applicable trinity is 'arbitrator, arbitrator, arbitrator'.[10] One reason for making a careful, judicious choice regarding an arbitrator is to avoid disappointment with the arbitral process *per se* as a dispute resolution mechanism. In addition, and more importantly, the wrong choice of an arbitrator establishes a logical pre-condition for a later challenge. Indeed, despite likely pressure from private investors and the host State alike, the arbitrator of 'best quality' seems to be the most credible one by preserving his or her independence and accountability.[11] Before expounding on arbitrator challenges in investment arbitration, as an introduction, we will provide a brief synopsis of qualities to look for in an arbitrator.

Generally speaking, 'arbitrators are selected and appointed from a market for international arbitration services.'[12] But what should a party look for on the shelves of this market? As regards the qualities to look for, little guidance can be obtained from institutional rules because of the

[9] A. Redfern, M. Hunter, N. Blackaby and C. Partasides, *Redfern and Hunter on International Arbitration*, 5th edn. (Oxford University Press, 2009), para. 4.14; see also S. Wilske, 'The Ailing Arbitrator: Identification, Abuse and Prevention of a Potentially Dangerous Delaying and Obstructing Tool', *Contemporary Asia Arbitration Journal*, 7 (2014), 279, 281; see D. Hacking, 'Arbitration Is Only as Good as Its Arbitrators', in S. Kröll, L. A. Mistelis, P. Perales Viscasillas and V. Rogers (eds.), *Liber Amicorum Eric Bergsten* (Alphen aan den Rijn, Netherlands: Kluwer Law International 2011), 223, 224.

[10] W. W. Park, 'Income Tax Treaty Arbitration', *George Mason Law Review*, 10 (2002), 803, 813. On arbitrator selection, see Chapter 14.

[11] Responding to criticism of the 'Perfectionists' that 'consider arbitrators to be "the businessman's court"... [with an] alleged lack of independence and accountability': Wilske and Raible, 'The Arbitrator as Guardian', 249, 253, 256; see regarding the arbitrators' role in international commercial arbitration in general Michaels, 'Role and Role Perceptions', 47, 48.

[12] C. Rogers, *Ethics in International Arbitration* (Oxford University Press 2014), para. 2.11.

wide discretion granted to the parties. The ICSID Convention defines three minimum requirements for the choice of arbitrators: qualifications, nationality and no prior involvement in the dispute. Article 14(1) of the ICSID Convention calls for arbitrators 'of high moral character and recognized competence in the fields of law, commerce, industry or finance, who may be relied upon to exercise independent judgment'.[13] For the parties' selection process, 'high moral character' refers to an arbitrator's state of mind and work ethic, while 'competence' refers to an arbitrator's academic or professional qualifications.[14] Since assessing an arbitrator's state of mind naturally can be a difficult task, parties are likely to turn to his or her publications, prior awards and available public statements when making their assessment of his or her suitability. As required under all major arbitration rules alike,[15] an arbitrator must be independent.[16] In addition, although not explicitly laid down in the text, the ICSID Convention also requires an arbitrator to be impartial.[17]

Moreover, the nationality of the arbitrators is an important criterion in investor-State disputes in particular.[18] Unless the parties agree otherwise, in ICSID arbitration, the majority of the arbitral tribunal must be of a different nationality than the parties in order to avoid any appearance of preferential treatment or bias in this regard.[19] Along the same lines, arbitrators should not have any prior involvement in settling the dispute, for example, as a mediator, so as to ensure that their first look at a case will be impartial and open minded.

13 For the appointment of arbitrators, Article 14(1) of the ICSID Convention is applicable according to Article 40(2) of the ICSID Convention.

14 J. Crawford, 'Challenges to Arbitrators in ICSID Arbitrations', *Confronting Global Challenges: From Gunboat Diplomacy to Investor-State Arbitration*, PCA Peace Palace Centenary Seminar, 11 October 2013, 2.

15 Article 11(1) of the ICC Rules; Article 5(2) of the LCIA Rules; Articles 11 and 12(1) of the UNCITRAL Rules; see P. W. Egger, 'Independence, Impartiality and Disclosure in International Arbitration: Recent Developments', M. Roth and M. Geistlinger (eds.), *Yearbook on International Arbitration*, Vol. I (2010), 103, 105.

16 Article 14(1) of the ICSID Convention.

17 M. Kinnear and F. Nitschke, 'Disqualification of Arbitrators under the ICSID Convention and Rules, in C. Giorgetti (ed.), *Challenges and Recusals of Judges and Arbitrators in International Courts and Tribunals* (Leiden/Boston: Brill 2015), 34, 50; Crawford, 'Challenges to Arbitrators', 1; C. Giorgetti, 'Challenges of International Investment Arbitrators: How Does It Work, and Does It Work?', *World Arbitration & Mediation Review*, 7 (2013), 303, 306.

18 E.g. Article 6(7) of the UNCITRAL Rules; Article 13(5) of the ICC Rules; Article 6(1) of the LCIA Rules.

19 Article 39 of the ICSID Convention.

It is worth noting, however, that when having a say in the process, each party will seek or lean towards the appointment of a person it expects to be somewhat favourably predisposed to its case without actually being biased.[20] Admittedly, parties can dispose of this allegation if in fact

> [T]he typical arbitrator is cosmopolitan; he [or she] speaks at least English and French and frequently additional languages, and appears worldwide. His [or her] national origin is frequently regarded as a handicap and may preclude him [or her] from proceedings in which his [or her] compatriots are parties.[21]

So does nationality no longer matter? On the contrary, people prefer something they are familiar with. Consequently, parties favour arbitrators who share a similar cultural or legal background that they consider to be favourable to their case, at least as long as the arbitrator is not yet fully perceived as a 'global citizen'.[22] In addition to general geographical vicinity, such a background might encompass factors such as 'religion, economic ideology and social environment, all of which may condition an arbitrator's way of thinking'.[23]

As regards further hard facts, to ensure an effective and functional arbitration, other aspects the parties might want to consider when 'choosing' their arbitrator could be his or her expertise in international investment, public international law and international trade law, as well as the arbitrator's reputation.[24] Likewise, when agreeing on a presiding arbitrator, a wise choice might seek to balance the deficiencies or, to put it positively, to augment the strengths of the arbitral tribunal to reflect a wide range of the necessary expertise.

Apart from having experience in conducting or presiding over complex international arbitrations, parties should also take into account pure technicalities such as time constraints, that is, the arbitrator's availability to focus on the case and act in a timely manner – or with a slightly

[20] M. Hunter, 'Ethics of the International Arbitrator', *Arbitration*, 53 (1987), 219, 223.

[21] Michaels, 'Role and Role Perception', 47, 54 (footnotes omitted).

[22] For the arbitrator's *entre deux chaises* as national and global citizen, see Michaels, 'Role and Role Perception', 47, 50 *et seq.*; D. Bishop and L. Reed, 'Practical Guidelines for Interviewing, Selecting and Challenging Party-Appointed Arbitrators in International Commercial Arbitration', *Arbitration International*, 14 (1998), 395, 401; Redfern and Hunter, *International Arbitration*, paras. 4.52 *et seq.*

[23] Bishop and Reed, 'Practical Guidelines', 395, 402.

[24] Redfern and Hunter, *International Arbitration*, paras. 4.65 *et seq.*; M. Kinnear, 'Appointment to Arbitral Tribunals at ICSID', American Bar Association, Section of International Law, *International Arbitration Committee Newsletter*, 1 (2013), 35; Rogers, *Ethics in International Arbitration*, para. 2.35.

different emphasis – his or her physical and mental fitness.[25] Depending on the specific facts of a case, special qualifications, such as special technical knowledge, certain language skills or level of proficiency, could be taken into consideration.

(2) *The Legal Standard for the Challenge of Arbitrators*

Since arbitration is a private dispute resolution mechanism mostly without judicial review and appeal,[26] the integrity of the arbitral process is of the utmost importance for ensuring its acceptance by the parties, its efficiency and its legitimacy.[27] Therefore, the quality of the arbitrators, that is, their independence and impartiality throughout the proceedings, is essential. Challenges, that is, the removal of an arbitrator, can be described as

> [A] device to maintain minimal standards of independence and impartiality in arbitrators. Challenge is an exceptional and serious mechanism; it is a process that has been rarely initiated and even more rarely has resulted in a decision.[28]

While noting that a challenge should be an extraordinary recourse, recent developments sow doubt about its 'rare initiation'.[29] In contrast: concerns are voiced that challenges are overused and that most of the challenges are unmeritorious.[30]

25 Wilske, 'The Ailing Arbitrator', 279, 284; Kinnear, 'Appointment at ICSID', 35.

26 See Chapter 5.

27 Cristani, 'Challenge and Disqualification of Arbitrators in International Investment Arbitration: An Overview', *The Law and Practice of International Courts and Tribunals*, 13 (2014), 153; C. M. Baker and L. Greenwood, 'Are Challenges Overused in International Arbitration?', *Journal of International Arbitration*, 30 (2013), 101, 102.

28 D. Caron, L. Caplan and M. Pellonpää, *The UNCITRAL Arbitration Rules: A Commentary* (Oxford University Press, 2006), 187.

29 S. Finizio and C. Salas, 'Expert View: Challenges to Party-Appointed Arbitrators: Crying Foul', *Commercial Dispute Resolution*, 4 (2013), 64: 'Of 26 published treaty decisions on challenges to arbitrators, 24 have been since 2007.'

30 Harris, 'Arbitrator Challenges', 1; only seven per cent of challenges brought under the ICC Rules and approximately ten per cent under the LCIA Rules result in a removal of the arbitrator, Baker and Greenwood, 'Are Challenges Overused?', 101, 102, 109; under the ICSID Convention, only one out of forty-two challenges succeeded by 2012; see K. Daele, *Challenge and Disqualification of Arbitrators in International Arbitration* (Alphen aan den Rijn, Netherlands: Kluwer Law International 2012), para. 4-084; B. Vasani and S. Palmer, 'Challenge and Disqualification of Arbitrators at ICSID: A New Dawn?', *ICSID Review*, 30 (2015), 194, 195.

The balance between the need for the institution of challenge, on the one hand, and avoiding an adverse effect on the efficiency of the arbitral proceedings, on the other, must be carefully kept, especially in the field of investor-State arbitration, where the number of challenges (without merit) has increased significantly and bears the touch of a wilful obstruction of the arbitral process, that is, a deliberate guerrilla tactic.[31] Before analysing the topic of issue challenge, the twin qualifications of arbitrators and the challenge mechanism in investment arbitration together with the 'normal' grounds for challenge, that is, in contrast to arbitrator issue challenges, will be introduced.

(a) Applicable Standards and Procedure

The arbitrator's independence and impartiality – the so-called twin qualifications – are rooted in the principle of *nemo iudex in causa sua* combined with the mantra-like maxim that 'justice must not only be done but must be seen to be done.'[32] Both are of particular importance in the investment arbitration context because in most, if not all, cases public interest is involved, and the decision might have far-reaching effects on the home State's economy and citizens, which often distinguishes it from commercial arbitration.[33]

[31] E.g. Argentina brought challenges against the entire tribunal, the presiding arbitrator or the other party-nominated arbitrator in *Sempra Energy International* v. *Argentine Republic* (entire tribunal); *BG Group plc* v. *Argentine Republic* (party-nominated arbitrator), *National Grid plc.* v. *Argentine Republic* (party-nominated arbitrator), and *Suez and others* v. *Argentine Republic* (twice against the same party appointed arbitrator); none of them was successful. Similarly, Venezuela has initiated approximately ten challenges in ICSID arbitrations since 2010; see S. Perry, 'Fortier under Fire Again for *Valasek* Ties', *GAR News*, 15 April 2015; for Venezuela's latest challenge of Mr Yves Fortier after his co-arbitrator Mr Alexis Mourre resigned following an earlier challenge by Venezuela in *Fábrica de Vidrios Los Andes, C.A. and Owens-Illinois de Venezuela, C.A.* v. *Bolivarian Republic of Venezuela*, ICSID Case No. ARB/12/21; for the use of challenge proceedings as a guerrilla tactic, see G. J. Horvath, S. Wilske, H. Nettlau and L. Leinwather, 'Categories of Guerrilla Tactics', in G. J. Horvath and S. Wilske (eds.), *Guerrilla Tactics in International Arbitration* (Alphen aan den Rijn, Netherlands: Kluwer Law International 2013), 3, 10 *et seq.*

[32] Baker and Greenwood, 'Are Challenges Overused?', 101, R. K. L. Chung, 'Conceptual Framework of Arbitrators' Impartiality and Independence', *Arbitration*, 80 (2014), 3.

[33] Often, however, the distinctions between investment arbitration and commercial arbitration are exaggerated for self-serving purposes; see S. Wilske, M. Raible and L. Markert, 'International Investment Treaty Arbitration and International Commercial Arbitration: Conceptual Difference or Only a "Status Thing"?', *Contemporary Asia Arbitration Journal*, 1 (2008), 213; see e.g. decisions involving the Argentina crisis; Harris, 'Arbitrator Challenges', 1.

In ICSID proceedings,[34] the procedure for challenges differs from other institutional rules. The challenge is not decided by an arbitral institution or a designated appointing authority.[35] Though not free from criticism,[36] under the ICSID Convention, the challenge is decided by the co-arbitrators unless the sole arbitrator, the majority of the tribunal or the entire tribunal is challenged.[37] The decision is reached in the absence of the arbitrator in question and by means of an informal, non-adversarial procedure.[38] If the majority of the tribunal or the tribunal in its entirety is called into question,[39] the challenge is decided by the Chairman of the ICSID Administrative Council(Chairman).[40]

Any challenge must be brought 'promptly, and in any event before the proceeding is declared closed'.[41] The grounds for challenge should be laid down in a formal document addressed to ICSID's Secretary-General,

34 The following analysis will focus on the rules under the ICSID Convention since it is the institution most frequently used for investment disputes but will refer to other arbitration rules if necessary and if this offers added value.

35 See e.g. Article 11(3) of the ICC Rules (ICC Court); Article 10(2) of the LCIA Rules (LCIA Court); Article 11 of the UNCITRAL Rules.

36 Voiced criticism mainly questions the uninfluenced decision of the truncated tribunal since the investment arbitration community, the 'elitists', is very small and its ties are strong; see L. Malintoppi, 'Independence, Impartiality, and Duty of Disclosure of Arbitrators', in Peter Muchlinski et al. (eds.), *The Oxford Handbook of International Investment Law* (Oxford University Press, 2008), 789, 828.

37 See Article 58 of the ICSID Convention; Redfern and Hunter, *International Arbitration*, paras. 4.116 *et seq.*

38 See Rule 9(4) of the ICSID Arbitration Rules; see also C. Schreuer, L. Malintoppi, A. Reinisch and A. Sinclair (eds.), *The ICSID Convention: A Commentary*, 2nd edn. (Cambridge University Press, 2009), Article 58, para. 10.

39 See e.g. *Quiborax S.A., Non-Metallic Minerals S.A. and Allan Fosk Kaplún* v. *Plurinational State of Bolivia*, ICSID Case No. ARB/06/2, Decision on Respondent's Proposal for Disqualification of the Three Members of the Tribunal of 6 July 2010; proposal to disqualify the entire tribunal in *Victor Pey Casado and President Allende Foundation* v. *Republic of Chile* (unpublished), which was rejected for the president of the tribunal and accepted for the co-arbitrator who had not yet stepped down on recommendation by the Secretary-General of the PCA; see Schreuer et al., *The ICSID Convention*, Article 58, para. 16.

40 See Article 58 of the ICSID Convention. According to Article 5 of the ICSID Convention, the chairman is *ex officio* the president of the World Bank. In case of a possible conflict, for example, if the challenge relates to a former World Bank employee, under unwritten institutional practice, the chairman will consult the Secretary-General of the PCA, as happened in *Generation Ukraine, Inc.* v. *Ukraine*, ICSID Case No. ARB/00/9, Award of 16 September 2003, paras. 4.8 *et seq.*; and *Siemens AG* v. *Argentine Republic*, ICSID Case No. ARB/02/8, Award of 6 February 2007, paras. 31 *et seq.*

41 Rule 9(1) of the ICSID Arbitration Rules. In the event that the grounds for challenge only become known after the closing of the proceedings, such grounds have to be addressed in a request for the annulment of the award according to Rule 50 of the ICSID Arbitration Rules.

who then forwards it to the members of the tribunal, the other party and the chairman, if applicable.[42] Given that the proposal for disqualification must be raised between the constitution of the tribunal and the closing of the proceedings,[43] the notion of a 'prompt' challenge is somewhat broad but nevertheless subjects any challenge to certain time constraints. While noting that saving any reasons for disqualification for the annulment proceedings is not considered timely,[44] no definite time limit exists.[45] Hence, parties should file their proposal for disqualification as early as possible after the grounds become known to them.

In order to increase transparency, ICSID requires reasoned and well-founded decisions and encourages their publication with the consent of the parties.[46] The standard publication of challenge decisions, as will be emphasised later, would be a helpful and necessary development in international investment arbitration since it would clarify the applicable standard under the ICSID Convention and enhance consistency and predictability.

(b) 'Normal' Grounds for Challenge

There are roughly two scenarios of 'normal' allegations of bias. The first scenario involves connections and relationships between the arbitrator and a party or its counsel.[47] As a general prerequisite, there must be some objective nexus between the party and the arbitrator. Whereas some cases may be clear,[48] other cases are not as clear-cut, and a qualitative element should be required in addition to the objective relationship since

42 Rule 9(1) and (2) of the ICSID Arbitration Rules.

43 See Article 57 of the ICSID Convention, Rule 9(1) of the ICSID Arbitration Rules; see also Schreuer et al., *The ICSID Convention*, Article 57, para. 8.

44 See *CDC Group plc* v. *Republic of Seychelles*, ICSID Case No. ARB/02/14, Decision on Annulment of 29 June 2005, para. 53.

45 In *Suez, Sociedad General de Aguas de Barcelona S.A. and InterAguad Servicios Integrales de Agua S.A.* v. *Argentine Republic*, ICSID Case No. ARB/03/17, Decision on the Proposal for the Disqualification of a Member of the Arbitral Tribunal of 22 October 2007, paras. 18 *et seq.*, the other members of the tribunal found that filing a challenge fifty-three days after the purportedly disqualifying event was not prompt.

46 See Rule 48(4) of the ICSID Arbitration Rules; Schreuer et al., *The ICSID Convention*, Article 48, paras. 120 *et seq.*; ICSID Secretariat, 'Suggested Changes to the ICSID Rules and Regulations', Working Paper, 12 May 2005, 9; ICSID Secretariat, 'Possible Improvements of the Framework for ICSID Arbitration', Discussion Paper, 2004, 9.

47 For a detailed analysis, see L. Markert, 'Challenging Arbitrators in Investment Arbitration', *Contemporary Asia Arbitration Journal*, 3 (2010), 237, 254 *et seq.*; Daele, *Challenge*, 398 *et seq.*

48 See *Holiday Inns S.A./Occidental Petroleum Corporation* v. *Kingdom of Morocco*, ICSID Case No. ARB/72/1, in which one of the arbitrators accepted a position as a non-executive director of claimant.

> The fact of an alleged connection between a party and an arbitrator in and of itself is not sufficient to establish a fact that would establish a manifest lack of that arbitrator's impartiality and independence. Arbitrators are not disembodied spirits dwelling on Mars, who descend to earth to arbitrate a case and then immediately return to their Martian retreat to await inertly the call to arbitrate another. Like other professionals living and working in the world, arbitrators have a variety of complex connections with all sorts of persons and institutions.[49]

Regarding the requirement of a qualitative element, any business relationship of the arbitrator or his or her firm must have an element of proximity as well as an element of time. Hence, one should evaluate how close the business contact is and whether the relationship is in the past or still active and ongoing. In the annulment proceedings in *Vivendi* v. *Argentina*, it was disclosed that the firm of one of the arbitrators was advising one of the parties in a minor, unrelated matter without any involvement of that arbitrator. The remaining arbitrators did not have any doubts as to the arbitrator's unbiasedness since he had immediately and fully disclosed the relationship, had no personal attorney-client relationship with the claimants and the advice concerned a specific transaction in contrast to general legal or strategic advice.[50] To determine when a certain *de minimis* threshold is crossed as regards an arbitrator's business relationship to a party, the so-called *Suez* test – which establishes four helpful criteria for any challenge decisions: proximity, intensity, dependence and materiality – might come in handy.[51]

The second scenario concerns a possible relationship with a party's counsel. In *SGS* v. *Pakistan*, Pakistan's appointed arbitrator had previous

[49] Using these words, the other members of arbitral tribunal dismissed the second proposal for disqualification on different grounds against Professor Gabrielle Kaufmann-Kohler (under the ICSID Convention and Article 10(1) of the UNCITRAL Arbitration Rules) in *Suez et al.* v. *Argentina*, para. 32; in a nutshell, the challenge was sought on the basis that the arbitrator was a supervisory board member of an investment bank that was a small-stake shareholder in two of the claimants. It was confirmed that the investment bank held participations in a variety of investments. The arbitrator had no knowledge of this fact and had no influence on the bank's investment decisions. Moreover, the bank's remuneration resulting from that participation was *de minimis* compared to its overall portfolio.

[50] *Compañia de Aguas del Aconquija S.A. and Vivendi Universal S.A.* v. *Argentine Republic*, ICSID Case No. ARB/97/3, Decision on the Challenge to the President of the Committee of 3 October 2001, para. 26; the ad hoc committee also clarified in this decision that the provisions of the ICSID Convention and the ICSID Arbitration Rules dealing with the disqualification of arbitrators apply, *mutatis mutandis*, to annulment proceedings in case a party asks for the disqualification of a member of the ad hoc committee; *ibid.*, para. 8.

[51] *Suez et al.* v. *Argentina*, para. 35.

(successful) experience as counsel in other arbitrations in which Pakistan's counsel had served as the presiding arbitrator.[52] Pointing out the close (investment) arbitration community, the unchallenged arbitrators found the need for 'something more' that would reliably indicate that an arbitrator might not exercise independent judgment in the case at hand.[53] Similarly, challenges on the basis of multiple appointments as arbitrator for one party or by the same law firm in unrelated cases have been unsuccessful.[54] Hence, it should be noted that it is rather difficult for a party to establish the 'something more' that is the straw that breaks the camel's back, since this must be supported by solid evidence instead of mere inferences.

C. Application Scenarios of Arbitrator (Issue) Challenge in Current Practice

Turning to a special area of challenges that seems to be *en vogue*, we will briefly critically assess the notion of arbitrator issue challenge before we review the different scenarios in practice in search of current best practice.

(1) The Unhelpful Vagueness of the Notion of 'Arbitrator (Issue) Challenge'

In investment arbitration, an increasing number of so-called 'issue challenges' have arisen with the potential to affect the credibility of the system as a whole.[55] Before reviewing case law in which issue challenges have

[52] *SGS Société Générale de Surveillance S.A.* v. *Islamic Republic of Pakistan*, ICSID Case No. ARB/01/13, Decision on Claimant's Proposal to Disqualify Arbitrator of 19 December 2002.

[53] *SGS* v. *Pakistan*, paras. 402, 404.

[54] *Azurix Corp.* v. *Argentine Republic*, ICSID Case No. ARB/01/12, Decision on the Application for Annulment of the Argentine Republic of 1 September 2009, para. 9, challenge brought by Argentina regarding Mr Andrés Rigo Sureda also serving as arbitrator in *Siemens* v. *Argentine Republic*; see also *ConocoPhillips Company et al.* v. *Bolivarian Republic of Venezuela*, ICSID Case No. ARB/07/30, Decision on the Proposal to Disqualify L. Yves Fortier, QC, Arbitrator of 27 February 2012; *National Grid plc.* v. *Argentine Republic*, UNCITRAL, Decision on the Challenge to Mr Judd L. Kessler, 3 December 2007; for Ms Brigitte Stern's multiple appointments by Venezuela and its external counsel, see Thomson, 'Stern Faces New Challenge over Repeat Appointments'.

[55] See e.g. *Blue Bank International & Trust (Barbados), Ltd.* v. *Bolivarian Republic of Venezuela*, ICSID Case No. ARB/12/20, Decision on the Challenge to José María Alonso of 12 November 2013; *Caratube International Oil Company LLP and Devincci*

occurred, it is necessary to define the notion of arbitrator issue challenge, which must not be misinterpreted as the similar notion of conflicts of interest. Apart from the topic of arbitrator challenge as such, the vague term 'arbitrator issue challenge' is, on its own, rather unhelpful when it comes to providing an idea of which problems it covers. While there is no accepted definition, it was explained in a recent decision that

> The basis for . . . a challenge invoking an 'issue conflict' is a narrow one as it does not involve a typical situation of bias directly for or against one of the parties. The conflict is based on a concern that an arbitrator will not approach an issue impartially, but rather with a desire to conform to his or her own previously expressed view.[56]

Thus, without giving a clear understanding of the notion of issue challenges, it can be inferred that 'arbitrator issue challenge' refers to an arbitrator's understanding of a case in connection with previous cases. As understood by scholars and practitioners alike, 'issue challenge' generally involves an allegation that an arbitrator is biased or predisposed not towards a party but regarding a specific (legal or factual) issue central to the dispute.[57] Parties generally develop this concern based on an arbitrator's former rulings, his or her activities as counsel, his or her academic writings or general public expressions of his or her view, which give the (reasonable) impression that he or she adheres to his or her existing views regarding certain legal or factual aspects and, in doing so, is not impartial.[58] Dealing, basically, with an arbitrator's experience or involvement in the subject area, such terms as 'doctrinal predisposition' or 'prejudgment' have been considered as an alternative to better outline its contents.[59]

The topic of arbitrator issue challenge is particularly relevant in investment arbitration as compared to international commercial arbitration. The persons involved in investment cases – for better or for worse – form

Salah Hourani v. *Republic of Kazakhstan*, ICSID Case No. ARB/13/13, Decision on the Proposal for Disqualification of Mr Bruno Boesch of 20 March 2014; *CC/Devas (Mauritius), Ltd., Devas Employees Mauritius Private Limited, and Telcom Devas Mauritius Limited* v. *Republic of India*, UNCITRAL, Decision on Respondent's Challenge to the Honourable Mark Lalonde as Presiding Arbitrator and Professor Francisco Orrego Vicuña as Co-Arbitrator of 30 September 2013.

56 *CC/Devas* v. *India*, para. 36; see also A. Ross, 'Time to Rename "Issue Conflicts"?', 7.

57 ICCA, 'Discussion Draft', para. 2.

58 *Ibid.*

59 The notion of 'doctrinal predisposition' was discussed but then rejected by the ICCA Task Force arguing that no arbitrator will or should approach a case with a mental *tabula rasa* but instead should bring into the proceedings his or her educational and regional background and experience, for example, which is a desired consequence; see *ibid.*, para. 18.

a small and elite community constantly switching between the roles of counsel and arbitrator in different matters. In contrast to commercial arbitration, awards and decisions are regularly made public, giving the interested reader an idea of the decision-making of the tribunal and, in so doing, giving them 'ammunition'[60] for a possible challenge. Without having a binding system of precedents *per se*, consecutive tribunals tend to rely on previous decisions as a reference in order to achieve consistency and to place their decisions on a firm foundation to achieve greater legitimacy. Investment cases generally involve similar or even identical standards which have to be interpreted and applied by the arbitrators.[61] Thus, the legal issues arising out of investment treaties are relatively specialised in nature but at the same time very similar as regards content. This situation raises concerns regarding an arbitrator's impartiality relating to his or her previous decisions matching or resembling the issues of a later arbitration. As a result, how to approach the topic of arbitrator issue challenge is not to search for a comprehensive – naturally vague – definition but instead to analyse situations in practice in which the threshold of a natural predisposition based on experience is overstepped.

(2) *Is There a Current Best Practice?*

When taking a closer look at the possible content, different issue challenge scenarios – which could give rise to a successful challenge in investment arbitration – can be identified in practice. With a view towards predictability and credibility as objectives in ISDS, it makes sense to establish a threshold, that is, to give shape to the ambiguous notion of issue challenge by defining when the line is crossed.[62] Therefore, it is equally important that the ISDS system not be paralysed by frequent issue challenges to arbitrators without merit whilst effectively responding to justified concerns in respect of an arbitrator's predisposition.

Pursuing this line of analysis, three different scenarios will be distinguished in the following: an arbitrator's scholarly publications or general public expressions of his or her opinion; an arbitrator's professional affiliation, that is, his or her firm might represent clients in different

[60] Markert, 'Challenging Arbitrators', 237, 361. [61] ICCA, 'Discussion Draft', para. 10.

[62] See E. Cárenas and D. W. Rivkin, 'A Growing Challenge for Ethics in International Arbitration', in G. Asken (ed.), *Liber Amicorum Robert Briner* (Paris: ICC Publishing, 2005), 191; M. Hwang and K. Lim, 'Issue Conflict in ICSID Arbitration', *Transnational Dispute Management*, 8 (2011), 1.

proceedings with similar legal or factual questions; as well as an arbitrator's prior involvement as counsel or arbitrator.

(a) Prior Academic Publications and Public Expressions of Opinion

While noting the importance of voicing academic views and opinions on substantive legal issues on a general level, a distinction must be made between this and commenting on specific aspects of a case for which an arbitrator has been nominated.[63] Taking into account his or her prior publications or public statements, the arbitrator must be legitimately expected to decide each case with an open mind on the basis of the specific facts and provisions before him or her. However, it is worth noting that the emphasis should be on an open mind and not an empty one. Or, in the words of the US Supreme Court, 'Proof that a justice's mind at the time he [or she] joined the court was a tabula rasa … would be evidence of lack of qualification, not lack of bias.'[64]

Perenco v. *Ecuador*[65] is an example of a successful challenge regarding an arbitrator's expression of public opinion for or against a party. In this case, Judge Charles N. Brower, the acting arbitrator appointed by claimant, made critical remarks regarding Ecuador's non-compliance with interim measures ordered by two ICSID tribunals in an interview[66] after the commencement of the arbitration.[67] Thus, when giving the public interview, according to the Secretary-General of the Permanent Court of Arbitration (PCA), the 'combination of the words chosen … and the context in which he [the arbitrator] used them'[68] tipped the scales of

[63] *IBA Guidelines on Conflicts of Interest in International Arbitration*, 23 October 2014: Under item no. 4.1.1, 'Green List' of the 2014 *IBA Guidelines on Conflicts of Interest*, the previous publication of legal opinions concerning an issue arising in the arbitration does not trigger any duty of disclosure.

[64] *Republican Party of Minnesota* v. *White*, 536 US 765 (2002), 777, 778.

[65] *Perenco Ecuador, Ltd.* v. *Republic of Ecuador and Empresa Estatal Petróleos del Ecuador (Petroecuador)*, ICSID Case No. ARB/08/6, Decision on the Challenge Concerning Judge Charles N. Brower of 8 December 2009.

[66] The article is titled 'A World-Class Arbitrator Speaks!' and was published in the August 2009 issue of *The Metropolitan Corporate Counsel*.

[67] After rendering a decision on provisional measures in *Perenco* v. *Ecuador*, in this publicised interview, Judge Brower mentioned Ecuador's non-compliance with provisional measures ordered by ICSID tribunals while at the same time making reference to 'recalcitrant host countries' and Libya's expropriations which led to the 'hot oil' litigation; *Perenco* v. *Ecuador*, para. 27.

[68] *Ibid.*, para. 48.

raising justifiable doubts as to the arbitrator's impartiality in the view of a reasonable and informed third party.[69]

Based on prior academic publications, it was argued in *Urbaser* v. *Argentina* that an arbitrator's decision on important legal aspects of the case was already predisposed.[70] As regards the applicable standard, however, the remaining arbitrators expressed that the issue must be

> [S]pecific and clear enough that a reasonable informed third party would find that the arbitrator will rely on such opinions without giving proper consideration to the facts, circumstances, and arguments presented by the Parties in this proceeding.[71]

It was the view of the remaining arbitrators that, in addition to academic writing, without further supporting evidence in the form of a certain connection between the voiced position and the party, taking a position does not suffice to dispute an arbitrator's ability to impartially decide the individual dispute based on the particular facts.[72] Following this line of reasoning, favourably referring to a third party's view in a public presentation, which would be to one party's detriment in a certain case, is likewise not sufficient to prove the arbitrator's lack of impartiality.[73] Whereas academic writing in

69 Similarly, in *Burlington Resources, Inc.* v. *Republic of Ecuador*, ICSID Case No. ARB/08/5, Decision on the Proposal for Disqualification of Professor Francisco Orrego Vicuña of 13 December 2013, para. 80, the arbitrator was successfully disqualified for his written critique of respondent's counsel's disclosure of information regarding a prior case. Hence, the line between making a general statement and making specific reference to a case was crossed by painting an unfavourable picture of or criticising one party and its counsel.

70 *Urbaser S.A. and Consorcio de Aguas Bilbao Bizkaia, Bilbao Biskaia Ur Partzuergoa* v. *Argentine Republic*, ICSID Case No. ARB/07/26, Decision on Claimant's Proposal to Disqualify Professor Campbell McLachlan, Arbitrator of 12 August 2010, paras. 21 *et seq.*: the challenge of Professor Campbell McLachlan resulted from two of his publications (the book *International Investment Arbitration: Substantive Principles*, which he co-authored with Laurence Shore and Matthew Weiniger in 2007, and a journal article, 'Investment Treaties and General International Law', in *International & Comparative Law Quarterly* (2008), 361) allegedly favouring respondent's position with respect to important issues in the present case, for example, the application of most favoured nation (MFN) clauses to dispute settlement provisions and the arbitrator's comment on the necessity defence in the *CMS* decision by the annulment committee.

71 *Urbaser* v. *Argentina*, para. 44.

72 *Ibid.*, para. 45. Regarding even critical views on issues relevant to a particular case, this view was supported in *ST-AD GmbH* v. *Republic of Bulgaria*, Enforcement of Arbitral Award, Higher Regional Court of Thüringen, 21 November 2013; see 'Bulgaria Obtains Enforcement of Costs Award: Court Dismisses Investor's Belated Allegations of Arbitrator's Bias Due to Issue-Conflict', *IA Reporter*, 14 February 2014, para. 3.

73 *Repsol S.A. and Repsol Butano S.A.* v. *Argentine Republic*, ICSID Case No. ARB/12/38, Decision on the Proposal for Disqualification of Arbitrators Francisco Orrego Vicuña and Claus von Wobeser of 13 December 2013, rejected by the President of the ICSID

and of itself is not sufficient to warrant disqualification, it could amount to a pre-judgment that crosses the line when combined with other circumstances relevant to the particular case. In the only successful challenge decision based on scholarly publications, *CC/Devas* v. *India*, one of the arbitrators publicly defended the approach he had taken on a certain topic in a prior award that was likely to become relevant in present proceedings.[74] By publicly defending his view, the arbitrator created – in the opinion of the president of the International Court of Justice (ICJ) – the impression that he would automatically seek to confirm his view in the present case without considering the facts with an open mind.[75] Hence, a successful challenge might be possible on the basis of an arbitrator's prior public statements or publications if they are more than just general remarks and appear to indicate that his or her views are set in stone.

(b) Concurrent Activities as Counsel: A Possible Conflict with Acting as Arbitrator?

Concerns with regard to an arbitrator's impartiality could also be based on the arbitrator's former activities as counsel. In *St Gobain* v. *Venezuela*, claimant's concern was that one arbitrator might argue for Venezuela

> [B]ecause he [the arbitrator] has argued the same, or similar, issues in favor of Argentina in the past and potentially in the future, and in doing so, that he will not have sufficient regard to the merits of this case.[76]

The unchallenged arbitrators did not see the challenge as substantiated since '[i]t is at the core of the job description of legal counsel . . . that they

Administrative Council, paras. 26 *et seq.*, 86; in another unpublished decision of *Saipem S.P.A.* v. *People's Republic of Bangladesh*, ICSID Case No. ARB/05/7, Decision on Jurisdiction and Recommendation on Provisional Measures of 21 March 2007, Mr Christoph Schreuer's scholarly writing was also not found sufficient by itself; see Schreuer et al., *The ICSID Convention*, Article 57 para. 32.

74 *CC/Devas* v. *India*, para. 58: The reason for the challenge by Respondent was that both arbitrators (Professor Orrego Vicuña and the Honourable Marc Lalonde) had served together on two tribunals (*CMS* v. *Republic of Argentina* and *Sempra* v. *Argentine Republic*) which dealt with the issue of 'essential security interest' that was possibly relevant to the current case. Additionally, Professor Vicuña defended his view on this issue in an article following the awards.

75 *CC/Devas* v. *India*, para. 64: 'The later article in particular suggests that despite having reviewed the analyses of three different annulment committees, his [Professor Vicuña's] view remained unchanged.'

76 *Saint-Gobain Performance Plastics Europe* v. *The Bolivarian Republic of Venezuela*, ICSID Case No. ARB/12/13, Decision on Claimant's Proposal to Disqualify Mr Gabriel Bottini from the Tribunal under Article 57 of the ICSID Convention of 27 February 2013, paras. 77 *et seq.*

present the views which are favorable to their instructor and highlight the advantageous facts of their instructor's case.'[77] The tribunal was right to distinguish between taking up arguments as counsel in previous proceedings or as arbitrator in an award, since the former does not necessarily represent the counsel's personal view, while the latter might.

This can be different, however, if the activities as arbitrator and as counsel coincide. In the well-known case of *Telekom Malaysia* v. *Ghana*, one of the arbitrators, Professor Emmanuel Gaillard, represented a client in an annulment proceeding in which Ghana was the respondent while simultaneously serving as arbitrator in a case in which Ghana was relying on that award. After Professor Galliard resigned from his position as counsel, the deciding authority saw no further grounds for tension.[78] In *Blue Bank* v. *Venezuela*, the concurrent service as arbitrator and counsel was regarded as grounds for challenge – even for two different persons belonging to the same law firm – if there is overlap between the issues and respondent states involved.[79] In this case, a partner of Baker & McKenzie's Madrid office was appointed as arbitrator, while lawyers from two other offices of the firm acted as counsel against Venezuela in a different investment arbitration.[80] In addition to a possible financial interest deriving from the firm's global remuneration system for partners, the arbitrator could decide, based on the similarity of the issues involved, on questions relevant to the other case handled by the firm.[81]

77 *Saint-Gobain* v. *Venezuela*, para. 80. Previous activities as counsel were also not seen as sufficient in *Universal Compression International Holdings, S.L.U.* v. *The Bolivarian Republic of Venezuela*, ICSID Case No. ARB/10/9, Decision on the Proposal to Disqualify Professor Brigitte Stern and Professor Guido Santiago Tawil, Arbitrators of 20 May 2011.

78 District Court of The Hague, Civil Law Section, Provisional Measures Judge, Challenge No. 13/2004, Petition No. HA/RK 2004, 667; and District Court of The Hague, Civil Law Section, Provisional Measures Judge, Challenge No. 17/2004, Petition No. JA/RK 2004, 778.

79 *Blue Bank* v. *Venezuela*, paras. 67 *et seq.*; in *Grand River Enterprises Six Nations, Ltd. et al.* v. *United States of America*, NAFTA/UNCITRAL, concerns regarding concurrent duties as arbitrator and advisors of parties in an international forum were confirmed as grounds for challenge, but the assertion that representation of a party is tantamount to supervising students on a similar topic was rejected; see letter from ICSID Secretary-General Ana Palacio to Professor James Anaya, 23 October 2007, available at http://ita.law.uvic.ca (accessed 25 February 2016).

80 *Longreef Investments A.V.V.* v. *Bolivarian Republic of Venezuela*, ICSID Case No. ARB/11/5.

81 *Blue Bank* v. *Venezuela*, para. 68. Unfortunately, the challenge decision did not consider the possibility of an 'ethical wall' shielding the arbitrator from the firm's activity in the other case.

In addition, although aware of the issue of concurrent service as counsel and arbitrator, that is, the 'double hat' dilemma, the International Bar Association (IBA) Arbitration Committee refrained from including it in the 2014 'IBA Guidelines' and instead only touched on the topic in the Introduction.[82] Under the 'IBA Guidelines', it is left to the arbitrator himself or herself to decide whether to disclose circumstances that might give rise to justifiable doubts as to his or her impartiality based on his or her having a 'dual role'.[83] As a result, while previous services as party representative in similar circumstances seem to be acceptable, the simultaneous service as arbitrator and counsel raises justifiable doubts as to an arbitrator's ability to render an impartial decision.[84]

(c) Multiple or Repeat Appointments: Prior Involvement of Arbitrators in Similar Factual Circumstances

A different scenario is multiple appointments in cases with similar factual circumstances. This scenario similarly raises concerns regarding an arbitrator's impartiality and independence. As regards impartiality, an arbitrator's ability to render an unbiased decision with an open mind might be called into question due to his or her consecutive involvement with the same or at least similar substantive and procedural issues. At least it seems understandable that such an arbitrator (in particular, if he or she is a busy one) would cut short the analysis of a standard legal problem that he or she has recently already given considerable thought to when reaching a particular solution. Jan Paulsson eloquently addressed this concern by stating, 'We long for shortcuts. Lazy thinking is so sweet.'[85] However, one might wonder whether another term for this condition is not simply 'experience' and his or her most valuable asset, seeing as the arbitrator has already thought through some or all of the major issues in investment arbitration and was appointed for that very reason.

In addition, multiple appointments by the same party or law firm might negatively affect an arbitrator's independence if they appear to

[82] E. Zuleta and P. Friedland, 'The 2014 Revision to the IBA Guidelines on Conflicts of Interest in International Arbitration', *Dispute Resolution International*, 9 (2015), 55, 61; see *IBA Guidelines*, 'Introduction to Part II', para. 6.

[83] Zuleta and Friedland, 'The 2014 Revision to the IBA Guidelines', 55, 61.

[84] At the recent ICCA-HKIAC summit in May 2015, Mr Nassib Ziadé and Mr V. V. Veeder, both participating in a panel discussion, agreed that arbitrators who are hearing a case should not act as counsel in other investment treaty cases simultaneously; K. Karadelis, 'Hong Kong Summit Focuses on the South-South Trade', *GAR News*, 14 May 2015.

[85] Paulsson, 'Metaphors', 615, 618.

be an arbitrator's main source of income.[86] In such a scenario, the arbitrator might have a substantial financial interest in the outcome of the cases. In light of this, it has been suggested that the ICSID issue guidelines regulating the repeated appointments of certain individuals to remove any doubts as to their impartiality.[87]

In *Tidewater* v. *Venezuela*, a challenge based on multiple appointments of an arbitrator by the respondent state was rejected. The sole fact of several appointments by the same party in – concurrent or consecutive – cases dealing with similar legal or factual issues did not suffice to raise justifiable doubts as to an arbitrator's impartiality.[88] With regard to multiple appointments, another challenge was recently brought against the arbitrator appointed by claimant, Mr Bernard Hanotiau, in *Aktau Petrol* v. *Kazakhstan* and declined by its co-arbitrators.[89] Despite the non-disclosure of the disqualification proposal's basis, it is conspicuous that Mr Hanotiau served in two other cases where treaty jurisdiction clauses similar to the one in the present case have been at issue.[90] More importantly, these jurisdiction clauses were interpreted favourably to claimants by the arbitral tribunals, rejecting the requirement of litigation in the host State's domestic courts prior to arbitration.[91]

A different assessment might be warranted in cases where the involved facts are so similar that an arbitrator might be prejudiced due to the knowledge he or she gained during his or her other involvement. Here the concern does not so much stem from the similarity of the facts but from an external knowledge that is exclusive to this

[86] Regarding Professor Brigitte Stern's record of appointments by Venezuela and the law firm Foley Hoag, see Thomson, 'Stern Faces New Challenge over Repeat Appointments'; S. Perry, 'Stern Challenged over Montenegro Appointments', *GAR News*, 1 May 2015.

[87] Karadelis, 'Hong Kong Summit Focuses on the South-South Trade'.

[88] *Tidewater, Inc. et al.* v. *Bolivarian Republic of Venezuela*, ICSID Case No. ARB/10/5, Decision on Claimant's Proposal to Disqualify Professor Brigitte Stern, Arbitrator, 23 December 2010, paras. 64 *et seq.* Another challenge against the same arbitrator on the multiple involvements was likewise rejected in *Universal* v. *Venezuela*, paras. 83, 84.

[89] *Aktau Petrol Ticaret A.S. and Som Petrol Ticaret A.S.* v. *Republic of Kazakhstan*, ICSID Case No. ARB/15/8, Decision on Proposal of Disqualification of Arbitrator Bernard Hanotiau, 9 November 2015 (unpublished); D. Thomson, 'An Open Mind, Not a Blank Mind'; 'Hanotiau Survives Challenge by Kazakhstan', *GAR News*, 26 November 2015.

[90] These cases were *Muhammet Çap & Sehil Inşaat Endustri ve Ticaret Ltd. Sti.* v. *Turkmenistan*, ICSID Case No. ARB/12/6; and *Rumeli Telekom A.S. and Telsim Mobil Telekomunikasyon Hizmetleri A.S.* v. *Republic of Kazakhstan*, ICSID Case No. ARB/05/16; Thomson, 'An Open Mind, Not a Blank Mind'.

[91] L. E. Peterson, 'Kazakhstan Makes a Move to Unseat Bernard Hanotiau in Pending ICSID Arbitration', *IA Reporter*, 22 July 2015.

arbitrator. Applying this line of reasoning, a challenge succeeded in *Caratube* v. *Kazakhstan* when the remaining arbitrators inferred that the challenged arbitrator might be 'privy to information that would possibly permit a judgment based on elements not in the record in the present arbitration'.[92] This view was confirmed in *EnCana* v. *Ecuador* for an arbitrator sitting in parallel proceedings involving the same bilateral investment treaty.[93] Thus, the concern does not arise from the multiple appointments as arbitrator but from the arbitrator's access to privy information in cases involving the same or very similar factual circumstances or legal issues.

(3) Critical Evaluation of Current Practice

It is certainly true that investment arbitration must strive for a high level of legitimacy and credibility, in particular, in the absence of an appeal mechanism, in order to safeguard the authority of tribunals. However, the current debate and the booming number of arbitrator issue challenges[94] raise doubts as to whether all the challenges brought are actually driven by a party's justifiable doubts concerning an arbitrator's impartiality. As a consequence, in light of the challenge proceedings analysed, it would be wrong to assume that every initiated challenge is evidence of a party's doubts in respect of an arbitrator's independence or impartiality.[95] Instead, it must be critically noted that in certain instances the challenge procedure is quite openly used as a tactic to delay the proceedings.[96] If 'delay' is considered to be synonymous with 'control',

[92] *Caratube* v. *Kazakhstan*, para. 89.

[93] *EnCana Corporation* v. *Republic of Ecuador*, UNCITRAL, Partial Award on Jurisdiction of 27 February 2004, para. 43, referring to *Occidental Exploration and Production Company* v. *Republic of Ecuador*, LCIA Case No. UN3467.

[94] See note 55; Vasani and Palmer, 'Challenge', 194; M. Kirtland and B. Sabahi, 'Recent Challenges to Arbitrators in Investment Treaty Cases: Is There an Emerging Trend?', *16(1) IBA Arbitration News 2011*, 172; Hwang and Kim, 'Issue Challenge', 1.

[95] Harris, 'Arbitrator Challenges', 1, 13.

[96] C. Giorgetti, 'Challenges of Arbitrators in International Disputes: Two Tribunals Reject the "Appearance of Bias" Standard', *Proceedings of the American Society of International Law*, 16 (2012), 20, referring to the proceedings in *Abaclat and Others* v. *Argentine Republic*, ICSID Case No. ARB/07/5, in which the latter challenged two arbitrators on the day each side was supposed to file its submission; S. Wilske, 'Arbitration Guerrillas at the Gate: Preserving the Civility of Arbitral Proceedings when the Going Gets (Extremely) Tough', *Austrian Yearbook of International Arbitration* (2011), 315, 316; S. Luttrell, *Bias Challenges in International Commercial Arbitration: The Need for a 'Real Danger' Test* (Alphen aan den Rijn, Netherlands: Kluwer Law International, 2009), 3.

then, indeed, such issue challenges represent a viable means for the state to 'reassert control' over the proceedings by delaying them.

Regarding a challenge based on an arbitrator's academic writing, scholarly publications of a more general nature should not be seen as negatively affecting an arbitrator's impartiality. Instead, access to publicly available decisions and commentaries of writers with practical experience is important for the further development of investment law. Or, to put it differently, should academic writing in investment arbitration be dominated by bookworms, ivory tower residents and writers who have never been privy to the decision-making process of either an investor or a host State? Or should every publication by an arbitrator be followed by the disclaimer, 'For the avoidance of doubt, I will not express any views. In fact, I have no views. In the event that anything I will say nevertheless would be deemed to constitute a view, such view is not mine.'[97] In-depth knowledge of the practice and decision-making process can be invaluable and should not be replaced by the more theoretical writings of pure academics.[98]

Thus, it should be vigorously avoided that the impending danger of a challenge discourages an arbitrator from producing academic writing that is sufficiently detached from a particular case.[99] To the contrary, arbitrators should be able to voice critical views in order to improve the current investment system. Accordingly, what should be decisive for a challenge's chances of success is the character of an arbitrator's arbitration-related writing, such as, for example, the professional context and the pursuit of academic independence.

Likewise, the complaint of repeated service as arbitrator or as counsel without further inferences seems to be in contrast with predictability and legal certainty – other values desired by the parties when choosing their

97 See Nils Eliasson's droll disclaimer at the IBA Annual Conference in Tokyo on 24 October 2014, as reported by Sarah Grimmer, 'Investment Arbitration', *Arbitration News*, 20(2) (September 2015), 20.

98 Admittedly, in the words of Nobel Prize laureate 2016 Bob Dylan, a writer who has nothing to say often has nothing to lose; that is, he or she can speak or write openly without tactical manoeuvring; see 'Like a Rolling Stone', *Columbia Records* (1965) ('When you ain't got nothing, you got nothing to lose. You're invisible now; you've got no secrets to conceal'). However, this should not be taken as an argument for leaving academic writing exclusively to the 'ivory tower' residents either – in particular, as some professorial writing in the field of investment arbitration is often a barely concealed application to investors or host States for appointment of the author as an expert or arbitrator.

99 This view was confirmed in *Urbaser* v. *Argentina*, para. 48; see also Schreuer et al., *The ICSID Convention*, Article 57, para. 32, regarding the case *Saipem* v. *Bangladesh*; *Suez et al.* v. *Argentina*, para. 36.

dispute resolution mechanism and arbitrator.[100] What remains necessary is that from the point of view of an objective third party, the arbitrator still appears capable of distancing himself or herself from his or her prior service.

D. The Way Forward: Possible Solutions and Limitations

Having regard to recent discussions, the search for possible solutions instead of stand-alone criticism is the preferred way forward with a view to the continued success of international investment arbitration. The obligatory publication of challenge decisions (and the underlying reasoning) would be a logical starting point. This would provide positive support in the current discussion on transparency in the investment arbitration regime.[101] More importantly, the publication of challenge decisions would further clarify the meaning of the standards applicable to the arbitrator's independence and impartiality under the ICSID Convention and other arbitration rules, thereby creating greater legal certainty. Likewise, if they knew a decision on a given challenge was going to be publicly available, arbitrators would be encouraged to thoroughly substantiate this decision, which would also enhance its quality.

Another idea would be to tackle the issue of possible challenges right at the beginning of arbitration. As mentioned earlier, the community from which arbitrators in investment arbitration are chosen is (still) a relatively small and exclusive circle. A positive consequence is that this results in a group of people with great expertise. Yet, as touched on earlier, it raises concerns about the decisions-makers' impartiality and independence.[102] The tension between expertise and bias leads to a paradox. On the one hand, a party appoints 'its' arbitrator from the 'circle' in order to achieve

[100] In search of predictability regarding the party-nominated arbitrator, the ironic reversal of an arbitrator issue challenge was brought forward to the US courts, where Argentina requested that an award be set aside, arguing that in the award the arbitrator had decided differently than he previously had with regard to the necessity defense; see *Republic of Argentina* v. *BG Group PLC*, Petition to Vacate or Modify Arbitration Award, 715 F.Supp. 2d 108 (DDC 2010) (No. 08-0485 (RBW)), 2008 WL 6047403.

[101] J. Sackmann, 'Im Schatten von CETA und TTIP', *SchiedsVZ*, 2015, 15; S. W. Schill, 'Transparency as a Global Norm in International Investment Law', Kluwer Arbitration Blog, 15 February 2014; K. Yannaca-Small, 'Transparency and Third Party Participation in Investor-State Dispute Settlement Procedures', OECD Working Papers on International Investment, No. 2005/1; see, in particular with respect to challenge decisions, ICCA, 'Discussion Draft', para. 165.

[102] See Section B(2)(a).

maximum certainty and predictability as to how the arbitrator will decide certain legal issues central to the case. Recently, a party even challenged its arbitrator in set-aside proceedings because the arbitrator had adopted a different view in other proceedings with respect to the same issue.[103] Obviously, this party was more interested in a predictable arbitrator than an open-minded one. One might doubt that this party's position is an absolute exception to the rule. On the other hand, when it comes to the arbitrator appointed by the opposing party, the first party will take the view that any predisposition should lead to a successful challenge due to the lack of impartiality.[104] These double standards shed doubt on the fair-mindedness and logic of quite a few critics.

Instead of constantly appointing the 'members of the circle', the circle should at least be extended to include new, virgin arbitrators, that is, allowing 'new blood' to enter the cadre of arbitrators, which is at any rate necessary because the most frequently appointed and desired arbitrators will not get younger.[105] Similarly, 'Thinking things through is hard work', and new (and younger) blood might well be more enthusiastic about thinking one step further.[106] In practice, the list of arbitrators at the ICSID could be opened to include 'new' people, thereby enlarging the pool of arbitrators as well.[107] This would not automatically lead to their – desirable – appointment by the parties, but it would add to the variety and might offer an alternative to undecided parties. For the future viability of the investment arbitration system, the circle of arbitrators must be enlarged out of necessity. It is not a natural law that only the experienced arbitrator who has decided a minimum of a hundred or so cases will be a good arbitrator. In contrast, for example, due to his or her case load in parallel proceedings or physical and mental condition, he or she might not be able to focus on a case like a newcomer who needs to

[103] *Argentina* v. *BG Group*.

[104] To follow up on *Argentina* v. *BG Group*, at the same time, Argentina initiated several challenges based on an arbitrator's alleged predisposition due to his prior involvement (see e.g. *Suez et al.* v. *Argentina*; *Repsol* v. *Argentina*) and opposed a challenge to its own arbitrator on the grounds of scholarly writing in *Urbaser* v. *Argentina*.

[105] This was emphasised in respect of the US Supreme Court judges by D. R. Stras and R. W. Scott, 'Retaining Life Tenure: The Case for a "Golden Parachute"', *Washington University Law Review*, 83 (2005), 1397, 1437, 1436–7; see S. Wilske and M. Stock, 'Rule 3.3.7 of the IBA Guidelines on Conflicts of Interest in International Arbitration: The Enlargement of the Usual Shortlist?', *ASA Bulletin*, 23 (2005), 45, 51.

[106] Paulsson, 'Metaphors', 615, 616.

[107] Along this line of thought, Mr Nassib Ziadé, CEO of the Bahrain Chamber of Dispute Resolution argues that ICSID 'has a responsibility to diversify its pool of arbitrators'; Karadelis, 'Hong Kong Summit Focuses on the South-South Trade'.

build up his or her reputation.[108] Thus, adopting a more restrictive approach, regulations regarding the parties' appointment of arbitrators could be introduced. Similar to the 'IBA Guidelines',[109] provisions could limit the number of times a party appoints a certain person as its arbitrator, thereby avoiding any appearance of malicious intent, such as a possible pre-judgment or financial interest, from the outset.

In addition, disclosure – and the timing thereof – is still a valuable remedy for any possible doubt as to an arbitrator's impartiality that exists at the beginning of or arises during the arbitral proceedings. Allowing the parties to know about prior involvements, professional affiliations and academic engagements could be an efficient way to build confidence if this ends up helping to reduce further unnecessary challenges.

Against the background of the TTIP discussions, the current 'sparking' idea of an investment court as a standing body that is also incorporated in the European Commission's latest TTIP proposal does not appear to be a desirable short-term option.[110] Just as before, the same people would repeatedly decide on similar factual and legal issues. A standing investment court would simply result in an establishment of the current status quo with the 'usual suspects' acting as (permanent) decision makers. The criticism would merely shift to a different adjudicating body. So, what could the different options be – appointment for life like the

[108] Regarding the physical conditions, see Stephen R. Bond, 'The International Arbitrator: From the Perspective of the ICC International Court of Arbitration', *Northwestern Journal of International Law & Business*, 12 (1991), 1, 6; Wilske, 'The Ailing Arbitrator', 279, 281 *et seq*. An enlargement of the circle, however, is criticised by one quite pessimistic writer as encouraging 'a race to the lowest common denominator'; S. Nappert, 'Bias in International Commercial Arbitration versus Investment Arbitration: Are There Different Standards? Should There Be?', in A. Rovine (ed.), *Contemporary Issues in International Arbitration and Mediation: The Fordham Papers* 2009, Vol. II, 152.

[109] *IBA Guidelines*, under Rule 3.3.8 'Orange List', it might give rise to justifiable doubts if the arbitrator has been appointed more than three times within the last three years by the same counsel or the same law firm.

[110] EU Commission, press release, 12 November 2015 (announcing that 'the EU has formally presented to the US its proposal for a reformed approach on investment protection and a new and more transparent system for resolving disputes between investors and states: the Investment Court System'); see also C. Tietje, 'Ein internationales Handels- und Investitionsgericht für CETA (und TTIP)?, *Policy Papers on Transnational Economic Law*, 42, March 2015; S. Hindelang, 'Study on Investor-State Dispute Settlement (ISDS) and Alternatives of Dispute Resolution in International Investment Law', in Directorate-General for External Policies, Policy Department, *Investor-State Dispute Settlement (ISDS) Provisions in the EU's International Investment Agreements*, Vol. 2: *Studies*, 39, 102 *et seq*.

US Supreme Court judges or instead service for a limited period of time?[111] Either way, accountability would be limited even further. Being a permanently appointed arbitrator of the standing investment court rather appears to fuel one's ambition to write legal history more than it does to motivate him or her to approach each case with an open mind. Limiting the appointment to a six-year term, renewable once, as is currently discussed, would force each member of such investment court to think about his or her professional future after the end of the appointment. In this case, it might not be far-fetched to assume that such a judge might bear his or her own career in mind when dealing with global companies in dispute proceedings during (at least the last years of) his or her appointment, thereby possibly speculating about a future professional opportunity.

Appointing only 'Methuselahs' who will have their professional life behind them or (retired) judges[112] does not seem to be an attractive option either. Furthermore, as can be seen from experience with appointments to other standing international tribunals such as the European Court of Human Rights (ECtHR), states might not put forward the most suitable or experienced candidates but instead make political appointments.[113] In light of the criticism of ECtHR judges, it appears rather doubtful that a standing investment court would improve the quality of decisions and enhance the transparency and legitimacy of investment dispute settlement.

Yet, for a standing investment court, it will be essential to ensure the proportional representation between experienced and new arbitrators as well as different cultural and legal backgrounds. Moreover, there was

[111] The side effects of securing judicial wisdom by means of appointments for life, that is, the physical and mental condition, have already been described, see note 105.

[112] Along these lines, Hindelang strongly suggests providing for tenured judges, at least at an appeal level regarding the EU's investment agreements; see Hindelang, 'Study on Investor-State Dispute Settlement', 39, 102, 114; judges elected for such a prominent position will in general be experienced (but certainly not in investment arbitration) – if not elderly. As an example for the downside to using (ex-)judges in arbitration, see the case of the Indian ad hoc arbitration practice as described by Wilske, 'The Ailing Arbitrator', 279, 290.

[113] A. von Bogdandy and C. Krenn, 'Zur demokratischen Legitimation von Europas Richtern', *Juristenzeitung* (2014), 529, 537; N. P. Engel, 'Mehr Transparenz für die Wahrung professioneller Qualität bei den Richter-Wahlen zum EGMR', *Europäische Grundrechte-Zeitschrift* (2012), 486; *ibid.*, 'Richterwahl beim EGMR und Qualifikationen der von den Regierungen nominierten Richter-Kandidaten', *Europäische Grundrechte-Zeitschrift* (2010), 368, 369; see for Germany S. Wilske, L. Markert and L. Bräuninger, 'Germany', *Getting the Deal Through: Investment Treaty Arbitration 2016*, available at https://gettingthedealthrough.com/area/60/investment-treaty-arbitration-2016 (accessed 25 February 2016), 1, 4.

a reason for moving away from courts towards the now flourishing system of investment arbitration, and that must be kept in mind. In other words, just as Nils Lofgren concludes that 'somehow when the lights went out I got myself through the night, yes I did . . . cause the sun hasn't set on this boy yet',[114] the arbitration community will have to continue to struggle for some time in a Sisyphean manner with the ideal of the impartial and independent, extremely experienced, 'has seen it all' arbitrator who is – at the same time – predictably predisposed to one party's position but has never before adopted such a position in any case, legal debate or academic writing.[115]

[114] Nils Lofgren, 'The Sun Hasn't Set on This Boy Yet', *Hip-o Select* (1975).

[115] Cf. R. Woolley, 'Is Arbitrator Impartiality a Myth?' *Global Arbitration Review News*, 9 June 2015.

INDEX

For EU product safety concerns, contact us at Calle de José Abascal, 56–1°,
28003 Madrid, Spain or eugpsr@cambridge.org.

www.ingramcontent.com/pod-product-compliance
Lightning Source LLC
LaVergne TN
LVHW011530200926
848484LV00001B/220
* 9 7 8 1 1 0 7 1 7 2 6 5 4 *